Between Justice
and Beauty

Between Justice and Beauty

Race, Planning,
and the Failure of Urban Policy
in Washington, D.C.

Howard Gillette Jr.

The Johns Hopkins University Press
Baltimore and London

For My Native Washington Sons
Ellery and Felix

© 1995 The Johns Hopkins University Press
All rights reserved. Published 1995
Printed in the United States of America on acid-free paper
04 03 02 01 00 99 98 97 96 95   5 4 3 2 1

The Johns Hopkins University Press
2715 North Charles Street
Baltimore, Maryland 21218-4319
The Johns Hopkins Press Ltd., London

Library of Congress Cataloging-in-Publication Data

Gillette, Howard.
    Between justice and beauty : race, planning, and the
failure of urban policy in Washington, D.C. / Howard
Gillette, Jr.
        p.   cm.
    Includes bibliographical references (p.   ) and index.
    ISBN 0-8018-5069-X
    1. Urban policy—Washington (D.C.)   2. Washington
(D.C.)—Social conditions.   3. Washington (D.C.)—
Politics and government.   4. City planning—Wash-
ington (D.C.)   5. Washington (D.C.)—Race relations.
I. Title.
HN80.W3G55   1995
307.76'09753—dc20   94-45938

A catalog record for this book is available from the British
Library.

Portions of Chapter 8 appeared in an earlier version as "A
National Workshop for Urban Policy: The Metropolitani-
zation of Washington, 1946–1968," *The Public Historian* 7,
no. 1 (1985) : 7–27. Copyright 1985 by the Regents of the
University of California; reprinted by permission.

Frontispiece: Photo by Charles Hine, from *Neglected
Neighbors,* reproduced in Scott Nearing, *Poverty and
Riches* (1916).

Contents

Illustrations

Illustrations

Preface and
Acknowledgments

Voters entering the polls in Washington, D.C., in November 1992, considered more than just the election of the next president of the United States. Attracting most intense discussion and controversy was a referendum issue calling for the restoration of capital punishment, a measure the United States Congress had forced on the ballot after the murder of a legislative aide in a residential area near the Capitol. District voters rejected the referendum by more than a two-to-one margin. The same day residents of the city's poorest and most neglected ward overwhelmingly elected as their representative to city council former mayor Marion Barry, who only recently had been released from prison after serving six months for a crack cocaine conviction. Barry's victory evoked jubilant response from supporters, who hoped that he would deal with the social problems besetting their city.

The linkage between issues of crime and poverty in Washington was familiar enough. The capital punishment referendum, actively pursued by Senator Richard Shelby, a conservative white southerner seeing assurance that federal business would proceed in safety, nonetheless bore the familiar markings of "law-and-order" candidates, who over the years had directed their antagonism at the nation's poor, largely black, inner-city residents. Marion Barry, on the other hand, as a black former civil rights activist whose prosecution by federal officials gained him sympathy from those same inner-city residents, tapped deep-seated aspirations for empowerment and equal justice.

Reaction to these two crimes and these two choices on the ballot emerged from sharply differentiated experiences, beliefs, and aspirations, oppositional forces that were assured confrontation in the nation's capital. Ever since the federal government had begun exercising constitutional jurisdiction over the territory set aside for federal business, it had assured the presence of national authority in Washington affairs. By intentionally setting out to make a city in the federal district, Congress had assumed for itself a role in urban policy. Although public officials from the start had maintained high expectations for the District of Columbia as a model city for the new nation, federal oversight of Washington in practice proved uneven at best and at times disastrous. To some degree, such failures were the product of incompetence or indifference.

But a long view of relations between city and capital suggests a deeper and more profoundly disturbing revelation: what happened in Washington, D.C., was what the nation wanted. The cause of the urban policy failures that have left vast parts of Washington with neither safe streets nor a livable environment lies not in local circumstances but in national choices. Given the opportunity to pioneer programs in Washington for social welfare as well as physical improvement, the federal government made decisions time and again that left the city the worse for its efforts. Even as it created an aesthetically pleasing monumental core at the heart of Washington, it allowed many of the surrounding neighborhoods to fall into the social and physical decay now considered endemic in urban areas. Such results were not inevitable, as the history of Washington reveals.

The two large trends in national urban policy—one to improve the physical environment, to make cities beautiful; the other to improve conditions of social welfare, to make cities just—were not always at odds. In Washington the French planner of the city, Pierre Charles L'Enfant, insisted that the new city be useful as well as commodious, a place of expanding economic opportunity as well as a physical symbol for the new republic. During Reconstruction, local Republicans supported by Congress devised an expansive program of public works to employ newly liberated and enfranchised African Americans in order to secure their civic as well as partisan loyalty. During the Progressive Era, when architects employed elements of L'Enfant's plan to promote the idea of a city beautiful concentrated at the urban core, social reformers urged the public to attend to the social needs of the city's "neglected neighbors." Similar arguments animated the campaign for urban renewal after World War II, when planners called for improvements that would achieve social as well as aesthetic goals. The emergence of a black power movement in the 1960s necessarily changed the terms of social advocacy, but even then activists sought to use planning tools to improve physical structures in the name of social justice and political empowerment.

Despite these promising efforts to link social welfare with aesthetic improvements, the two strands of urban policy ultimately led in different directions. As demographics changed, as organizations crystallized around separate causes, and as the factor of race sharpened the debate over what could and should be done in urban areas, reform efforts splintered. What one set of leaders achieved in the name of social justice was often undone by those who followed. In Washington, even the election of a black activist as mayor failed to reverse a pattern by which the social advances of one period were undercut in the next. Caught between opposing forces for beautification and social justice, Washington gained two identities: one closely associated with the federal presence, visited annually by millions of tourists and known as the city beautiful; the other consisting of the city's indigenous neighborhoods, many of them beset by inadequate housing, soaring levels of poverty and crime, and social disorder.

Despite its special political standing, Washington should not be viewed as a passive victim of federal control. Its development has been thoroughly contested, both in the ways different national figures have attempted to direct its fate and in local efforts to set the city's own agenda. Whether it was Pierre L'Enfant's dramatic plan for the city, Congress's effort to impose Reconstruction policies on Washington after the Civil War, or the highway lobby's effort to bind city and suburb through a dramatic expansion of throughways into the District, policies for Washington have provoked controversy and attention.

Washington, of course, represents a special case in American history. No other part of the country experiences the same dominant federal presence, either physically or politically. Still, the very fact of federal control over its local affairs makes Washington's story exemplary. What federal authorities have provided in the way of programs for Washington most often has reflected their national goals for urban policy. State legislatures have played an intermediate role in other cities; in Washington, the relationship between national and local authorities has been direct. Here triumphs could be recorded and failures not ignored. Here, in short, is a crucible for evolving urban policy and a place whose history reveals the shortcomings of even the best of intentions.

In a period when specialized monographs dominate advanced scholarship, it may seem old-fashioned to attempt a city's whole biography, albeit on a selective, interpretive basis. If the past held no influence on the present, I would not have undertaken the task. But in Washington, as I believe is also true in other cities, historical forces have a way of influencing ideas and attitudes long after an understanding of their context has been lost. This is especially true in Washington as long as Congress retains the power of exclusive jurisdiction. The effects of the government's historical relationship with the city show up daily, in debates over the placement of structures according to the L'Enfant plan, over efforts to assign fiscal responsibility for providing services, and in interpreting social relationships. Yet the absence of any shared sense of the historical circumstances that shape those debates makes it difficult either for permanent residents or for more transitory government officials to deal effectively with the problems they face. Without such understanding, efforts to revive civic culture remain weak at best. By bringing together material over time and across subject matters usually treated in isolation, I want in this study to provide a framework for understanding the roots of Washington's history. By examining how the federal government has tried but failed to make Washington a city "worthy of the nation," I explore not just the problematic relationship between capital and city but also between the nation and its cities.

★ ★ ★

In the years I have worked on this book, I have incurred many debts, none deeper than to George Washington University, which granted the sabbatical leaves that launched this study and helped bring it to a conclusion. In addition, I received a grant from the university's Center for Washington Area Studies providing me the help of two dedicated research assistants, Margaret Henry and Stephen Want, during the 1989–1990 academic year. A summer research grant from the university in 1991 allowed me to investigate redevelopment in Shaw.

Many librarians have assisted with this project over the years, most notably Roxanna Deane and her staff at the Martin Luther King Jr. Public Library; Philip Ogilvie and Dorothy Provine at the District of Columbia Archives; and at George Washington University's Gelman Library Department of Special Collections, Francine Henderson, Cheryl Cherneaux, and David Anderson. My thanks also go to former Special Collections staff William Keller, now at the Milton S. Eisenhower Library at the Johns Hopkins University, and Matthew Gilmore, of the King Library. Anne Meglis, former librarian at the District of Columbia Office of Housing and Community Development, deserves special thanks, not just for saving so many important materials and making them available, but also for her comments on parts of an earlier draft. The major portion of the library she nourished for so long has been moved to the District of Columbia Archives.

I have been blessed at George Washington with the opportunity to work with a particularly talented group of students. My debt to them is abundantly acknowledged in my citations of their work, but those who deserve special thanks for doing so much to break new ground in Washington history are William Bushong, Jessica Elfenbein, Elizabeth Hannold, Susan Klaus, Jane Levey, Melissa McLoud, Druculla Null, Helen Ross, and especially Katherine Schneider Smith, who read and commented extensively on the first draft of this manuscript.

To my colleagues Frederick Gutheim, who died as work on this book entered the final phase, and Richard Longstreth I owe special thanks. Fritz, more than anyone, drew me to issues central to urban and Washington history. Richard, who is always a sensitive and acute critic, read a portion of the draft at a critical point in its formation. I am grateful as well to Walter Fauntroy for making available portions of his papers at George Washington's Gelman Library and for reviewing the chapter on Shaw. Peter Reimer, now retired from the Redevelopment Land Agency, read the same chapter and made many useful comments. Early in my

Preface and Acknowledgments

work Darwin Stolzenbach made available information he had been gathering for a history of the Metro subway system, materials now available at the Gelman Library. Jerome Paige commented extensively on an earlier draft of the material on Marion Barry, and Pamela Scott made many helpful suggestions for the early chapters. At the Johns Hopkins University Press, Robert Brugger provided many good insights as to how best to sharpen the focus of this study as well as encouraging me to tackle the subject. David Schuyler of Franklin and Marshall College and a second, anonymous reader provided many helpful suggestions for strengthening the text. Finally, my deepest appreciation goes to Margaret Marsh, whose intellectual, emotional, and moral support for this book, as in life, are valued beyond telling.

Locus of the
New Republic

2   In determining to fashion a new capital out of the wilderness, the founders
of Washington, D.C., had the opportunity to mold a place entirely to their
liking. At an early stage, they thought boldly. They embraced a grand plan
for a new city at the heart of the federal district, anticipating that its advan-
tageous location on the Potomac River would generate the commerce and
subsequent growth necessary to achieve the expectations of that plan. Success demanded a close partnership between federal and local interests, and
that seemed assured from the active role George Washington, Thomas
Jefferson, and other leaders of the new republic played in the capital. Almost from the start, however, those high expectations were compromised.

Despite the best intentions of its founders, Washington less than its
rivals benefited from government largess in the early republic. Elsewhere
city governments and state legislatures promoted urban growth, aggres-
sively supporting internal improvements to hasten trade and investing in
the physical plant of cities. While Congress maintained a relationship to
Washington akin to that between other cities and their states, it lacked the
same loyalty to its urban constituents. By delaying investments in internal
improvements, the federal government dampened Washington's prospects
for economic self-sufficiency. With the city lacking the anticipated revenues of trade, Congress assured its dependency on federal funding for physical improvement. But lacking the will to pay for services not directly related to its own functioning, the government proved doubly parsimonious.
As a result, while the nation clung to hopes that a beautiful and magnificent
city would soon emerge, Washington retained the reputation more of an
unkept village.

Even as Congress remained reluctant to spend money on the new city, it
played an active role in Washington's affairs, not the least in attempting to
regulate race relations. In accepting the prevailing laws along with the land
ceded to the new federal district by Maryland and Virginia, Congress assured at the capital not only a significant black presence but the practice of
slavery. Since the capital's location had been tied from the start to slavery by
those seeking to protect their interests from government interference, the
issue was bound to affect Washington as it more bitterly divided the nation.

Under pressure from those who saw Congress's power of exclusive jurisdiction as a means of securing one measure of social justice through the emancipation of slaves held in the District of Columbia, the capital became quite a different symbol than the city's founders had envisioned. By the time of the Civil War neither the concerns of race nor physical development had been resolved fully. It remained clear through Washington's early history only that the two issues would remain inseparably linked.

To change a Wilderness into a City, to erect and beautify Buildings &ca. to that
degree of perfection, necessary to receive the Seat of Government of so extensive
an Empire, in the short period of time that remains to effect these objects is an
undertaking vast as it is Novel, and reflecting that all this is to be done under the
many disadvantages of opposing interests which must long continue to foment
Contention among the various Branches of the Union—the only expedient is to
conciliate, and interest the Minds of all Ranks of People of the propriety of the
Pursuit by engaging the national Fame in its Success, evincing in its progress that
utility and Splendor, capable of rendering the Establishment unrivalled in greatness by all those now existing, by holding out forcible inducements to all Ranks of
People.

> Pierre Charles L'Enfant to Thomas Jefferson,
> February 26, 1792

The establishment of a permanent capital for the new nation in 1790
was an event of immense importance. Forged at a critical point in the early
nation-building process, the compromise that located the federal district
on the Potomac River after years of contention between the states promised, as George Washington put it, to unify the country by creating a port
city capable of exploiting to national advantage the rich agricultural hinter-
land of the western frontier. As it emerged from the wilderness, this new
city could aspire to the status of New York or Philadelphia, or even London
and Paris eventually. But even more was anticipated. By casting Washington
as a symbol for the nation, the city's designer, the French architect and engineer Pierre Charles L'Enfant, expected it to inspire national pride through
the beauty of its buildings and magnificence of its physical plant. Exem-
plifying national aspirations for grandeur, Washington would prove viable
enough economically to serve federal needs for years to come. Beauty would
be yoked to enterprise.

In fact, nothing like that happened in Washington's early history, and in
this failure lay the central contradiction in the founders' hopes for the new
capital. Created as a city to inspire respect through the realization of an

aesthetically powerful and inspiring physical presence, Washington instead fell victim to the constraints of its peculiar political culture, a city of magnificent but hopelessly failed intentions.

Washington's symbolic role followed most powerfully from L'Enfant, whom George Washington called upon in 1790 to design the new capital. Imbued with America's revolutionary fervor out of his own participation as a military volunteer in the conflict, L'Enfant described to Congress in 1784 his hopes for a capital sufficient "to give an idea of the greatness of the empire as well as to engrave in every mind that sense of respect that is due to a place which is the seat of supreme sovereignty." Five years later he wrote President Washington of the unprecedented opportunity for America to choose its own site for a capital. Noting that the nation as yet lacked the means "to pursue the design to any great extent," he nonetheless urged that any plan "should be drawn on such a scale as to leave room for that aggrandizement and embellishment which the increase of the wealth of the Nation will permit it to pursue at any period however remote."[1]

L'Enfant's first surveys of the area generally designated for the new capital immediately impressed him with the beauty of the site and convinced him of the importance of building on that advantage. As he wrote Washington's chief agent in the area, Secretary of State Thomas Jefferson, his intent was to "unite the usfull with the comodious & agreable viewing."[2] To do this, he conceived of making ornamental even such a basic urban function as a canal intended to link shipping activities in the existing town of Georgetown with the superior deep water port envisioned for the Potomac's Eastern Branch, or Anacostia River. Other uses of water would help beautify and embellish the capital in ways equal to the leading urban centers of Europe. A great avenue would extend from Georgetown to the Anacostia "laid out on a dimension proportioned to the greatness which . . . the Capital of a powerful Empire ought to manifest."[3] Given the excuse to plan a large city at the heart of the federal district, appropriately named after Washington himself,[4] L'Enfant conceived of creating strong relationships between the two central nodes of government. In locating the Capitol a mile and a half distant from the president's house and other public buildings, L'Enfant raised some practical concern about the difficulty of conducting federal business,[5] but such an arrangement, he argued, would by "giving them reciprocity of sight and by making them thus seemingly connected, would promote a rapid settlement over the whole extent."[6] Each element of L'Enfant's plan for Washington, as he wrote Jefferson, represented his intent to "delinate on a new and original way the plan the contrivance of which the President has left to me without any restriction soever."[7]

Although some critics have described L'Enfant's vision for Washington as symbolically inappropriate for the new republic and too grand for its undeveloped site,[8] Pamela Scott makes a strong case that the French engineer, far from slavishly replicating forms from abroad, consciously designed a city to represent the new democratic experiment in America. By imposing a carefully orchestrated set of diagonal boulevards on the standard grid, L'Enfant's plan created a complex system of private neighborhoods and public ceremonial spaces. To each of the latter, he assigned a symbolic function. The grand avenues, designated an extraordinary width of 160 feet, would assume the names of the states. These L'Enfant arranged within the city of Washington to represent both geographic location and each state's prominence in the process of nation building. Massachusetts, Virginia, and especially Pennsylvania, with its associations both with the Declaration of Independence and the signing of the Constitution, gained the most prominence. Avenues named after other states with prominent roles in ratifying the Constitution, notably Delaware and New Jersey, intersected with the Capitol. At the same time, in devising means to create squares at the intersection of diagonal avenues with the grid, L'Enfant intended to provide locations for state buildings, thereby giving them the same symbolic importance in the capital city that they held in the federal system.[9]

Scott finds confirmation for her interpretation in an anonymous essay that appeared in 1795, believed to be written by Stephen Hallet, L'Enfant's draftsman in 1791 who later worked on the construction of the Capitol. It argued that the capital's size and central location was, like the city plan, an expression of national union: "To found a City in the center of the United States, for the purpose of making it the depository of the acts of the Union ... which will one day rule all North-America ... is a grand and comprehensive idea ... a temple erected to liberty." Seeing the symbolic significance of L'Enfant's calculated street plan in its relationship to the Capitol, it added, "Here he fixed the center of the city, as the city is the center of the American Empire, and he rendered the edifice accessible by more than twenty streets which terminate at this point. Each street is an emblem of the rays of light which, issuing from the Capitol, are directed toward every part of America, to enlighten its inhabitants respecting their true interests."[10]

Initially L'Enfant had no reason to believe his intentions to build a city to serve as a new seat of empire were out of line with those of his federal sponsors, not the least George Washington. Active as a young man in promoting the prospects of the tobacco town of Alexandria, Virginia, and the Potomac River more generally, Washington played a quiet but no doubt crucial role in securing the Potomac location for the new capital. As early as 1770 he advocated opening the river to better navigation by clearing its channel of rocks and building a system of bypasses around its major falls, a goal he attempted to put into effect by establishing the Potomac Company in 1784. He described the project as "the channel of commerce" for "the trade of a rising empire," one that could save the nation by forming a link to

Plan of the City of Washington by Andrew Ellicot after Pierre Charles L'Enfant. Engraving by Thackeray and Vallance, March 1792. Courtesy Geography and Map Division, Library of Congress.

western rivers capable of "binding these people to us by a chain which can never be broken."[11] Thomas Jefferson shared Washington's enthusiasm, becoming involved in the improvement of rivers in Virginia as a young man and arguing in 1784 for a state tax to that end, saying of the Potomac, "This is the moment . . . for seizing it if ever we mean to have it. All the world is becoming commercial."[12]

George Washington, as much as anyone, was responsible for extending the boundaries of the new city of Washington. While initially it appeared that the city would be concentrated in a much smaller space, he clearly intended to expand the area, both to appease the interests of competing landowners in the area and to provide a site equal to his grand vision for the city. As he wrote L'Enfant April 4, 1791,

LOCUS OF THE NEW REPUBLIC

It will be of great importance to the public interest to comprehend as much ground (to be ceded by individuals) as there is any tolerable prospect of obtaining. Although it may not be *immediately* wanting, it will nevertheless increase the Revenue; and of course be beneficial hereafter, not only to the public, but to the individual proprietors; in as much, as the plan will be enlarged, and thereby freed from those blotches, which otherwise might result from not comprehending *all* the lands that appear well adapted to the general design.[13]

Jefferson's early notes reveal every bit as much passion for prescribing the details of urban development, from the size of lots to the height of buildings and their arrangement on the street.[14] Writing L'Enfant in April 1791, Jefferson urged "very liberal reservations" for public buildings "on the back of the town," so as to be "of no injury to the commerce of the place, which will undoubtedly establish itself on the deep waters towards the Eastern branch and mouth of Rock Creek." The same day he indicated to George Washington his intent to circulate in the federal district plates of "about a dozen or two of the handsomest fronts of private buildings" with hopes that "it might decide the taste of the new town."[15] Like L'Enfant, Jefferson maintained an overriding concern with balancing the useful with the ornamental, a concept Julian Boyd asserts he had imbibed from his classical education.[16]

It is true that when Jefferson passed along his relatively modest conception of how the city might look in March 1791, L'Enfant reacted intemperately, calling the proposal "tiresome and insipid" and attacking the gridiron approach so closely associated with urban development in America for annihilating the natural advantages of Washington's site and threatening to injure the success of the undertaking.[17] But such was not the central factor of their disagreement. By all indications, Jefferson himself conceived his sketch as only the first step in outlining the city. He never objected to L'Enfant's bolder concept, and he must have taken some satisfaction from L'Enfant's decision to incorporate his concept of public gardens along the Potomac River into what finally became the Mall.[18] Indeed, even after L'Enfant had been dismissed without finally completing the map detailing his ideas, Jefferson maintained the chief elements, excising only the sites for state squares.[19] While L'Enfant complained bitterly about alterations in his plan, the most telling of which was the absence of his name from the 1792 version, the scope and the intent of the federal city remained virtually intact.[20] The source of their disagreement lay not in the scale or design of the undertaking but in the decision on how to finance it, and in this lay the source of Washington's fundamental difficulty.

Given the conception he shared with Washington and Jefferson of the new capital as an engine for commercial development as well as a fitting symbol for the nation, L'Enfant concluded that the country ought to be

Thomas Jefferson's Plan for the
City of Washington, March 1791.
Courtesy Geography and Map
Division, Library of Congress.

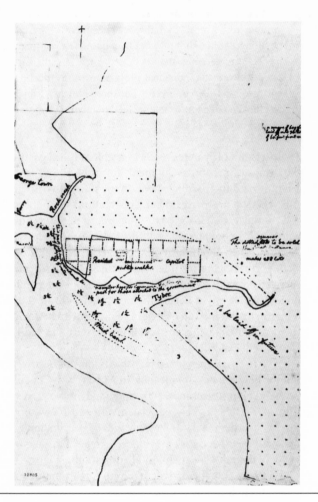

willing to invest in the project. He favored issuing sufficient government
bonds to construct public buildings and lay out the necessary infrastructure of roads, walkways, and the like. Once started, he believed, such improvements would attract substantial private investment, and from a grouping of small hamlets, or paper cities, as John Reps calls them, Washington
would emerge virtually simultaneously as a thriving metropolis.[21] But while
L'Enfant had the luxury of creating urban space that would place each state
in symbolic harmony with the others, Jefferson was acutely concerned
about divisions between the states and the jealousies that had only recently
been aggravated by the long and bitter controversy over the location of the
capital.[22] Fearing that burdening the states with the additional costs of

constructing the capital would only make matters worse, he advanced, and President Washington accepted, the alternative approach of raising the necessary revenues from the sale at auction of land the government would purchase from the local proprietors.[23] To do this effectively it was necessary to have an accurate map of the territory, and in efforts to secure one from L'Enfant for the first government sale lay the source of the friction that ultimately led to L'Enfant's dismissal.

By midsummer 1791, President Washington was pressing L'Enfant to have a map prepared in time for the first government sale slated for October 17. L'Enfant retorted that he needed more time to put into place the full details of his design, including the placement of the canal he believed was essential to spur the movement of trade within the new city. By withholding the map on the assumption that sales would not be harmed, when they were, L'Enfant provoked the anger of the president as well as the commissioners who had been designated by the Residence Act to supervise the capital-building process. By taking the additional step of ordering the house torn down of the nephew of one of the commissioner's relatives, Daniel Carroll of Duddington, on the pretext that it blocked the way of a projected street and an important square, L'Enfant severely undercut his position.[24] Yet Washington only mildly rebuked his planner, writing L'Enfant, "Having the beauty, & harmony of your Plan only in view, you pursue it as if every person, and thing was *obliged* to yield to it; whereas the Commissioners have many circumstances to attend to, some of which, perhaps, may be unknown to you; which evinces, in a strong point of view, the propriety, the necessity & even the safety of your acting by their directions."[25] Instead of reprimanding him for destroying Carroll's home, he asked the commissioners to delegate L'Enfant more authority.

Washington, it appears, was so anxious to avoid giving the enemies of the Potomac location any opportunity to rescind the Residence Act that he chose to protect L'Enfant in hopes of getting his as-yet incomplete plan rather than dismiss him.[26] When out of exasperation Jefferson finally instructed L'Enfant to submit to the commissioners' authority, L'Enfant, who had been used to taking his directions from the president directly, refused. Again ignoring the immediate pressure to sell the land, he defended his plan as the best means of overcoming national divisions by enlisting the "National Fame" in the city's success. For directly thwarting the president's request, Jefferson informed L'Enfant, his services had been terminated.[27]

The task of completing the map of Washington fell to Andrew Ellicott, who had worked with L'Enfant to survey the new territory. He too clashed with the commissioners, indicating that L'Enfant was not entirely to blame for his own misfortune. Ellicott's own version of the map, when completed in 1792, was not sufficient to improve sales of lots, however, and the government finally had to resort to loans after all.[28] Once in hand, public funding allowed the capital-building process to begin in earnest, but delays and disappointing results from land sales meant that the capital city was anything but ready when the new government arrived in 1800.

★ ★ ★

The first reactions, in fact, to the new capital as the government moved from Philadelphia in 1800 were highly critical. Reviewing the city's unpaved streets, the incomplete buildup of structures along major thoroughfares, and the lack of amenities by then commonplace and considered essential to modern standards of living in the nation's leading cities, Congressman Richard Griswold of Connecticut called Washington "both melancholy and ludicrous . . . a city in ruins."[29] Secretary of the Treasury Oliver Wolcott wrote his wife, "I do not perceive how the members of Congress can possibly secure lodging unless they will consent to live like scholars in a college, or monks in a monastery."[30] Brought to Washington to supervise public works, engineer Benjamin Henry Latrobe complained about the effect of delays in building as workers who might otherwise have settled in the city, finding their hopes for employment dashed, were forced to "inhabit the half-finished houses, now tumbling to ruins, which the madness of speculation has erected." He called Washington an "enormous baby of a town."[31]

Washington's shortcomings prompted not just criticism but suggestions that the capital be moved. As early as 1808, Representative James Sloan of New Jersey, citing the inconvenience of location and expense of erecting public buildings, offered a resolution to return the capital to Philadelphia. The resolution failed after provoking debate for a week,[32] but the issue emerged again after British soldiers devastated the capital in 1814. Bankers intervened with sufficient funds to rebuild public buildings and thus to retain the capital in Washington.[33] But as late as 1838, British visitor Harriet Martineau, declaring Washington "a grand mistake," described western efforts to move the capital to a more central location, noting that "the Cincinnati people are already speculating upon which of their hills or table-lands is to be the site of the new Capitol." Impressed as she was with the Capitol itself, she expressed dismay at its surroundings, "so sordid are the enclosures and houses on its very verge."[34] Charles Dickens provided the most devastating epithet for Washington, labeling it a "City of Magnificent Intentions" laid out with "broad avenues that begin in nothing and lead nowhere" and space wanting "only houses, roads and inhabitants."[35]

None of these problems were anticipated immediately in government circles because of the assumption that the close association of federal with local concerns would guarantee proper attention to city needs. Thomas Jefferson's administration quickly revealed the fault in that logic. As he had done in the original planning of the capital, Jefferson maintained a running correspondence with local agents charged with building up the city. In recognition of his interest, the school board, established in 1804, unanimously elected him their president. A number of local statutes designated the president, in title if not in name, as the chief authority in attending to local needs.

Almost from the start, however, Congress compromised Jefferson's capacities to act. To an 1803 letter from the city commissioners stating the belief that in allocating funds for public buildings Congress clearly intended to provide for roads to connect them, Jefferson provided a discouraging reply. Such funds, he reported, related only to maintaining the highway between the Capitol and other public buildings, which he interpreted to mean only Pennsylvania Avenue. This, he said, was "expressly explained to me by a member who moved the insertion of these words, and by others. Sincerely desirous of promoting the interests of the city and of Georgetown . . . I should have been happy to have it in my power to improve their communications with each other & with the country round about them: but no such power has been given to me."[36] When the issue arose again in 1807, Jefferson responded, "We cannot suppose Congress intended to tax the people of the US. at large for all avenues in Washington and roads in Columbia."[37] Given the restraints on his authority, Jefferson was more inclined to apologize to Congress for allowing the commissioners to overspend in their zeal to improve the city than he was to intervene, either to encourage improvements or to prevent private intrusions on the plan of the city.[38]

Such problems were anticipated immediately on the arrival of the first Congress in a series of articles by Augustus Woodward, who had recently moved from Alexandria to Washington. Writing under the pen name "Epaminondas" in the *National Intelligencer*, Woodward warned against the mixing of great with small concerns that would inevitably follow from placing Congress in control of city affairs. Moreover, he pointed to congressional failure to specify what portion of local expenses it would bear. Could it be believed that Congress would lavish its resources upon "this favorite child" without such provisions clarified in law?[39] In what might be imagined as a response to these concerns, Congress granted the city its own charter in 1802, authorizing a mayor appointed by the President of the United States and a bicameral city council, both branches to be elected by white male property owners, according to an amendment of 1804. Congress, however, withheld all powers that were not specifically delegated to the new corporation. Only gradually did it expand those powers by responding to local petitions to issue licenses, to provide for the superintendence of public schools, and to compensate the mayor. The Council subsequently enacted its own ordinances to regulate public markets, carriages, and places of amusement; to provide assistance to the poor; and prohibiting swine and geese from running at large in the city.[40]

In 1820 Congress granted the city a new charter, which in addition to establishing the popular election of the mayor every two years, authorized other powers, including the right to establish a board of health; to establish night watches and erect street lamps; to supply the city with water; and to authorize an annual lottery of up to $10,000, a measure pressed by city officials seeking additional funds for public improvements.[41] The charter also committed the federal government for the first time to pay its proportion of the cost of street and sidewalk improvements in front of public squares or reservations, but without specific appropriations beyond the proceeds from the sale of public lots.[42]

The expansion of municipal powers gave city officials more tools to pursue development, but throughout the early part of the century the operation of public affairs remained largely voluntary and consensual, in a manner more consistent with a villagelike community based on shared social values than a modern urban corporation based on law. The first act relating to fire authorized the purchase of three fire engines but failed to provide any appropriation. As a result, the council put the burden of protection on individual householders by requiring them to have on hand their own water buckets, one for each floor of the building. The mayor could spend no more than $50 for the purchase of ladders and fire hooks, which were informally designated for "such citizens as shall be disposed to take care of them and use them." A single fire engine was to be located near the center market, for general use by the community. By an additional act passed in 1804, fire companies were organized in the city's four wards under the supervision of citizen committees appointed by the mayor to serve without pay.[43]

A year later local residents petitioned Congress for funds to purchase engines, hoses, and ladders "for the material protection" of the United States, but Congress responded only by making the Treasury Department's lone fire engine available to the city. In 1811 the city supplemented private subscriptions to purchase an engine for the Columbian Fire Engine Company, and in 1815 it appropriated another $175 for the purchase of additional ladders and fire hooks as well as $25 for engine maintenance. It was not until 1822, however, that the city made any provision to provide the private companies with an adequate water supply by appropriating funds for reservoirs.[44] In 1818 the council authorized construction of reservoirs to be filled with spring water in each quadrant of the city. But officials dropped the plan a year later because the city lacked adequate funding. Once again Washington residents observed the federal government responding to its own interests alone: it located new firehouses next to the Capitol and the White House.[45]

Although a health officer had been authorized and appointed in 1819, it was not until 1822 that the council established a board of health as granted under the 1820 charter. In line with the board's voluntary standing, the budget remained at only $15 a year. The council extended regulatory oversight by creating in 1828 the office of surveyor, whose responsibilities to "stake out and mark the lines and proper graduations, according to the plan of the ... city" also included supervising the gradation of streets and keeping good records. Although provided with a salary of $800 a year, the surveyor could anticipate further remuneration from fees ranging from 50 cents to $2.00 each for surveying and recording lots.[46] A growing awareness of the environmental hazards to good health encouraged the council to provide the following year for a system of ward commissioners charged, in addition to supervising local improvements, with removing nuisances from the streets. In 1844 the council laid down further restrictions on nuisances and authorized scavengers to remove wastes. Typical of the premodern city, these scavengers received no salaries, as they were expected to take their compensation in the form of the manure they collected and sold.[47]

Street lighting, which had been provided Congress in the years it was located in Philadelphia through some hundred lamps, did not exist in Washington at all when the federal government arrived in 1800. Although the city council appropriated $100 in 1801 for placing lamps "on the most public avenues and streets," it failed to provide appropriations for their maintenance and supply. Not until 1819 did the council begin to provide annual appropriations for that purpose in response to negative accounts from visitors to the city and to a member of Congress who complained publicly that on his way home one evening he had been forced by the nature of darkness to slip and slide by barrels and piles of bricks strewn along Pennsylvania Avenue. As late as 1830 municipal lights were lit only during the months Congress sat in session in order to save money. A year later the council abandoned street lighting entirely for the rest of the decade.[48]

Street improvements remained just as uneven. In asking whether Congress should create a new authority to supervise public buildings and paved walks, Congressman Henry Clinton Martindale of New York compared Washington's streets clogged with "liquid mud" unfavorably to other cities known to be "kept in a state of decency, and comparative neatness."[49] Congress remained reluctant, however, to provide funding adequate to local needs. In 1834, for instance, in considering a bill to complete improvements on Pennsylvania Avenue, Congressman James Parker of New Jersey warned that a $200 item designed for removing dust and mud from the street surface "might prove an entering wedge to future demands on Congress." According to the report of the debate, Parker

> had no idea that Congress should take upon themselves the functions of scavengers to the good City of Washington. Was it, he inquired, necessarily to follow, that because they had, at an expense of one hundred and fifty thousand dollars, made a Macadamized road, they were to have this duty entailed upon them? If so, it was better they had not directed it to be constructed at all. He thought the people of Washington should do as the people of other

City of Failed Intentions

cities did, namely: keep their own streets in repair, and keep the dust out of their own eyes.[50]

While other members of Congress came to the city's defense, the *National Intelligencer* could report a year later that as Pennsylvania Avenue entered Georgetown it terminated "in a half-formed cut, through a precipitous sand-hill, which to the right overtops the road, in all the rugged and unseemly barrenness in which it has been left by the spade of the laborer; and if [a visitor] rides in an omnibus or carriage, the chances are against him but he will get his bones half dislocated, or the vehicle upset, in one or the other of the enormous ruts with which this nonpareil piece of road is disfigured."[51]

The limits placed on the development of Washington's physical facilities were typical of those employed in other major cities. By practice, regulation of streets remained extremely fluid throughout the first half of the nineteenth century. Typically, trash littered throughways, which suffered further congestion from animals wandering free.[52] Garbage collection, which remained in the hands of private companies, proceeded unevenly at best. Property holders along affected routes were required to pay the costs of proposed changes before work could begin. It was not until 1852 that New York City acquired authority to issue bonds in advance of such improvements, thus speeding the expansion of the city's built-up sector.[53] Before midcentury, cities typically let contracts to private companies to provide essential services like water and gas, with anything but satisfactory results.[54] Washington stood out from other cities, however. State legislators could be every bit as meddlesome in local affairs as congressmen were in Washington, but on requests for public improvements they tended to accede to the requests of local officials.[55] In no way was this more evident than in the desire to advance internal improvements to enhance trade: first roads and turnpikes, then canals, and ultimately railroads. In this regard, Washington's peculiar political culture set it apart in such a manner as to compromise its ability to be competitive.

★ ★ ★

From the outset, promoters of the new capital pointed out the importance of trade to its development. Otherwise, a commentator in the *Hartford Courant*—believed to be Noah Webster—said, "neither grants of money, nor acts of Congress, will have the least effect. We may expend ten millions of money in erecting accommodations for people, but if the place is not naturally designed for business, people will not live there."[56] To be successful, an 1804 pamphlet urged, Washington should follow Baltimore's successful rise as a port by diversifying trade rather than relying on a single product as Alexandria and Georgetown had done with tobacco. By building a canal across the city, as L'Enfant had proposed, connecting the Potomac River in Georgetown with the superior port facility on the Eastern Branch, Washington could well expect to divert "most of the flour, corn, &c. now carried by wagons to Baltimore" into its own facilities. Trade would bring draymen and boatmen to the city, who would build houses or rent them,

> as wood for burning of bricks, stone, lime, coal, flour, &c. will be landed there, instead of bringing them from the extremities of the city, . . . as these will require shops and warehouses. . . . As the city, not long ago a wilderness, becomes independent of Alexandria and George-town, it will progress in a compound ratio. No sooner is a canal formed through a town or city, than stores, &c. are erected on its banks.[57]

The federal government eventually built a city canal, thereby enhancing the natural trade advantages promised by the river site. True to his earlier beliefs, Jefferson continued to promote Washington's commercial potential, not the least through the support of canals. Writing from Paris, where he had made a fortune as a shipping agent and broker by slipping American cargo into the country, Joel Barlow said of Jefferson on the occasion of his inaugural that one of his foremost objectives was to "improve the domestic state of the nation by his system of small canals, which shall take the place generally of roads, and cut . . . the expense of interior transit."[58] In his annual message for 1806, Jefferson proposed to sustain duties on foreign luxuries so that the proceeds could be applied to "the great purposes of the public education, roads, rivers, canals. . . . By these operations new channels of communication will be opened between the States; the lines of separation will disappear, their interests will be identified, and their union cemented by new and indissoluble ties."[59] Treasury Secretary Albert Gallatin's 1808 plan authorizing the federal government to invest in a vast network of turnpikes and canals, intended to bind the nation together through better trade and communication, represented the culmination of arguments that federal leadership on a nonpartisan basis offered the best hope for national prosperity.[60]

Sectional rivalries, however, quickly undercut any hope that westward expansion would extend outward from Washington. The states, in addition to objecting to concentrating so much power under central authority, quickly perceived their own advantages through patronage and investment in public works. Congress rejected efforts by New Yorkers to secure national funding for a system of internal improvements that failed to include the Potomac region, but the state soon showed what it could do by itself. Completion of the Erie Canal in 1825, with such returns as to repay its debt five years into operation,[61] immediately demonstrated the benefit of state public works. Although a young John C. Calhoun in 1817 and President John Quincy Adams in 1824 attempted to revive Gallatin's concept of nationally directed

City of Failed Intentions

investments in trade networks, the states were not interested. Instead, they looked to their own legislatures to make the public subscriptions in stock that could make their cities competitive with New York.[62]

The phenomenal success of the Erie Canal finally prompted Congress to investigate supporting a similar public investment for the District of Columbia. Engineers who had worked on the Erie Canal reported that the project would be extremely expensive, however, thus dampening initial enthusiasm for the project. A concerted effort in 1825 finally overcame resistance. Under John Quincy Adams's prodding, Congress revived George Washington's dream of a canal as a national project, one that would extend all the way to the Ohio River.[63] Congress backed the effort by subscribing $1 million to the Chesapeake and Ohio Canal Company—the largest federal commitment to such a mixed enterprise project to date. In addition, it assured foreign investors that as supervisor of the District, it backed the C&O's credit. Formally organized in June 1828 with the help of an additional subscription of $500,000 from Maryland, the Chesapeake and Ohio Canal Company broke ground July 4 the same year.[64]

The cities of Washington, Alexandria, and Georgetown eagerly embraced the canal, placing great hope in its prospects for boosting the local economy, thereby providing the funds necessary to complete the task of building up the area. In seeking authority for Washington to subscribe to $1 million and Georgetown and Alexandria $250,000 in shares of canal stock, the cities expressed confidence that "as the canal is extended, the revenue arising from its use will be augmented, and every augmentation of that revenue will proportionally reduce the necessity of taxation, to supply the interest on the several corporation loans; as will the gradual increase of the population and wealth of the Corporations, diminish the proportion of the assessed tax to the number of people, and the amount of property upon which it is charged."[65] In his 1829 report to the city council, Washington mayor Joseph Gales noted, "to the success of the Chesapeake and Ohio Canal I look with hope and confidence for the establishment of a commerce, and the influx of a population, which will indemnify this city for all its expenditures and reward the courageous enterprise with which it embarked its funds and its credit upon this great adventure."[66]

Despite considerable debate in ward meetings held throughout the city over the propriety of adding to its debt, the Washington city council purchased the City Canal from Congress, authorizing an additional $50,000 expenditure to insure that barges could move though the city from the canal terminus in Georgetown to deep water on the Eastern Branch. Alexandria, in turn, fearing that its isolation would result in lost trade, committed funds to connect its port with the C&O by building its own canal along the Potomac's southern bank, crossing the river at Georgetown on an aqueduct bridge.[67]

The timing of the C&O venture was inauspicious, however, not just

because the Baltimore and Ohio Railroad broke ground for the nation's first major rail line the same day, but also because Congress, under the influence of small-government Jacksonian Democrats, quickly determined to end the practice of subscribing to stock in private internal improvement companies. When in 1830 the canal company sought further help from Congress because its funds were depleted by delays and underestimates of expenses, legislators put off acting on the request, saying it was best to determine first the relative merits of railroads and canals.

Typically, District newspapers invested deep faith in the canal. "If we were inclined to prophecy," the *Alexandria Gazette* declared in 1830, "we should much rather hazard our skill on the probability that the rail-road will benefit by the canal, than the canal by the railroad."[68] Likewise, the

National Intelligencer, in defending the canal from a pro-railroad editorial in a Baltimore paper, claimed that "the world is wide enough for both of us; and why should we be jostled in our quiet and unobtrusive course to the West, in search of its inexhaustible mineral, animal, and vegetable productions by the exchange of which in commerce Baltimore herself will be enriched?"[69] The world, however, was hardly wide enough for both, as Baltimore fought to establish its dominance over western trade. The two companies reached a literal impasse at the entrance to the Potomac Valley at Point-of-Rocks, forty-eight miles above Georgetown and east of Harpers Ferry, when each secured an injunction against further work until the legal right-of-way through the gorge had been established.[70] In the ensuing political as well as legal contest, the railroad pressed every advantage, in Congress as well as in the Maryland assembly. Early in 1833 Washington's leading citizens, protesting the railroad's efforts to block congressional funding for the canal, complained about "the gratuitous interposition of the railroad company to dry up the fountains of your liberality" and argued that "the destruction of the canal project would involve our city and our citizens in one common and irretrievable ruin."[71]

Although the canal finally won the legal battle in December 1831, delays in construction were costly, not just to the canal company but to the ambitious cities of the District as well. When the anticipated profits of trade failed to materialize and the cities found themselves unable to meet their obligation to pay the interest on a canal loan secured from Holland by Secretary of the Treasury Richard Rush, they turned to Congress for help in 1833 and 1834. The request for funds launched a particularly heated debate in Congress, with the first round directed at funding the Alexandria canal extension to Washington. Although part of the debate dealt with the purely logistical question of the propriety of building a canal alongside a river, it assumed larger dimensions as members of the House of Representatives quarreled over how much Congress had already done to assist the District of Columbia. While John J. Allen of Virginia charged that Congress had not so much as returned in funds the money that was received on the original cession of land from Virginia to the District, James Harlan of Kentucky, in charting loans as well as grants to the District, claimed, "There is not a convenient footway, or a piece of ground highly beautified and ornamented, which has not been done out of the public treasury."[72]

Washington's hopes received a major boost in February when New Jersey senator Samuel Southard reported that the Committee on the District of Columbia had approved a bill for relief. Pointing to debts exceeding $1.8 million, Southard described as "abhorrent" the prospect that Washington, having exhausted its revenues, might be forced to surrender its charter "and thus be left upon the hands of Congress to dispose of, govern, and sustain as may best suit their own views of what is proper for the capital of the Union." While concentrating to some degree on the immediate problem of the debt owed Holland, Southard accepted the broader argument of the Washington memorialists that in this instance as in others Congress had imposed its will on the city for national purposes, and now it was obliged to back that commitment financially. In particular, Southard accepted the argument that the federal government had failed to pay its fair share of improving city streets. Noting that the plan of the city was formed by public authorities, he declared, "It is a plan calculated for the magnificent capital of a great nation; but oppressive from its very dimensions and arrangements, to the inhabitants, if its execution to any considerable extent is to be thrown upon them."[73] Having paid itself only some $36,000 for land within the city, the government had acquired property worth more than $2.5 million, a sum which, had it been taxed, would have equaled twice Washington's indebtedness. "The committee are of opinion," Southard reported, "that the Government was bound by every principle of equal right and justice to pay a proportion of the expense incurred upon this subject."[74]

Such an argument was not entirely new. As early as 1826, in a petition seeking territorial government for the District, a committee of thirteen headed by Virginia's Richard Bland Lee argued that government property, if taxed, would yield $30,000 annually, enough to pay the cost of the local government.[75] In 1828, in debate over funding improvements to Pennsylvania Avenue, Senator John Eaton of Tennessee pointed to the discrepancy between the funds generated by the sale of government lots and the funds spent to improve the District. Asking whether it was fair or proper "for the citizens to be subjected to the expenses of improving and enlarging the town, making and keeping in repair the streets and avenues, whilst the government . . . shall . . . contribute nothing to that end," he urged that unappropriated lots and grounds be set apart as a fund for improving the streets and avenues and for establishing common schools.[76] There was a new implication in the Southard report—that since federal government property equaled in value that of the rest of Washington, Congress should pay at least half the expenses of improving the city. So encouraged were some members of the city council by the report that in July they considered an act that would have assessed and taxed for public improvements government property within the District at the same rate as property owned by individuals.[77]

The city council tabled the tax bill in deference to arguments that Congress might react negatively at a time when it was considering petitions for assistance. When Congress considered relief again in the spring of 1836, it narrowed the question of government responsibility to its liability for the canal loan alone. Arguing for complete assumption of the debt, a Senate report asked rhetorically why Congress would permit "a weight to rest upon the District, which can only produce the effect of cramping all its energies and retarding most seriously its growth in wealth and popula-

City of Failed Intentions

tion. . . . That the fortunes of the towns must advance in all ways, when the canal is made, may without hazard, be asserted."[78] The bill faced opposition in the House of Representatives, especially from Jacksonians who questioned the propriety of pouring money into the federal city. The House, by a close vote, rejected a potentially crippling amendment, but it also rejected, without a count, a proposal to set aside for the city's benefit all remaining unsold government lots. Congress finally assumed the full canal debt of $1.5 million in May 1836.[79]

Although reassured by Congress's decision, corporate authorities in the three District cities still struggled with developing an adequate economic base to underwrite urban development. Maryland further enhanced the prospects for the canal company with loans for $2 million in November 1835 and $3 million in 1836, but under the terms of the second bill the corporations of the District were required to surrender their stock to Maryland. Washington officials reacted angrily, declaring that Maryland, under the influence of the Baltimore and Ohio, was responsible for delays in the canal's construction:

> Year after year, while this corporation was exhausting its means and oppressing its citizens to carry on this canal, Maryland was taxing the ingenuity of her ablest men to defeat the canal; surveying routes for a cross-cut; strengthening the railroad, the great rival of the canal company; demanding the right to cut a canal through this city; and, in every way, seeking to secure to herself every advantage from the investment of this corporation; and never relaxing these efforts until she was well assured that this was the only practicable means of bringing into use the great wealth of her mountains.[80]

Editorials in the *Intelligencer* urged the city representative in the canal company to fight the surrender, but the city finally turned over its stock. When the federal government again refused additional aid, the company had to turn to Maryland again, securing by a single vote in the legislature an act giving the state control of the company, thereby authorizing it to issue its own mortgage bonds. With guarantees of $300,000 from Virginia, $25,000 from Georgetown, and $50,000 from Washington for new construction, the canal finally reached Cumberland in 1850. The canal terminated 160 miles short of the original Ohio Valley goal, however,[81] and in the meantime, the city suffered the irony of welcoming, in 1835, the only rail connection it could secure, a branch line of the Baltimore and Ohio.[82]

Lack of support from Congress prompted calls for withdrawal from the District from the two cities that predated its establishment. Boosters of both Georgetown and Alexandria complained about the lack of support from and sometimes active interference by the federal government in their efforts to build trade. Although the drive for retrocession in Georgetown did not lead to anything more than a sympathetic government report,[83] it continued to gain momentum in Alexandria and in Congress, where the chief supporter of the bill, Virginia representative Robert Hunter, made a number of legal as well as political arguments but focused the heart of his case on Alexandria's commercial interests. With imports declining precipitously, population stationary since 1820, and a preferred channel in the Potomac blocked by a bridge thrown up by the government, Alexandria had grounds for complaint against Congress. The city's prospects, Hunter asserted, would have been different had it remained in Virginia: "She would have been the flourishing depot of the commerce of the western portion of that State—the keystone in a great arch of commercial interests which would bind eastern and western Virginia together—a common bond, perhaps the golden link, which, to a great extent, would have united the interests and healed the divisions of the two sections of that State."[84]

A consistent supporter of retrocession, the *Alexandria Gazette* argued that completion of the canal was a matter of importance to the whole state. It promised to make Alexandria one of the most important ports in the country where "manufacturing would at once spring up and flourish—the coal trade would induce extensive and lucrative business relations with the great northern emporiums."[85] The Virginia Assembly not only accepted Alexandria back into the state but also promptly relieved the city with a large subscription in Alexandria Canal Company stock and a subsequent guarantee of some of the company's bonds.[86] Thus offered what both Georgetown and Washington had variously sought without success, not just self-government, but the active support of a state legislature for internal improvements, Alexandrians voted overwhelmingly in favor of retrocession, setting off a wild celebration in the town.[87]

★ ★ ★

Despite its sometimes troubled relations with Alexandria, the Washington city council passed a resolution opposing retrocession, charging that it would prove to be the first step in an effort to move the District elsewhere, "whereby total ruin and destruction would be brought upon the industrious and patriotic citizens of Washington."[88] The statement represented one more sign of government by reaction, but the effect of Alexandria's retrocession was more positive. Spurred by the dire consequences that could follow from the dissolution of the District of Columbia, the council assumed for itself a more active role on issues of urban development. Early in 1848 a member of the common council introduced a resolution calling for the development of general guidelines for improvements. A year later the same body passed a resolution calling on the ward commissioners to list proposed improvements according to priority, along with their costs, in advance of filing requests for payment.[89]

Also in 1848, the council reorganized the board of health. Although members remained virtual volunteers, being restricted to payment of $1 per meeting up to $12 a year, they were given additional powers to determine

nuisances and have them removed. The secretary's salary was set at $25 a
year and increased three years later to $100. In 1850 the council reorganized
the system of ward commissioners, dividing the city into two districts, each
under a single salaried commissioner who assumed the responsibilities
once given to scavengers. In 1852 the board attempted to solve the problem
of streets used as dumping grounds for slops and garbage by encouraging
residents to use tubs designated for refuse at certain locations. That measure failing, the board turned to contractors to remove the wastes. In 1856 it
took an additional step to standardize its operations by appointing a health
officer at a salary of $1,500.[90] The council provided detailed requirements
for the removal of wastes in 1850, adding laws to prohibit burial grounds
within city limits in 1852 and restrictions on lumber yards and slaughterhouses in 1858.[91] And in 1848, some thirty years after the precedent set by
Baltimore, Congress authorized the establishment of the Washington Gas
Works to light the city. By the eve of the Civil War Washington had eight
hundred public gas lamps, many of them erected and maintained by the
federal government.[92]

Constance Green describes Washington in the antebellum period as "a
community caught unprepared for expansion, a village formerly controlled
by two or three hundred knowledgeable property-owners which found
itself suddenly converted into a burgeoning city run by inexperienced men
who did not know what they wanted or how to get it."[93] But Green's own
figures on expenditures suggest that by 1850 city officials were exercising
greater control over Washington's fate. The proportion of city funds spent
for public works rose sharply from a level of under 18 percent in 1848–49 to a
level of 33 percent or greater throughout the 1850s. These included significant increases for street grading and lighting from 12.3 percent to 24.4 percent between 1848–49 and 1853–54. Expenditures for health also rose, from
only 0.6 percent in 1848–49 to 3.7 percent in 1853–54.[94]

Even the federal government made a few significant steps toward upgrading the physical city. In response to a delegation of influential Washingtonians, including Mayor Walter Lenox, financier William W. Corcoran,
and Joseph Henry, secretary of the new Smithsonian Institution, President
Millard Fillmore promised to improve Washington's central park, the Mall.
Although conceived by Jefferson and L'Enfant as a "grand avenue" central
to beautifying the capital city, this 150-acre area had been largely neglected
to the point where it was described as a "bleak inhospitable common."
Although acts of 1812 and 1820 vested powers in the president and city
council to improve public lots in the city, under the sale of the City Canal to
Washington in 1832, parts of the Mall were subject to development as building lots.[95] Undoubtedly aware of this possibility as well as the threat posed
by wastes collecting in the Potomac a short distance from the White House
(believed responsible for the sudden death from typhoid fever of his predecessor Zachary Taylor), Fillmore directed the commissioner of buildings to

invite the nation's leading horticulturist and landscape expert, Andrew Jackson Downing, to prepare a plan to landscape the Mall. Seizing the opportunity to demonstrate the utility of parks in the heart of cities, Downing accepted the commission, proposing to translate L'Enfant's original intent into a series of six linked gardens.

In order to provide the "healthful interval" and "relief" from Washington's built-up areas, Downing designed, in the words of Therese O'Malley, "an irregular landscape of hilly terrain, varied gardens, and changing vistas," which was intended to contrast with Washington's symmetrical classical federal buildings and straight broad avenues. This romantic treatment, he suggested, was intended to exert an "enchanting influence, by which the too great bustle and excitement of our commercial cities will be happily counterbalanced by the more elegant and quiet enjoyments of country life."[96] In describing his hopes to make the Mall the first *"real* park in the United States," Downing expected to establish a national model as a "Public School of Instruction in everything that relates to the tasteful arrangement of parks and grounds."[97] Harper's magazine prematurely seized upon Downing's proposition as promising "the transformation of the marshy and desolate waste into a National Park." In fact, the same correspondent had to report seven years later that since Downing's untimely death in an 1852 steamboat accident, little had been done to execute his plan.[98]

More immediately successful was the effort, again pressed on Congress by local residents, to improve the city's water supply. For years they had to secure their own water from wells and springs. An ordinance of 1812 authorized the mayor to sink wells upon the petition of two-thirds of the residents of any ward, but as was the usual custom, the costs were to be borne by those benefited by the improvement.[99] In 1830 architect Robert Mills, who spent much of the decade designing monumental buildings to adorn the new capital, presented to Congress a full report on Washington's need to secure a better water system, to deal with fires as well as to provide adequate supplies for cleaning and drinking.[100] The following year Congress authorized construction of pipes to bring water from a spring two miles north of the Capitol to supply public buildings, a boon to local residents only in that some of them proceeded to tap the pipes.[101] Congress remained reluctant to make any major appropriation, however, prompting Mayor Seaton in 1849 to complain that Washington had fallen well behind other cities. Mills backed his complaint in communications appearing in the *Intelligencer* the same year.[102] A number of Washington citizens petitioned Congress for action a year later.

It took a fire in the Library of Congress in 1851, which threatened to burn the highly combustible Capitol dome above it, to move Congress to appropriate $5,000 to plan for an adequate water supply. Placing the work under the direction of a young and self-assured army engineer, Montgomery C. Meigs, Congress authorized a new system originating at Great Falls, some fourteen miles above the city. Inaugurated in 1853 and completed only over a nine-year period, the system of pipes over rough terrain represented a major breakthrough as the largest federal expenditure—more than $2.5 million—on the capital city to date.[103] The new system required the city to begin addressing a vital element in city planning, the challenges of distributing fresh water and channeling off waste water, both sewage and drainage. Washington still lagged behind other cities, but with federal intervention the city assumed the basis of a modern system, a fact underscored in city expenditures for laying water mains, which soared from a figure consistently below 4 percent of total municipal expenses in 1848–49 to 19.2 percent a decade later.[104] In 1859 the city council established the new office of water registrar at a salary of $1,200 "to exercise a constant supervision over the use of waste." Five years later Washington added a water board with responsibilities to set regulations for laying water mains and service pipes and installing fireplugs and hydrants.[105]

By the time the Civil War had convulsed the capital with the overwhelming demands on its physical plant, Washington had achieved the framework for modernization. The lack of adequate paving for its broad streets, the use of the Washington Canal as an open sewer for much of the city's refuse, and the incomplete design of the Mall served to remind observers, however, that the grand vision for a beautiful and magnificent city conceived by its founders remained tantalizingly unrealized. Viewed in terms of population alone, Washington had failed to keep pace with its rivals for commercial hegemony. Compromised in their own aspirations for empire, Alexandria and Georgetown failed to grow at all during the antebellum period. Although Washington's population increased, it could best be compared to an as yet relatively isolated entrepôt like Pittsburgh, whose late start did not prevent it from surpassing Washington in rate of growth at midcentury. As Washington's nearest rival, Baltimore ascended to the dominant position in the region, the product as much as anything of its success with the B&O Railroad and its advantage over the C&O Canal.[106]

Members of Congress could argue with some effect that they had been generous in their grants to the fledgling District cities. Compared, however, to the investments by New York in the Erie Canal, Pennsylvania in its system of state works, or Maryland in the B&O, Congress had failed to support the District's young cities, except under a state of emergency, with the Dutch ready to put the capital city on the auction block. The vision that underlay George Washington's hopes for the District of Columbia and L'Enfant's grand plan for a booming city core boosted by trade and not government alone thus remained largely unrealized at midcentury. At particular fault was Washington's unique political culture. While the close relationship between capital and city clearly offered some possible advantages, in practice it retarded growth and stifled development.

If revolutionary changes be made in the local law of the District . . . instead of a free negro population of perhaps 14,000 in the current anomalous condition of the country the District of Columbia cannot fail to become at once the harbor for at least 50,000 negroes, practically freed as an incident of the war. With such a population, without especial restraining laws, Washington will be rendered almost uninhabitable to the white man. . . . The abolitionists of Congress who can see naught worthy of their sympathy in the condition of any class in any community but the negro class, will of course continue their tinkering experiments upon the local affairs of the District of Columbia, until they make it nothing less than a hell upon earth for the white man.

Washington Star, December 11, 1861

Congress's intimate ties with Washington meant that it controlled the fate not just of the city's physical development but of its social relationships as well. No such relationship was more central in the first half of the nineteenth century than race. And while Washington's status as slave territory linked its experience with the South, its subjection to federal power left it open to the influence of Northern abolitionists. As the national struggle over slavery heightened, it swept Washington into the controversy, making it a central battleground for the future of race relations in America.

Created out of two states with the largest slave populations in the South, the District of Columbia contained from its origin a significant black presence. As Maryland increased the pace of emancipation in the early 1800s and a Virginia law of 1806 required blacks to leave the state within a year of achieving their freedom, Washington's free black population rose significantly.[1] While Washington ranked below other major cities in the absolute size of its free black population, by 1840 it nonetheless ranked ahead of the. others in terms of the total black proportion of its population, a position it retained right up to the eve of the Civil War (table 1). Moreover, fears that the black population would grow even larger spurred authorities to restrict its movement.

The city's first black code, passed in 1808, imposed a $5 fine on blacks

Table 1

Free Black Population by City (and % Total)

	1800	1820	1840	1860
Philadelphia	4,210 (10.2)	7,579 (11.9)	10,507 (11.2)	22,500 (3.9)
New York	3,499 (5.8)	10,368 (8.4)	16,358 (5.2)	12,500 (1.5)
Baltimore	2,771 (10.4)	10,326 (16.5)	17,967 (17.6)	25,000 (11.7)
Boston	1,174 (4.7)	1,687 (4.0)	2,427 (2.6)	2,000 (1.2)
Charleston	951 (5.1)	1,475 (6.0)	1,558 (5.3)	3,200 (7.9)
Washington	123 (3.8)	1,696 (13.0)	4,808 (20.6)	9,209 (15.0)
Cincinnati	20 (2.7)	1,475 (4.5)	2,240 (4.8)	3,731 (2.4)

Source: 1800–1840 figures appear in Leonard P. Curry, *The Free Black in Urban America, 1800–1850: The Shadow of the Dream* (Chicago: University of Chicago Press, 1981); 1860 figures were compiled from local histories.

out after 10 o'clock in the evening. Following a petition to Congress in 1810 seeking to guard against "the disorderly and tumultuous meetings of slaves and free negroes," the city in 1812 authorized jail sentences for those caught out at night and attending "disorderly" meetings. Free blacks were required to carry certificates of freedom at all times, and while this provided them some protection against kidnapping, they were prohibited from disturbing the peace and playing games of cards or dice and required to secure permits for balls or dances. Under the terms by which the city charter was renewed in 1820, free blacks were required to register their freedom papers with the mayor and to secure the testimony of one "good and responsible free white citizen" of personal acquaintance that they lived peaceable and quiet lives. They were required to post a $20 bond for good behavior and against the possibility that they might become a charge on the corporation.[2] In 1827 the city extended the rules governing free black behavior, requiring annual registration with the posting of a bond for good behavior and self-support.[3] A year later all persons of color were prohibited from visiting the Capitol "without necessary business." The city set fines for offenses by free blacks and authorized whipping slaves who violated established standards of decorum.[4] Somewhat more permissive than similar codes in the South, Washington's regulations conformed closely to laws enacted to restrict black freedom in the North. The growing attention that Washington received from abolitionists tested, however, the protection that Washington's whites sought from the city's code.

In 1830 abolitionist William Lloyd Garrison targeted the District as "the first citadel to be carried" and considered publishing his new publication,

The Liberator, in Washington. The decision of Benjamin Lundy to move his antislavery publication, *The Genius of Universal Emancipation,* from Baltimore to Washington encouraged Garrison to locate his paper in Boston instead. But the establishment of an abolitionist society in Washington in 1831 and Nat Turner's rebellion in neighboring Virginia the same year prompted defensive actions in the District, including the first regulations in Georgetown for regulating free blacks. Among the list of offenses was the subscription to or possession of books or papers "calculated to excite insurrection or insubordination among the slaves or colored people ... and particularly a newspaper called the *Liberator.*" The 1836 version of this black code cited the *Liberator* as an extreme example of literature "calculated to incite insurrection or insubordination among slaves or colored people."[5]

White fears seemed to be confirmed in 1835. In August of that year, a slave owned by the widow of Architect of the Capitol William Thornton, in a drunken state, allegedly attempted to murder his mistress. Rumors quickly spread that the man had a number of abolitionist documents in his possession at the time of the attack, a charge magnified a week later with reports that a young Northern teacher recently arrived in Georgetown, Reuben Crandall, had circulated incendiary abolitionist literature.[6] The news provoked white attacks on blacks. In three days of civil disturbance, some homes, a school, a church, and the fashionable home of a mulatto restaurateur, Beverly Snow, were badly damaged. Rumors that Snow had made derogatory remarks about the wives and daughters of artisans on strike at the Navy Yard helped fuel the mob. Confining himself to jail for his own protection, Snow denied the charge, provoking an anonymous response in the *National Intelligencer,* which the paper only identified as "a respectable citizen," who charged, "We have already too many free negroes and mulattoes in this city, and the policy of our corporate authorities should lend to the diminution of this insolent class, and the increase of the whites." Pointing to a motion hastily introduced before the city council during the disturbances to prohibit shop licenses to blacks, he proclaimed, "If they wish to live here, let them become subordinates and laborers, as nature has designed; if they aspire higher, let them remove to the North, and flourish under the patronage of their friends, the abolitionists."[7]

Although blacks were the ones who suffered during the period of disorder, the result of the attacks upon them was the tightening of existing black codes in Georgetown as well as Washington through new restrictions on their livelihood as well as their social activities. Washington's 1836 modification of its black code increased the number of white witnesses of character to five and required a bond of $1,000 "conditioned for his or her good and orderly conduct, and that of every member of his or her existing family," to be renewed every year. It prohibited all secret, private, and religious meetings beyond 10 o'clock at night and banned blacks from operating taverns and eating establishments. Associated ordinances in Georgetown

The Specter of Race

in 1835 and Washington City in 1836 denied licenses to blacks for any trade other than driving carts or carriages, acts both intended to deter further immigration of free blacks to the city and to discourage those already in residence.[8] Although Chief Judge of the Circuit Court William Cranch upheld an early challenge to the law, which proved difficult to enforce and was subsequently modified to reduce the number of witnesses to one and the bond to $50, the restrictions on employment appear to have had some effect. While a few notable blacks made dramatic breakthroughs in business, economic opportunity for blacks declined between 1823 and the Civil War. As a whole they remained tightly confined to the lower occupational rungs of the economy.[9]

The violence in Washington appears to have had some correspondence to similar attacks in other cities to drive blacks out of businesses sought after by whites. The anger of the Navy Yard artisans suggests that conclusion as well as the effect the restrictions placed on employment. Blacks and whites in Washington were not, however, in the same kind of direct competition for jobs they faced in industrializing cities in the East and Middle West.[10] Washington confined blacks largely to hotel and domestic service and unskilled laboring positions not actively sought after by whites but deemed sufficiently important to the functioning of the city to have influenced a congressional report opposing colonization, lest those positions be lost only to be filled by refugees from Southern slavery.[11] Although there was some competition for positions on public works, the virtual exclusion of blacks from federal employment helped remove the sharp edge of job competition between races, even as it assured a bifurcated economy.[12] Beyond the immediate effort to punish Snow and the few black entrepreneurs with his standing, the new codes appear to have been more directly a part of the national response, frequently punctuated by rioting, that accompanied the American Anti-Slavery Society's effort starting in the summer of 1835 to flood the country with abolitionist literature and with petitions to Congress for emancipation in the District.[13]

As the dominant local paper, the *National Intelligencer* stressed this point. Running its account of the riots under the title "First Fruit," the *Intelligencer* described the offending slave as

> venting the most ferocious threats, and uttering a tissue of jargon, much of which was a literal repetition of the language addressed to the Negroes by the incendiary publications above referred to. Believing that his bloody purpose was in part at least, if not altogether, the effect of those publications, and that such deeds must be the natural consequence of their dissemination, we have concluded, not, however, without some hesitation, to make the occurrence public, as well for the information of our northern fellow citizens at large, as for that of the Fanatics themselves, who may not be aware of the tendency of their labors.

Like the mayor, who responded immediately by prohibiting the further assemblage or meeting of any blacks, slave or free, the paper appeared more concerned about the threat to the city's reputation than the damage inflicted on blacks. "We grieve to have to publish such things, of our hitherto peaceable city," the paper stated. "We could not have believed it possible that we should have to see the Public Offices garrisoned by the clerks with United States troops posted at their doors, and their windows barricaded, to defend them against citizens of Washington." Urging the agitators to consider "the fatal tendency of their conduct to the vital interests of the city" and to leave the administration of justice and "the reform of defective regulations" to proper authority, the paper placed the blame on outside agitators, notably what it branded "a demoniacal design, on the part of a fanatical individual to stir up our negro population to insurrection and murder" to "the terror of the women and children, and enduring injury to the character of the city, if not utter ruin to all its hopes and prospects."[14]

The courts ultimately acquitted Crandall of the charges that the *Intelligencer* was all too quick to levy against him, but that did not eliminate the paper's expressed fears about abolitionism. It filled its columns with reported incidents of abolitionist agitation, even as it commended other meetings "repudiating the doctrines and rebuking the schemes of the fanatical Abolitionists."[15] As it reprinted an article from a Boston paper claiming that slaves were better off in the South than free blacks as well as a number of whites in the North, it editorialized, "We hope to see public sentiment in the North manifest itself as pointedly, and as generally against the designs of the Abolitionists, with regard to this District, as against their insane interference with the subject of Slavery elsewhere."[16]

Perhaps most revealing, the *Intelligencer* reprinted a July 4 oration delivered in New Bedford, Massachusetts. Although taking the usual Northern stand against slavery itself, the speaker nonetheless urged his audience to respect the interests of Southern gentlemen, who were in a better position to know black character and capacity. Besides, he claimed, in a reference bound to attract the attention of Washington readers, should the slaves be freed, they "would run riot in the intoxication of freedom. . . . Robbery, pillage, devastation, and blood, would be the first fruits of an indiscriminate release." For those who would respond to the reformist spirit, he urged that attention be redirected abroad, where "Humanity calls upon you, to go into the streets of Manchester and Birmingham and there lecture the People upon the disease, poverty, misery, and death inflicted upon the operatives."[17]

Congress revealed its sympathy with such attitudes among Washington whites in an 1836 report on a resolution that it ought not interfere in any way with slavery in the District of Columbia. Calling such interference "unwise, impolitic, and dangerous to the union," the report condemned abolitionists, who, it charged, had no interest in the District of Columbia.

The Specter of Race

"Who does not perceive," it asked rhetorically, "that under such circumstances the district would constitute at once a neutral ground upon which hosts of free blacks, fugitive slaves, and incendiaries, would be assembled in the work of general abolitionism; and that, from such a magazine of evil, every conceivable mischief would be spread through the surrounding country." Charging that slaves were unfit for freedom, the report predicted that emancipation would spawn vice, immorality, and licentiousness. Either whites or blacks would be forced to leave the South, or, even more likely, it continued, "blacks would every where be driven before the whites, as the Indians have been, until they were exterminated from the earth." The committee, chaired by Representative Henry Pinckney of South Carolina, prompted a new practice, the so-called gag rule, which required that petitions calling for emancipation in the District be automatically tabled without debate. Congress faithfully followed the practice for most of a decade.[18]

The Pinckney report claimed that Washington's local residents had offered no support for emancipation whatsoever. Such was not entirely the case. In 1827 more than one thousand Washingtonians signed a petition calling for the gradual end to slavery, claiming that the institution "impairs prosperity and happiness of this District and casts the reproach of inconsistency upon the free institutions established among us."

> The existence among us of a distinct class of people, who, by their condition as slaves, are deprived of almost every incentive to virtue and industry, and shut out from many of the sources of light and knowledge, has an evident tendency to corrupt the morals of the people, and to dampen the spirit of enterprise, by accustoming the rising generation to look with contempt upon honest labor, and to depend, for support, too much upon the labor of others. It prevents a useful and industrious class of people from settling among us, by rendering the means of subsistence more precarious to the laboring class of whites. It diminishes the resources of the community, by throwing the earnings of the poor into the coffers of the rich; thus rendering the former dependent, servile, and improvident, while the latter are tempted to become, in the same proportion, luxurious and prodigal.[19]

The Committee on the District of Columbia buried the petition, but statements issued by the grand jury of Washington County in 1828 and 1829 against the slave trade and an additional petition to Congress to abolish slavery and the slave trade in 1833 generated enough interest in the subject to launch a congressional investigation into the domestic slave trade in Washington and the use of Washington and Alexandria jails for the safekeeping of slaves who were about to be sold. The report, issued in 1836, recommended against emancipation, arguing that it would serve to bring thousands of blacks into the District. Citing a report from the grand jury of Washington County, which had taken up the problem of runaways, it agreed with local sentiment that no change would be practical until the slaves could be removed to Africa.[20]

The effect of the 1835 riots was apparently sufficient to harden public opinion against any form of emancipation. An 1839 petition submitted to Congress from some two hundred Washington residents protested against any further agitation on the subject:

> It is not that your memorialists are slave-holders that they present these views to your honorable bodies; many of them do not own slaves, and some of them might be forbidden by conscience to hold any but these, nevertheless, unite with others in this prayer to your honorable bodies, not only from the just respect due to the legal rights of those of their neighbors who do possess slaves, but from a deep conviction that the continual agitation of the subject by those who can have no right to interfere with it is calculated to have an injurious influence on the peace and tranquillity of the community, and upon the well being and happiness of those who are held in subjection.[21]

When the House Judiciary Committee showed some sympathy with free blacks who had been held in prison for failure to produce their freedom papers, a resolution in the city council opposed any change in the law, arguing that it worked well enough and that any change would make Washington a haven for blacks.[22] Although antagonism to the slave trade continued, support for emancipation quickly dissipated. Moreover, after 1835 white citizens withdrew the helping hand so necessary to assist the black community. While nearly half the schools that had opened for free blacks before the riots that year were run by whites, from 1836 to 1861 only two of twenty-four black schools were opened by whites.[23] In a city where legal restrictions continued to tighten, the most moderate stance, shared by the *National Intelligencer,* favored colonization, a position to which Washington blacks themselves were decidedly antagonistic.[24]

In 1848 the city was rocked once again, this time by news of a daring escape by Washington slaves aboard the ship *Pearl.* The incident started when a free black resident of Washington, fearing that the manumission of his wife and children might be reversed by the courts, sought assistance from friends in Philadelphia to flee the city. It ended tragically when he and fellow escapees were captured after one of their number revealed their plans to authorities. Believing that the whole affair was the product of an abolitionist conspiracy, an angry mob turned first on the jail that held the ship's captain, then on an outspoken antislavery Whig congressman from Ohio, Joshua Giddings, who had reportedly visited the escapees in their cells and offered assistance, and finally on Gamaliel Bailey, editor of Washington's second antislavery paper, the *National Era.*

While the city faced immediate fear of civil disorder, members of both houses of Congress entered the fray. One member, William T. Haskell of

Tennessee, charged that other congressmen had actually "been engaged . . . in the deliberate attempt to scatter the seeds of insurrection and insubordination, if not rebellion, among the slaves in this District."[25] Not to be intimidated, Giddings entered congressional debate over slavery in the District by calling for a local referendum on the question that would include black men as voters. When challenged on black participation, he said he would accept an amendment to his proposal that would declare black men ineligible if white slaveholders were excluded as well.[26] Although order was restored after three nights of potential violence, the effects of what was considered outside agitation continued to grate on Washington's conservative white residents.

While these arguments for emancipation in the District found little enthusiasm in Congress, more support could be found for terminating the slave trade there, including that of Henry Clay, who presented a petition from the city council and the mayor supporting the position. Claiming that the move should satisfy South as well as North, the chief architect of the 1850 compromise stated that he had "shared in the horror at this slave trade in this District, and viewed it with as much detestation as any of those at the North who complain of it." Congressman Robert Hunter of Virginia, the architect of Alexandria's retrocession from the District, was among those who opposed the provision. Pursuing the forced argument that blacks would suffer from the want of the right to emigrate, he revived the more standard argument that the act would prove the first step toward emancipation.[27]

Elimination of the slave trade under the Compromise of 1850 drew much support in the Washington press, but tough provisions for capturing and returning fugitive slaves provoked immediate controversy and several violent clashes. One household slave who failed to reveal the hiding place of a runaway in his quarters was jailed, while some whites physically resisted efforts of traders and bounty hunters to seize blacks on Washington streets. But Senator Charles Sumner's effort to interfere with the Fugitive Slave Act drew sharp criticism from the *Washington Star*, which in commenting on riots over the return of fugitives from Boston, noted sarcastically:

> A few silly old women shrieked, and a few crack-brained persons groaned at the shocking idea of a person claiming and obtaining possession of his property, no matter where found or by whom retained; but their ravings did not, at first, prove contagious. It was not until Sumner and his tribe, until Giddings and his followers, sent forth appeal after appeal to the people to resist the law and to smite its officers, that the worst of feelings of the worst of men were excited into brutal action.[28]

Generally the Washington press remained sympathetic to slavery where it existed and defended Southern property rights over meddlesome interference from abolitionists.

Despite efforts to mute controversies surrounding Washington as a potential site for social experimentation, issues regarding race simply would not go away, as revealed in the reaction to the founding of Washington's first high school designed specifically for black women. Excluded under Washington's first bill to provide free education, which was passed in 1804, free blacks had nonetheless managed to attain a considerable measure of education through schools supported by private subscription, starting in 1807. No other black community in America supported more private schools than Washington.[29] Educational opportunities for blacks lagged well behind those available to whites, however, thus offering an ideal location for missionary work. The leading figure attracted to this end was a white teacher from New York State, Myrtilla Miner. Deeply influenced by abolitionism herself and supported personally as well as financially by feminist Lucretia Mott and abolitionists Wendell Phillips and Arthur Tappan, Miner opened her school in 1851. However, when she sought the assistance of John F. Cook, a black clergyman and leading educator among Washington's free blacks, Cook urged her to look for white support instead, claiming that his people had "neither vote nor voice."[30]

The reaction of whites in Washington was overwhelmingly hostile, including that of a Washington lawyer whom Miner quoted as saying, "We are not going to have you Northern abolitionists coming down here to teach our Niggers. We know better what to do with them than you do."[31] Forced by local reaction to move her schoolhouse three times in her first three years in Washington, Miner complained that she habitually retired each night with the expectation that it would be torched before morning. Looking for a safe place for herself, she found that "many ladies refused to take me to board because I would teach colored girls." Even an early supporter, Mayor Walter Lenox, eventually turned against her, publishing a letter in the *Intelligencer* condemning the school both for threatening to attract black migrants to the city and for instilling dissatisfaction with their social condition once they arrived. "With this superior education," he claimed, "there will come no removal of the present disabilities, no new sources of employment equal to their mental culture; and hence there will be a restless population, less disposed than ever to fill that position in society which is allotted to them."[32] Miner held her ground, however, retorting that it was the failure to educate blacks that would threaten the prospects for peace:

> If left in ignorance, no wise counsel can stay the tide, should they rise in their might and desperation, to roll back the flood of power that deprives them of privileges, which, ignorant as they are, they know to be the "inalienable right" of every honest person who treads American soil. This you have taught them without schools, and now they must be enlightened and awakened to a full consciousness of things as they are; of the difficulties to be met, and of the best mode of disposing of them.[33]

The Specter of Race

Miner found her efforts in Washington thwarted, however, as even such a staunch friend of abolition and the education of blacks as Sayles Bowen, a founder of the city's Republican party, disassociated himself from the school and opposed efforts to grant it a federal charter.[34]

Although made predictable by the presence of slaves in Washington, Miner's harsh reception was not unlike what she could have expected in the North, where by the 1830s statute or custom relegated black children to separate schools in nearly every community. Although Ohio began to tax blacks locally to support public schools in 1821, they were denied admission to those schools until 1829. So hostile was the reaction of local officials, however, that the state legislature repealed the act two years later, leaving blacks to attend schools, as they did elsewhere in the North, in private academies or in inferior separate facilities.[35] So negative was the reaction to Prudence Crandall—Reuben's sister—in her efforts to establish a school for black girls in Connecticut that she was forced to abandon the effort and to try again in Illinois.[36] While some portions of Massachusetts permitted publicly funded integrated schools, it took a massive effort by abolitionists working with Charles Sumner finally to break down racial barriers in Boston in 1855. Subsequent efforts to assure integration in Providence and Philadelphia failed.[37] More broadly, free blacks in the North lacked such basic liberties as the right to vote or to serve on juries. In a rare exception, the Free Soil Party used its power in the Ohio legislature in 1849 and 1850 to repeal laws barring black testimony in courts and requiring blacks to post bond when entering the state.[38] More typically, the law strictly confined black freedom in the North. Leon Litwack has summarized the situation on the eve of the Civil War:

> Having excluded the Negro from profitable employments, the whites scorned his idleness and poverty; having taxed him in some states for the support of public education, they excluded his children from the schools or placed them in separate and inferior institutions and then deplored the ignorance of his race; having excluded him from various lecture halls and libraries, they pointed to his lack of culture and refinement; and, finally having stripped him of his claims to citizenship and having deprived him of opportunities for political and economic advancement, the whites concluded that the Negro had demonstrated an incapacity for improvement in this country and should be colonized in Africa.[39]

As long as Southerners remained in Congress, Washington's anti-abolitionists found allies for maintaining their restrictive policies over blacks. In 1860, Republicans, citing the good work of Miner, attempted unsuccessfully to pass a bill enabling blacks who paid taxes to be entitled to the benefit of public schools.[40] With the outbreak of war, however, the complexion of Congress changed. Assuming majority power, Republicans reversed antagonism to supporting black education, passing first without opposition a law detailing a portion of local taxes paid by blacks to the use of their own schools and then expanding the pool of funds available to a portion of all local taxes paid.

Locally elected officials did what they could to resist the will of Congress. While James Grimes of Iowa, as chairman of the Senate District Committee, pointed out that blacks had contributed $3,600 in taxes to schools they could not use, under the 1862 school bill the council allotted to colored schools only $265 in 1862 and $410 in 1863. In the same years, the council funneled a total of $65,000 to white schools.[41] When Congress forced the resignation of Mayor James B. Barrett for refusing to take a loyalty oath, he was succeeded by Richard Wallach, a Whig who in his unsuccessful race for mayor had been tainted with sympathizing with the "black Republican party." Wallach nonetheless stood with his conservative constituents by refusing to allocate payments required by Congress to black schools.[42]

Without adequate funds, colored schools had to rely on the assistance of private philanthropy. This, the local radical papers commended heartily. When the Freedman's Relief Association opened the city's first free school for blacks, the *Washington Chronicle* boasted:

> The corner of the curtain that hides the crowded events that are to characterize the history of the colored race of our hemisphere has already been lifted, and here in Washington city the colored people are slowly but surely being rescued from the bondage of mind, as well as body, which has so long enthralled them. The Bensons and the Douglasses that are to emerge from this school and kindred others will in themselves furnish the most powerful weapons with which to combat the ignorance and prejudices of men.[43]

As Radical Republicans pressed for the end of slavery in the District, local residents predictably opposed that change too. Fearing that emancipation would assure that Washington would be overrun with black refugees from the South, the *Star* asked for amendments to the black codes instead, claiming that they worked well enough to help the free black community prosper. Estimating that the arrival of up to fifty thousand blacks would make the District of Columbia almost uninhabitable, the *Star* charged that abolitionists in Congress were intent on making "it nothing less than a hell upon earth for the white man."[44] The *National Intelligencer,* while finally recognizing the right of Congress under the power of exclusive jurisdiction to emancipate the city's slaves, nonetheless sought to have the question submitted to a vote of eligible Washington residents first, a position Abraham Lincoln had taken as a young congressman in 1849.[45]

Although no such referendum took place, the board of aldermen, while disclaiming any intent to interfere with federal policy, nonetheless declared that "a large majority of the people of this community is adverse to the unqualified abolition of slavery in this district." It directed its committee

The Specter of Race

on interests before Congress to seek safeguards "against converting this city, located as it is between two Slaveholding States into an asylum for free negroes, a population undesirable in every American community, and which it has been deemed necessary to exclude altogether from some even of the Non-slaveholding States."[46] Even the radical paper the *Chronicle,* employing terms that had become common throughout the North, sought to assure its readers that "emancipation does not mean equality; liberty does not mean license. . . . [There are] certain laws of nature which no law of Congress can controvert." Following passage of the bill, which offered owners approximately $300 in compensation for each slave, the *Chronicle* claimed that blacks "will scarcely realize the difference between a condition of modified servitude and a condition of complete independence."[47]

Although the battle against Congress over emancipation appeared lost, local Democrats took every opportunity to keep the race issue alive. Even before passage of the emancipation bill in April 1862, Alderman Thomas Lloyd used a military request to lift the ban on nighttime travel on blacks as an excuse to raise the specter of tumult in the city. To the argument that the continuation of such laws was a nuisance, Lloyd asked a series of rhetorical questions: "Would the gentleman have negroes vote in the city; their children mingle in the schools, and throw aside all the natural barriers between the white and the Negro?" For himself, the *Star* reported, "he was in favor of colonization, and thought that subject had better be considered as soon as possible, as the city was already overrun with free negroes, who proved to be the most disorderly class of people we have at night, notwithstanding the law forbidding their appearance after 10 o'clock."[48]

Appealing to the conservative sentiment of established Washington residents, Democrats running for local office in the 1862 elections condemned abolitionists for "injury and oppression of the white race" and spoke out against "the odious task" of schooling black children.[49] Condemned in turn as the paper of proslavery by the Radical *National Republican,* the *Star,* though Republican, warned against abolitionist efforts to enforce social equality, charging it would "inevitably end in bloodshed amounting to a war of the races that will exterminate the race for whose benefit it is unwisely sought to be entailed on the country."[50] Even staunch Unionists, in seeking to protect the rights of freedmen, remained wary of social experimentation. When local whites pilloried blacks who signed up to fight in the war, the *Chronicle* charged that such hate against races was "unworthy of the age and of us a people." The paper considered it necessary nonetheless to reassure its readers that there "need be no assimilation with the colored races, either red or black; there never will be, never can be in these United States; but that is no reason why they should not be treated with humanity and kindness, especially when they are freely offering us their services against the enemies of our flag and country."[51]

Such political sentiment convinced congressional radicals to extend rights for blacks in ways that even the rare success of Massachusetts had been unable to achieve. Reacting angrily to incidents provoked by the continuation of the Fugitive Slave Law, Congress, after two years' effort, abolished the offensive measure in 1864.[52] Rights granted under the emancipation bill, by allowing blacks to testify before a claims commission, paved the way for subsequent legislation opening District courts for their use.[53] In addition, Massachusetts senator Henry Wilson successfully reorganized the District judiciary, despite a petition signed by forty-eight lawyers who opposed it.[54] Wilson also sought to eliminate all discrimination according to color in the District, a goal heatedly debated in Congress and fiercely resisted in Washington. The *Star* retorted that such sweeping laws could scarcely be intended to help the people of the District so much as they were devised for political effect: "While we shall cheerfully sustain thoughtful, well-balanced and discriminating changes in our whole judiciary system, we shall deprecate anything of the sort which are likely to be neither more nor less than revolutionary experiments at the expense of the only community lawfully at the mercy, in such matters, of the experimenters."[55]

Senator Charles Sumner, also of Massachusetts, secured other rights for blacks in Washington. Appalled by the practice of Washington's street railways prohibiting blacks from riding inside the cars and requiring them to stand on the front of the platform with the driver or to ride on the roof, he managed in 1862 to get a ban on racial restrictions on one minor line.[56] He pressed for ending discrimination on all public transportation in the District, but not without provoking resistance even from his own party members, including Senator James Grimes, author of the landmark 1862 bill to make funds available to educate black children. More committed to equal opportunity for blacks to learn in separate schools than to their right to mingle equally with whites in public spaces, Grimes argued that the highest quality blacks in the District did not want to ride in desegregated cars but preferred to be "permitted to occupy undisturbed the cars which the company have dedicated to their own use." The real outrage, Grimes charged, was not segregation but "the interference of white men with cars devoted to the exclusive use of colored people." The Senate passed a bill forbidding discrimination in Washington streetcars by a majority of one, but the measure died in the House.[57]

Against the backdrop of the Radical agenda in Congress lay the social turmoil brought about with the massive influx of refugees from Southern battlefields, immigration that appeared to confirm even the worst specter whites could conceive of seeing the city overrun with destitute newcomers. Labeled "contrabands"—literally confiscated property[58]—these blacks, often arriving with nothing more than the clothes on their backs, trickled in at first to temporary quarters housing about four hundred at Duff's Row behind where the Library of Congress now stands on Capitol Hill. The federal government, in an effort to retain slaveholding Maryland's loyalty,

The Specter of Race

refused to grant runaways from that state contraband status. But by claiming to be from Virginia or by finding Union troops willing to harbor them, many Maryland slaves also found refuge in the city.[59] News reports in Baltimore and Washington claimed that between one hundred and two hundred slaves were moving from Maryland's Montgomery and Prince George's counties, which were adjacent to the District, into Washington each week. According to the *Star*,

> The owners of slaves in Prince George's say that it is almost useless to bother with them, that they are a source of continual trouble, having to be watched at all times. Several instances have occurred where the owners have overtaken on the road a part of their slaves making their way up, and have contented themselves by picking out the most valuable ones, and allowing the others to go. Others let the fugitives "slide" unmolested, giving themselves no uneasiness, expressing the belief that they will wish themselves back again.[60]

The tide continued despite Maryland senator-elect Reverdy Johnson's threatened challenge to the constitutionality of the law ceding territory for the District and Maryland governor Augustus Bradford's protest that federal authorities had failed to release custody of runaways from his state. By mid-1862, Washington authorities had given up attempts to further pro-union sentiment in Maryland by avoiding any action that might be construed as an attack on slavery there. To yet another complaint from Governor Bradford in May, U.S. Attorney General Edward Bates replied indifferently, "In these distempered times I am not at all surprised to hear that slaves in the border states are using all available means to escape into free territory."[61]

With the spring military campaign in Virginia, the number of refugees swelled, forcing the army to open a new site, Camp Barker, to accommodate them. In September 1861 alone, fourteen hundred new refugees arrived. By 1862 the total had reached four thousand, while in Alexandria some additional one thousand crowded into an old schoolhouse, a former slave pen, and "several tenements that can hardly be called a shelter." Disease and hunger among the contraband prompted both federal authorities and Northern philanthropists to seek additional areas in which to provide food and shelter. By 1863, the army had established contraband camps on both sides of the Potomac River that accommodated as many as ten thousand refugees at any one time.[62]

Such numbers spurred sometimes hysterical commentary about the inability of the local community to absorb them. In expressing his fear that the growing number of free blacks would prove a burden on the city, Mayor Wallach said that he would care for local blacks in need but that he could not provide assistance to the ranks of refugees. "The contraband and emancipated slaves already number by the thousands," he declared, "and many of them are idle, dissolute, and reckless, and to impose on this city the

Former slaves known as contraband set to work on Washington's defense building a stockade around the Orange and Alexandria Railroad complex and unloading provisions at the nearby Alexandria Canal, ca. 1862. Mathew Brady Collection, courtesy National Archives.

burthen of supporting the multitude who would be thrown upon it would be an intolerable grievance, absent all provision for its care, and exhaust its taxables." A Washington paper, quoting the *Rochester (New York) Union* for April 26, 1862, added further fuel to popular concern by reporting, "Just about these days there seems to be quite an influx of strange colored persons in our city. Each is telling some large story about his escape from slavery and his sufferings. These persons come here expecting to be taken care of by 'white folks,' and disappointed in that expectation, resort to means for a living not countenanced in this community."[63]

The newly arrived contrabands, men and women, were anxious to work and assumed many of the hard jobs whites were unwilling to take in and

The Specter of Race

around military encampments. Pay was often delayed or did not come at all because government employers reasoned that "sustenance & freedom" were compensation enough. But demand for labor quickly pushed wages up above the $10 a month established by military order in July 1862 to as much as $20 or $25 a month.[64] Many of the freedmen were destitute or infirm, however, and subject to private and government charity. To counter charges of idleness and expense like those leveled by Mayor Wallach, the government established a $5 a month tax on the federal wages of contrabands for a fund to assist blacks in need. While blacks appeared to accept the idea in principle, its effect was harsh in a time of rising prices, and they objected as well to having no control over the disbursement of funds.[65] Chief Quartermaster of the Department of Washington Elias Greene defended the fund by arguing that it countered criticisms that blacks constituted only a drain on public funds. Moreover, he argued:

> Remit the $5 tax, and the old state of things is restored.—Instead of being gathered together in one place, where they can be economically provided for, and properly trained; the colored people who come within our lines will be scattered in sickly camps, through the city, as has been the case heretofore; living a life of idleness at the public expense; subject to the most demoralizing influences; and in return for the moral contamination they receive, from contact with the worst class of citizens; spreading the small pox, and other infectious diseases, to which they are extremely liable, when living idly in crowded barracks in the close air of the city.[66]

With the demand for labor to execute the war at its height, the government finally abandoned the tax. But efforts to keep contrabands apart from built-up sections of Washington, and thus out of sight of critics, continued as Greene promoted the opening of a new camp on Mason's (now Roosevelt) Island. There, in addition to securing "the salutary effects of good pure country air, and a return to their former healthy avocations as 'field hands,'" Greene promised a reduction in the threat of disease.[67]

As the war drew to a close, Washington entered a critical historical juncture. The huge black population, swollen to some forty thousand from the eleven thousand listed in the 1860 census, demanded attention. A bill of rights had been secured in law, but Republicans saw even greater possibilities. "This is a moment for changes," Charles Sumner wrote a colleague. "Our whole system is like molten wax, ready to receive an impression."[68] As the *Chronicle* put it, "The great anti-slavery party of our nation owes it to themselves, now that we have completed the destruction of slavery, to see to it that the national capital shall not only be the seat of freedom, but shall also be occupied and surrounded by a prosperous, enterprising and progressive population." To that end, the paper urged not just the franchise for black men but also a municipal government dedicated to ending all discrimination.[69] Although Washington was hardly equivalent to rebel territory, the resistance of the city's white population to rights for freedmen prompted Radical Republicans to exercise the power of exclusive jurisdiction to treat the city as though it were under Reconstruction. Seen as an unprecedented opportunity to advance their goals, Washington beckoned as a grounds for new social programs, but not without the opposition of entrenched prejudices which bitterly resisted any hint that emancipation would also suggest equality.

Seat of

American Empire

11

The Civil War vastly expanded the reach of federal power even as it stimulated the growth of the capital city. In line with the goal not just to preserve the Union but to make it more perfect, Radical Republicans attempted to put their social philosophy into effect in Washington, which though not conquered territory was considered a slaveholding area sympathetic to the South and thus ripe for Reconstruction. Federal interventions into such central matters of civic life as the enfranchisement of black males set a precedent for different kinds of interventions in the form of long-delayed physical improvements. Reconstruction thus offered opportunities to satisfy both the social aspirations of free blacks and the demand for increased investments in physical development. With the termination of Reconstruction and the institution of a federally appointed government in 1874, however, social programs came to a halt. Henceforth, Washington's development would be placed in the hands of experts captivated by the goal of upgrading the physical city and extending amenities to outlying residential areas. This approach gained acceptance not only from local white residents but nationally, as Washington was compared favorably to other major cities with their boss-ridden machines.

The City Beautiful movement that emerged at the turn of the century was built on these goals, its advocates conceiving Washington as a showcase for the nation that would be made possible by creating a distinctive monumental core. At the same time, however, the drive for social uplift associated with one wing of Progressive reform directed new attention to Washington's poorer residents, especially the large number of blacks crowded into the city's back alleys. Expressing confidence in the beneficial effects of a good environment, social activists sought to make the city's residential quarters every bit as beautiful and healthful as the monumental core. The resources for such efforts were limited, however, and given the powerful institutional backing for the City Beautiful philosophy, they could not command equal national attention. By the time of the New Deal, the creation of a monumental core was nearly complete, but the city's poorer residential areas remained very much in the shadow of the Capitol, in the words of social reformer Charles Weller, "neglected neighbors."

The cover of Charles Weller's *Neglected Neighbors* (1909), showing slums in the shadow of the Capitol.

Reconstruction: Social and Physical

The rebellion has effected revolutions in many instances, and none more signally than Washington. The outside American world begins to look in upon this microcosm. People come here from all the Northern States, not simply to get and hold office, but to get and hold lots and houses. For every traitor who has deserted, ten honest people come here to settle down and occupy ten times his former space. With this people come nerve and enterprise and ambitious activity. They find slavery abolished and the old slave owners fled or quiescent. They see that the Capital, so long contended for by the rebels, and so bravely held by the patriots, is now, as it were, forever set like a precious jewel in the very center of the diadem of the Republic. . . . The capital of a great Republic should not only be the freest but the most progressive and beautified in the world.

Washington Chronicle, June 3, 1864

With peace Washington set the stage nationally for the freedmen's enjoyment of new rights. The city faced competing demands, however, most notably from the need to address the war's devastating wear and tear on its physical fabric. An additional goal voiced for the period, then, was physical improvement. To a considerable degree the politics of the postwar era, including the District's short-lived experiment in territorial government, tied together the potentially charged issue of advancing opportunity for blacks with the physical reconstruction of the city. For most of the immediate postwar period, Republicans promoted both goals, despite differences in priorities within their ranks. As Reconstruction evolved, however, Republicans divided, and ultimately the commitment to physical development triumphed over social advances.

The issue of granting the franchise to black men animated fierce debate after the war, and in this Washington quickly emerged as the focal point. During the spring of 1865 Republicans in Congress pressing for universal manhood suffrage believed they had the support of President Andrew Johnson. On May 29, however, the president issued his North Carolina Proclamation, setting up a new government without extending the suffrage. Leaving that decision to voters clearly hostile to the idea, Johnson issued similar proclamations for seven other Confederate states. When Iowa, Wisconsin, and Connecticut in the North rejected extending the franchise, Radicals turned to the District as a opportunity to advance their cause.[1] Senator Charles Sumner tried to secure universal manhood suffrage in Montana early in 1865, and when that failed he attempted to secure that right in the District of Columbia in conjunction with the renewal of Washington's charter. Noting the difficulty in securing extensions of the vote in the North, Sumner's Radical colleague in the House, Benjamin Wade, advised him that it was impractical to press the issue in Washington, despite attention given to a petition signed by twenty-five hundred black Washington residents, who pointed to their role as soldiers and taxpayers as evidence of their readiness for the vote.[2] Sumner continued his effort, however, considering it a symbolic move intended to inaugurate "a policy not only strictly for the District of Columbia, but in some sense for the country at large." Arguing that there would be "more harm in refusing than in conceding the franchise" to blacks who, he stated, were about "as intelligent as the Irish just arrived," he fended off a woman's suffrage amendment, by which, he claimed, the bill would be "clogged, burdened, or embarrassed."[3]

The reaction among Washington's racially conservative white politicians was immediate and decisive. In debates in the city council over drawing up a resolution putting the issue of universal manhood suffrage before the city electorate, one councilman urged a quick resolution lest "the nigger bill" pass the Congress before city residents could be heard from. Another member, citing antagonism to the black vote in Connecticut, defended his own opposition to the measure by arguing that the black man "had no more qualification to vote than a brickbat."[4]

As the December 21 date set for the referendum approached, rival Republican papers, the Star and the more radical Chronicle, debated the question. The Star opposed giving black men the vote, saying that whites would be degraded by extending the "highest privilege of citizenship to those unready for the responsibility." Claiming that "the proposition is plainly the opening of a war on the rights of white laboring men," the Star asked rhetorically that if there were already those whites who debased the vote, how could one argue for "adding to it . . . illiterate negroes, not one in a thousand of whom could tell if his ballot was upside down or upside up?"[5] Although favoring the measure, even the Chronicle maintained a vision of the franchise that would exclude the transient contrabands and those who did not hold property.[6]

Such arguments carried little weight with Radical Republicans in Congress. Sumner reacted in the Senate to the resolution in the city council by producing a petition signed by a number of District whites favoring the extended franchise and stating harshly that whites in opposition to the measure were "in respect to the colored people . . . no better than squatters, and it is our duty to dispossess them."[7] A leading proponent of distributing confiscated land to the freedmen, Congressman George Julian of Indiana, openly seized on enfranchising blacks as a way of punishing Southern rebels. Building on widespread knowledge of the split loyalties of District residents during the war, he charged:

> A very large majority of the white people of this District have been rebels in heart during the war, and are rebels in heart still. . . . Meaner rebels than many in this District could scarcely have been found in the whole land. . . . Congress in this District has the power to punish by ballot, and there will be a beautiful, poetic justice in the exercise of this power. . . . Nor shall I stop to inquire very critically whether the negroes are fit to vote. As between themselves and white rebels, who deserve to be hung, they are eminently fit.[8]

With blacks excluded from participating and some local Radicals urging voters in favor of extending the franchise to stay away from the polls entirely, District residents overwhelmingly voted against the measure, 6591-35 in Washington City and 712-1 in Georgetown. Never a sympathizer with Radical measures in the Congress, Mayor Richard Wallach wrote the president of the Senate, "This vote, the largest, with but two exceptions, ever polled in this city, conclusively shows the unanimity of sentiment of the people of Washington in opposition to the extension of suffrage to that class." Supporters of the extended franchise, he claimed, were confined to those "who, with but little association, less sympathy, and no community of interest or affinity with the citizens of Washington, receive here from the general government temporary employment."[9] The *Star* praised the vote and Washington's local leaders, saying, "while willing to grant the negro every right due him before the law, they are not prepared to make a farce of the right of suffrage, by giving it to an ignorant mass of negroes, who know no more how to exercise it than the cattle of the field they so lately herded with." In the same issue the paper published a minority report from the House Judiciary Committee, which claimed, "It is degrading the people and the District to permit a class of poor weak-minded negroes, who have no idea of government, many of whom have just emerged from a state of slavery, to exercise the highest political privilege given to man upon earth, to wit, the elective franchise." Such a move, the report argued, would lead to the election of a black mayor as, echoing earlier such charges, it claimed, "negroes would soon flood the District and give them a majority."[10]

Although the House passed a suffrage bill, Andrew Johnson bolstered local opposition by saying he would not force the franchise on any jurisdiction that opposed it. On February 7, 1866, the *Star* provided a detailed account of a dramatic encounter between a delegation of blacks and the president, in which Johnson and antislavery leader Frederick Douglass respectfully but forcefully stated their opposing views. As Douglass threatened to take his case to the electorate, Johnson replied equally firmly that while he considered himself a friend of the colored man, "I do not want to

51

adopt a policy that I believe will end in a contest between the races, which if persisted in will result in the extermination of one or the other."[11] Privately he revealed a less eloquent antagonism to his visitors, telling his secretary, "I know that d——d Douglass; he's just like any nigger, & he would sooner cut a white man's throat than not." Days later Johnson attracted a sizable rally of support from local whites on the anniversary of George Washington's birthday, where a resolution passed that the declaration that "all men were created equal" was "never intended as placing the African race on a civil, social or a political level with the Caucasian."[12]

The franchise bill was not expected to pass the Senate, but deteriorating relationships between Johnson and Congress affected the District's fate. Until February 1866 Johnson had the support even of the *Chronicle*, which, though continuing to press for an extended franchise, chose to believe that its view of maintaining some electoral restrictions was consistent with the president's position. His veto of the Freedman's Bureau Bill with military sanctions attached proved a dramatic shock, however, forcing the *Chronicle* into direct opposition to Johnson. Sharing a sense of mortification with a number of moderate as well as Radical Republicans, the paper asked rhetorically whether the evidences of Southern treachery and mistreatment of blacks was to be overcome by the arguments of Democrats. "This message of President Johnson will fall like the cold hand of death upon the warm impulses of the American people who have given so much of their treasure and their blood to the cause of the Republic and have reposed such unstinted and unquestioning confidence in the Executive."[13] The next day Lot Morrill of Maine, chairman of the Senate District Committee and one of those most offended by Johnson's veto, reported the District franchise bill out of committee without amendment.

Congress took no action on the bill until December 1866, when it received renewed attention following a sharply acrimonious campaign that pitted congressional Republicans against Johnson's permissive Reconstruction policies. More conservative Republicans argued that the franchise for black men should be restricted to taxpayers, or at the very least, as one senator argued, to those among blacks just arrived from "the lowest type of barbarism" who could read and write. The Senate majority rejected such arguments, however, passing the bill on December 19 without either property or educational restrictions and adding to it a punitive clause barring from the franchise "persons who may have voluntarily given aid and comfort to the rebels in the rebellion."[14]

On January 7, 1867, Johnson vetoed the District suffrage bill, stressing in a lengthy message his reluctance to override the views of those who had voted in the city's referendum and his belief that blacks were not yet ready for the franchise. Claiming that newly freed slaves were not as well prepared for citizenship as immigrants who still faced a number of restrictions, he warned against admitting a new class of voters not qualified for the exercise of the elective franchise lest they "weaken our system of government."[15] Both houses of Congress quickly overrode the veto by a near unanimous vote among Republicans, showing how greatly isolated Johnson had become from his own party. The *Star,* for its part, expressed its willingness to give the system a chance, saying that although it was "frankly opposed to increasing the number of ignorant, thriftless and shiftless voters any where," it did not deem it proper to wage obviously ineffectual opposition to the well-known purpose of Congress. On a more positive note, it said it was more important to improve the lives of freedmen than to give in to extreme demands of Southern leaders who sought to override the results of the war.[16] Within weeks, blacks went to the polls for the first time, in Georgetown. To its relief, the *Star* reported a lack of incident, noting that "the colored voters exercised their new privilege with becoming modesty" and "whether acting from their own prompting or under judicious advice, voted for and elected good men."[17]

The subsequent campaign in Washington placed race at the forefront, as Republicans pointed to emancipation as the key to reviving the capital by "throwing aside the dead weights which have retarded the progress of the city and made it a first-class village when it should have been a splendid metropolis." "Commercial and material necessities, no less than political considerations," the *Chronicle* editorialized, "should impel our citizens without distinction of party to cut loose from the men who are identified with a party into whose creed we look in vain for those great principles of political equality and material advancement which have made the great cities of the North and West the wonder and admiration of the world."[18] Conservatives, on the other hand, warned variously against allowing the city to fall under the rule of "unlettered negroes, who have no interest in the government of the city" and those hustled to the polls "fresh from the cornfields of Virginia."[19] Noting that "of course our main reliance is on our colored friends," Republicans pressing for enforcement of sanitary rules, provisions for the poor, and active support for public schools led the field for local office by some two thousand votes, taking five of eight seats in the upper board and sixteen of twenty-one seats in the lower board of the city council.[20]

National hostility to black suffrage, as revealed by Republican losses in the 1867 off-year state elections, made Washington's 1868 mayoralty race an important test of Radical principles. As the Republican candidate, Sayles Bowen was thoroughly identified with Radical politics. A native New Englander who was dismissed from his first government job, as a clerk in the Treasury Department, for circulating documents against the extension of slavery, he actively participated in the national Republican campaigns of 1856 and 1860. Rewarded with a series of appointments by President Lincoln, he championed both public schools for blacks and their enfranchisement, joining the debate on that issue with a highly charged open letter in the *Chronicle* in December 1865. Asking who supported the referendum

Reconstruction: Social and Physical

resolution passed by the council with "such indecent haste," he claimed that it was every traitor who left the city during the war, who took up arms against the government, who sympathized with the rebellion or denounced emancipation. "Here let the National Legislature set an example," he wrote, "by repealing all laws making any distinction on account of color, and securing alike to the white and black man equal suffrage, equal rights, and equal privileges."[21] In supporting Bowen's election, the *Chronicle* assumed an equally militant tone, charging that "the partial triumph of last year must be rendered complete. The outer line of entrenchments was then captured; the inner citadel must now be stormed, and the corrupt ring, which in the past has had possession of it, be dispossessed. When this is done we shall soon see a great and beneficial change in the management of our municipal affairs."[22]

The opposition, choosing not to assume the tainted Democratic label, simply called themselves anti-Radicals, urging all "conservative citizens" of the District to "restore peace and prosperity" by supporting their ticket. Referring to what it considered better times, when Democratic administrations supported major public works programs, the *National Intelligencer* commented:

> It has been the misfortune of the city that since the administrations of Presidents Fillmore and Pierce, when the construction of the aqueduct was commenced, and that of many public buildings with the extension of the Capitol, and the building of structures for charitable purposes, but little has been done for Washington. . . . All the nuisances of the city, like the canal, might have been removed by the multitude of contrabands who swarmed in this region, and have been supported in idleness by the Freedmen's Bureau, had Mr. Stanton so willed it. . . . All the avenues and streets might have been lined with trees, and graded and drained by the half or quarter labor of the band of negroes who have been and are fed, lodged, and clothed at the public expense.[23]

As both sides strove to register voters favorable to their position, Democrats charged that Republicans were importing blacks from Maryland and Virginia, while Republicans complained that their opposition was illegally recruiting soldiers stationed temporarily in the area.[24]

By all accounts, blacks voted solidly with the Republicans, while a late move to strike a number of Irish soldiers from the rolls by the Republican registrar may have given Bowen the number of votes he needed to win by a margin of only 83. In any event, neither Mayor Wallach nor the Democratic Board of Aldermen initially acknowledged Bowen's election, putting the Radical program at a disadvantage from the start.[25] Republicans chose, however, to cast the victory as a clear triumph over Southern rebel interests and a vindication of the right of black males to vote. "Those who have been described by our opponents as being too ignorant and degraded to intel-

ligently exercise the right of franchise," Bowen told an appreciative crowd
celebrating his election, "have shown that neither the seductive power of
money, the artifices of wily politicians, threats of discharge from employment, ill-treatment, nor promises of work or patronage has served to change
a colored voter in our midst, or caused him to go over to the ranks of his
old oppressors and vote for the candidates of the 'white man's party.'" In
line with his acknowledged support from blacks, who reportedly contributed eighty-two hundred of the eighteen thousand votes cast, Bowen promised rewards in the form of schools and improved public facilities as well as
employment "at remunerative wages and prompt pay."[26]

The transition to an integrated party was not entirely smooth, as shown,
for instance, when one Republican declined nomination for the Board of

Reconstruction: Social and Physical

Aldermen in 1868, saying he was not yet ready to run on the same ticket with blacks.[27] The *Star* lost no chance to comment sarcastically on the heated and sometimes raucous debate, which drew newly empowered blacks into party deliberations. And yet, without denying the difficulties, Republicans pressed forward, over consistent Democratic opposition, with a broad agenda directed at blacks, including elimination of the term *white* from every passage where it occurred in the charters and laws for Georgetown and Washington and passage of two civil rights bills to insure accommodation of blacks in restaurants, bars, hotels, and places of amusement.[28] Under pressure to promote blacks to citywide office, Republicans nominated and elected John Cook as register of wills in 1869 and ran black candidates in every ward. On the particularly difficult issue of integrating public education, which divided blacks as well as whites, Republicans secured from Congress increased public funding for separate black schools. Bowen initially opposed a consolidated school system. By the time of his first message to the city council in 1869, however, he had fully embraced integration. "The distinction of color is no longer recognized in our charter, nor at the ballot-box, in the courts of justice, the lecture-room, the hall of public amusements, or the public conveyance," he stated. "It should be eliminated as speedily as possible from our school system."[29]

What infused the Republican party with life was the deep appreciation among blacks for the opportunity to participate in local politics and the expectation throughout party ranks, central to the period, that the fruits of victory would be political jobs.[30] Both in his campaign and in his inaugural address, Bowen committed himself to an ambitious program of public works, a central tenet for any local administration struggling with the unfinished business of capital building and a logical choice for party building through patronage. To petitions from blacks complaining that racism kept them from finding work, Republicans responded with jobs as well as charitable contributions.[31] But with appropriations blocked in the Board of Aldermen, as each party struggled for control, and the carryover of considerable debt from the previous administration, Bowen's powers were limited. Seeking to redeem the Washington Canal from its condition as an open sewer, he said he much preferred to institute a full program of sewers instead of just cleaning the canal, but funds did not allow it.[32] Pressed both to advance improvements and to employ many of his black supporters during the hard winter months of his first year in office, Bowen had to go to Congress to secure special funds for public works.[33]

Despite its lack of enthusiasm for his social agenda, the *Star* was initially positive toward Bowen. During Bowen's 1868 campaign for mayor, the paper declared him as fit as his opponent, and in 1869 it chastised the Citizen's party's opposition ticket for putting up only Democratic candidates. The paper's chief objective, as it revealed in countless editorials, was the physical improvement of the city, a goal made all the more pressing by a growing threat instigated by western members of Congress that the capital might be removed to a more central location.[34] Shortly after Bowen's election, the *Star* charged in an editorial under the title "Removal of the Capital" that "the improvement of the city should be our text from this date. Washington could better afford to have a debt of ten millions than to be in its present condition." Among the priorities the paper listed for the city were the paving of Pennsylvania Avenue, the reconstruction of the Center Market, which had been destroyed by fire, cleaning the Washington Canal, and controlling animals still allowed to run free in the streets.[35]

Both Bowen and his party were clearly in sympathy with the *Star* on these points. At a Republican ratification meeting of May 1868, banners appeared not just proclaiming "Equality before the Law" but also reading, "Give us a Republican government, and we will give you good schools, good drainage, and good streets."[36] In editorials supporting Bowen just before the election, the *Chronicle* coupled Radical rhetoric with an argument for improvements as the best way to reduce pressure to remove the seat of government. "It is for you to decide," the paper told its readers, "whether you will have Copperheadism and rebel rule, without appropriations from Congress and with the removal of the seat of Government staring you in the face, or Republican rule, with ample appropriations, a permanent seat of the General Government secured for Washington, and a relief from our existing financial embarrassments through the aid of our friends in Congress."[37] If the *Star* found fault with Bowen, it was one of emphasis, that in concentrating improvements in outer areas of the city, he neglected other priorities at the heart of the emerging business district.

As Bowen's campaign for reelection neared, however, the *Star* grew sharply critical. Following an essay castigating political rings throughout the country, it began a series of editorials criticizing Bowen, not for his social policies, but for alleged corruption in contracts. "The municipal government of Washington is a byword abroad and a scandal at home," a May editorial declared. "In a few years the taxes have nearly doubled, and the debt actually doubled. What have we to show for these oppressive burthens, but the glaring enrichment of a gang of personal partisans at public expense?"[38]

Citing an inherited debt of $800,000, Bowen in turn claimed for himself a cost-effective administration "untrammelled by corrupt cliques or combinations," which through public improvements had enhanced the value of public property "infinitely beyond their cost."[39] His defenders stressed the importance of expanded sewers, bridges built, gas and water mains laid, and schools constructed. A Republican convention renominating him for mayor stressed a number of social issues, but its formal resolution of support stressed "that spirit of improvement which shall tend to beautify the city and add to the material interests of the laboring men of the city."[40]

Race remained a central issue in the campaign, however, as blacks, who dominated a meeting to ratify Bowen as the Republican candidate, charged that bolters from the party intended to drive them both out of jobs and out of the city. Anthony Bowen, black social activist and minister, made clear the connection, in answering charges that the Bowen administration had hired blacks for unessential work. What did Sayles Bowen do? he asked. "The abolition of slavery threw into the city large numbers of famishing colored families. Mayor Bowen employed the male members of such families in the improvement of property, and thereby made it valuable, and kept you in so doing from starvation, thus benefiting both the poor and the rich. Reformers propose that no improvements shall be made: that Washington shall revert back to old slavery times."[41] Pointing with pride to Washington's rapid growth, a supporter predicted that the city of 150,000 would reach half a million in twenty years. And a banner paraded in a pro-Bowen rally read, "Washington for our Capital, St Louis for Lager Beer."[42] "If by any fatuity or blind zeal of faction, Mayor Bowen should be defeated," the *Chronicle* editorialized, "the administration of the city government would be in the hands of the party that ruled its destiny during the rebellion as faithful allies of treason. Would not such a victory blight the prosperity of the city, and close the doors of Congress against the continuance of the generous appropriations that have been thrift throughout all its borders?"[43]

The *Star* kept up its attacks, and true to its conservative position on race as well as its support for public improvements, it combined both positions in a May 2 endorsement of Bowen's opponent, Matthew Emory, a former Republican alderman, stonemason, and businessman. Arguing that the debt had doubled under Bowen's administration, the paper asked, to what end? "Streets opened up to the outskirts to benefit favorites . . . hardly a sign of substantial improvement. . . . Instead of encouraging the colored people to habits of industry and thrift, every effort has been made to degrade and enslave them . . . by vice and politics."[44]

The *Star*'s campaign against Bowen was strong on rhetoric but short on detail. Similar charges had been levied in each of the preceding campaigns for mayor. Bowen's agenda for city improvements as well as his language—having instituted one of the paper's favorite phrases as early as 1868, that the capital should be made worthy of the nation—coincided closely with that of the *Star*. An early-twentieth-century sketch of Bowen accurately described the improvements under his administration as "the inspiration and object lessons which led up to the adoption of the comprehensive system" adopted by the Board of Public Works under the city's brief experiment in territorial government.[45] The cause of debt, as the *Star*'s columns had frequently noted, lay as much in the hands of Congress as in local politics. So why did the paper turn against Bowen when it did?

One cause was the clever hand of Alexander Shepherd, subsequently referred to by historians as "Boss Shepherd" in line with his controversial role in the city's brief experiment in territorial government. Following a rapid rise in the plumbing and fitting business and a short stint in the Union army, Shepherd helped found Washington's first Board of Trade in 1865. An active promoter of increasing Washington's business and, by the mid-1860s, a part owner of the *Star*, Shepherd was speaking for the socially conservative wing of his party. Pitted against Bowen as early as 1867 in the contest for a seat on Washington County's governing body, the Levy Court, he was described by a Bowen ally as a man who "allows himself to be used as a club to beat the brains of the radicals."[46] Elected an alderman in 1869, Shepherd used the Emery campaign to give what he called his first political speech, a long indictment of Bowen's failure to live up to his promises for physical improvements offered in his inaugural address.[47] As the spearhead of the new Citizens Reform Association formed at the height of the 1870 campaign, Shepherd undoubtedly contributed to Bowen's loss, which came by a substantial majority of more than three thousand votes.

Emery responded to his election by embracing the cause of physical development. Stating in his inaugural address that the "great questions of universal freedom and universal suffrage" had already been settled, he expressed confidence "that these questions no longer concern us." Rather, he stated, "we are glad to be permitted to dismiss them and turn our attention to matters of more immediate local interest." These he cited as high debts and unnecessary partisanship, which demanded "economy and reform."[48] But even as he took office, Emery was undercut by an even more dramatic movement to reverse the social gains identified with Radical politics, the substitution of an entirely new form of government for the District of Columbia.

As early as 1865, Senator Lot Morrill introduced a bill to place the different governments of Washington under a single entity of a commission, to be appointed by the president. The bill may have been intended to give Republicans control over a city that was still under conservative rule, as it drew immediate support from the *Chronicle* and opposition from the more conservative *Star*. The effort nonetheless quickly generated heated criticism from white and black Radical Republicans, who felt it ran entirely counter to their drive to extend the franchise.[49] In contrast, the idea received a welcome reception from the Board of Trade, which took up a resolution favoring a similar form of government in 1867. Although one member pointed out that Congress was likely to resist revoking Washington's charter so soon after enfranchising the freedmen, the board passed the resolution anyway.[50] It was an amended Morrill bill that Shepherd and his allies resurrected in 1868 in the form of a proposed territorial government and commended to Congress in 1869.[51]

Radical Republicans stoutly opposed the proposed change, as first the city council passed a resolution opposing the idea and then Bowen testified before Congress against it.[52] Although some blacks saw the utility of a government designed to extend services to outlying areas in the District where they had been forced to locate because of high rents at the center of the city, most opposed the idea. At a Bowen rally in February 1870, when a speaker asked those assembled whether they would be willing to give up rights now held to a new form of territorial government, the crowd responded loudly, "No, never."[53] A recently inaugurated black paper, the *New National Era*, edited by Bowen supporter Sella Martin and Frederick Douglass, made its own case against territorial government, claiming that the idea represented an effort by conservatives to block the wheels of progress advanced by local Republicans: "The 'rabble,' so called, must be silenced, or, in plain Anglo-Saxon, the old fogies are opposed to negro suffrage; and as they cannot withdraw it, they seek to diminish, if not destroy, the opportunities for its exercise. Here is the whole secret of the recently inaugurated movement to take away our municipal government."[54]

Shepherd defended the proposed change by arguing that giving the federal government the power of appointments would insure a national stake in the new government. But even he had to tell critics that he would accept making some appointments subject to popular election.[55] Privately, he pressed for more centralized control, gaining particular support from the Board of Trade, which he commended for helping secure passage of what he called one of the most important measures for the welfare of the community ever proposed in Congress.[56]

The central argument for the new government was the creation of a board of public works responsible for physical improvement. The concept received a strong endorsement in strikingly modern language by Colonel William H. Philip, a signer, along with Shepherd, of the original petition to Congress seeking adoption of a modified Morrill bill. He wanted such a body charged with the duty of establishing "general, comprehensive and systematic plans for all general improvements." The *Star* adopted similar language, echoing Shepherd's argument that once given assurance of greater control of District affairs, Congress would finally provide the funds necessary for urban development.[57] Efforts by Radical Republicans to assure continuity with the first stage of Reconstruction failed, as Congress rejected George Julian's proposal to introduce a provision for woman's suffrage and Charles Sumner's call for a civil rights clause.[58] In helping defeat efforts to retain a fully elected government, Representative Burton Cook of Illinois, who reported the bill for the House District Committee asserted:

> Every man in the United States has a personal interest in the government of this District, and the theory of this bill is that the proper conservative influence in the government of the city may be secured by the appointment of a portion of that government by the authority of the United States. . . . The United States has vast property here, and while it is the capital of this great nation the interests of all the people should be represented in the government of the District.[59]

The bill incorporating a presidentially appointed governor, a board of public works, and an upper house of the legislature passed February 21, 1871. It went into effect June 1.

★ ★ ★

Although a number of Democrats, including financier William W. Corcoran, had supported the new government as a means of eliminating the partisanship as well as the influence of blacks that they believed had beset local affairs since the war, President U. S. Grant kept partisanship alive in Washington by appointing only Republicans to the new administration. Although Radicals complained at first that they had been passed over in early appointments to the Board of Public Works and in their choice of governor, the continued importance of the black vote to Republicans insured some continuity with the Bowen and Emory regimes. The appointed governor, businessman Henry Cooke, although not associated with Radical causes, quickly embraced the Radical social program, including integrated public schools.[60] Frederick Douglass lost his bid for the Republican nomination for the new nonvoting delegate's position to Congress to a relative outsider to Radical politics, Norton Chipman. Still, Douglass and his followers in the press remained magnanimous in defeat, supporting Chipman throughout the campaign.[61]

Cooke and the Republican Party strongly endorsed Charles Sumner's supplementary civil rights bill, and the legislature passed two landmark civil liberties bills. Even Shepherd, disappointed not to be named governor but fully invested in the new government as vice-president of the Board of Public Works, went out of his way to introduce Frederick Douglass warmly at a party gathering and to embrace Sumner's civil rights bill at a rally at Howard University.[62] But only the most naive would have failed to recognize that the emphasis of Washington government had shifted from liberties to bricks and mortar. As Democrats left out of the ranks of the new government reacted strongly in opposition, Republicans had little choice but to close ranks behind an ambitious program of physical improvements.

Cooke revealed the importance attached to public works when in June he announced a $6.25 million plan for laying sewers, grading and paving streets, planting trees, and removing unsightly nuisances. Because Congress backed away at the last minute from providing a set federal payment to the new territorial government, $4 million of the amount needed for improvements was to be paid by a bond issue. The remaining funds would be raised by assessments on private property. A petition presented to Congress by the Board of Public Works, while noting that "the aggregate of the accompanying statement may at first appear extravagant," promised nonetheless that new procedures requiring more exact estimates for work done and the substitution of centralized planning for the "casual repairs and local improvements previously done at an annual level of up to $300,000,"

Reconstruction: Social and Physical

would enhance property values more than enough to meet the expenses incurred.[63] Democrats attempted to block expenditures by bringing an injunction against the city's improvement loan. When Congress failed to provide the money requested, the territorial House of Delegates made available $500,000 in interim funds for improvements already started and called for a plebiscite to demonstrate popular support for the loan.[64]

The local Republican press quickly embraced the board's plans. For its part, the Washington *Star* commended the results as a proper extension of efforts started after the war to beautify the city. The paper praised the Board of Public Works for "instead of contenting themselves with patching broken pavements, agree[ing] upon a general system of street improvements and sewerage which would benefit all parts of the District." Likewise, the *Chronicle* commended the board, comparing its effort to the creation of Central Park in New York City, saying, "This is the result of starting on the right plan and giving the right men means and authority to push the work to completion."[65]

Giving voice to the opposition, a new Democratic paper, the *Patriot*, founded with the financial support of both William Corcoran and New York City's preeminent politician, William Tweed, responded by denouncing years of "onerous taxation . . . wilfully squandered or appropriated to the vilest uses of party." It charged in addition that "we are now threatened with new imposition of even a more formidable character, for the Ring into whose hands the President has sought to deliver the city is one of alarming proportions and unscrupulous designs." Choosing to see in Paris's reconstruction ill omens for Washington, it declared, "If Napoleon's director of public works, the 'magnificent Haussmann,' beat those figures, it is no wonder the French Treasury failed to supply the War Department with sufficient material to fight the Germans."[66] Although the financial implications of the *Patriot*'s attack were clear, Shepherd's advocates, instead of shying away from the comparison, embraced his identity with Napoleon's autocratic planner. "The Baron Haussmann here is the Board of Public Works," a writer for *Lippincott's* magazine pronounced. "Within its sphere this board has despotic power; it would be worthless with any less. . . . It makes bitter enemies by its inexorable exactions: the public cannot be served except at the expense of the individual."[67]

Defeated at the polls and thwarted in the courts, opponents of the new government submitted a petition to Congress in January 1872 charging that public works were not being executed properly, pointing specifically at the Washington Canal, which petitioners charged was threatening the city with inundation and pestilence. Continuing its staunch support of the new government, the *Star* defended the administration as committed to lifting the city "out of the mud and making it what it should be, as the capital of the nation."[68] Clearly miffed that the petition had not been circulated through him, congressional delegate Norton Chipman supported an investigation.

He managed, however, to thwart the creation of a special investigating committee by assigning the task to the Committee on the District of Columbia, a majority of which, the *Patriot* charged, "are so hampered by personal complications and partisan connections, that no serious and searching inquiry is to be expected."[69]

Chaired by Shepherd's close friend, H. H. Starkwater of Connecticut, the committee not surprisingly issued a report defending the administration's expenditures for public works. Recognizing that "in the anxiety to redeem the city from the charge of being behind," the new authorities had "become somewhat intoxicated with the spirit of improvement," the report claimed nonetheless that such improvements were fully justified. While noting that the board had entered upon government work "upon a scale so much greater than the resources of the District would justify," it concluded that "the plan of the board for the improvement of the District, in grading, paving, and parking the streets, will . . . if carried out as a whole, prove beneficial to the city and increase the value of real estate, as well as greatly improve and beautify it." The committee settled for a mild rebuke of the Board of Public Works by setting a cap of $10 million on District debt and stating that the government should not pursue its excessive newspaper advertising practices.[70] In December 1872 the House of Representatives warned that the city, having entered into $9 million in debt, was dangerously close to its limit. Members of the Senate contested the figure and managed to get Congress to appropriate $500,000 to defray the costs of improvements near government properties, and for the moment the crisis passed.[71]

Cooke resigned as governor in September 1873, giving way finally to the acknowledged authority in the District, Alexander Shepherd. The *Star* praised Shepherd extravagantly, saying, "It is sufficient to say that from his earliest boyhood he has had an honorable ambition to make the city of Washington worthy of its name." The theme reverberated in public meetings, when Republicans and businessmen commended Shepherd for his efforts "to improve the city . . . and to relieve us from the embarrassments which for the present cloud our prospect and in the effort you shall make to beautify and adorn the city of our birth or our adoption, and present it to the nation worthy the proud name it bears."[72] Republican victories in the fall elections prompted the *Star* to claim the results as an endorsement of the government and the Board of Public Works in "the improvements in progress under their direction" and a rebuke "to those who are endeavoring by their willful misrepresentations to block the wheel of progress and impair the credit of the District government."[73]

Shepherd's defense of high expenditures for public works was made more difficult, however, by the effects of the depression that followed the failure of the Philadelphia brokerage house owned by Henry Cooke's brother, Jay Cooke. Although a November report from the Board of Public Works claimed that Washington's debt was lower than any other major city's but

Boston, it could not ignore mounting obligations, which it placed at just over $4 million.[74] Responding to yet another appeal from disgruntled property owners, including both William Corcoran and Sayles Bowen, who claimed they sought only to secure more financially efficient means to assure Washington's future as "the most beautiful and attractive residence city in the world," Congress launched another investigation of the city in February 1874.

Covering three and a half months, the investigation established the debt at more than $18 million, well beyond the legal limit. Shepherd responded by reiterating claims made in the 1873 Board of Public Works annual report that the city had been hurt by unpaid taxes and by the lack of an adequate tax base. The investigating committee concluded, however, that the government had been a failure, recommending that all major positions and boards except the Board of Health be abolished and placed under the control of the Army Corps of Engineers.[75]

As might be expected, the Star defended the existing government, pointing out that the chief counsel to the investigating committee, Richard Merrick, had been an unsuccessful Democratic candidate for nonvoting delegate to Congress under the new government. In the equivalent of a bloody shirt commentary, an editorial for May 20 attacked Merrick, saying that "nothing should so much incense Mr. Merrick as to see clean streets, modern institutions, taste, ornament, and, in short, an elegant American capital where he hoped the dying cavalry of the rebellion would apply the torch, sack the public buildings, and put abolitionists and contrabands to the sword." A subsequent editorial reiterated the positive side of public improvements, saying, "One fact alone should reconcile the citizens of the country generally, that the agitation of the removal of the seat of government, so rapidly gaining ground when these improvements first began, has entirely ceased."[76]

On June 19, however, the Star suddenly shifted its position by embracing termination of the territorial government. In almost wistful tones, the paper responded that "the citizens of the District have grown so used to being bandied about from pillar to post by Congress, that they will accept the new provisional government with the same philosophy exhibited by the Parisians or the Mexicans, when they wake up in the morning and find themselves the subject of a King, emperor, president or counsel. . . . What they want now above all things, is to get the blocked-up wheels of business in motion, and it is hoped that the new bill will, to a certain extent, reflect this desideratum."[77]

The key to the Star's reversal on territorial government lay with its hopes for assistance in bolstering the city's finances, a prospect that President Grant encouraged in an October 1873 speech praising the Board of Public Works for helping Washington assume "the appearance of a capital of which the nation may well be proud" and calling for a "liberal policy"

64

Portrait of Alexander Shepherd, by German-born painter Henry Ulke, 1871, just as Shepherd took control of the new Board of Public Works and, through it, directed Washington's massive program of urban development. Courtesy Historical Society of Washington.

through which the federal government "should bear its just share of the expense of these improvements."[78] Just days before the *Star* reversed its position, the House Judiciary Committee endorsed a federal payment to the city. In terms closely associated with the Southard report of 1835, the Judiciary Committee, in noting that the city had been laid out on a scale not intended to saddle a small population with the expenses intended for national benefit, recommended that the government establish some well-defined basis for sharing the expenses of improvements and defraying current expenses.[79]

The joint committee of Congress established in June to draw up a suitable alternative to the territorial government reiterated the theme in its report of December 15, 1874. Stressing the national character of the capital as

Reconstruction: Social and Physical

"common ground" that should rise above "the zeal of partisanship," "local interest," and even the "necessities of commerce," the report urged virtually complete federal responsibility for the city's physical well-being: "The demands for expenditures, as indicated in the disposition of its avenues and streets and numerous squares, will necessarily be upon a scale beyond what might reasonably be imposed upon or drawn from the resources of a business and resident population.... These necessarily impose on Congress the duty of making provision for needful expenditures, as well as for their supervision, as for other branches of the public service." Listing every possible service for which the federal government might take responsibility, the report concluded that "this paramount authority, obligation, and duty of Congress in relation to the District is apparent."[80]

It took another four years to determine the exact form of financial support to the District. In reasserting its power of exclusive jurisdiction, however, Congress both embraced a particularly strong vision of postwar nationalism and, in the process, managed to place local politics in a purely administrative and thus subordinate role. Such an approach, anticipating some of the arguments of the Progressive Era, wiped out in one stroke the intensely active role of citizenship that had characterized all local jurisdictions in the aftermath of the Jacksonian revolution and left Washington residents subject to a system of administrative government not yet tested in the United States. Although Radical Republicans made a last-ditch effort to save black suffrage, and later both houses proposed limited forms of home rule, government by federally appointed commission finally became law as part of the Organic Act of 1878.[81] Indeed, by 1874, giving up suffrage in the District—and all the social baggage it carried—was considered worth achieving the longstanding goal of federal support for physical improvements.

Part of this dramatic shift in policy undoubtedly came in reaction to pressures from the race-baiting *Patriot*. In an 1872 editorial entitled "Our Black Rulers," the Democratic paper described Republican alliances with blacks as part of a ring "which would put to shame the worst of degraded Tammany." In terms reminiscent of those directed at Sayles Bowen in 1870, the paper charged, "Under the 'comprehensive plan' of the present Ring, thousands of negroes have been imported, and they, with the previous stock, compose the machinery by which the property, intelligence, and virtue of this community are now controlled, through the discipline and rascality of a few white plunderers." Pointing to white opposition to school integration, the *Patriot* lashed out later that year against congressional efforts to convert Washington "into a seat of experimental gardens for crude theories and absurd abstractions." The city, it claimed, had no obligation "to educate the children of mere sojourners, who have no intent of becoming resident citizens, and who feel no more interest in the prosperity of this capital than they do of Liberia, indeed, much less."[82] The shift in Republican philosophy was also grounded, however, in national trends.

In 1870, at the height of Radical strength, just as the Washington school board petitioned Congress to permit an integrated school in the city's Southwest sector, the Joint Congressional Committee on Reconstruction added a provision to Virginia's new state constitution prohibiting discrimination in selection for jury duty or attendance in public schools. Following the introduction of similar provisions to bills readmitting Mississippi and Texas to the Union, Charles Sumner drew the analogy to Washington by introducing legislation to require mixed schools in the city. Sumner's bill languished, but a year later James Patterson of New Hampshire reported the bill out of the Senate District Committee as a means to consolidate Washington's dual school system. Patterson, however, reported that while the committee majority favored the measure, he felt that it would "tend to destroy the schools of the city" and moved to strike the provision. Patterson's objections were sufficient to prevent any further action on the bill, and by 1873, when Sumner again attempted to get the bill passed, it was routed to the Senate Judiciary Committee, where its opponents knew it would die.[83] Both in congressional debate and in the fall political campaigns in 1874, Republicans, fearful of Democratic charges that Charles Sumner's civil rights bill intended to legislate an unwanted social equality, backed away from the most controversial element, school integration. Despite such caution, voters reversed a large Republican majority in the House and dealt radicalism its death blow as a national program.[84]

In the District, despite strong support for integration among the trustees for colored schools, as well as among blacks more generally, Republican leaders also abandoned the measure. Although Lewis H. Douglass, while completing his father's appointment to the upper body of the territorial government, introduced a resolution to integrate the schools in 1872, the bill never emerged from committee. A similar bill appeared in 1873 but was dropped when a black member of the lower house, John H. Brooks, opposed it on the basis that he was not sure integrated schools were legal.[85] Indeed, what was notable and of lasting effect for the city in the end was that all dominant parties, including the once radical journals, the *Chronicle* and the *National Republican,* settled on a political agenda of public improvements.[86] Blacks, and the social goals that had animated their entrance into District politics, including the drive for integrated schools, were thus thwarted for most of a century.

In such a context, it was hardly surprising that it was Shepherd and his agenda for public works that triumphed. He achieved his basic goals despite being forced out of office. If the territorial government did not survive, Shepherd nonetheless left behind impressive physical improvements, as described by a Washington guidebook of 1886:

In ten years from the time the Board of Public Works began its improvements, the city was transformed. The streets were covered with an almost

Reconstruction: Social and Physical

noiseless, smooth pavement. Fifty thousand shade-trees had been planted; the old rows of wooden, barrack-like houses had given place to dwellings of graceful, ornate architecture. . . . The water-works and sewer system were unequalled in the country. Washington had risen fresh and beautiful, like the Uranian Venus, from stagnation and decay.[87]

Although the charges that Shepherd had been guilty of boss rule quickly dissipated, in truth his role was much like that of a traditional boss. His impatience with procedure inevitably brought about charges of impropriety, both in evaluating the work done and the payments provided, most often decided on partisan grounds, to favorites. His close association with contractors through the emerging enterprise of city building, most notably those in paving and street railway companies, made him and his associates vulnerable to criticism.[88] The partisan *Patriot* not only revealed some of these improprieties but presaged the supervision of public works under a nonpartisan commission dominated by trained engineers.[89] Yet as telling as such criticisms were, it was Shepherd's argument for federally supported improvements and their direction under direct national supervision that emerged as conventional wisdom for Washington after 1874. As Shepherd put it so starkly some years later: "The re-establishment of suffrage here is an impossibility, and a belief that it may be attained some time in the hereafter is an absurdity. The District of Columbia is really a big government reservation, and the people who come here take up their residence with the distinct understanding that the United States government is the controlling influence in the direction of its destiny."[90]

Those who knew Washington before the Board of Public Works, under the leadership of Governor Shepherd, began the remarkable improvements, described elsewhere, and who have not visited the city since, can hardly imagine the great change that has taken place everywhere within its boundary. . . . The growth and development of Washington during the past ten years have been wonderful. Nearly all the old landmarks have disappeared, and out of a rude, unpaved, dilapidated town has risen a stately city, with most of the resources, the pleasures, the superiority of a metropolis. Once it was called in derision "the only child of the Nation," but now it has attained to a magnificent manhood, and is entirely worthy of the pride and admiration of its parents.

Picturesque Washington, 1884

The demise of Washington's territorial government ended any last expectations that the city might become a laboratory for forging new social programs and establishing new social relations. In place of Charles Sumner's vision for the future, Washington's leadership embraced earlier goals of growth and prosperity, standards that would be measured by the extension of residences throughout the whole of the District of Columbia and the buildup of the government's presence at the city core. Complemented by active neighborhood associations and the inception in 1889 of a new board of trade, government by commission dedicated itself to creation of what boosters came to call a "Greater Washington." The agents for this expansion of Shepherd's program for Washington lay in physical improvements, including the extension of streets, sewer lines, and streetcar lines into largely undeveloped Washington County, and the establishment at Rock Creek of a new park set apart to serve the entire area. Further efforts to reclaim the unhealthy flats along the Potomac River and to exercise control over the intrusion of railroad lines into the heart of the city lent support to claims that Washington was well on its way to becoming the most beautiful as well as the best governed city in the nation. "The capital has become a city," the *Star* proclaimed on the occasion of Washington's centennial in 1900, "with a city's duties, equipment and prospects. It has grown from a camp reluctantly pitched by most of the campers into a place of permanent homes, eagerly sought by sojourners, attracted by the city's charm of atmosphere or drawn by duty to spend pleasant months as veritable residents."[1]

The transitional period under commissioner rule that started in 1874 dragged on, lasting even longer than the territorial government it replaced. Necessarily, the commissioners made the restoration of Washington's finances their chief priority, but they maintained at the same time the general goal if not all the particulars of Shepherd's comprehensive plan for the city. The local press welcomed the new government as long as it stood by the federal commitment to provide the District with an annual payment matching local expenses. Emphasizing the importance of this provision, the *Star* declared in 1876, "The District people are not at all tenacious as to the form in which suffrage is allocated to them, so long as the 50 percent provision is secure." To this the new *Washington Post* added, "No sensible citizen cares a straw" for election, since the city would gain more from Congress without it.[2] Thus while a few diehard Radical Republicans continued to fight the loss of elective government, the Organic Act of 1878, which made the commission form of government permanent, easily passed both houses of Congress. Only one member, Representative Mark Dunnell of Minnesota, cited the end of suffrage in Washington as his reason for voting against it.[3]

The Washington press welcomed the change. The *Star,* in fact, reacted strongly against efforts in 1879 and 1880 to revive the territorial system. Asking rhetorically whether citizens could have forgotten the bad experience "under Murder Bay politicians," the paper concluded that it "saw no reason to expect that the same class of politicians will not spring up again should suffrage be revived." No friend of Radical Republicans, the paper ran another editorial entitled "Cultivating the Dangerous Class," which placed the blame for previous misfortunes squarely on the "idle, vicious element of the contraband population." Claiming that a number of this "dangerous class" remained in Washington just waiting the "return of the flush time of suffrage," the paper expressed its preference for what it called the current program of public improvements efficiently spent, not handouts for "the idle masses."[4] Throughout the last quarter of the century, the *Star* pointed with pride to Washington as a model of honest and efficient government in contrast to "boss rule" in other cities, a position for which it found considerable support in the national press.[5]

In this context, the *Star* supported the revisionist theory that it was the Radical Republicans, not Shepherd, who were guilty of taking Washington to the brink of ruin. Although Congress blocked President U. S. Grant's effort to appoint Shepherd to the interim commission governing the city and Shepherd was forced after declaring bankruptcy in 1876 to recoup his losses in Mexico, he quickly regained his reputation. As early as 1875, Senator Simon Cameron, who as secretary of war during the Lincoln administration had witnessed the pressures that rapid growth put on the city of Washington, claimed that because of the Board of Public Works "this city will go on and prosper and every year become more beautiful." Shepherd, he asserted, one day would be "pointed at as the master spirit who had the courage, intelligence, and vigor enough to combine the intellect of this town in favor of its prosperity." The same year, *Harper's* magazine, in an article entitled "The New Washington," chose to interpret the territorial period as an effort to overcome "riots and the suspension of improvements, which came with Reconstruction," stating that "between the two parties a conservative northern element felt obliged to save the common property and reputation of all."[6] In 1883, in the debate over federal appropriations for Washington, Senator John Ingalls of Kansas went out of his way to praise Shepherd, suggesting that the city erect a statue to mark his achievement.[7] Two years later, a scholarly account of Washington's governance praised Shepherd as a man who "brought many of the most rare and valuable qualifications of success to the office which he held as the real dictator of the office."[8]

A grand parade greeted Shepherd on his return to Washington in 1887. The *Star* subsequently presented a detailed analysis of how, despite the vilification of his enemies, he had managed to build up the city to the expectations of its founders. At the time of Shepherd's death in 1903, the *Star* testified to his enhanced reputation, stating, "He measured more accurately than most other men the meaning of Washington in the national equation. He deplored the bad conditions which had accumulated through decades of federal neglect and local inertia and helplessness." His problem, the paper implied, was not corruption but the natural resistance to change: "He realized that the man who should attempt the regeneration of the capital would incur enmity through running counter to selfish interests too narrow to appreciate the broader duty of citizenship."[9]

The consolidation of public support behind the Shepherd myth of benign improvement lends support to the argument that the goal of the Board of Public Works and its supporters was to promote Washington primarily as a government center, not as a commercial or industrial site. Shepherd insisted in filling in the Washington Canal, for instance, despite objections from local businessmen who argued that the decision would cut off the flow of goods arriving by the C&O Canal in Georgetown to the central city. While the decision to allow a new rail line to locate in the heart of the city must have helped mollify opposition, such decisions marked a clear transition to a city built for visitors and residents more than commerce.[10] Indeed, Henry Adams was not alone in suggesting in his 1880 novel *Democracy* that Washington was coming to be perceived as a refuge from the relentless commercialism of the Gilded Age. A guidebook for 1885 proclaimed:

Making a Greater Washington

At last it begins to look as though the student, the artist, the statesman, the retired trader, the man and woman of the world may find a place on this continent where escape from the din of money-grubbing is possible, where culture can shake hands with genius in all forms, where merit, not money or grandfathers, is the entree to society, where persons of leisure may hobnob with other persons of leisure and not be regarded as public nuisances, and where the stock market is not the chief end of man.[11]

To a considerable degree, Shepherd's program of public works had been especially designed to attract and hold prosperous residents in the city. In the West End, rising from Kalorama Hills along Rock Creek to the Georgetown border, an area popularly known as the Slashes was drained and graded to effect a transformation. This once dreary, unhealthy area, formerly occupied largely by black squatters, was now bought up by shrewd realtors for wealthy residents. "It is on this spacious plain," a city guidebook proclaimed, "but a few years ago, an almost valueless area of swamps, that those palatial mansions, the pride and boast of the capital, are erected."[12] To achieve high standing as a residential quarter, however, much more had to be done both to build on Shepherd's public works program and to extend it to the undeveloped residential sector of Washington County.

No modern city could be realized without proper attention to urban infrastructure, and in this the commissioners had much to do to make up for Shepherd's mistakes. Wooden pavements, which had found favor in other cities as well at the time, were unequal to the wear and tear of heavy traffic and had to be replaced soon after Shepherd's departure. Pennsylvania Avenue, the Engineer Commissioner reported in 1875, covered with a layer of decomposed wood, was in such a condition "that all vehicles shun it, and the Capitol is approached from the northwestern part of the city by the back streets." In order to repair the wood pavements thoroughly, he said, it was necessary to get rid of them.[13] More significantly for the city as a whole, Shepherd's biggest mistake may have been authorizing the construction of lateral sewers that had to run uphill to empty into main trunk lines. In the absence of effective pumping mechanisms at a time when most systems depended on gravity flow rather than steam pumps, Shepherd's effort was close to useless.[14] Among the Engineer Commissioner's first priorities, then, was the rebuilding of Washington's streets and sewers, projects that the *Star* warmly embraced without a sense of either embarrassment or irony. By 1890, in an accurate measure of the continuity of commitment to building up the city as expressed in the Shepherd years, Washington would have the luxury, compared to such regional centers as Baltimore, of being fully sewered with twenty-three thousand house connections to 255 miles of sewers.[15]

In Washington, engineers had to address overall issues of development, not just by providing sewers for the growing suburbs, but also by dealing with the problem of disposing of wastes dumped into the Potomac and Anacostia rivers. As early as 1875 the District Commissioners appropriated funds to clean up the poisonous marshes, but three years later they could still complain about "a vast undulation of rank vegetation" cumulating where sewers dumped the effluvia into the river.[16] The commissioners raised the issue again in 1879, prompting the *Star* to editorialize, "While such strides have been made in improving and beautifying the city, the offensive river flats have been allowed to remain a plague-spot and an eyesore, a strong discredit to the national capital."[17] A severe flood in 1881, which threatened the executive mansion as well as the entire river bottom portion of the city, caught the attention of Congress, which was told by the nationally recognized sanitary engineer George E. Waring Jr. that proper drainage of the city was essential to its health. The following year Congress appropriated $400,000 to reclaim the area under the direction of the secretary of war. Although litigation contesting just compensation for the property taken delayed completion of the work more than a decade, it was finally completed and secured, as Waring had urged, as a public park, in 1897.[18]

As long as the settled river bottom portion of the city remained a health hazard, elevated sites in the hills surrounding Washington City beckoned potential settlement. Before the Civil War, residential development outside Georgetown and the L'Enfant city concentrated in just a few small pockets. In 1854 an early Washington developer, John Van Hook, laid out the community of Uniontown in an effort to attract as residents workers located just across the Anacostia River at the Navy Yard. The effects of the war, in addition to the financial panics of 1857 and 1873, slowed development there, however.[19] The introduction of the city's first horse-drawn streetcars in 1863 prompted the *Star* to comment that many businessmen who formerly walked a great distance to and from the place of their daily duties would now find it unbearable should they be deprived of the opportunity to ride the streetcars.[20] Initial lines were developed, however, more for military purposes, to move men and material from Georgetown to the Navy Yard, than to facilitate the dispersal of residences outward. A few other subdivisions cropped up in Washington County in the 1860s, notably Mount Pleasant Village, Meridian Hill, and Pleasant Plains. But it was not until the 1870s, with the development of LeDroit Park, just north of the L'Enfant city near the new Howard University, that a fully developed suburb emerged. Tied to the city by a streetcar line which ran directly to the Treasury, LeDroit's planned amenities of planted trees, romantic architecture, and its own water and sewer lines succeeded in attracting as residents members of the city's growing middle class.[21]

In 1870 the *Washington Chronicle* envisioned the rapid expansion of Washington through rail extensions into the county in a process much like that encouraged by the consolidation of Philadelphia City and County in

Washington City and its early
residential subdivisions. Map
prepared by J. C. Entwistle, 1876.
Courtesy Geography and Map
Division, Library of Congress.

74

1854. Soon it will be possible, the paper claimed, for residents of Washington "to enjoy every advantage of city life in the country as thoroughly as any living in the heart of the metropolis."[22] Washington's retarded record of transportation improvement, however, slowed development. With only twenty miles of street railroads in 1870, the perimeter of the city had scarcely been breached. In 1860 the entire population of Washington County, the largely undeveloped portion of the District outside the cities of Georgetown and Washington, was only five thousand, 6.7 percent of the District total. Although the area had grown to seventeen thousand in 1870, it still represented only 9.6 percent of District residents. The introduction of the Metropolitan Branch of the B&O Railroad in 1873 spurred development of new outlying areas: Takoma Park in 1883, described in a local guidebook as a place "for quiet, social enjoyment . . . away from the vices of the city," and Brookland in 1887.[23] But Washington's role as a government center meant that one additional element was needed before the pace of expansion could quicken.

★ ★ ★

Washington's growth owed much to the expansion of federal jobs, up by 600 percent in the period from 1860 to 1880.[24] Although the *Star* responded critically to efforts to block a raise in clerks' salaries in 1867, commending the "many gentlemen and ladies of great intellectual ability" whose salaries "are totally inadequate," federal annual wages during the period, averaging $1,200 for men and $900 for women, were actually substantially better than could be found in comparable clerkships elsewhere. In 1870 such compensation was sufficient to allow two-thirds of families headed by a government clerk to live comfortably. In the same year, however, only a quarter of government clerks owned any real estate, the great proportion valued at less than $5,000.[25]

Although wage levels may have dampened home ownership in Washington, the *Star* believed, reasonably enough, that a more important factor was the lack of job security in government positions. In 1882 the paper argued,

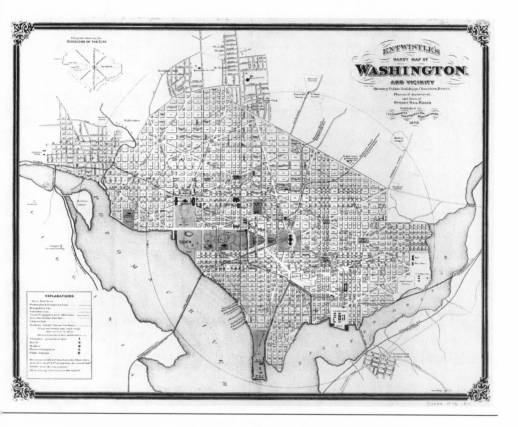

If civil service rules were in force here, and the government clerks were assured of being able to hold their places during good behavior, they would find some security in acquiring permanent homes in Washington and identifying themselves with the city. As it is, the large mass of the clerks feel their tenure of office to be so insecure that they hesitate about undertaking to buy homes for their own use, and are content to keep up a homeless existence in boarding houses or rented houses.[26]

Passage the following year of the Pendleton Civil Service Act establishing standard procedures for appointment and review of government employees outside the influence of politics appeared to provide homebuilding as well as home ownership the impetus it needed. Although few figures on

Making a Greater Washington

home ownership exist for the period, a guidebook for 1886 claimed that at least five thousand government clerks owned their own homes, in what would have been a significant increase over the figures for 1870.[27] With government expanding at an even greater rate than the population as a whole (table 2), Washington began to fill in what appeared in the first half of the nineteenth century to be the vast open spaces of the outer sectors.[28]

Not just historic in-town areas, like Capitol Hill, grew in response to the new law,[29] but also outer residential areas as they were brought within the orbit of the city by improved transportation facilities, especially with the first conversion of streetcar lines from horse to electric power in 1888. In Brookland, for instance, the proportion of residents in the professions jumped from only 30 percent in 1880 to 81 percent in 1900, a factor attributed to the introduction of rapid transit downtown.[30] Just to the west, out Seventh Street, developers announced plans to transform fifty acres of farmland into the new suburban neighborhood of Petworth. Like Brookland, such hopes relied on rapid streetcar transit, for as the *Star* reported in 1889, Brookland no longer seemed so far from the city since in a few months the Brightwood Street Railway, whose president was also one of the owners of Petworth, would reach the area.[31] Despite the temporary failure of its rail line in 1891, Brightwood itself, several miles farther to the north, saw its demographic base shift at the end of the century from a largely rural and agricultural community to one intimately tied to the downtown.[32] The purest form of marriage between railway and residential development emerged in Chevy Chase, Maryland, the result of Senator Francis Newlands's munificent investment. But other areas grew up as well along Newlands's Connecticut Avenue streetcar line, notably Kalorama and Cleveland Park.[33]

So powerful was the impetus that streetcars provided to growth that one builder complained:

> Real estate is just about as high as its going to be. Builders can't get any good land nowadays. A few days ago I went out about a quarter of a mile beyond the boundary to look at some land. When I asked the price it was one dollar a foot. You see, when it was proposed to extend the streets into the suburbs, real estatemen got up syndicates of speculators, and they bought up every bit of land they could on the line of the extensions with the expectation of making a big thing of it.[34]

Such speculation generated concern from the *Baltimore Sun*, among others, which in a front page article in 1886 noted the outcropping of "for sale" signs "in almost every direction on the drives out of the city." Charging that such lots were "undoubtedly in excess of real or prospective value," the paper stated hopefully that "the wisest of those who are looking ahead will not deceive themselves with the delusive idea that all the farms in the District of Columbia will in a few years be converted into town lots, but will

Table 2
Growth of Population and Civil Service

Year	Total Pop.	% Increase	Paid Civilian Federal Employment in DC		% Increase
1860	61,357		2,199	(1861)	
1870	109,092	77.8	6,222	(1871)	182.9
1880	147,491	35.2	13,124	(1881)	110.9
1890	230,402	56.2	20,834	(1891)	58.7
1900	278,785	17.4	28,044	(1901)	34.6

make their purchases in city property, which under any circumstances, can scarcely fail to appreciate." Nonetheless, the paper was forced to recognize that as a city of "magnificent distances" Washington was gaining credibility as a place that could reach a population of two million "within its present limits without the least crowding, without tenement-houses, and without encroaching in the slightest on its splendid parks, reservations and terraces."[35]

By 1890, the *Star* was reporting unprecedented purchases of suburban tracts at $3,000 and even $7,000 an acre.[36] In 1896, one petition to Congress seeking authority to extend a street railway to the zoo claimed that rapid transit to the area would increase property values fivefold and enrich the public treasury in the process. Similarly, a letter from *Washington Star* editor Victor Kauffman, citing the effect of rapid transit on the Columbia Heights area, said, "That seems to be a rather rapid growth and is very fair evidence of what might be expected of the whole section north of Florida Avenue as far as Rock Creek, were it supported with proper railroad facilities."[37] Prospects for improved transportation, though threatening change, nonetheless found considerable support among Washington residents. As W. F. Mattingly wrote the commissioners in 1899:

> Washington is growing rapidly. People in the near suburbs are becoming part of the population of the city, and in the near future, if they desire to enjoy the benefits and advantages of the city, they will be called upon to submit to the inconveniences incident to the growth of a city. If the people attempt to throttle every attempt that is made for public improvement the city will never grow. . . . I reside on a street on which an electric street car line is located, and would not have the line removed for a thousand dollars. People residing on such streets soon become used to the additional noise and pay no attention to it.[38]

With such pressure on land values, the pace of development accelerated, leaving the city as yet unprepared to exercise direction over the outward flow of its development. The city's streetcar system provided one such

Making a Greater Washington

compelling example of the need for central control. Other cities expressed similar concerns, but Washington's problems were complicated by the role of Congress as an intermediary. Throughout the 1870s and 1880s the process for initiating lines came privately, with Congress proving willing to grant franchises without considering much in the way of local opinion. As a result, the network of lines developed without plan or overall direction. As early as 1879, the District Commissioners' annual report for Washington urged immediate adoption of "a general and comprehensive plan for the location of street railways" to "avoid the multiplication of such corporations" as well as to prevent "the unnecessary occupation of streets by such roads."[39] It was not until 1893, however, that Senator James McMillan of Michigan introduced a bill granting landowners such simple rights as the public announcement of proposed lines and approval by the majority of property owners along the routes. McMillan subsequently pushed through a bill consolidating the lines, thus bringing more equitable fares to the overall system as well as more control over how railways would relate to development.[40] The *Star* actively supported McMillan's efforts to exercise control over the streets, endorsing the effort to "give the people of Washington and the hosts of tourists who annually visit the capital adequate transportation facilities which are now lacking."[41]

A problem associated with the quickened pace of growth was the lack of overall control over privately developed subdivisions. Because subdividers traditionally emphasized their own concerns without municipal direction or control, not one street in the first nine hundred acres of subdivision north of Boundary Avenue harmonized with the L'Enfant plan. So serious was the problem that in 1879 the Assistant Engineer Commissioner warned that random subdivision had to end or "the District government will be required at no distant day to expend large sums for damages incurred in straightening out the streets of these villages."[42] In LeDroit Park, for instance, developers had purposefully laid the streets off-line to those of the city, to enhance the psychological as well as physical distance between city and suburb, a statement that was made even more overt when residents surrounded their community with a combined cast-iron and wood fence. The *Star* backed the commissioners' efforts to exercise control over development, noting editorially in 1887, "When Washington shall cover the whole of the District it will not do to have half of the city with narrow streets running towards all points of the compass, especially ugly in contrast with the other half, which will be fully developed on the lines of the magnificent original plan."[43]

In 1888 the District Commissioners secured authority over new development by requiring that new streets conform with the city's original plan, stating hopefully that the new act "will prevent in the future any more subdivisions like LeDroit Park, Meridian Hill, Mount Pleasant, etc., being laid off, apparently at random, and without any reference to adjoining property and the proper extension of the city." The Engineer Commissioner stated the government's faith in the new act, claiming, "There is nothing which adds more to the desirability of Washington as a place of residence than well-constructed, smooth, wide country roads and suburban streets, over which people can comfortably ride and drive for health and recreation and which open up pleasant sections of country where people of limited means can build homes."[44] Developers in new subdivisions, like Petworth and Brightwood, responded by laying streets in line with those of the city. Parts of already developed areas underwent a quick transformation. Noting the impact of introducing well-defined city streets and squares, the *Star* in 1889 expressed satisfaction that it was "impossible to find the deep gullies, the nooks and glades," which once marked Kalorama. In nearby Washington Heights, it noted, "the valleys and the odd freaks and fancies of nature in the way of ravines and gullies that mark this spot will all be transformed into a level plain." The following year, the *Star* praised other subdivisions for adapting to new city regulations, which through wider streets and generous spaces could be "recognized to be the crown and glory of the plan of the city."[45]

Some existing development continued to stand in the way of full control, however. In 1889 the Engineer Commissioner criticized LeDroit Park's continued separatism, calling it "a thorn in the side of the District" for throwing itself across the northern part of the city and compelling everybody to go around it.[46] After residents restored the fence after it had been torn down several times in protest by blacks from nearby Howardtown, the commissioners finally required that the streets be open permanently to everyone. "With the opening of the streets," the press reported, "the park soon lost its former characteristics and became a part of the city with all its advantages and disadvantages."[47] Although the commissioners recognized that it would be too costly to realign LeDroit's streets to conform to Washington's city plan, they sought further authority to compel existing subdivisions to meet that standard, power they secured with the support of the Board of Trade through an additional highway act passed by Congress in 1893.[48]

Delays in platting the land and executing a plan, however, left the city seeking still further supervisory power, as a petition from the District Commissioners to Congress in 1898 indicated. Citing the failure of earlier acts intended to make of city and suburb a "harmonious whole," the commissioners sought to establish "a comprehensive plan for the whole district," in line with what they claimed was the practice in other cities.[49] When Congress resisted funding improvements in the District outside the city of Washington, *Star* editor and Board of Trade president Theodore Noyes reacted sharply. Calling on the federal government to pay its fair share, Noyes charged, "Either suburban Washington should be made a part of the capital in all respects or the section should be retroceded to Maryland and

Making a Greater Washington

permitted to develop on the natural lines of its own resources as a series of Maryland villages."[50] Congress refused, however, to provide its share in funding the improvements, thus marking the first time the federal government had failed to provide half of such costs since 1878.[51]

In fact, by 1900 Washington City had extended fully into the county. Even Georgetown, which had clung to its separate social and political identity, was fully incorporated into Washington City government in 1895. Similarly, after years of living with conflicting names of streets, by 1904 the city managed to push through that necessary rationalization to urban development.[52] Although investors had originally resisted such controls, they came to embrace the new rules, as a *Star* interview with local developer George Truesdell in 1890 indicated:

> "Why did you adopt the policy of making city improvements in the country?" Mr Truesdell was asked.
>
> "To make my property more attractive and saleable," he replied. "I found what every other owner of suburban property has discovered—that people would not leave the well-lighted and well-paved streets of the city, to any great extent, and build houses along mud streets in the country that were destitute of every city convenience. I found, moreover, that in the ordinary course of events it would take about twenty-five years to secure these improvements at the public expense, so I concluded to anticipate the future to some extent by providing them at my own expense, and I have never regretted that conclusion."[53]

In 1887 the *Star*, in noting the laying out of a seventeen-acre estate on Park Avenue in Mount Pleasant known as Rosemont, could describe the emergence of a "new city" that would soon equal in size the city proper.[54] Additionally the paper embraced an especially visionary picture of Washington, claiming, "Citizenship of the great Washington of the future, with its numerous and varied light manufactures giving it the wealth of Paris without the smoke of Pittsburgh, its vast population, its public buildings and institutions . . . and its general attractions as a place of residence indicated as well by miles of contract built houses as by the palaces of millionaires, will be a cause of congratulation and not of reproach."[55] Indeed, by the 1890s, the creation of a "greater Washington" was attracting wide attention. "The suburbs and the city so far constitute but one community," the annual report for the Washington Board of Trade declared in 1896, noting "that the health and well being of the suburbs cannot be ignored without injuring that part of the District known as the old cities of Washington and Georgetown."[56] Claiming in 1901 that Washington had the best streetcar system in the nation, the *Star* stated that "it is now possible to live in the suburbs without giving up essentials in the way of advantages to the family." A 1903 editorial pronounced that there was no longer any meaningful distinction between city and suburb.[57]

★ ★ ★

Although Washington's residential development came to be seen in the twentieth century as inevitable, it did not advance in the preceding years without serious impediments. A letter addressed to Senate District chairman James McMillan in 1896, in urging the extension of rail lines out Columbia Road to the Washington Heights section of Northwest Washington, complained that despite paying heavy taxes, the residents "so far have nothing in return except street lights, no fire protection, no police, no street cleaning, little or no street improvements except those we pay for, and many of us have been compelled to provide our own mains and sewerage. A private company now offers to give us what we need more than anything else, and it seems fair to urge you to let them give it."[58] Although Mount Pleasant's proximity to rail service along Fourteenth Street stimulated its growth, residents could still complain about service. One claimed, in a letter to Senator McMillan, that he could reach Baltimore, more than thirty miles from his home, faster than he could get to work downtown.[59]

Most devastating was the experience of Eckington, located in the newly emerging northeastern sector of the city, above Florida Avenue and east of North Capitol Street. Benefiting from a charter granted to the city's first electric street line, the Eckington and Soldier's Home Railway, the area surged with development. As the *Star* reported in 1889, "The hills have huge pieces chopped out of them, and their slopes and summits have been flattened to accommodate the houses to be built on them."[60] The incursion of the B&O freight yards nearby and new restrictions placed on overhead wires in the suburbs by the commissioners set back service by rail. Seeing investment lag, the chief developer of the area, George Truesdell, sold his streetcar shares and became a District Commissioner in 1894, only to return later to street railway operations without the burden of directing neighborhood development.[61] As commuting time lengthened and investment lagged, residents complained that developers had offered false promises that "no nuisances or objectionable places of any kind" would compromise the area. The lack of an integrated system, a petition charged, left passengers frustrated by having to make numerous transfers, all the while left exposed to inclement weather.[62]

As other residents of Washington neighborhoods before them had done, Eckington responded, in 1896, by forming a citizens' association. Lacking the franchise, these residents organized to take their case directly to Congress to protest the presence of the "well-known nuisances of round houses, machine shops, and even cattle yards" in their neighborhood. A similar strategy had been employed in Brightwood in 1891. Anacostia used the same device to secure from Congress assistance in upgrading the motive power of its streetcar line, also in 1896. Although the immediate focus of the North Capital and Eckington Citizens Association was improved rail service, like other associations it quickly broadened its mission to embrace

Making a Greater Washington

a variety of residential concerns, including fire and police protection and improved sidewalks, streets, and sewers.[63]

The formation of neighborhood associations, a practice that dated to 1871 in Washington, was one tool for residents to exercise control over their lives. But in a city whose parts were increasingly interdependent, such associations were ill suited to meet more cosmopolitan needs. Occasionally the active intervention of a neighborhood association contributed to a city-wide improvement, as in efforts of the East Washington Citizens Association to improve the malarial flats along the Anacostia River, a threat both to its own members and to the city at large.[64] More typically such associations remained bound to their own parochial concerns, arguing for some greater share of the amenities provided by central authorities, such as paved streets or sewers. When the city's Engineer Commissioner submitted the first proposal for a new union station, for instance, at Maryland and Virginia avenues, S.W., local improvement associations strenuously objected to the intrusion, arguing that the site should be farther to the east. When this location was selected some years later, the North East Citizens Association objected, calling the new station "hideous and monstrous."[65]

As quickened growth forced different neighborhoods into greater interdependency, it was hardly surprising that a new citywide organization formed, the Washington Board of Trade. Although announcement of its formation in November 1889 carried with it the usual booster attention to building up the economic interests of the city, it was no coincidence that the board's first president, Myron Parker, would have identified his organization's cause with residential development. Like the board's first treasurer, Brainard Warner, Parker was an active investor in real estate, especially in the Petworth and Brightwood areas. Undoubtedly aware of an unsuccessful effort among neighborhood associations to join forces in 1888 to influence congressional legislation, Parker cited the board's ability to speak with one voice as a necessary supplement to neighborhood activism, stating in his first annual report:

> Being governed by a Board of Commissioners appointed by the President, without the usual form of municipal government and without representation in Congress, the necessity for an organization like our Board of Trade representing without favor or prejudice all sections and interests of our city, was manifest to all. It was the common remark in both Houses of Congress that there was no general organization in Washington representing in a public, impartial, unsectional way, the necessity and wishes of the community.[66]

In a pattern common to the South, these boosters embraced civic as well as commercial goals in efforts to overcome every sign of backwardness.[67] Board officers favored the conservation of residential amenity over economic development at all costs. In its early years, the board set up a committee actively to recruit more industry to the city, but the committee typically reported that such development should not proceed at the expense of the city's natural beauty. As Brainard Warner put it, the board would promote only "such manufactures as would not be detrimental to the city in any respect."[68] In addition to supporting the 1893 and 1898 highway acts to control development, it promoted and secured strong legislation from Congress to control the smoke nuisance.[69] In 1894 the board opposed a bill that would have granted the Alexandria and Mt. Vernon Railroad rights to enter the city through the Potomac flats because the board was firmly committed to seeing that area become a park.[70] More important, in its early years, the board intervened at a critical juncture in the effort to establish an extended park along the valley of Rock Creek.

Originally proposed in 1867 as an alternative site for the executive mansion to escape the malarial swamps nearby, the idea languished for almost twenty years until another threat emerged, that of pollution in Rock Creek. With the sewers of Georgetown as well as the Northwest emptying into the creek, and additional urgent calls for sewerage facilities from the Mount Pleasant, Columbia Heights, and Meridian Hill neighborhoods, the *Star* charged that the valley, "if not speedily secured by the government, will be occupied for purposes that will convert it from a 'thing of beauty, a joy forever,' into a dangerous nuisance in the shape of foul open sewer, lined with a succession of slaughterhouses, breweries, dye-houses, hog-pens, privies, &c., polluting the creek with their excrement."[71] Although buoyed by the support of the preeminent landscape architect and designer of New York's pioneer Central Park, Frederick Law Olmsted, park supporters faced opposition in the House of Representatives from lingering hostility toward expenditure of federal funds for what some members conceived as a local improvement. It took a concerted campaign by the Board of Trade, working especially with Senator John Sherman of Ohio, to secure final approval of a bill setting aside two thousand acres and an appropriation of $1,200,000. To accommodate the House, the bill required owners of adjacent property to pay a "benefit" tax to help offset the normal national contribution of 50 percent to District improvement projects. While the *Star* complained about the expense to the District, it took pride that in preserving the picturesque beauty of the Rock Creek valley, the new park both adorned the national capital and prevented its surrender to real estate speculators and sellers of suburban lots.[72] Just as importantly, the Washington Board of Trade took a lead in the dominant issue of the period, asserting control over steam railroads operating in the city.

During the last quarter of the nineteenth century, public reports reiterated the terrible sacrifice that Washington had paid in the effort after the Civil War to attract additional rail service to the city. Angered by the high prices charged by the B&O, the city council in 1871 authorized the Baltimore and Potomac Railroad, a subsidiary of the Pennsylvania Railroad, to enter Washington. Initially the line planned to construct a depot south of

The city core before replanning.
Currier and Ives print, 1892,
showing different gardens as well
as a rail crossing on the Mall and
the lack of a defined federal
presence. Courtesy Geography
and Map Division, Library of
Congress.

the Mall. But within two weeks of securing its access rights, the railroad received additional authority to locate its tracks some three blocks to the north, extending its tracks across the Mall at Sixth Street, N.W. Although members of Congress as well as the Republican *Chronicle* and the Democratic *Patriot* protested the desecration of the Mall,[73] arguments that the depot would be less of a nuisance to residents of South Washington and more of a convenience to business congregating next to the new Center Market on Pennsylvania Avenue a block away carried the argument for the new location.[74]

The railroad's intrusion onto city streets provoked numerous complaints. Not only did the noise of steam engines disrupt the sylvan quality of the Mall, but the B&P freight operations quickly spilled over into the streets of South Washington, creating additional physical hazards to residents as well as through traffic. According to a petition submitted to the District Commissioners by Southwest residents in 1900, "The noise and confusion, together with dust, smoke, soot and cinders, necessarily incident to each operation, have increased so enormously in recent years as to constitute a nuisance almost intolerable to residents in the vicinity." Responding to complaints about the clamor, a railroad spokesman retorted that while the "noise from these gongs are not as sweet as village chimes," they marked "the progress of the world."[75] When, despite the protest of nearby residents, the B&P sought the right to construct a permanent freight yard in South Washington, it revived the old argument in Congress, backed by the *Washington Post,* that such a step was the only logical way of conducting business. The Board of Trade and its closely allied voice in the *Star* strongly protested the Atkinson bill granting the B&P its request. When the bill gained approval in 1890, the *Star* satirically quipped, "It would simplify matters if Congress should formally surrender its constitutional control of District affairs to the local railroads in respect to all questions." Washington, like a woman, the *Star* argued later that year, should remain "strong in beauty because of the absence of many things characteristic of a great commercial city."[76]

The depots of both of the city's rail lines were quickly perceived as nuisances. While the commissioners in 1878 blamed the B&O for retarding development of the city's northeast sector, they charged the B&P with disfiguring the Mall and obstructing improvements on the south side of the Capital. "It is not to be expected," they wrote, "that the surroundings of the Capitol can become what they ought to be while these two railway stations occupy their present sites."[77] In 1882 the commissioners began pressing for completion of a union station north of the Mall at Maryland and Virginia avenues, a position objected to not just by the railroads but also by a number of congressmen, including outspoken Representative Joseph Cannon of Illinois, who said he would "vote for no legislation that will permit the railroad, if the Government has rights, to move the depot or to fail to operate its track across the park, because I believe as one of the citizens of the country that the people should have the right to be carried into the heart of the city and into that depot."[78]

Although critics of the railroads continued to denounce intrusions on the Mall, including parked cars, piles of coal, and the B&P depot, which extended nearly half the distance of the Mall, the issue most characteristic of the arrogance of the rail lines came to be associated with their insistence on keeping their tracks at grade, despite abundant evidence of their threat to public safety. Such complaints reached back as far as 1875 in the first report of the city's Engineer Commissioner. In 1880 the commissioners called for a law to require steam railroads to enter the city below grade. A year later the Engineer Commissioner said he would allow the B&P depot

A crowd gathers in the aftermath of a rail accident on the B&O Railroad, August 17, 1887, one of many tragedies caused by the failure to regulate traffic through the city. Courtesy Washingtoniana Division, D.C. Public Library.

to remain at Sixth and Pennsylvania avenues, provided the company would deal with the grade issue. The railroads, with their allies in Congress, continued to resist pressures to act on both counts, prompting criticism from both the nascent Board of Trade and the *Star*, which claimed that more than one hundred people had been killed or mangled by B&P trains in Washington, some of them running at illegal speeds.[79] The Board of Trade provided a particularly strong statement in its annual report for 1894, declaring that even as efforts should continue to promote industry and manufacturing, "No expenditure of money should be spared, no vigilance remitted to secure for the citizens of this broad land a salubrious abiding place within its limits and an absolutely safe conduct over its thoroughfares. To this end the greed of individuals and the rapacity of corporations should be sternly and relentlessly antagonized and repressed."[80] Senator McMillan first introduced a bill to require the railroads to adjust their grades in 1893, and the commissioners prepared their own legislation in 1898.[81] The issue dragged on for the rest of the decade, however, making it one of the city's most glaring pieces of unfinished business for twentieth-century planners to address.

Even with that business unfinished, however, by the end of the century Washington had moved significantly toward its eventual standing as a modern metropolis. In the city core as well as in its neighborhoods, vast improvements were either in place or well on their way toward execution. The District Commissioners, working closely with the Board of Trade and taking account of neighborhood concerns, had effectively honed its governmental authority and set an ambitious agenda for the city's continued development. Washington could look forward to the celebration of its centennial as the nation's capital, an event that promised to confirm recent accomplishments and to extend the agenda for additional improvements.

87

The New Washington:
City Beautiful

By the patient and steadfast cooperation of all those persons charged with the upbuilding of the District of Columbia, a result may be attained such as has been reached in no other capital city of the modern world. The task is indeed a stupendous one; it is much greater than any one generation can hope to accomplish. The very hearty and intelligent cooperation that the plans have been [*sic*] received by the officers of the Government, the committees of Congress, and by the public generally makes it reasonably certain that the development of the National Capital will be prosecuted along the general lines proposed; and that the city which Washington and Jefferson planned with so much care and with such prophetic vision will continue to expand, keeping pace with national advancement, until it becomes the visible expression of the power and taste of the people of the United States.

> *The Improvement of the Park System of the
> District of Columbia,* Report of the Senate
> Committee on the District of Columbia,
> January 15, 1902

The Senate Park Commission plan for Washington, issued January 15, 1902, marked a critical turning point in the city's history. Although more than a quarter century passed before the park commission ideal was realized, it left an indelible imprint on the capital city. Built on the accomplishments of the Shepherd era, in drawing on the ideals of the emerging City Beautiful movement the report assumed new stature as the nation's first comprehensive plan and a catalyst for the nascent city planning profession.[1] By urging a distinctive identity for Washington's core, it promised to link parks and public buildings in a scheme that would embrace the highest standards of magnificence and beauty as well as provide a powerful symbolic statement for the federal presence. In setting the government symbolically as well as physically apart from the city around it, however, the plan institutionalized the division between city and capital that made even more difficult persistent local problems.

The dramatic turn of events that resulted in the formulation of a new vision for Washington owed much to ongoing efforts to modernize city services. But the chief influences on the new plan for the capital lay outside the city, in the aesthetic influences of the World's Columbian Exposition of 1893 and efforts in the architectural profession to assert a role in the physical planning of Washington, as well as a more general drive to raise Washington's stature to that of other world capitals following the international prominence that the nation gained in winning the Spanish-American War. Although the Park Commission described its plan as "the most comprehensive ever presented for the development of an American city,"[2] it actually represented a turn toward a more specialized vision for the city. The commission's recommendations, it is true, extended beyond Washington's city limits to envision a regional network of parks and parkways. It provided the framework for redoing the city's core area to a standard considered suitable for the nation then taking its place at the head of world affairs. But in emphasizing the monumental, practically to the exclusion of the residential city, the commission and its successor, the Commission of Fine Arts, narrowed the purview of planning.

Charles Moore, the influential secretary to Senator James McMillan and the Park Commission he established, explained the commission's rationale by arguing that by the turn of the century Washington had reached an appropriate crossroads to undertake a new step in its development. "That the time has come for beautifying Washington none can doubt," he wrote in the introduction to the collected papers of the proceedings of the annual conference of the American Institute of Architects (AIA) for 1900. "Those necessary matters of civic economy which must precede adornment either have been completed, or at least provision for them has been made." As evidence, he cited the public works accomplishments of the late nineteenth century, including a comprehensive sewer system, the water filtration plant, and the extended system of highways, as well as the new Rock Creek Park and reclamation of the Potomac River flats. With these projects serving to show "how comprehensive and varied is the movement now in progress for the development of Washington," Moore argued, it was now time to apply more aesthetically imbued principles to the ornamentation of the capital city's monumental core.[3] Senator McMillan voiced a similar view by suggesting that the city might employ a body of experts to lay out parks similar to the plan used to complete Washington's system of sewers.[4] In this, both men were clearly influenced, as were the members of the commission, by the event each of them had helped shape, the 1893 World's Columbian Exposition in Chicago.

As early as 1890, at its first annual meeting, the Washington Board of Trade had seized the occasion of the forthcoming centennial celebration of the location of the capital at Washington as an excuse to introduce a new set of physical improvements to the city. Secretary Alexander D. Anderson proposed, among other improvements, extension of the White House, a new National University, the planting of centennial trees in a new Columbus Park, and the building of a memorial bridge to Arlington, a project which subsequently received support from the secretary of war and the Congress.[5] It was up to the *Star* to put such bold ideas in the specific context of the fair. In August 1893, the paper's real estate column called for a "comprehensive plan" according to the world's fair precedent, including the consolidation of public buildings on the south side of Pennsylvania Avenue. The paper restated the fair's inspiration in a subsequent editorial pressing for a new municipal office building, commenting that construction "will be unsatisfactory if it fails to reach the elevated ideals of a people who appreciate more than ever before since it has seen what architectural genius did for the World's Columbian Exposition."[6] As the term *City Beautiful* gained favor in the national press, the new magazine *Municipal Affairs*, citing the precedent of the Chicago fair, proposed Washington as the ideal site to demonstrate the value of comprehensive planning.[7]

America's quick military victory over Spain in 1898 not only helped propel the nation onto the world stage politically but renewed interest in elevating the physical status of Washington to that of other world capitals. Boosted by the good works accomplished during the temporary possession of Cuba, the *Star* by 1900 could call the military occupation there an object lesson for reform at home. Likewise, the Washington Board of Trade could assert that the war and its aftermath had confirmed its faith that as the body politic expanded to Puerto Rico, Cuba, and the Philippines, government machinery operating in Washington would increase, thereby helping develop the government's city, nation, and capital: "The bloodshed of the Revolution created the Federal Union and the Capital. The bloodshed of the Civil War developed a nation and a national city. The bloodshed of the war with Spain washes out all traces of the civil struggle, reunites the national elements, and expands and promotes the nation and the national city."[8]

Both the Chicago exposition and the Spanish-American War encouraged bold thinking about Washington's future, but it was the occasion of the centennial celebration itself that proved the turning point in the city's history. Starting in October 1908 and continuing for the next two years, a committee of nine prominent citizens discussed various proposals for providing a permanent memorial to the occasion. Among the most popular ideas were the construction of a memorial hall and a memorial bridge across the Potomac to Arlington. Local citizens, with President William McKinley's support, applied to Congress for formal assistance, but legislation languished throughout 1899 and 1900 until James McMillan, the conscientious chairman of the Senate Committee on the District of Columbia, stepped in. Participants in an ad hoc meeting February 21, 1900, again took up familiar projects, most notably a memorial bridge. Following a midday break, however, a subcommittee headed by McMillan reported back an alternative: the extension of the White House, as previously recommended by the Board of Trade, and the creation of a three-mile-long Centennial Avenue from the foot of Capitol Hill across the Mall to the Potomac River.[9]

McMillan's "grand thoroughfare," as he called it, was the design of Chicago architect Henry Ives Cobb, as revealed in a long article in the *Inland Architect* for March 1900, which called for dramatic changes in Washington. Detailing problems with the design and location of prominent public buildings in Washington, in addition to supporting the Centennial Avenue, architect F. W. Fitzpatrick called for an art commission staffed by "a competent body of unbiased specialists" to oversee federal, state, and municipal architecture, statuary, decoration, and improvement of parks. An associated editorial, endorsing the movement to "permanently beautify the national capital," supported using the centennial to promote harmonious groupings of public buildings.[10]

McMillan's proposal provoked immediate local opposition, however, most notably from the *Star*, which in a series of editorials and articles complained that the plan both would compromise the Mall's function as a park and make nearby Pennsylvania Avenue a virtual backwater. McMillan's plan, the paper claimed, would "despoil the park, . . . cut it in twain by an inartistic street and . . . change its character entirely." Under the headline "Would Be Sacrilege" two days later, the *Star* quoted Secretary of Agriculture James Wilson as saying, "I would just as soon cut down all the shade trees in Washington and sell them for cord wood as to run a boulevard through the Mall." Challenging McMillan's proposal to line Centennial Avenue with new public buildings, Wilson charged that "not an inch of public park should be utilized for public building sites."[11] With McMillan's help, the Centennial Committee secured a provision in May in the Senate appropriations bill to provide a commission of experts to report back in December on plans for enlarging the executive mansion and improving the area between Pennsylvania Avenue and B Street, S.W.[12] The *Star* reacted sharply, saying that inclusion of the Mall in the area for consideration was designed to boost the idea of the Centennial Avenue while preventing any possible improvement to Pennsylvania Avenue.[13]

The *Star*'s position on preserving the Mall as a park was closely associated with Board of Trade president John Joy Edson's strenuous effort to link the Mall with the centennial celebration. In 1899 Edson declared, "No other labor of the centennial year is more inspiring or more promising of notable results in increasing the attractiveness of the Capital than that of developing Washington as the city of parks and the forest city by a vigorous campaign for the series of connected reservations."[14] But the paper gave a new twist to the issue by linking it to the 1893 fair, printing a suggestion in February 1900 that every state be encouraged to construct its own building along Pennsylvania Avenue. Referring specifically to the central feature of the world's fair, Mrs. F. M. Bradley suggested, "In the center of this reservation let there be a magnificent court of honor, extending perhaps from 3rd

91

The New Washington: City Beautiful

to 15th streets, with lakes, fountains, colonnades and statues, with handsome buildings ornamented by the best of American architects and artists." What Chicago had offered the nation as an object lesson, she claimed, "will not bear legitimate fruit unless and until the glories of 1893 are rivaled in the great governmental park in the capital city of the new world."[15]

Franklin Webster Smith, a Bostonian greatly influenced by Frederick Law Olmsted's pioneer work designing a metropolitan park system there, petitioned Congress as early as 1891 to authorize the grouping of monumental buildings around proposed new facilities for national galleries of history and art. Further influenced by the world's fair, he adopted his proposals for consideration in 1900 as part of the centennial celebration. Like Mrs. Bradley, he proposed the inclusion of state buildings from the fair in space that he urged should be cleared for the purpose along Pennsylvania Avenue. In addition, he laid out an ambitious plan for public buildings, including a new executive office building—allowing the old White House to be converted to office use—a system of parks, a memorial bridge to Virginia, and the introduction of public baths.[16]

For its part, the *Star* favored a plan for the Mall, solicited by army engineer Theodore Bingham and offered by Samuel Parsons Jr., which proposed the creation of a complex of elliptical or oval boulevards. Building on his association with Calvert Vaux as landscape architect of New York's Central Park at the end of the nineteenth century, Parsons's proposal reiterated the romantic view of parks as pleasure grounds that should be "set apart and isolated as completely as art can contrive it from the sight and sound of the surrounding city." Immediately criticized by a number of prominent Washington architects, the Parsons plan nonetheless gained the *Star*'s endorsement both for proposing to remove from the Mall the railroad tracks and the station that had intruded since 1872 and for preserving the concept of the park as a refuge from the city around it. "Mr. Parsons' scheme," the *Star* editorialized on December 1, 1900, "disregards the suggestion that a straight, broad thoroughfare be cut through the Mall from end to end, spoiling the beauty derived from curves and irregularity, and largely reducing its total park area. He plans a series of artistic drives which will afford convenient access from one part to another and yet will preserve the semblance of park and forest which a rigid street would utterly destroy." In addition, the *Star* praised Parsons for promoting its own preference for public buildings sited along the south side of Pennsylvania Avenue, thereby ridding the area as well of a notorious slum.[17]

Although historian Jon Peterson, in calling attention to the importance of McMillan's Centennial Avenue idea, suggests that he was acting in cooperation with the Pennsylvania Railroad in providing a grand approach to the company's proposed new terminal on the Mall, that appears unlikely. A letter in the files of McMillan's Senate District Committee from Pennsylvania Railroad president A. J. Cassatt specifically objected to the Centennial

The Mall as envisioned in a petition that Franklin Webster Smith submitted to Congress in 1900, a coordinated series of "national galleries of history and art" drawn to scale to the great architectural buildings of the ancient world. Courtesy Prints and Photographs Division, Library of Congress.

Avenue for cutting back the space that the railroad might have to build.[18] More likely, McMillan, like other leading critics of the railroad, had resigned himself to trying to make the best of a bad situation. By November 1899, the impasse in the effort to get both the Baltimore and Potomac and the Baltimore and Ohio lines to remove their tracks from grade appeared finally to be over, as the *Star* reported that the Pennsylvania's Cassatt was ready to work with Congress and the District Commissioners to secure an agreement. For the Baltimore and Potomac, the reward was an affirmative answer to its request to build a new and larger depot on the Mall to accommodate its growing business. For the B&O, the incentive to take up tracks would be a $1.5 million payment.[19]

Colonel Theodore Bingham, the Army Corps of Engineers officer re-

The New Washington: City Beautiful

94

sponsible for overseeing public buildings and grounds, opposed Cassatt's proposal to build a new station for the B&P. In a report dated January 1900, he charged that George Washington's "noble plan" had already been "almost irreparably injured" by the presence of the railroad on the Mall. "Considering that this park was specially reserved in the formation of the city by our immortal President Washington, it does seem unpatriotic, and even irreverent, that Washington's ideas should not be carried out," he charged. "It is, in my humble judgment, the national interests and the interests of this city, as the capital of our great nation, and not merely the local commercial interests, which should govern the consideration of this entire question of rail road terminals within the District."[20] In a separate report to Congress, the District Commissioners took another position, however, choosing to stress the convenience of the proposed new station to street rail traffic in the city and the improvement to local traffic which the introduction of an elevated viaduct would offer. In the report of the Senate District Committee, McMillan sided with the commissioners, arguing that the city had become adjusted to buildings on the Mall, "and to disturb them now would be not only a practical impossibility, but also would be, in the opinion of the committee, highly undesirable. By virtue of the proposed changes this occupation will be greatly improved so far as sightliness is concerned, and as a result the visitor to the National Capital will not only be landed nearer to the heart of the city, but also his first impressions of the city will be of the pleasantest possible character."[21]

The B&P proposal proved controversial in the Senate as well, where Richard Pettigrew of South Dakota complained that an elevated dike some twenty feet in height would "cut the park absolutely in two, besides destroying the view."[22] McMillan responded by defending the elevated tracks not just as structurally sound but also as a necessary means of solving the persistent grade issue. "We are asking them to do away with these grade crossings on account of which the loss of life has been very great," he said in the railroad's defense. "The Committee on the District of Columbia have been at work for many years trying to frame a bill satisfactory alike to the District, to the railroad, and to the property owners. As satisfactory a bill as

can reasonably be hoped for has been presented." When another senator questioned the lack of a union depot in pending legislation, McMillan responded defensively, "I have talked to the officers of the railroad companies about it, but I found that there was no use in trying to bring them together."[23]

In the House debate six months later, Representative William Cowherd of Missouri defended the traditionally romantic vision of the Mall, arguing that "a lightning express is quite incompatible with a green garden and singing birds." Congressman Richard Powers retorted that tourists in the city would be impressed with the vision of seventeen trains arriving daily at a magnificent station, asking rhetorically, "the gentleman does not expect that the visitors would spend their whole time looking at parks?" Congress-

The New Washington: City Beautiful

man Joseph Babcock, speaking for the House District Committee, claimed the proposal would "result in making the grandest and most convenient terminals enjoyed by any city in the world." While it was not a perfect plan, Congressman William Hepburn of Iowa added, "I believe it is the only feasible one. It is the only one that probably can pass the two houses."[24] Even the strongest critics of the railroad assumed that some form of central station was necessary. Despite petitions from nearby property owners urging Congress to drop a railroad request to place a freight facility on Garfield Park near the Mall, even Congressman Cowherd, in defense of the Mall, was willing to sacrifice the park.[25]

The railroad controversy reached a peak just as another group, the American Institute of Architects, attempted to influence the future development of the city. Under the influence of its politically astute national secretary, Glenn Brown, this organization chose to schedule its national meeting in Washington in conjunction with the centennial celebration. Imbued with a desire to advance high standards of professionalism in the field, Brown and his allies from other parts of the country—most notably Daniel Burnham and Charles McKim, architects given particular prominence at the Columbian Exposition—had argued for a national competition for the design of public buildings in Washington. When Theodore Bingham revealed both the Parsons plan for the Mall and his own concept of how the White House ought to be extended, architects led by Brown mounted a vocal assault in the press, building on earlier arguments that government engineers like Bingham were not qualified to engage in such important architectural business.[26]

Even as the local press used the occasion of the centennial to commend Washington for overcoming "indifference and injustice" to launch "an era of municipal development which is a marvel of results and promise,"[27] architects meeting the same day attacked the city's failures, especially to achieve a distinctive core. In line with the AIA's orientation toward public buildings, a number of speakers, fully imbued with the example of the Columbian Exposition, argued for more systematic and aesthetically pleasing groupings of federal structures. Howard Walker of Boston captured the interest in federal planning represented in the group by arguing that "the city of to-day has grown too large to be picturesque; its avenues are too broad, its spaces too vast, its distances too great. Accident must give place to intention, or the general effect of the city will be haphazard, incongruous, and incomplete." Washington, Glenn Brown argued, should give itself the advantage of "a proper and artistic grouping" of public buildings, adapting a standard of beauty that had been set by L'Enfant and realized in many cities abroad. Frederick Law Olmsted Jr., who had assisted his father as landscape designer of the 1893 Columbian Exposition, used his direct link with the fair to challenge Parsons's design and what he called "a mere commonplace boulevard," in clear reference to the Centennial Avenue proposal. Following the example of the Tapis Vert at Versailles, he called for "an immensely broad and simple space of turf, with strong flanking masses and architecture, and shaded driveways." Countering the Parsons approach of offering a retreat from modern life—an opportunity that he said had been offered by the new Rock Creek Park—Olmsted suggested instead a Mall that would "form a contributing part in the effect of grandeur, power and dignified magnificence which should mark the seat of government of a great and intensely active people."[28]

Following a number of comments that Washington's future should be entrusted to a body of experts competent to evaluate "the aesthetic as well as the material and economic conditions" of the city, the AIA passed a resolution urging Congress to create a commission to plan "the location and grouping of public buildings, the ordering of landscape and statuary, and the extension of the park system in the District of Columbia." The architects quickly moved to secure political support for their vision for Washington, sending in the last hours of their meeting a delegation to petition Senator McMillan for their cause. Three days later McMillan responded by offering Senate Resolution 139, "To Provide a commission to consider certain improvements in the District of Columbia." The accompanying report, drafted by Glenn Brown, urged the restoration of the L'Enfant plan for the Mall and formation "of a general plan connecting the park system, as well as devising broad principles in which all parks shall be treated."[29] Like the previous proposal attached to the civil appropriations bill in May,[30] the proposed commission included an architect and a landscape architect. As the third member, in obvious response to the architects' plea, McMillan substituted another architect for the chief engineer of the army. Gone too was specific reference to treatment of the Executive Mansion and the area between Pennsylvania Avenue and B Street, S.W. Instead, reflecting the concerns of the architects' meeting, there was a new focus, "the location and grouping of public buildings and monuments to be erected in the District of Columbia and the development and improvement of the entire park system of said District."[31]

McMillan revealed his debt to the architects' approach, both in Resolution 139 and his defense of it in light of an alternative offered by Senator George Frisbie Hoar the same day. Hoar's bill, which listed a series of specific projects, including a memorial bridge, suitable boulevards, and a plan for condemning and improving the land south of Pennsylvania Avenue for the construction of government buildings there, would have created an advisory board of public works to report to Congress a general plan for the improvement of the city.[32] Clearly it represented an effort to build on Alexander Shepherd's board of public works.[33] As such, it drew the support of the District Commissioners, who described it as more suitable for the comprehensive treatment of the city than Resolution 139. Urging their own inclusion on the ten-person board, along with the chairs of the Dis-

The New Washington: City Beautiful

trict committees of the House and Senate, they argued that the city's future would be better handled by members "thoroughly familiar with the conditions prevailing" than by "outsiders which will have to become acquainted with the whole subject after their appointment."[34]

McMillan's report January 18 endorsing Resolution 139 ignored the commissioners' argument. Finding his inspiration in Chicago rather than locally, he looked to the world's fair as a model for showing "how an artistic plan may be devised and carried out so as to be a source of national pride and a means of national education. What has been achieved temporarily in the midst of commercial cities may be realized permanently in this noncommercial city." Arguing that the Chicago fair had demonstrated the utility of small commissions and attaching to the report Glenn Brown's own argument for the coordination of parks with public buildings, McMillan claimed to have the support of the AIA as well as of the Washington Board of Trade.[35]

The appearance of rival bills in Congress raised fears among architects that the commission of experts on which they pinned their hopes would lose out to other alternatives. According to Moore, McMillan's resolution fell victim to a "multitude of councillors." In executive session on March 8, however, after the adjournment of Congress, McMillan secured authorization for his committee to "report to the Senate plans for the development and improvement of the entire park system of the District of Columbia." Reduced in its apparent mission as well as authority, the revised resolution was the best that McMillan and his allies could secure under the circumstances.[36]

The ties between what would come to be called the Senate Park Commission and the world's fair were quickly secured, as McMillan selected first Daniel Burnham, the exposition's supervising architect, then Frederick Law Olmsted Jr. They in turn chose Charles McKim, another veteran of the fair, as the third member, subsequently adding another fair associate, sculptor Augustus Saint-Gaudens.[37] Throwing himself into the work, Burnham made clear his own sense of continuity with the fair, writing Secretary of the Treasury and former chair of the Chicago board of directors for the fair Lyman Gage, "I do not think anything that has come into my life since the World's Fair promises such a delightful vista."[38]

In the months that followed, members of the Park Commission surveyed sites in Washington and other American locations which they believed could have influenced the original Washington plan, including the colonial capitals of Williamsburg and Annapolis. Convinced by Glenn Brown's argument of the importance of restoring L'Enfant's plan to its original intent, the commission nonetheless had to deal immediately with the most volatile contemporary issue in Washington, the accommodation of the B&P Railroad on the Mall. Although Congress finally approved the grade legislation bill in February, with its commitment to an enlarged station on the Mall, neither McKim nor Burnham found that acceptable. Told by McMillan to accept that decision as given, Burnham and McKim nonetheless lobbied Pennsylvania Railroad president Cassatt to remove his station to a site south of the Mall. Although Cassatt reacted angrily to pressure from Burnham, telling him he was interested in an architectural design for the new station and no further advice, the Pennsylvania's acquisition that spring of the B&O, and thus its consolidation with the B&P, made the prospect of a union station more attractive. Cassatt told Burnham that if Congress would help pay the expenses associated with relocating, he would consider consolidating his line at the site already authorized for the B&O northeast of the Mall near the Capitol.[39]

Cassatt must have considered such help necessary. Although the *Washington Post* pressed for acceptance of the bill as passed by both houses of Congress in December, the *Star* and its Board of Trade allies remained hostile to any subsidies to the rail lines. At the conclusion of the House debate the *Star* commented, "There was absolutely nothing logically to be said in favor of the B&O million and a half gratuity, except that the public had presented to the Pennsylvania road two million dollars' worth of land, to which it was not entitled, and consequently, not having this amount of land in the vicinity of the B&O tracts to run over to that corporation it became the duty of the public to make up in cash from the public purse a like undeserved gratuity to the B&O."[40] With the union depot finally agreed on at a meeting between Cassatt and Burnham in London in July, the chief obstacle to an improved park plan had been removed.

No doubt the commission's trip to Europe in the summer of 1901—taken, according to the commission, to trace earlier influences on L'Enfant—colored the specifics of their final recommendations. Both Rome and Paris provided particularly compelling models for refashioning Washington's core as both a ceremonial space and a proper location for new government buildings. Burnham and McKim were already well under the influence of European taste, as represented in the classical styles promoted by the Ecole des Beaux Arts in Paris and realized in the 1893 world's fair. Through photographs Olmsted took abroad, the Park Commission provided illustrations of how the Potomac River could be beautified by quays, following the examples of Paris or Budapest, or how the malarial swamps along the Anacostia could be turned into a pleasure ground, after the example of Henley in England.[41]

The ideas for the commission had been well formed before the European trip, however, in each member's participation in the 1893 exposition, in the campaign for better public buildings in Washington, and in the 1900 AIA convention. Specific precedents for the plan derived from the parks work of the Olmsted firm, in Washington as well as in Boston, Hartford, and Brookline, Massachusetts, where the firm was located. Moreover, members of the commission were intimately connected to the City Beautiful

The New Washington: City Beautiful

movement, which envisioned for America a public life of the street, the park, the square, or the mall adorned with monuments, memorials, and public buildings.[42]

In line with the emerging Progressive Era view of the importance of rousing public opinion for needed reforms, members of the McMillan Commission fussed over the presentation of their report, hoping to make it acceptable to a wide audience,[43] and committed themselves to unveiling their plans through an exhibit at the new Corcoran Gallery of Art. The key to the exhibit lay in two large models of the city core, one as it existed, the other as planners envisioned its future. Plagued by increased costs for the models and delays in its execution,[44] members of the commission managed nonetheless to open the exhibit on the January 15, 1902, deadline. An appreciative audience, including President Theodore Roosevelt and Secretary of War Elihu Root, whose jurisdiction included Washington's parks, attended.[45]

Despite its claims for comprehension, the commission report released at the time of the exhibit confined itself largely to the two elements originally envisioned in Resolution 139, "the location and grouping of public buildings and monuments to be erected in the District of Columbia and the development and improvement of the entire park system of said District." "By connecting existing parkland and carrying the park system to the outlying areas of the District and across the river as far as Mount Vernon and Great Falls," Frederick Gutheim writes in summarizing the report, "it addressed the regional character of the city. By grouping public buildings in formal compositions, the McMillan plan created a highly concentrated central core. It gave the city an 'official' architecture as well as a plan."[46] As Burnham put it, "We all realized that the important thing to obtain was that sort of beauty which arises from an orderly arrangement of all the buildings and other monumental structures to be erected by the government in the city, and this could only come about by following a well considered plan."[47]

The report, reflecting Olmsted's contribution, called for a complete reorganization of the Mall, as he had proposed at the 1900 AIA meeting, away from the romantic landscape fiercely defended by Bingham and the *Star* in favor of more formal and monumental precedents set in Europe, especially the Champs Elyseés in Paris. Following Root's suggestion, the report called for the kind of reconstruction of the south side of Pennsylvania Avenue the Board of Trade had proposed. The commission endorsed the creation of an improved bathing facility along the Potomac and the provision of additional recreational facilities on newly filled ground south of the Washington Monument. But for the most part it was buildings and grounds, not people, that captured the commission's attention. It communicated its special vision most dramatically in a painting commissioned for the exhibit at the Corcoran Gallery. Standing out at the center of the paint-

ing was a white city, very much in the image of the Chicago fair, while the rest of Washington stretched out without clear detail, a virtual brick wilderness. Although the report harked back to L'Enfant, its call to treat the city as a work of civic art was bold and innovative. Under its inspiration, even the most mundane aspects of urban utility—lighting posts, alarm boxes, and advertising spaces—could be accorded aesthetic treatment.

Following the introduction of the plan, its chief supporters mounted an aggressive campaign to secure a positive public reception. Noting that Washington "exists only for the country at large; its local interests not dependent upon its national functions are in effect nothing," Olmsted stressed the opportunity for achieving a consistency of design unavailable in other cities.[48] Charles Moore and Glenn Brown tied the plan's design to the

The New Washington: City Beautiful

emerging City Beautiful movement, and Daniel Burnham, citing the example of Haussmann's Paris, struck a chord that would become intimately associated with the movement, that beauty would pay in returns from tourism and general city use.[49] Burnham provided the most forceful—and nationalistic—rationale for the commission's reconceptualization of the city core. Echoing Senator McMillan's determination that no undertaking "be allowed to invade, to mutilate, or to mar the symmetry, simplicity, and dignity" of the capital city, Burnham proclaimed in the February 1902 issue of *Century* magazine, "People bid their wise men not alone to safeguard them from foreign invasion or internal corruption, but to remove and forever keep from view the ugly, the unsightly and even the commonplace."[50]

Despite the initially favorable reaction to the Park Commission report, its supporters faced considerable obstacles. The *New York Times* architectural critic Montgomery Schuyler could downplay costs, which he described as millions the planners did not care to estimate, by stating, "The point is to have a plan that you believe in, that is based upon study of what has been found most admirable of its kind in the world, in those examples of the art of city making which 'have pleased many and pleased long. . . . ' Whatever it may cost Uncle Sam to do all this, it will cost him nothing to say now that he believes in it, that he means to do it in good time, and that in the meantime whatever he does in the way of public architecture or public embellishment he will do in accordance with it."[51]

But opposition to funding such grand improvements in the House of Representatives, especially from newly elected speaker Joseph Cannon of Illinois, limited what the commission could do. Noting that the commission plan had never been adopted by Congress, Cannon argued that such improvements could go forward only as fast as the city was willing to pay the usual 50 percent.[52] Still stung by Congress's initial refusal to pay its share of improvements in the suburbs, the *Star* reacted angrily to the idea that the city should pay for embellishments that were intended to be national in character. Charging that Cannon had "virtually locked the project behind a door of financial impossibility," the paper claimed:

> It is barely possible that the District, being squeezed to the core in taxation, and skimping on all legitimate municipal expenses, depriving itself in part of schools and policemen and firemen and other necessities of civic life, and neglecting its sewerage, grade crossing, and water supply needs might save a million a year out of its revenues which could apply to the capital improvement fund. It would be grossly unjust to impose on the District one-half the cost of a great national improvement. While the people of the District will benefit incidentally from the extension of the park system, and enjoy the aesthetic betterments provided under the commission's plans for the improvement of the public grounds, the property of the United States, yet those items are logically, by no process of reasoning, to be placed upon the half-and-half basis.[53]

The most immediate result of the commission's recommendations was one for which the groundwork had been laid before its report, the construction of the new Union Station. Praised in the commission report for offering an "impressive gateway to Washington," the station, by its massive size and distinctive Roman style of architecture, was intended to set the standard for new buildings. Cannon opposed legislation authorizing government funds to assist the Pennsylvania, but the reimbursement measure passed anyway, in February 1903. Although compared to the Capitol, which it was intended to complement, the station clearly emerged, as did the new plan for Washington, under the immediate influence of the 1893 Columbian Exposition. The *Architectural Record* made this point as the station neared completion in 1905: "The White City is vanished like a beautiful

The New Washington: City Beautiful

dream, but its chief designer, grown greater with the years, has produced in this building a structure which surpasses the most beautiful of the ephemeral creations of the vanished city."[54]

Members of the commission were quickly called on to serve as jurors for other projects, including a new municipal building on Pennsylvania Avenue and a memorial to U. S. Grant. As early as December 1901, members corresponded about the establishment of a permanent park commission that might oversee their plan. But Senator McMillan's death in August 1902 represented an immediate setback to their hopes. As Olmsted wrote McMillan's secretary, Charles Moore, "I fell at once to wondering, fearfully, how seriously this irreplaceable loss would set back the movement upon which we have all come to set our hopes. . . . I have never expected any sudden transformation scenes in Washington, but I do hope for very material progress in the next twenty years and I know it won't come of itself. So I feel as though I ought to be out hustling for it some where."[55] Olmsted's fears were quickly realized when he discovered that architects completing a new addition to the Soldier's Home, where presidents had traditionally taken summer retreats, were operating in ignorance of the Park Commission's recommendations for the site.[56] Within months commission members were sufficiently defensive about their status to decide that they had to bring attention to the fact that they no longer acted in any official capacity.[57]

The vulnerability of the Park Commission's vision for Washington was demonstrated in 1903 when Secretary of Agriculture James Wilson directly challenged the commission's plan for the Mall. Wilson's proposal for a new building for his department on the south side of the Mall greatly compromised the Park Commission's determination to keep the vista between the Capitol and the Washington Monument free from obstruction. Declaring that his view was based on George Washington and Pierre L'Enfant's intent, Burnham warned of the dire consequences that would follow Wilson's decision, writing, "If one of these buildings be now created on the Mall, but not on its true axis, then a state of disorder will have been made permanent and a systematic arrangement of the public space will have been made impossible hereafter." One or two such precedents, he claimed, "will make it impossible for the people to realize any good scheme whatever for public beauty in Washington."[58]

Secretary Wilson challenged Burnham's contention that the city's planners intended the Mall's open space to extend a full 850 feet across.[59] In hearings before a subcommittee of the Senate District Committee, Wilson's representative complained that because the Mall's axis was diagonal to the city grid, the commission's ambitious 850-foot goal left the department an impossibly small lot of 250 feet to build on. He pointed out that the Park Commission plan would necessitate the removal of the Smithsonian Institution castle building as well, since it compromised the plan more than the Department of Agriculture's projected building, a charge Daniel Burnham confirmed by saying, "We frankly confess that in our opinion it ought not to stand in the way of a grand improvement." Asserting the moral if not legal authority of the commission, Burnham further challenged Wilson's desire to maintain the Mall as a natural rather than a formal site by arguing: "We do not feel that it can with propriety be left in its natural state. We do not feel that in the midst of a great city, which has formality all about it, that informality should become the rule. We think with the Capitol at one end and the monument at the other, which are the most formal things in the world, the treatment between these structures should be equally formal."[60]

Following Wilson's directive, army engineers staked out a plot within 300 feet of the Mall's center point and managed to convince President Theodore Roosevelt, an enthusiast for the Park Commission plan, that the building would not compromise its intent. This provoked a strong reaction among supporters of the Park Commission's vision for Washington, including Charles Moore, who had retired to private life in Detroit after McMillan's death. Writing Olmsted in reaction to the controversy, he admitted he was "more concerned for the immediate future of the plans than I am quite willing to admit. The trouble over the location of the Agriculture Building is a warning of what may happen any time, when trouble is least expected."[61]

Together Park Commission members orchestrated an active campaign to pressure Congress into overturning existing plans for Agriculture. Enlisted in addition to the presidents of Harvard and Columbia universities was Charles Mulford Robinson, chief national spokesman for the emerging national City Beautiful movement. Stressing the capital's importance to the nation, Robinson wrote:

> Washington is looked upon as representative of the country at large, as having almost as great an interest for the citizens of Maine, California and Florida as for those who live within its borders. . . . Its plan, when announced, commanded the artistic approval of the country, and has stirred the imagination of the people, while touching at least upon almost every problem involved in the improvement of cities. Thus is it reasonable to attribute much of the strength of the present [City Beautiful] movement to this commission.[62]

A petition directed at Congress on behalf of the Park Commission's position in March 1904, claiming that Washington "does not belong to the District of Columbia, but to the citizens of the forty-five States of the Union," charged that the proposed Agriculture building would "seriously interfere with and actually prevent the development of the original plan of the city of Washington as laid out in 1790 by President Washington and P. C. L'Enfant."[63]

A delegation of architects including Glenn Brown helped convince Roosevelt to change his mind. Addressing the annual meeting of the AIA in 1905, Roosevelt responded to the architects' plea by saying that any public building should be "erected in accordance with a carefully thought-out plan adopted long before, and it should be not only beautiful in itself, but fitting in its relations to the whole scheme of public buildings, parks, and the drives of the District."[64] Under the leadership of Senator Francis Newlands, they secured a bill in Congress limiting placement on the Mall to no closer than 400 feet from its center.[65] Relieved, Moore wrote Olmsted, "the immediate peril seems to be averted." He warned, however, that "the campaign is only begun."[66]

Indeed, with that controversy overcome, supporters of the plan found themselves challenged by an old ally in the effort to site a memorial to U. S. Grant. Seeking to introduce more formalized plantings, following from European baroque style, especially as represented in such formal spaces as the Champs Elysées in Paris, advocates of the new memorial generated a severe reaction. Under the headline, "City Beautiful Committee to Wipe out Mall," the *Star* denounced the sacrifice of old trees to the "idealization of artificial ideals, imported from France's formal system of municipal beautification." Denouncing "slavish imitation" of the French, the *Star* charged that the only excuse for the proposal "appears to be a mathematical harkening after the straight line and an insatiable longing to substitute for the natural beauties of Washington the empty desolution of a Parisian square." To make the object of its scorn specific, the paper carried a cartoon showing the members of the Park Commission, headed by McKim blowing a horn—his own—marching on the Mall bearing a set of squared box hedges to replace the existing trees there.[67]

Members of the Park Commission managed finally to placate opponents of the memorial adjacent to the Botanic Garden site. An even more difficult controversy developed over the placement of a suitable memorial to Abraham Lincoln. The Park Commission had made such a memorial a keystone of their plan, locating it on filled land at the west end of the Mall, where they also envisioned a grand memorial bridge, also classical in style, extending across the Potomac to Arlington. Once again, Joseph Cannon proved an obstacle, proclaiming that he would "never let a monument to Abraham Lincoln be erected in that god-damned swamp."[68] Much to his fellow commissioners' dismay, Daniel Burnham appeared to break ranks with the original recommendation by responding to requests in Congress to provide a possible treatment near Union Station. Privately he held to the Park Commission's original recommendation, reassuring Olmsted in 1908 that he did not see how a memorial to Lincoln could be placed in the neighborhood of the station. "Of course we must stand together in anything that is done in Washington," he asserted.[69] Publicly Burnham remained more open, undoubtedly because he wanted authority to extend the station grounds. In a telegraph message to Architect of the Capitol Elliott Woods, a protégé of House Speaker Cannon's, Burnham indicated that he felt Congress was the best judge of the most appropriate site; com-

106

pleting the Union Station composition was the most important factor, "no matter what name it bears."[70] Stating his own preference for the Potomac site, Burnham nonetheless reiterated in a subsequent letter to Woods the importance that the Park Commission had also accorded to providing an impressive gateway to the city. "That we should have secured so beautiful a building to stand forth as the symbol of legislative authority in America is a piece of national good fortune, and the most beautiful possible setting for this beautiful dome is none too good."[71]

The difficulties that the nationally oriented promoters of the City Beautiful in Washington had securing ideal sites for the Department of Agriculture and the Grant and Lincoln memorials spurred their desire to create a permanent agency to implement their vision for the new Washington. "What we need in Washington is a system," Burnham wrote Moore. "When work affecting our plan is afoot it should be someone's business to know about it and to promptly post all of us."[72] In 1907 Theodore Roosevelt attempted to form just such an organization by appointing the commission members, along with the superintendent of the Library of Congress, as an unofficial board of consultants. When this proved unsatisfactory, at the end of his term Roosevelt named a Council of Fine Arts consisting of thirty prestigious members drawn from around the country. According to Charles Moore's unpublished account, Roosevelt recognized that Congress would not initiate such an idea itself, but, he claimed, he could by executive order appoint his own advisers in the execution of artistic projects. Although Roosevelt expected his successor, William Howard Taft, to accept his action, the council convened only once. After unanimously affirming the Park Commission's recommendation for the site for the Lincoln Memorial, the commission adjourned, never to meet again. When the civil appropriations act reached President Taft for his signature March 1, 1909, it contained a clause forbidding payments for services or expenses of the commission. Once again, Joseph Cannon, feeling excluded from Park Commission activities, retaliated to block efforts to institutionalize its plan.[73]

Success finally came the following year when Taft approved formation of a much smaller National Commission of Fine Arts. Its power was limited to advising government agencies on statues, fountains, and monuments in the District of Columbia. To assure continuity with the Park Commission, both Burnham and Olmsted were appointed members, while Charles Moore assumed the role of secretary. Reaffirming the importance of the Chicago world's fair, other key figures from the exposition joined the new commission as well, most notably Francis Millet, who had served as Burnham's chief artistic adviser in 1893.[74]

Establishment of the Commission of Fine Arts represented an important step in institutionalizing City Beautiful principles in Washington and the nation. Describing the 1902 Park Commission report as an "aesthetic Magna Carta," a writer for *Munsey's* magazine described Washington as the "focus of national sentiment" and "the realized dream of a triumphant democracy, clad in beauty and power."[75] The hopes of large and small cities focused on Washington, according to City Beautiful leader J. Horace McFarland, where planning had created "a permanent civic exhibit" and "the model community of America."[76] While the commission's role was purely advisory, it managed to institutionalize efforts which to date had been voluntary and unofficial. It led the fight to locate the Lincoln Memorial by the Memorial Bridge and enforced the classical design that members of the Park Commission had favored. It pressed to keep federal buildings within the orderly plan laid out by the commission as well as grouping them between the Mall and Pennsylvania Avenue. The commission gained authority through a 1913 executive order to renew all proposed federal structures that might affect the appearance of the city. With the commission thus in place, as Frederick Gutheim has written, official Washington was at last rising to the expectations that the nation held for it as a "renewed city" serving "as a unifying force, a national image with which the country could associate its role as a world power. When implemented, this idealized city would look like the capital of a new kind of America—clean, efficient, orderly and, above all, powerful."[77] As the controversy over the Grant Memorial had indicated, however, city and national interests were not always seen as one, despite the local press's enthusiasm for the basic concepts of the Park Commission plan. As the Fine Arts Commission and later complementary agencies became stronger, the distance between city and capital would grow, and thus the first decade of the twentieth century marked the triumph of a largely national ethos over local interests.

Reform:
Social and Aesthetic

We cannot truthfully boast of or take pride in our capital city until we improve the conditions of our slum property and remove the festering plague spots which are equally a menace to the health and morals of the community. . . . It may be a work meriting all praise to beautify a portion of the city in which we live, enhancing the value of property and of elevating human life. . . . But how incomparably better is the merit of the effort and toil spent in uplifting frail members of the human family.

> William F. Downey, "How to Benefit the
> Poor in the Slums," *President's Homes*
> *Commission*, 1909

If our country wishes to compete with others, let it not be in the support of armaments but in making of a beautiful Capital City. Let it express the soul of America. Whenever an American is at the seat of his Government, however traveled and cultured he may be, he ought to find a city of stately proportion, symmetrically laid out and adorned with the best that there is in architecture, which would arouse his imagination and stir his patriotic pride.

> President Calvin Coolidge, quoted in the
> *Annual Report of the Public Buildings*
> *Commission*, 1930

In 1901 Charles Weller, executive secretary of the Associated Charities of Washington, urged the Senate Park Commission "in formulating plans for the systematic beautification of our city to give especial consideration to its poorer neighborhoods." Weller received a polite response to his letter, and the commission included in its report his recommendations for more neighborhood playgrounds and their linkage with schools, as well as larger recreational parks and expanded bathing facilities. The commission paid some attention to residential neighborhoods, albeit stating its concern by pointing to the way the Capitol had become surrounded "in the main by private buildings, many of them of the most squalid character or by neglected stretches of land used as dumping grounds."[1]

To Weller's plea for the elimination of the dilapidated alley houses that honeycombed the interior of the city's older quarters—what Weller called "the saddest blot on our national capital"—the report remained silent. When Senator McMillan described the "grave problems" facing Washington, he did not identify large numbers of poor living in substandard housing and struggling at inadequate wages as Weller had in his communication to the commission, although he had been largely responsible in 1896 for the reorganization of Washington charitable work in an effort better to respond to those conditions. Rather, the "grave problems" that concerned McMillan and his successors over the next quarter century lay, in his words, in "the location of public buildings, of preserving spaces for parks in the portions of the District beyond the limits of the city of Washington, of connecting and developing existing parks by attractive drives." While he added the need of providing for "the recreation and health of a constantly growing population," the commission's perspective remained overwhelmingly shaped by aesthetic rather than social considerations.[2]

As a planning document, the Park Commission report's relatively narrow focus was not surprising. Even other major plans that followed, notably for Cleveland in 1903 and Chicago in 1909, while more encompassing, paid scant attention to residential neighborhoods.[3] Charles Mulford Robinson, the highly influential publicist of the City Beautiful movement, revealed its diffident attitude toward residential neighborhoods when he wrote in 1904, "We may reasonably assert . . . that civic art need concern itself only with the outward aspects of the houses, and therefore that for such details—sociologically pressing though they are—as sunless bedrooms, dark halls and stairs, foul cellars, dangerous employments, and an absence of bathrooms, civic art has no responsibility, however earnestly it deplores them."[4] Washington's special status as a governmentally oriented city, lacking the kind of immigrant concentrations characteristic of industrial cities, made the Park Commission's focus on the monumental core all the more appropriate. Such, at least, has been the standard historical interpretation of the plan and its legacy.

The context of the plan ought not be forgotten, however. Far from lacking the kind of social problems characteristic of other cities, Washington gained national as well as local attention for the sorry conditions of its "poorer neighborhoods." As a major contributor to the formation of the McMillan Commission, the Washington Board of Trade led efforts to improve social conditions, especially in housing, both before and after the Park Commission's presentation. Two years before President Taft appointed the Commission of Fine Arts, Theodore Roosevelt named the President's Homes Commission to investigate and report on the causes of poverty in the nation's capital. The first national planning conference, held in Washington in 1909, in devoting much of a whole session to Washington as a model city, dealt with the city's social as well as its aesthetic concerns. Yet by the mid-1920s, while such social reform efforts continued, they were increasingly treated outside the realm of planning. For Washington, which marked in the first thirty years of the twentieth century a triumph in physical planning, the reasons for the neglect of social reform deserve explanation.

Although Washington's poorest residents attracted considerable charitable support as well as the active intervention of the Board of Health, which was established under the territorial government in 1871,[5] interest declined sharply during the Gilded Age that followed. The Board of Health was abolished in 1878, the result, according to an early–twentieth-century social activist, of "ignorance and greed."[6] An occasional guidebook entry or article would note the presence of the poor—almost always identified as black—living in dilapidated hovels, usually located in one of the many alleys in the older portions of the city. Such notice was couched not in shocking but in picturesque terms, a kind of quaint reminder that Washington was not entirely composed of ambitious clerks moving into new brick homes.[7] As the city grew in the latter part of the century, the painter Delancy Gill captured a number of these sorry structures for posterity before they gave way to the march of development. His purpose, like those in the print media, was to record, not to change, conditions that had come to be accepted as part of the modern urban landscape.[8]

Attitudes toward the poor and the conditions they lived in began to change in the 1890s, as they did around the country. Growing awareness of the negative effects of unhealthy environments, combined with a quickened social consciousness, drew the attention of activists and journalists. In 1890 the *Washington Star* began to run a series of moralistic exposés of terrifying social conditions under such titles as "Among the Poor" and "Among the Hoodlums." Under the subhead "A Sad Picture," the first of these articles read:

> In a filthy back yard, a disease breeding hole, some one had at some time put up some boards in such a manner as to give a poor imitation of a very poor cow shed. In that three people lived after a fashion. The floor sagged as one walked over it. The dirt was so thick everywhere that nothing short of a shovel could ever have made any impression. The room was perhaps eight by ten feet square, for there was only one room there. In it was a bed, covered with a dirty tick and without a vestige of bed clothes. Close by the bed was a little stove that was all but falling apart. One tiny pane of solid glass let in a little of the sunlight that was making the outside world glorious. On the bed sat a young colored woman. She was clad in the scantiest manner. The waist of her dress was of torn calico and open wide that she might nurse a little brown baby, showing that there were no other garments beneath. A more miserable picture one could not imagine. This little shanty fairly reeked of despair.

Reform: Social and Aesthetic

Continuing, the reporter asked his "gentle readers" whether money given to the Associated Charities was not well spent on such needy recipients of their benevolence.[9]

Such dramatic imagery continued to shape reports directed at stirring public interest. While the object of social commentary in other large cities like New York, Boston, or Philadelphia focused on improving immigrant quarters, Washington critics pointed largely to the lot of poor black residents in the city's back alleys. Numbering some twenty thousand according to police reports in the late nineteenth century, these concentrations of poverty were the result of the crowding that followed the mass migration of freedmen into the city after the Civil War.[10] A *Star* reporter said that she was moved to investigate alley conditions in 1896 after reading a report issued by the Associated Charities. Describing the horrible conditions encountered, she then turned directly to her audience for sympathy, writing:

> No human being could be other than stunted physically and morally amid such surroundings, yet the woman not only had no complaints to make, but she was proud of herself and of what she had. I saw myself and my belongings in her and hers as in a broken mirror, and I realized as I have time and again that there is a "submerged" within each human heart that must be changed before society can reap a benefit from any attempted reform. Every desire I, or you, have and every effort I, or you, make to accumulate worldly goods are extending the influence of a common human nature that in the alleys disorders and debases mankind with an accumulation of positive filth.[11]

Increasingly, social commentary emphasized public health. New discoveries in bacteriology revealing the personal factor in spreading disease led to more efforts to control not just material sources of filth but contact between healthy and diseased human beings.[12] The *Star*'s description of the conditions of a crowded portion of the Southwest sector prompted city authorities and the voluntary Sanitary League to intervene. In 1893 the paper reported that conditions had improved, although it pressed additionally for the introduction of public bath houses, following precedents in England and other American cities.[13] A report issued by the House of Representatives in 1892, which complained that back alleys were often filled with vicious classes of people of unclean habits over whom it was impossible to exercise proper police or sanitary regulation, prompted Congress to prohibit the erection of new houses in alleys less than thirty feet wide and not supplied with sewers and water mains.[14]

Intervention by Congress virtually shut down new construction in alleys, but existing conditions continued to provoke concern. One effort to respond to the plight of alley dwellers was the establishment in 1894 of the Washington Civic Center, a coalition of civic and charitable organizations modeled after Chicago's Civic Federation. Embracing the emerging view that the effects of environment rather than faults of individual character lay at the root of poverty, the Civic Center incorporated all the techniques that would come to characterize Progressive reform at the turn of the century: thorough investigation of social conditions; informing and developing public opinion; and enforcing existing sanitary laws and promoting further legislation as needed. The Civic Center's leaders, who included officers of the Board of Trade, spoke optimistically of achieving their goals in Washington, since "there is no municipal obstruction to the perpetuation of good."[15]

The Civic Center's committee on housing, chaired by George M. Kober, dean of Georgetown University's medical school, conducted a preliminary investigation of the alleys in 1896. The following year, the committee secured the financial support of the Women's Anthropological Society to hire Clare de Graffenried, a special agent with the U.S. Department of Labor, to conduct a more thorough survey. Her report, issued in 1897, eschewed the dramatic personal story in favor of statistical tabulations. Blaming congested housing conditions for both high incidences of disease and immorality, Graffenried claimed that inhabited alleys helped make Washington one of the most unhealthy cities in the nation. Pointing to widespread reliance on unkept privies as just one of the many health hazards in alleys, she described conditions as "truly appalling, in view of the facts that Washington is supposed to be a modern city, with no nuisances and with appliances up to date for urban needs." She objected to the closed-off quality of blind alleys for "shutting off small communities from the outside world and which are calculated not only to promote sickness, but also immorality and crime."

As solutions Graffenried offered an agenda that would be reiterated for much of the next quarter century: converting the alleys to minor streets, or at least opening them up by cutting through to the main streets; subjecting alley dwellings to thorough investigation; condemning those found unfit for continued habitation; and seeking capital investment in alternative low-cost housing. Making clear her belief in the importance of actively intervening to improve the poor's environment, she commented, "These country negroes, could reach higher standards; but as it is in their hidden retreats, they dwell in a state of arrested development . . . the poor man, bound to the treadmill of daily toil, requires all the agencies that can be provided."[16] Responding to the report, the *Star* commented that it had "repeatedly indicated the danger that lurks in the local slums, which, while less menacing than those of some other cities where enormous tenements are permitted, with their inevitable accompaniments of disease and vice, are nevertheless worthy of close reformatory attention."[17]

One typical response nationally to the exposure of such conditions was the largely negative one of imposing stricter building codes and seeking expanded powers to tear down unfit buildings. Washington housing reformers sought such powers over the next decade, but at the same time they

Reform: Social and Aesthetic

embraced the more positive role of seeking to provide additional housing at affordable costs. Working together with the Central Relief Committee, a body appointed by the District Commissioners to investigate living conditions of the poor, the Civic Center, the Women's Anthropological Society, and the Board of Trade organized a meeting in February 1897 to generate interest in providing housing for the estimated fifty thousand people dwelling in crowded and unsanitary homes in the alleys. Keynoting the meeting was George Sternberg, surgeon general of the army and an expert on the germ origin of disease. Drawing on Graffenried's examination of alley conditions, Sternberg cited Washington's high rank in deaths from typhoid fever—seventh nationally and double that of New York City. He warned that "such diseases, if once given a foothold here, would spread like wildfire." His plan was first to build sanitary homes to accommodate some five thousand of the alley dwellers, then to invest a board with the power to condemn and remove unsanitary houses.[18]

The District Commissioners responded by drawing up a bill asking Congress to create a tenement house commission with authority to condemn unsanitary buildings. The *Star* once again responded enthusiastically, proclaiming that "a city like Washington should have no slums. Its poor should have clean, wholesome homes, supplied with all the requisite facilities for preserving health. Overcrowding is unnecessary in a city laid out upon the spacious plan of Washington, and great tenements have no excuse for existence here." Stating its confidence in the expertise brought together under the commissioner's bill, the paper assured property owners that condemnation procedures would be fair and that homes maintained at a high level of cleanliness would "prove better investments in the end than rookeries upon which a minimum is spent for repairs."[19] In one of a series of hearings on the issue, Board of Trade secretary John Joy Edson joined fellow businessmen in pressing for minimum standards of light and air in Washington dwellings, saying, "It is humiliating for us to admit that the capital city of the nation has more tuberculosis cases than any other city . . . and that, in proportion to population, more infants die here than any other city in the country."[20]

When Congress delayed action in providing the powers of condemnation sought by the District Commissioners, Sternberg, Kober, and their associates forged ahead on the complementary goal of providing better homes by organizing the Washington Sanitary Improvement Company on April 9, 1897. Following the lead of other housing reformers, most notably New York's Elgin Gould,[21] whom they brought to Washington to address potential investors, the company directors limited dividends to 5 percent (as compared to the 10 to 20 percent received by alley property owners). The savings from limiting dividends were to be utilized in the form of lowered rents. Arguing that such investments would still offer good returns, company organizers nonetheless described their work as philanthropic housing, indicating the priority they placed on social betterment over personal profit. While Sternberg admitted that he had some difficulty raising the initial $25,000 necessary to begin operations, the company managed nonetheless to purchase its first property in May. By the end of the year, the company had secured sixteen flats, which were rented out at the relatively modest cost of $9.50 to $12.50 per month. By 1900 the company owned a total of forty-four houses, accommodating 88 families in the two-flat structures the company set as its standard.[22]

By 1904 the company housed 140 families, 30 of whom were black. Since the overwhelming majority of alley dwellers were black, the company clearly did not direct its attention to those in greatest need. Hoping to attract investment to grow, the company stressed housing "the better class of wage-earner." Justifying a trickle-down approach, which anticipated that poorer groups would move up the housing ladder as it rehoused some of those "worthy recipients," the company affirmed its position in its annual report for 1905 by stating, "It is confidently believed that in work of this character it is always best to begin at the top."[23] Apparently unconvinced by their own rationale, however, housing reformers organized a second company, the Washington Sanitary Housing Company, in 1904, limiting dividends to 4 percent so as to benefit lower ranks of workers—as Kober put it—"day laborers, laundresses and other humble wage-earners." Although the company's petition to secure a charter stated its mission as providing housing for those displaced by the condemnation of alley homes, Sternberg's continuing insistence that the company would not provide charity "for the idle and the dissolute" but opportunity to "those who pay their rents and take reasonable care of their apartments" meant that the company would still find it difficult to accommodate those most in need.[24] In a letter published in the *Star*, Sternberg directly stated his belief that new housing should not go to slum dwellers but "to industrious and respectable who are living in less desirable housing which is not unfit for habitation."[25]

The failure of housing reformers to attract substantial funding limited the impact of their effort. Significantly enough, however, by the turn of the century they had succeeded in garnering wide support, from the Board of Trade, the Washington *Star*, the District Commissioners, and even President Theodore Roosevelt. In his first annual message to Congress in 1901, Roosevelt urged that inhabited alleys—"the existence of which is a reproach to our Capital city"—be converted to minor streets "where the inhabitants can live under conditions favorable to health and morals."[26] The movement's ties to the emerging national Progressive movement were strong enough that a Washington citizens' committee formed to improve housing conditions in 1902 under the auspices of the Associated Charities was able to recruit as a member Leonard Wood, who was known for implementing sanitary reforms in Cuba as its military governor.[27]

Housing reformers made the case, with considerable success, that the

Reform: Social and Aesthetic

health and prosperity of the whole city depended on rooting out problems in alleys which could easily spread to other locations. In a statement reflecting both the comfortable status of the reformers and an awareness of their own self-interest, the Civic Center annual report for 1907 warned, "These dwellings often house our servants, and a large part of the washing is done there, and thus the filth and disease germs which infest these houses are not confined to their inhabitants, but are carried into our own homes."[28] They even managed to tie their campaign to an image of a City Beautiful well before the Park Commission made that goal its special cause. When Board of Trade president S. B. Woodward, a founder of the Woodward and Lothrop department store, opened a March 1897 meeting on housing conditions, he declared it was vitally important that there should be no slums in the most beautiful capital in the world.[29] Senator McMillan, who was himself an investor in the Washington Sanitary Improvement Company, announced early in 1902 his desire to pursue better city health through an attack on unsanitary buildings.[30]

It was hardly surprising, then, that Charles Weller, as the new director of the Associated Charities, would approach the Park Commission to promote the cause of improved sanitary and housing conditions. When he found his appeal for dealing with inadequate housing ignored, he turned for help to leaders in the emerging social settlement movement. Among those he tapped was Hull House director Jane Addams, with whom he had worked in Chicago. As the keynote speaker at the 1902 annual meeting of the Associated Charities, Addams declared that Washington's unsanitary conditions were inexcusable. She commended Washington women, already well represented among various social improvement committees in the city, for their involvement, saying, "If it is womanly to nurse those who suffer from diphtheria and from conditions that spring from conditions of filth, then it is womanly to prevent conditions that cause these diseases."[31]

Weller took his case directly to President Roosevelt the following December.[32] Not incidentally, he recruited Roosevelt's close associate Jacob Riis, the journalist acclaimed for exposing New York's slum conditions in his 1890 book, *How the Other Half Lives,* to address the Associated Charities annual meeting the same month. With only a few days in Washington to investigate conditions, Riis stormed through the city's slum areas, presenting his findings to the Senate District Committee as well as to the Associated Charities. Washington's slums, he charged, were worse than New York's, worse, indeed, than almost any in the world. "I confess I had no idea there were such things as I saw in this city yesterday when I went in several alleys and witnessed the way the colored people are living," he said before Congress. "The inside of these houses is too dreadful to even conceive." Later that evening he declared at the Associated Charities meeting, "The blind alleys you have here in the national capital are a menace to the civic health and are breeding places of vice and crime. You cannot suffer these places to

116

An unidentified alley scene, early twentieth century, one of many surviving images showing blacks living in inadequate housing and in an unsanitary environment. Courtesy Washingtoniana Division, D.C. Public Library.

continue in existence and do your duty to your city or to yourselves. The influences they exert threaten you, for the handsome block in whose center lies the festering mass of corruption is rotten to the core. The corruption spreads, my friends, and you will pay the bill."[33] Blaming Congress for failing to extend the necessary powers of condemnation to the city, the *Star* editorialized: "It is intolerable that the capital should further endure the menace involved in its inability to protect itself from disease and shame. If there is one city in the United States which should have the power to keep itself clean and pure, it is Washington, and if yesterday's revelation of filth and disreputable congestion serves to advance the day of purification, it will have been well worth the humiliation involved in the disclosure."[34]

After his friend Riis invoked his friendship on the housing issue, Presi-

Reform: Social and Aesthetic

dent Roosevelt urged Congress once again in his annual message for 1904 to act on the city's requests for improved housing and sanitary conditions. But when key members of Congress continued to oppose proposed legislation on the matter, Roosevelt's personal secretary responded cautiously to Weller's plea for the president's further intervention. The president, he wrote, remained concerned, but "he has found by experience that he can not make a habit of interviewing Senators on particular subjects, especially after he has discussed the subject fully in his message."[35] Not to be discouraged by the lack of national leadership, local activists continued to press reticent senators with the threat that as District residents they were not immune to the threat of disease. John E. Hayford made just such a point in a letter to Senator William M. Stewart, writing, "Your home, as well as mine and that of every other resident of Washington is daily menaced by the more or less direct avenues of transmission of disease from unsanitary dwellings of the laboring and servant class."[36] Finally, in 1906, Congress granted the District Commissioners the powers they sought to condemn inadequate housing. Reiterating the common theme of the period, a *Star* editorial, "Evolving a Model City," commended the bill's passage, stating, "There is a gratifying unanimity of opinion that Washington, by virtue of its position as the seat of federal government, should be made perfect in equipment."[37]

Even as the Park Commission's recommendations were generating national attention in architectural circles, Washington housing reformers gained encouragement from national housing leaders. Among these was Lawrence Veiller, leader in New York tenement reform efforts and considered the first professional housing expert in the nation, who wrote that plans to beautify the city offered "a tremendous opportunity to eradicate your slums."[38] Charles Weller affirmed his own leadership role in the movement by writing about Washington's housing problems, first in a 1906 article for *Charities and the Commons* and subsequently in his 1909 book, *Neglected Neighbors*. In his writing Weller shared Veiller's conviction that improved housing was essential to the alleviation of poverty and the revitalization of civic responsibility. In 1902 he had asserted, "Among all the services which philanthropy may render, none is of more fundamental importance than to gradually raise the standard of life among the people by promoting the improvement of their homes. This attacks the causes of poverty and clarifies the sources of good citizenship. Improved homes mean decreased expenses for workhouses, jails, criminal trials, police protection, and charitable relief."[39] In contrast to those proponents of the City Beautiful movement who sought to inspire good citizenship through the creation of monumental buildings,[40] Weller and his associates urged a more direct route to social improvement in attacking the immediate living conditions of the poor. A comprehensive plan, Weller argued, should encompass "the steady, progressive, uncompromising elimination of all the evils represented by the alleys, tenements and shanties of the national capital."[41]

With new powers to eliminate poor housing, reformers discovered the problems that followed when philanthropic investments in new structures could not keep pace with demolitions. With as many as eight hundred houses condemned in the first two years under the 1906 bill, George Sternberg began to describe the dire consequences of a "house famine" that would leave the poor worse off despite the best intentions of housing reformers.[42] Prompted by these concerns, the committee on housing of the Associated Charities pressed for the creation of a presidential commission to investigate and act on the housing shortage. President Roosevelt named just such a commission in 1908, recruiting James Bronson Reynolds as its chair. As former head of New York City's University Settlement and the New York State Tenement House Commission when Roosevelt was governor, Reynolds was part of a reform network that included Veiller and Riis. His appointment so assured the Associated Charities' committee on housing that it voted to turn its records over to the new commission and then disband. Continuity was assured when key committee members Weller, Sternberg, and Kober were named consultants.[43] Establishment of the commission drew the *Star*'s praise as it reiterated the persistent belief of the Progressive Era, that "moral conditions will inevitably improve if the physical surroundings of the ignorant class of people are bettered." "There should be just as good citizenship at the back gate," it added in a subsequent editorial, "as in the front of the house."[44]

As the commission's work began, Sternberg chose to play on the inconsistency of expenditures for government buildings while Washington's slums continued to fester. Addressing a meeting of the Monday Evening Club, an association of social workers and philanthropists dating back to 1896, he charged, "The members of the Senate and House are providing themselves with marble palaces; the national Museum is to be housed in a magnificent new building. But our poor neighborhoods seem to have been neglected until President Roosevelt took up the matter and finally appointed the President's homes commission."[45] Reiterating the middle-class fear of the spread of contagion, the Homes Commission report nonetheless gave visible attention as well to the needs of the city's poor black alley dwellers. At an early stage in his investigation of slum conditions, Reynolds had indicated that the city would be better off if poorer residents were driven from the city. After receiving a rebuke from the *Star*,[46] however, Reynolds took a more humane approach. Noting that of the 1,056 persons displaced under new powers of condemnation, 1,042 had been black, the Homes Commission report called for governmentally assisted housing. Such a program, it recognized, could not be instituted nationally, but Washington's special status required assistance, in the form of either appropriations or loans.

Reform: Social and Aesthetic

The Homes Commission further recommended that all unsightly and unsanitary property should be condemned and purchased by the government and improved in a uniform manner, and that inexpensive and healthful habitations should be erected for the poor.[47]

The national meeting on city planning held in Washington in 1909 brought together activists committed to improving social conditions in cities as well as to making them more beautiful. Health issues, especially relating to congestion in unsuitable housing conditions, proved a rallying point for social workers, writers, architects, and planners, who would subsequently pursue more specialized agendas. In the opening session, George Sternberg joined key organizers of the convention from the Commission on Congestion of Population of New York City to denounce slum conditions, saying of Washington, "Insanitary homes will eventually be eliminated in this city by condemnation and decay, but unless new homes are built to take the place of these, the tendency to overcrowding and all of its accompanying physical and moral evils will be greatly increased."[48]

On May 22, in a sign of Washington's symbolic importance to the nascent national planning movement, the convention passed a resolution calling for the adoption of a comprehensive plan for the city and the appointment of a committee to promote that goal before Congress. In notes that met Frederick Olmsted Jr.'s approval, the author of the resolution, J. Randolph Coolidge, cited congestion, the dearth of small parks and playgrounds, the clash of different municipal authorities, and greed as obstacles to making American cities as sightly and as healthy as the great cities of Europe. Olmsted, however, provided a telling commentary, in which he appears to have agreed with an objection to appointing Jane Addams, one of the organizers of the conference, to the committee, "because her name would not be influential with Congress and because she is illogical in argument." With his own contribution confined at the conference to describing the largely aesthetic town planning ideas he had recently surveyed in Germany, Olmsted was already distancing himself from the kind of social issues that Coolidge had cited in his resolution and with which social activists like Addams were particularly identified.[49] In further affirmation of the tensions between reformers pursuing social as opposed to largely aesthetic goals, George Kober used the occasion of congressional hearings prompted by the national planning conference to challenge the Park Commission's vision for Washington, saying, "I believe the question of housing or the transfer and location of factories, are more important than the buying up of large areas for parks."[50]

Although other signs of diverging agendas emerged at the city planning conference, the problem was not immediately apparent in Washington, where the immediate reaction was to reinforce the association between social betterment and beauty. A new committee on municipal art formed by the Washington Board of Trade under the chairmanship of architect

George Oakley Totten saw no inconsistency, for instance, in calling both for more suburban parks and for improved sanitary housing. Commenting on the effect of the 1909 planning meeting, the committee proclaimed in the Board of Trade's annual report that year, "Much has been done in Washington in the matter of the erection of monuments to the great deeds and memorable deeds of the past. It is not undervaluing the influence of these 'silent teachers of patriotism,' to say that work in this direction will not take the place of the duty of a city to give its citizens sanitary housing, open space and clean and pleasant streets."[51] Indeed, both the board and the closely allied *Washington Star* merged the two ideas in calling for the conversion of back alleys to parks, starting with the notorious Willow Alley in the city's Southwest sector.[52]

In what would become a common theme in urban development throughout twentieth-century Washington experience, the *Star* urged support for its position by contrasting the squalor of the alley to the shining dome of the Capitol plainly visible from the site. Congress, it charged, "cannot escape its responsibility for the existence of these human pestholes."[53] A report prepared for the National Civic Federation released in 1912 reiterated the theme by placing the caption "Washington, the City Beautiful" under the picture of a cluttered and deteriorating black alley. "The casual visitor to Washington thinks we have one of the most beautiful cities in the world," Grace Bicknell wrote. "He does not suspect the cancer within, for there are few cities which have so concealed their slums."[54]

By 1913 the city had converted Willow Alley to a park, but efforts to effect multiple conversions stalled. Undoubtedly the movement suffered when Charles Weller departed in 1908 for charitable work in Pittsburgh. His leadership role was assumed by Charlotte Hopkins, a native Washingtonian who had served on the Associated Charities' Committee on the Improvement of Housing Conditions. It was not until Woodrow Wilson's election and Mrs. Hopkins's success in engaging Ellen Wilson in the housing cause, however, that interest in the subject gained enough support to effect new legislation. Following the lead of Hopkins and Mrs. Wilson, a growing stream of Washington's most socially prominent women made their way into back alley tours.[55] Not surprisingly, their efforts gained the attention of President Wilson, who telegraphed one women's gathering in 1913 his support for "the great task of clearing away the slums" by urging a "systematic and comprehensive plan, worked out by the District authorities with the full authority and support of Congress."[56]

When Congressman William Patterson Borland of Missouri took to the House floor in May that year to respond to the "heroic efforts" of the women who had investigated the slums and called for the creation of new homes for the "industrious poor," he was interrupted repeatedly by applause.[57] The *Star* responded by charging, "It is a duty which the District owes itself to provide proper dwelling places for those who are now living in

"Washington, the City Beautiful." Illustration from Grace Vawter Bicknell, *Inhabited Alleys of Washington, D.C.* (1912).

the alley slums." Noting plans to demolish alley housing serving several hundred people, the paper urged subscriptions for alternative housing, warning that without such housing the city could experience extended deterioration as the problem spread to areas still "free from taint."[58] Building on this momentum, Mrs. Wilson's deathbed request to eliminate the alley nuisance in August 1914 finally helped to secure federal action. Congress overcame its preoccupation with the war breaking out in Europe long enough to pass a stringent act calling for the complete demolition of all alley dwellings by July 1, 1918.[59]

Wartime demands for additional housing made implementation of the alley act impractical, however. There simply were no new homes for alley dwellers to find. Faced with the deadline that would necessitate the eviction of fifteen thousand alley dwellers, organizers of the Emergency Housing Association urged the expansion of limited dividend housing, securing support in Congress for issuing $6 million in bonds for that purpose.[60] The solution resorted to, however, was simply to extend the deadline, and with the emergency removed, interest in the alley issue receded during and immediately after the war. As late as 1924, Mrs. Hopkins attempted to revive efforts to close alleys by organizing a new limited dividend company to absorb the alley population by building a thousand affordable homes a year, but nothing came of the proposal.[61] When a 1927 court decision compelled the District to pay for all demolished buildings, work stopped. Recognizing that further displacement from alleys would cause hardship, supporters in Congress introduced bills for federal financing of low-cost housing.

The *Washington Daily News* attempted to revive the alley elimination campaign, charging that the flaw in city improvement efforts remained the alley dwellings, which the paper described in familiar language as "a festering sore that has gone unhealed while statesmen, legislators, artists, architects, public-spirited citizens, have planned the city beautiful. . . . Some of the same money, the same effort, and the same genius that is building this most beautiful of capitals must go into cleaning up the city's back yard."[62] This last effort also failed, however, as planners, utilizing the aesthetic standard of the City Beautiful, directed attention back to the still unrealized goals of the Senate Park Commission.

★ ★ ★

Early ideas for the Park Commission had included the goal of extending design controls from public to private structures in residential neighborhoods. Suggested both by Burnham in his initial notes for the commission's work and in Montgomery Schuyler's review of the Corcoran exhibit,[63] the cause was taken up seriously for the first time by District Commissioner Henry B. F. MacFarland in 1909. Writing in *American City,* MacFarland complained that while public buildings had conformed to high aesthetic standards since 1902, the same was not so for private structures, many of which were "positively ugly." MacFarland proposed that design controls be imposed once 90 percent of the property owners affected agreed to restrictions on land use and height limitations. He promised to seek the help of the commissioners "in the effort to prevent such private building as will ruin the looks of the city."[64] The *Star* commented favorably on the idea, arguing that such controls were necessary "to prevent the city from becoming half beautiful in public buildings and half ugly with private construction."[65]

Although no public action immediately followed MacFarland's proposal, Montgomery Schuyler raised the issue again in 1912 by arguing that "when the question is of the beauty of a capital which largely lives by its beauty, collectivism must prevail over individualism."[66] Schuyler wrote at a time when the Commission of Fine Arts was attempting to secure more uniform design of District schools. Disappointed in the results, the commission wrote the District Commissioners in 1916, "Where the architecture is of so heterogeneous a nature, similarity in public buildings would add much to the impressiveness of the city." Under the chairmanship of Charles Moore, the commission launched an active effort to attain better controls for the "harmonious development" of the capital.[67] The first step was the institution of a zoning law, following the pioneer effort in New York in 1916. The Commission of Fine Arts stated its hope that such zoning would equalize real estate values, "and then the national capital should grow into a symmetrical arrangement of public and private utilities and conveniences of living." Although fought initially by the business community, zoning quickly gained approval for helping maintain some measure of order over development.[68]

Zoning proved, however, as in other cities, only a limited measure for planning. Through the efforts of the American Civic Association, a national improvement organization born out of the aesthetic concerns of the early City Beautiful movement, support quickly grew for additional powers to direct Washington's physical development. To carry out this task, the association supported the creation of the Committee of 100 on the Federal City. Aware of the way in which Glenn Brown had effectively directed a similar committee to organize national support for the Senate Park Commission's preferred site for the Lincoln Memorial at the west end of the Mall, the new organization established committees in seventy-five cities to marshal support for instituting greater controls over Washington's development.[69]

Formed in 1923, the Committee of 100 was chaired by Frederic Delano, a successful businessman who had actively promoted Burnham's 1909 plan for Chicago. While subsections of the committee's preliminary report urged new dwellings for those of modest means, the relocation of alley dwellers, and a comprehensive network of neighborhood parks, the emphasis fell squarely on the city's monumental core. Sounding every bit as nationalistic as Burnham had in 1902, Delano declared that since Washington was "the Federal City of America and not simply the creation of those who live in it, who can neither control its government nor effectively deal with its larger problems, public opinion of the entire country must understand it and delegate to proper hands the duty of dealing with it." Noting the inadequacy of zoning to maintain the high standard of federal buildings throughout the city, the report called for tight government restrictions over design. "To raise standards of private building and to prevent a 'boom town' appearance," it said, "the full force of any government agency, of all financial interests, of educational publicity and of nation-wide moral pressure should be exerted to impose upon private interests their responsibility to the nation."[70] The report also urged tight controls over highways and the development of whole neighborhoods." Praising the report for asserting "organized control of every activity that might affect the future development of Washington," the *Star* called it "the first definitive step toward carving out a program to make the national capital the world's most beautiful city."[71]

Although referring to local neighborhoods, Delano's remarks pointed to the aesthetic rather than the social concerns of Washington residents, and true to that emphasis the Committee of 100 reverted back to the Park Commission's concentration on parks and buildings. With the support of the Board of Trade, the committee pressed federal authorities to establish a permanent park commission. In congressional hearings in 1924, Fred Coldren, speaking both as chairman of the Board of Trade's Committee on Parks and as vice-chairman of the Committee of 100, charged that since 1901 the city had acquired only six of the fifty-three tracts recommended in 1901. Compared to eighteen other major cities, the value of park property in Washington was last, at just over $5 million, compared to $287 million in New York and $60 million in Chicago. As a subsequent witness, Frederic Delano testified that Chicago's success derived directly from recommendations in its 1909 plan to acquire a forest reserve outside the city of fifty-five thousand acres of land, 60 percent of which had been acquired by the early 1920s.[72]

Coldren's figures were raised again in support of the bill, both in a favorable report out of the Senate[73] and in debate in the House of Representatives. When Representative Thomas Blanton of Texas complained about adding yet another federal amenity for what he described as "the pampered, selfish, spoiled public in Washington," Congressman Charles Underhill of Massachusetts picked up the themes promoted by the Committee of 100, saying that "if you are going to have a beautiful city in Washington for your constituents to visit and enjoy and be proud of, you have got to take the chance now, get this land and preserve it before it is covered with buildings, necessary as they may be in some portions of the city of Washington."[74]

As finally approved on June 6, 1924, the bill creating the new park commission authorized expenditures of $1 million over each of the following twenty years to acquire new lands in Washington as well as in adjacent portions of Maryland and Virginia. The bill paid special attention to the protection of Rock Creek and its tributaries, to the conversion of sites previously used for fortifications during the Civil War in the hills surrounding the city, and to the connection of these sites through a park boulevard. In testimony to the bill's federal intent, the commission was composed entirely of federal officers: the chief of engineers of the army, the chairmen respectively of the Senate and House District committees, the officer in charge of federal public buildings and grounds, the director of the National Park Service, and the director of the United States Forest Service. Praising the new bill for offering planning on a comprehensive basis, the *Star* concluded that it affirmed the sentiment that "the growth of Washington shall be regulated by a program which will extend to the new Washington the general principles of the original plan of the city."[75] Buoyed by the precedent set in Washington, Boston landscape architect Arthur Shurtleff wrote, "If our federal city shall become an inspiring example of sustained interest and intelligent action in city planning, the benefits will spread in some measure to every city in the land."[76]

Despite progress in dealing with the nagging problem of coordinating federal planning with urban development, planning proponents quickly concluded that the new commission lacked sufficient powers as well as money. Following the example of a number of other cities, the Committee of 100 launched a campaign to create a separate planning commission. A Senate report issued on February 3, 1925, pointing to overlapping functions among government agencies and a lack of orderly development of a city that "should have the most beautiful and well arranged Capital in the world," favored creation of a Federal City planning commission. A subsequent report in the House of Representatives stressed the need to build on the Park Commission plan but to extend it to reach beyond parks and public buildings to other physical elements: playgrounds, school sites, and especially highways.[77]

An independent planning commission met some opposition, however, including that of Frederick Olmsted Jr.[78] In a compromise between various organizations supporting the effort, proponents of a revised bill agreed to extend the membership of the existing park commission by the appointment of four experts in planning, one of them to be a native of the city, to serve without compensation. The new bill, drawn up by Frederic Delano in association with various proponents of civic beauty, as approved in 1926, changed the name of the commission to the National Capital Park and Planning Commission to reflect its extended purpose. In response to demands for a more comprehensive approach to planning, it assumed the functions of the highway commission established in 1898 and promised to relate more effectively highway development with park planning.[79] Olmsted quickly indicated that he was willing to serve and joined Delano as two of the first civilian representatives on the commission. Together they assured continuity with the City Beautiful emphasis both of the Park Commission plan and the subsequent campaigns of the Committee of 100.

During debate on the planning commission bill, one member of Congress complained that his proposal for an expanded federal buildings program had not been acted upon.[80] This goal had been stated strongly at the 1900 AIA convention and incorporated in the Park Commission's 1902 report. As the federal work force grew, the issue gained attention, as in 1904 when it was the subject of extended consideration in Congress and the press. Walk down Pennsylvania Avenue, the *Star* suggested. "In front of the Capitol, in sight of it, there are insanitary buildings, buildings which would be torn down in almost any second-class city in the country because of their unhealthy condition and character."[81] In 1909, the Board of Trade complained that delegates to an international convention "were forced to find their way between cow sheds and stands crowded with country produce" to get to a meeting hall near the Mall.[82] The Commission of Fine Arts made the group of monumental federal buildings a priority shortly after its inception.

Despite the high costs of renting space for the overflow personnel of growing agencies, however, Congress remained reluctant to spend large sums on capital improvements. Only at the height of the war emergency, when federal employment in the District soared to fifty-five thousand, did Congress respond to further prompting from the Commission of Fine Arts to establish the Public Buildings Commission to deal with the issue.[83] It promptly called for funds to consolidate all major agencies along lines recommended by the Park Commission. The Public Buildings Commission's concern was largely practical, but it was also aesthetic, for it accepted the Park Commission's contention that such quarters should be both practical—built of fireproof materials—and beautiful. Moreover, it embraced expansion of the city's park system on the basis that it would afford the means of recreation to thousands brought to Washington from throughout the country who were "required to work under conditions strenuous, unusual, and detrimental to the nervous system."[84]

Finally, as Congress approved the National Capital Park and Planning Commission (NCPPC) in 1926, it authorized a substantial $50 million federal buildings program for Washington, half of which was to go to clearing land between Pennsylvania Avenue and the Mall for construction of what was to become the Federal Triangle public buildings project. The project had the advantage not only of consolidating government personnel in a central location but, as U. S. Grant III later remarked, of providing Washington's "first great urban development and slum clearance project."[85]

In yet another affirmation of Washington's ties to the City Beautiful movement, Secretary of the Treasury Andrew Mellon, under whom the work was to proceed, named Daniel Burnham's partner in the 1909 Chicago plan, Edward Bennett, as supervising architect.[86] At last, the *Star* proclaimed in an editorial entitled "A Year of Capital Making," "Architectural unity is assured by simultaneous connection of individual building projects. Harmony is guaranteed by the co-operation of the various agencies." The Public Buildings Commission called the program an important step in "the ultimate development of the National Capital to realize the dreams of statesmen, architects, artists, engineers, and nature lovers who have sought to crystallize in material form the 'City Beautiful' which is to express the soul of America."[87]

Early reports of the National Capital Park and Planning Commission indicated once again, however, that objectives for parks and parkways were difficult to achieve. Not only did it become a challenge to reconcile con-

128

flicting highway plans, but the acquisition of parks continued to lag. As director of the NCPPC, U. S. Grant III could complain in 1927 and again in 1928 that decisions by public as well as private authorities were made on the basis of superficial study, without the advantage of careful or comprehensive planning, a position backed by President Herbert Hoover.[88] To secure additional tools for the beautification of the capital city, the planning commission pressed for and secured two additional bills, both passed in 1930. The Capper-Crampton Act granted the commission additional powers to buy open space in the region in advance of development, while the Shipsted-Luce Bill prohibited new construction adjacent to public buildings or parks that might be incompatible with existing structures.[89]

At last, it appeared, the goal of making private interest bend to public goals seemed at hand. As the NCPPC annual report for 1930 noted, "For the first time, the commission has a definite basis upon which to go to the states, counties or private parties to secure their cooperation in carrying out approved projects."[90] District property owners objected to the Shipsted-Luce Bill because it narrowed personal liberties and added to growing dangers of government interference in Washington, but planners insisted that it provided an essential control, "protecting the investment of the people of the United States in their public buildings and grounds."[91] Press reviews generally agreed. As a writer for *Technology Review* noted, "The city beautiful has become the city useful. . . . In this era of unregulated city growth with its concomitant evils of noise, congestion and stench, Washington is emerging as the antithesis of all that—a liveable, healthy, useful city."[92]

Although use of the term *comprehensive plan* was not new to Washington—going back as far as the campaign to establish a board of public works for the city in 1870—it assumed institutional authority only in the first quarter of the twentieth century. Used frequently before World War I as an inclusive concept to cover social as well as physical components of city improvement, by 1930 "comprehensive" planning had assumed a narrower focus. Accepting the rationale of the Park Commission and its advocates that Washington's future depended on the beauty that could secure national loyalty and attract tourism, government leaders, as Calvin Coolidge's

claim cited in the 1930 annual report of the Public Buildings Commission indicated, remained unabashedly unapologetic about adhering to a City Beautiful standard, even at a time when the term had come under considerable criticism in other parts of the country. As NCPPC planning director Charles Eliot wrote in a 1931 essay, "Let other cities, in their plan and skyline, express the commercial, industrial or pleasure-seeking purposes that they primarily serve. . . . let us, in . . . planning the Federal City, assert the right of our cities to the pursuit of beauty."[93]

The City and   III

the Modern State

Slums not compatible with monuments: The wrecker's ball over the Washington Monument, mid-1950s. Courtesy District of Columbia Department of Housing and Community Development.

The New Deal ushered in a period of activism in national government that is now considered central to the American way of life. Given the devastating effects of a depression, especially in the nation's cities, it was no surprise that Franklin Roosevelt's administration would intervene in Washington, not just to extend the public works program considered necessary to serve the growing federal establishment, but also to rectify glaring social needs, most notably in housing. When public housing proved inadequate to the task, subsequent administrations developed new means to direct private investment into poorer neighborhoods. Washington, in fact, provided the first opportunity to work out national ideas for federal investment in redevelopment through passage of a landmark act in 1945. The first full experiment under the new law, the redevelopment of the entire Southwest sector of the city, gained wide attention as a model for the nation. But federally supported redevelopment, though it intended to combine social uplift with physical improvements, proved damaging to the social fabric by displacing poorer residents and adding to the problems of older residential areas.

The advent of the Great Society, with its emphasis on funding local organizations directly as a means of empowering them to solve their own problems, offered an alternative approach to redevelopment, one that was taken up in the Shaw neighborhood directly north of the old downtown. When federal policies shifted away from such grass-roots approaches, Washington nonetheless gained an opportunity under a newly instituted form of home rule to achieve the kind of social uplift through physical improvements envisioned in Shaw as city government came under the leadership of civil rights activist Marion Barry. Assuming power at a time when national leadership was moving away from the needs and interests of cities, Barry capitalized on his opposition to federal power to establish his dominance over Washington politics. At the same time, however, he squandered his opportunity to redeem the promises of his early years in office. By embracing a political strategy that emphasized an emotionally charged racial symbolism without accommodating the city's most urgent social needs, Barry

helped divide Washington even more than it had been when he entered its government. Through a host of federal programs passing down from the New Deal, Washington was more tied to federal support than it had ever been, but it found itself, even with home rule, well short of achieving the social rehabilitation of its neediest residents.

If Washington is to represent us fairly among the great world capitals; if it is to have the appeal it should have to the pride and affection of our own people, it must provide dignified, spacious, comfortable living conditions for those whose work calls them here or whose inclination prompts them to become residents. The prestige and appeal of the capital do not lie wholly in its governmental structures, but do lie largely in its dwellings. The latter cover by far the largest part of its area and in many ways make the strongest and most lasting impression.

John Ihlder, to the National Capital Park and
Planning Commission, September 21, 1929

If the movement [for housing reform] gains headway it is conceivable that from the ashes of this depression new cities may rise, and that new standards of comfort, cleanliness and beauty will replace the cheap, slovenly hovels that mar every city.

Washington Star, editorial, April 20, 1930

Historians have frequently criticized Franklin Roosevelt's administration for its shortcomings in advancing urban planning. For all its attention to national planning, the New Deal remained largely indifferent to physical planning in local areas, a factor no less true of Washington than the rest of the country.[1] Roosevelt's term of office brought with it, however, attention to social needs largely missing at the national level for the previous twenty years. By responding especially to the nation's housing crisis through the creation of public housing, the New Deal broke new ground in social policy. By making Washington a leading example, the national government inspired hope for the solution of one of the city's as well as the nation's most intractable problems. Washington's experience revealed, however, the limits of public housing reform, as it failed to satisfy either those the policy was intended to help or the most vociferous critics of substandard housing.

In October 1929, with the nation suffering from the outset of the depression, U. S. Grant III, executive officer of the National Park and Planning Commission, wrote Frederick Olmsted Jr. to announce that the commission, after a period of indifference to housing problems, was about to take up the issue. For fifteen years the District Commissioners had attempted to rid the city of alley dwellings, he charged, but "they have allowed themselves to be checkmated in their very weak effort to obtain results from the original law. . . . It is evident that somebody else has to do something about it, and that is why our Commission is making the investigation and preparing legislation."[2] Undoubtedly Grant's interest in the alley dwellings was spurred by his association with housing activist Charlotte Hopkins[3] and by the publication in January 1929 of a new study of alley conditions by Howard University professor William Henry Jones. The report represented a new departure in the cooperation of black and white civic leaders, including Mrs. Hopkins, but it retained the moralistic overtones of the earlier era by denouncing "a certain retrograde kind of Negro culture. They are now the habitats of a class of people who are unable, or do not wish to measure up to white cultural standards."[4]

To promote new action in Washington's festering slums, Grant turned to John Ihlder, one of the pioneers in a new generation of professional housing advocates. Inspired to enter the field through a meeting with Jacob Riis, Ihlder first commented on housing reform as a reporter for the *New York Evening Sun*. Following a stint as secretary of the Municipal Affairs Committee of the Board of Trade in Grand Rapids, Michigan, Ihlder returned to New York in 1910 to serve as field secretary for the new National Housing Association under the tutelage of its founder, Lawrence Veiller. A three-year appointment as director of the Philadelphia Housing Association, a private philanthropic organization, brought to his attention the plight of war workers, especially blacks recently arrived from the South. Recruited with Mrs. Hopkins's support to head the new Department of Civic Development for the U.S. Chamber of Commerce in 1920, in 1925 he formed a joint committee with the American Civic Association to investigate ways finally to eliminate slum buildings in Washington's back alleys.[5] He played a role in drafting the bill to create the National Capital Park and Planning Commission and was one of those Olmsted recommended for inclusion on the first board. Passed over for that position, Ihlder left Washington to head the Pittsburgh Housing Association in 1927. In response to Grant's invitation, he served as a consultant to the NCPPC on housing until his return to the city in 1933.[6]

Echoing the criticism of the Progressive Era that alleys were bad influences both because they were unsanitary and because "they are hidden [and thus] they either breed or attract a population addicted to anti-social practices," Ihlder urged the planning commission in the first of a series of reports to take immediate action. Setting the problem in the context of urban development, he argued that rapid growth and increased reliance on the automobile were altering traditional land use. Congestion at the city's core placed a new premium on the conversion of older buildings to other uses. "Old slum areas," he said in 1932, "may not contain suitable sites for housing, and may better be devoted to other uses." Some old buildings might give way to commercial use, while others might be reconstructed to offer government employees suitable places of residence close to their work.[7] With modern sanitary facilities and attractive housing accommodations offered close to business and government activities, there would be a rejuvenation of the social character, not only of in-town residential areas, but also extending outward to the Southwest and Southeast sections of the city. Alluding to the seminal contributions of Pierre L'Enfant and Senator James McMillan, Ihlder declared that the challenge the NCPPC now faced was to redesign the 250 squares that contained inhabited alleys.[8]

Ihlder recognized the potential problems associated with displacing the city's poorest black residents from their alley homes, noting that "there are differences among the colored people, and it is not proposed to give respectable colored neighborhoods a new character by flooding them with undesirable new tenants."[9] He argued nonetheless that since a housing shortage no longer existed in the city, the alley dwellers should be relocated. Tenants, he suggested, need not expect to stay in the same section of the city, as it was "established practice for families to improve their living conditions by moving from one section to another." The concentration of blacks at the city core was encroaching on nearby white neighborhoods. To relieve the problem, he suggested, the planning commission should concentrate on the elimination of alley slums, the provision of suitable alternative housing for the alley population, and, through housing rehabilitation, the relief of pressure on better neighborhoods.[10]

As early as 1929 Ihlder proposed a new bill intended to eliminate alley dwellings. The *Washington Star* took up the cause, writing in a 1930 editorial, "While tens of millions of dollars are being spent for magnificent public structures to make the model capital of the world, business and residential Washington should not be permitted to present the aspect of slums."[11] Meeting with the District Commissioners, President Herbert Hoover called for legislation on "model city lines" for not just beauty but also social betterment and welfare.[12]

The following year both the National Capital Park and Planning Commission and the District Chapter of the American Institute of Architects endorsed new legislation that incorporated Ihlder's ideas. Headed by Louis Justement, the AIA committee on housing urged both the creation of a new District Housing Board to supervise those limited dividend corporations that might provide alternative, low-cost housing and the wholesale redevelopment of older sections of the city. Noting that conditions in blighted areas were not yet "alarmingly low," Justement warned that "present tendencies, if allowed to continue, will convert our present blighted areas into slum areas." The best response to the downward trend, he claimed, was "the consolidation of relatively large parts of a blighted area under one ownership and the renovation or rebuilding of the buildings on a large scale

A New Deal for Washington

basis."[13] The alternative, he suggested in a subsequent article, would be that "existing blighted areas will continue to degenerate into slums and new areas will be developed in the suburbs, constantly draining the population of the older city."[14] Urging the adoption of powers of eminent domain, he pressed for the reconstruction of whole neighborhoods as a unit.

Such an approach, which was gaining adherents through publicity attending the neighborhood planning concept advanced by Clarence Arthur Perry,[15] received further collaboration in the form of a memo to the planning commission from Ihlder's mentor, Lawrence Veiller, who wrote in 1933,

> It is believed that the only way in which the character of the class of people living in a neighborhood heretofore a slum can be changed is with a complete neighborhood change. In other words, that the occupants of the new dwellings must find in their neighborhood complete fulfillment of the usual needs; mothers must find the right kind of associates and playmates for their children; the right kind of schools, the right kind of recreation facilities; the right kind of shops; the right kind of amusements. In addition it is not to be expected that people of even the white collar class will wish to have to journey through an extensive slum district to get to their homes.[16]

In April 1932 the Washington Council of Social Agencies held a conference on eliminating alley dwellings chaired by planning commission chairman Frederic Delano and addressed by both Ihlder and Charlotte Hopkins.[17] In October Ihlder followed up, with encouragement from the AIA, by preparing legislation intended to study Washington's slum conditions with funds made available under Hoover's Reconstruction Finance Corporation. With the election of Franklin Roosevelt as president in November, housing efforts attracted renewed attention. In response to Charlotte Hopkins's invitation to tour local slums, reviving the tradition set by Ellen Wilson, Eleanor Roosevelt replied, "If you will let me know when the bill in which you are so interested is going to be presented, the President says he will invite the House and Senate leaders and heads of Committees to drive through the alleys with him, and he rather expects the bill will pass."[18]

To gain public support for the bill, Ihlder helped organize the Washington Housing Association, a group of prominent local citizens, headed by Mrs. Roosevelt as honorary chair. Although the Senate passed the bill in 1933, the House did not, and by the end of the year it was clear to Ihlder that establishment of the National Recovery Administration under President Roosevelt necessitated changes in the original bill. Noting the need to reconstruct not just the alleys but also the surrounding areas on block fronts, he encouraged changes in the legislation to encompass whole city blocks.[19] The effort subsequently attracted substantial support, most notably from the National Recovery Administration's Housing Division chairman, Robert Kohn, who asked NCPPC chairman Frederic Delano to join him in establishing a housing committee that might make Washington "a sort of proving ground for this sort of public works project."[20] Also important was the active support of Senator Arthur Capper of Kansas, whose speeches and writing on alley life extended Charlotte Hopkins's concern about disease in the alley dwellings. "Sanitation," he claimed in 1933, "is practically unknown in these hidden alleys."[21] U. S. Grant III added his judgment that alleys were "a public danger and a nuisance" in a November news article that included a drawing illustrating how a typical inhabited alley near Union Station could be converted to include "tea gardens catering to the guests of [nearby] hotels, and garage space for their cars."[22]

The Capper-Norton Alley Dwelling Bill passed the Senate in February 1934, but the House of Representatives held it up after the Bureau of the Budget challenged a plan to draw funds from the unexpended balance of the U.S. Housing Corporation.[23] Once it was agreed to make funds available through the Public Works Administration instead, the bill went forward and was signed by President Roosevelt at a ceremony featuring Charlotte Hopkins, on June 12. Saying that he had always been interested in improving housing and beautifying the capital city, Roosevelt noted that he too hoped that the legislation would serve the purpose of making Washington a model for the rest of the country.[24]

As finally approved, the Alley Dwelling Act established a new Alley Dwelling Authority (ADA) with powers to condemn property, as Ihlder had hoped, within any square or block containing an inhabited alley and to convert such areas "in the interest of community welfare." Improvements could include conversion from residence to a business or community center and could be accompanied by street paving or alley enlargement, demolition or construction of buildings, and furnishing of utilities. To pursue this work, Congress allocated an initial $500,000 in Public Works Administration funds.

Despite its focus only on Washington's back alleys, the act made the ADA in effect the nation's first local housing authority. As a report in *American City* noted, its "broad powers of excess condemnation to make over at will whole blocks" was without precedent in the United States in "its combination of purpose and the breadth of power which it confers. One must look to slum clearance experience in Great Britain and on the Continent to discern striking similarities."[25] The new legislation set a new deadline of 1944 for the total elimination of alley dwellings, and while the *Star* noted the difficulties involved in providing alternative housing, it concluded optimistically that ten years should be enough time for the displaced to "be absorbed, rather than picked up and transplanted bodily to some new section set apart."[26] The *Post* identified relocation as an "admittedly delicate" problem, questioning whether construction costs for the two Public Works Administration housing developments announced to date could be kept low enough to stay within the range of alley dwellers.[27]

A New Deal for Washington

Appropriately, John Ihlder became the director of the new authority. Recognizing the requirement as established in the 1918 legislation to "care for the alley population" as well as to eliminate unsanitary alley dwellings, Ihlder quickly announced that he would not proceed with demolition of existing housing until substitute housing could be found. NCPPC chairman Delano strongly reinforced his position, writing Ihlder, "The experience that has happened repeatedly is that the people whom it is hoped to help by slum improvements have been driven out of their quarters, and a people from a higher stratum of society have taken their places. . . . I am very doubtful whether this helps the situation."[28] Ihlder drew on figures showing that unemployment brought on by the depression had forced increasing numbers of blacks to locate in alley dwellings. He expressly ruled out turning alleys into playgrounds, as some had previously recommended, but constraints in his budget kept him from providing much in the way of alternative housing. As part of the compromise which cleared the Alley Dwelling Bill, the authority's debts had to be self-liquidating. In order to sustain rents, some alleys were to be converted to commercial purposes, with only a few being upgraded as residential quarters. Despite such limitations, Ihlder and his colleagues cherished the widely circulated belief among public housing advocates that, as he said, "with dwellings of a different type, the character of the people will be altered."[29]

In an effort to achieve this more ambitious goal, Ihlder petitioned to have the authority's power extended to develop alternate sites outside the alley areas and to authorize borrowing. Under the National Housing Act of 1937, the ADA became eligible to receive funds as the local housing authority, and in 1938 Congress amended the Alley Dwelling Act to enable the ADA to serve as the District's authority in funding low-cost housing. Two housing projects—one for whites, the other for blacks—were authorized, although only the latter, Langston Terrace on Benning Road in Northeast Washington, was funded.[30] Discussions about new construction included a commitment to find alternative housing for those dislocated. Changes in the inner city, however, made the particular job of finding adequate residences for those in need, particularly blacks, virtually impossible.

The rapid expansion of government during the New Deal placed considerable pressure on the local housing market. In the absence of rent controls, prices rose sharply, and as predicted in 1925 when wartime controls were lifted,[31] the city's poorest residents had the most difficult time finding adequate housing. Not only did the use of substandard alley dwellings continue, but the physical expansion of government, with the attendant razing of a number of residential buildings, contributed to the housing squeeze.[32] To make matters worse for the city's poor blacks, government officials began to look to alley sites situated near downtown office buildings as potential locations for new residential quarters for federal workers. While a proposal to build an entire new federal city of apartment buildings on the

140

A man finds temporary shelter in the midst of Washington's notorious Southwest alleys. Photo by Marion Post Wolcott, 1941.

north side of Pennsylvania Avenue got nowhere,[33] as early as 1932 Ihlder recognized the potential attraction of alley sites for government workers. Even as Congress debated the 1934 Alley Dwelling Bill, Washington's Public Utilities Commission reported that "government employees would welcome the erection in the downtown area of modern, well-built, low cost apartment houses."[34] In 1937 competition for space near government locations downtown came to a head.

★ ★ ★

During the 1930s a number of New Dealers rediscovered the residential charm of Georgetown, and a private restoration effort gathered momentum there.[35] The conversion of multiple-unit homes to single residency

A New Deal for Washington

brought with it the displacement of a number of black families, a process that spread into the adjacent neighborhoods of Foggy Bottom and the West End in the latter part of the decade. There, private rehabilitation met public efforts under the ADA to clear and rebuild on a number of alley sites. Caught in the middle were blacks who lived in the area, many of them for several generations.

Originally the ADA intended to relocate blacks from dilapidated alley dwellings into new buildings constructed nearby. But white residents of the area, recognizing the growing desirability of in-town residences, challenged the decision, thus drawing Ihlder into controversy around the proposed replacement of alley dwellings with public housing at St. Mary's Court in Foggy Bottom. At a meeting in March 1937, members of the planning commission reviewed arguments from whites that reserving the St. Mary's Court apartments would retard progress toward revitalizing Foggy Bottom. Noting that six thousand blacks lived in the West End, many of them needing better housing, the planning commission reaffirmed the ADA's decision to stand by black occupancy.[36] The black press picked up the issue, however, as the *Washington Tribune* ran a headline in July, "Whites Say Negro Occupancy of ADA Project Would 'Retard Progress.'"[37] In response to several heated letters from E. H. Harris, president of the Lincoln Civic Association, with whom he had sustained debate over ADA policy for more than two years, Ihlder called a hearing on the matter in October. Harris's charge that the ADA would "annihilate the Negro from erstwhile Foggy Bottom," where he had lived and worked for seventy-two years, marked in tone and substance criticisms that he carried to President and Mrs. Roosevelt and to members of Congress.[38]

Although the ADA stood by its decision to maintain St. Mary's Court for blacks, it did not satisfy either Harris or the Lincoln Civic Association, which in 1939 called for the authority's abolition. Noting that the proposed new War and Navy departments between Twenty-first and Twenty-third streets would displace three hundred families, Harris charged that "the object of slum clearance certainly does not mean driving people from shelter with no regard as to how they shall exist. It certainly does not mean routing, colonizing, and depriving Negro people of homes."[39] A year later in hearings to consider making the ADA a permanent agency, the Lincoln Civic Association claimed that in the seven years of its existence the ADA and the federal government had demolished 173 houses and produced only one 24-unit replacement, figures that Ihlder challenged.[40] In March 1942 blacks again called for the abolition of the ADA, claiming that the authority had "disregarded human habitation by removing dwellings, scattering and not rehousing former tenants" and shattering "the faith and confidence of colored citizens."[41] Such criticism offended Ihlder, who complained in a 1940 diary entry:

Some Negroes have only one desire, full racial equality. They see in public housing an opportunity to advance a step further by demanding that there shall be no distinction of race in any public housing property. . . . In the District of Columbia and in Congress the preponderant opinion is so strongly against this that such a policy adopted by the ADA would kill it. When I tell these Negroes that our policy is to assure an adequate supply of good low-rent dwellings for all people irrespective of color, but that I propose to build for Negroes in areas now occupied by Negroes . . . they say it were better to leave conditions as they are. Then I go, as I did yesterday afternoon with Professor Frazier of Howard [University], to visit some of the old houses we have just bought. In one five room house with one room vacant, are four

A New Deal for Washington

families, six adults, thirteen children . . . , toilet frozen and broken, water supply frozen. We are to leave these people . . . until white opinion will accept Negroes as next door neighbors, as fellow tenants in any apartment building?[42]

The competition for space only got worse as the nation, trying to avoid war, nonetheless worked in 1940 and 1941 to build up its defenses. In the process, the spur to government growth provided by the New Deal accelerated, thereby deepening Washington's housing crisis. Although an increase in housing starts in 1941 could be credited with serving long-term needs, Defense Housing Coordinator Charles F. Palmer described the District in November as the nation's leading housing problem.[43] Even before Pearl Harbor, Palmer requested $15 million in new public funds for housing in the District, a proposal the Star supported because of emergency conditions, despite its strong preference for private initiatives. With America's entry into the war, Palmer announced an additional housing program intended to produce twenty-two thousand home and apartment units and fifteen hundred dormitory spaces within six months.[44]

New housing, which Palmer discussed with local realtors before making his plans public, was intended to serve government needs, not to overcome the long-term problems of poor conditions. New units were to be located in Arlington, Virginia, and Southeast and Southwest Washington, close to government employment on both sides of the Potomac. These quarters were presumably for whites, as the government indicated that a portion of the dormitory space—450 units—would be reserved for blacks in quite different locations, near the colored YMCA and Howard University. In February Palmer announced an additional $18.9 million allocation out of funds authorized for defense housing after Pearl Harbor for the construction of portable units to be installed by the ADA.[45]

The war thus pressed on local and federal authorities a number of temporary measures designed to alleviate the immediate housing shortage, but in the process activists returned to the theme of rebuilding blighted areas. Even as news of Pearl Harbor broke, speakers at the annual meeting of the Washington Housing Association complained that the beauty of the capital had been blemished by the continued existence of slum areas. One has to look a long time at the White House or the National Gallery of Art, John Fahy, chairman of the Home Loan Bank Board, claimed, "to ease some of the disturbing impressions from one's mind" left from a walk through the deteriorating Southwest section of the city.[46]

Fahy undoubtedly chose the Southwest example carefully, for within a month the Star reported an ambitious plan drawn up by the federal Home Owners Loan Corporation to rebuild that entire residential area—eighty-five city blocks—at a cost of $32 million. Supported by John Ihlder, the plan went to Defense Housing Coordinator Palmer for approval. The report, drawn up by Arthur Goodwillie, with the assistance of Ihlder, the

144

St. Mary's Court in Foggy Bottom, before and after improvements, from the Alley Dwelling Authority Annual Report, 1937. Courtesy Washingtoniana Division, D.C. Public Library.

Washington Housing Association, Howard University faculty, and the District Commissioners, stressed the advantages of increasing the number of housing units available close to the 90,450 federal jobs in the immediate vicinity. But the report also pointed to the advantages of eliminating alley slums. As the *Star* reported, "Such a program would supply a number of valuable by-products. It would eliminate what is perhaps the city's largest slum area, one that is within sight of the Capitol, and assure all the attendant benefits which accompany such an elimination."[47]

In attempting to help solve the demand for housing by war workers, the Goodwillie proposal indicated that some of the indigenous population of the area—much of it black—would have to find accommodations elsewhere. The report emphasized a need to minimize displacement, suggesting that rehabilitation proceed in stages so as to allow local residents to move into new units as constructed. In giving preliminary approval to the plan in February, the National Capital Park and Planning Commission also considered the potential problems of displacement, but Ihlder's own testimony indicated that the persistent need to clean up the city took priority, since he claimed that the city had more to fear from the spread of disease from unsanitary conditions than from possible bombing.[48] Not surprisingly, black Southwest residents condemned the plan, calling for the entire abolition of the ADA in a public meeting in March. "The group was warned by its leaders," the *Star* reported, "that constant vigilance must be maintained to protect the homes of those residents of Southwest Washington who wish to remain there rather than be moved to some outlying section of the city."[49]

The Goodwillie report was never implemented, not because of black protest but because Congress failed to authorize an extension of the Lanham War Housing Act to provide additional funds for the District. In 1942 all funding for public housing in the District ended as the ADA was directed to shift its attention to the construction of temporary, demountable housing units for war workers in open spaces. In 1943 the authority's name and function altered, as it gained power as the National Capital Housing Authority (NCHA) to build new units throughout the metropolitan area. Much of Ihlder's immediate effort thus went into negotiating new units for various suburban jurisdictions, most of which resisted an innovation they feared would contribute to the decline of property values.[50]

While the elimination of alley dwellings thus had to be suspended, as it had been during World War I, critics of slum conditions kept up their campaign for action. In March 1943 members of the Public Health Committee of the House Committee on the District of Columbia toured Washington alleys, with District Commissioner Guy Mason reporting that the slums should be torn down as soon as alternative housing was available.[51] In Senate hearings on Washington's housing needs the following month Bernard Wycoff, of the Washington Housing Association, called for an investment of $5 million to clear slums, while Ihlder testified that reconstruction should not be left to the postwar period. A *Star* editorial in May placed a high priority on slum clearance.[52]

During the summer of 1943 Ihlder pressed to restore the NCHA's authority to build public housing, along with its $5 million appropriation, and to commit the federal government to a twenty-year program to reclaim Washington's slum areas. To drive home his case, he launched yet another series of tours for public officials through the city's most dilapidated residential sectors. Although alley dwellings remained the chief object of concern, by now, Ihlder claimed, blight had spread to block fronts through the entire central city, to the extent that forty thousand dwellings needed to be either rehabilitated or torn down.[53] The most serious problem, he and others charged, was faced by the city's black population, which was increasingly beset by displacement, especially through government expansion. In January 1944 an official of the Washington Urban League made this point in directing Eleanor Roosevelt through a tour of black residential areas in both Washington and northern Virginia, where the new Pentagon building had displaced a number of black residents. In August, the new biracial Citizens Committee on Racial Relations identified housing for blacks as the city's most pressing social problem, citing especially the failure to find adequate replacement housing for those who lost homes to demolition.[54]

Despite Ihlder's difficult relationship with blacks in the 1930s, the first stirrings of a powerful civil rights movement lent credibility to his efforts to secure government funding for the NCHA. As hearings on the future of housing and redevelopment opened before Senator Harold Burton of Ohio in October 1943, Ihlder's effort received the endorsement of the Washington Urban League, the *Washington Post,* NCPPC chairman U. S. Grant III, District Commissioner John Russell Young, and Senator Arthur Capper, who proclaimed, "We will have to work out a system to provide decent homes for these people living in alley dwellings and other substandard housing."[55]

But the effort to expand the agency's power elicited sustained opposition from both white citizens' associations and homebuilders' organizations. In December the Federation of Citizens' Associations demanded the abolition of the NCHA. Charging that the agency was neither responsive to local concerns nor cost-effective in building low-income housing, the federation called for a new slum clearance agency to be appointed by the District Commissioners. Three days later, the Southeast Council of Citizens' Associations, objecting to plans to place temporary war housing for blacks in their neighborhoods, seconded the call for a new agency.[56] Despite an editorial retort from the *Washington Post* that it had been demonstrated repeatedly that private builders had not provided low-income housing when needed,[57] the council pressed its position. It even brought forth supporting testimony from black homeowners in the area as evidence that their objections were based on a desire for sound building practices, which had nothing to do with race.[58] Extending the argument, Joseph Decker, speaking for the Federation of Citizens' Associations, accused the NCHA of seeking "another grab of funds" to cover up "9 years of failure to make any appreciable dent in the alley problems."[59]

An even more formidable obstacle to NCHA funding was the opposition of powerful real estate and building industry groups seeking to deal public housing a mortal blow. "If Congress can be persuaded to end the NCHA's work," a December homebuilders' newsletter declared, "that same Congress, acting as a national legislature, may more easily be persuaded to end the whole national public housing program." In summoning allies in the real estate industry, a circular issued the same month called public

A New Deal for Washington

housing one of the most serious problems ever to menace private enterprise.[60] In response, realtors offered a wave of testimony before the Burton committee opposing the Ihlder proposal for additional public funds for slum clearance. On February 1, a homebuilders' spokesman, Robert Gerholtz, described the NCHA rebuilding plan as a step toward socialism.[61]

The opposition of realtors, and especially the executive secretary of the National Association of Real Estate Boards, Herbert U. Nelson, must have been particularly difficult for Ihlder. For some years, the two men had exchanged friendly letters, each accepting proper roles for both public and private housing. Nelson subsequently promoted the ADA as a national model that could provide public housing without subsidy and invited Ihlder to participate in the NAREB's Committee on Housing and Blighted Areas, which promoted an early form of private redevelopment.[62] Nelson broke with Ihlder, however, shortly after the ADA expanded its authority to exercise the power of public domain. Following a speech in which Ihlder stressed that the problem in housing lay with serving the poor, Nelson retorted that he believed "the housing problem for the middle income group today is just as severe in many ways as it is for the low income group due to the disorder into which our cities have fallen."[63] After a somewhat testy exchange of letters, quite out of character with previous correspondence, Nelson reversed his earlier position, stating emphatically that "we should have no public housing whatever."[64]

After a month of hearings, Senator Patrick McCarran of Nevada, who had just stepped down as chairman of the Senate District Committee, proposed a bill authorizing a loan of $20 million for slum clearance. Calling for legislation that would declare substandard buildings "injurious to public health, safety, morals, and public welfare," he claimed that subsidy was justified because inadequate housing could not be razed until new housing was provided for occupants.[65] His proposal was forwarded to the Burton committee for consideration and endorsed by McCarran's successor, Theodore Bilbo of Mississippi. But opposition to Ihlder continued to mount, as both white citizens' groups and black defenders of public housing called for a new local agency to take up the mission of low-cost housing.[66] The situation worsened when Eleanor Roosevelt commented that public housing in Washington ought to be desegregated, to which the spokesman for the Anacostia Citizens' Association retorted, "We, the permanent taxpayers, resent the meddling interference of Mrs. Roosevelt in our civic affairs. We feel that any errors committed in settling our housing problems will not affect Mrs. Roosevelt after she has gone back to Hyde Park, New York."[67] Senator Burton asked the two sides to seek compromise legislation, but negotiations broke down, and on May 17 Senator Millard Tydings of Maryland introduced the Homebuilders' Association's bill incorporating what it called a "Washington plan" to grant private builders priority in conducting slum clearance.[68]

Ihlder grew discouraged at the lack of allies for public housing, but finally the presentation of alternative legislation from the housing industry brought other organizations to his defense, most notably unions that had played a historic role in bringing public housing to the height of its strength in the National Housing Act of 1937. In addition to the Congress of Industrial Organizations, the NAACP and the National Public Housing Conference joined to form the Council on Community Planning, with the primary goal of defending the NCHA program.[69] This support was enough to establish at least a stalemate.

The issue was taken up in yet another set of hearings, chaired by Senator Robert Taft of Ohio, and again the lines of division held fast. Homebuilders and their allies among the white citizens' associations continued to assert that private builders could do a better job providing housing for low-income residents than any public authority. Moreover, Harry Wender, chairman of the Federation of Citizens' Associations, charged that whites would support no further public housing unless it were to be segregated.[70] Representatives of black civic associations, pointing to displacement from both public building and private rehabilitation, stated their express fears of further displacement if redevelopment were put in private hands. "I can see the government acquiring land and taking over whole Negro communities," one speaker charged, "and the trend has been to wipe them out in the District of Columbia, rebuilding and changing its occupancy altogether."[71]

As the issues of public housing and redevelopment were joined, planners assumed a more important role. Initially, members of the NCPPC, most notably its chief spokesman, U. S. Grant III, actively defended the NCHA from its opposition. Grant called the builders' redevelopment bill "the most dangerous piece of legislation I have known of being introduced with reference to the District of Columbia in my 43 years' connection with it."[72] Grant actively supported public housing. But the commission had its own goal for the postwar era, to establish a more central role for comprehensive planning. Grant revealed this objective in a letter to Senator Capper in 1945.[73]

To promote the commission's case, Grant enlisted Alfred Bettman, a Cincinnati planner with service as a consultant to the commission over the years, to draw up an alternative bill. As one who envisioned the housing problem in terms not of slums alone but of the broader conditions of blight, Bettman favored retaining a role for public housing, but one that would place overall control for redevelopment in a new agency.[74] Bettman failed to negotiate a compromise bill with Herbert Nelson of the National Association of Real Estate Boards. The District of Columbia Redevelopment Act of 1945 as finally approved gave the planning commission, however, the control over redevelopment it wanted while still giving the homebuilding lobby much of what it wanted as well. Although the new bill differed to an extent from the Washington Plan advanced by homebuilders, it contained the essential element of giving the first right of redevelopment to private investors. In addition, redevelopment was to be carried out under the purview of a new entity, the Redevelopment Land Agency, which would assemble land parcels for improvement, offering them to private bidders on a subsidized basis. The right of eminent domain, which Bettman and other planners had argued for, was shifted from the NCHA to the new agency, thereby depriving the NCHA of the ability to secure its own sites. With the NCHA left only as the builder of last resort, Ihlder bitterly told one of his antagonists, "You fellows have gotten all you asked for . . . it is now up to you."[75]

Although some claim has been made for Chicago as establishing the precedent for redevelopment under largely private direction as supervised by local planning agencies,[76] Congress's intimate involvement in setting a policy for the District of Columbia made Washington the true test of future policy. While subsequent annual reports of the NCHA dutifully emphasized the agency's role as only a supplement to the private sector, Ihlder made no secret that he considered his claims throughout the public hearings confirmed that the private sector would not adequately meet the need of low-income residents. In the postwar period, a series of articles and reports, including one by a young black NCHA staff member, Walter Washington, reiterated the critical housing needs of the city's blacks.[77] The problem was made more difficult, Ihlder pointed out, by the congressional requirement that all demountable wartime housing would have to be removed within two years of the armistice. To meet the housing shortage, Ihlder repeatedly asked for new funding for public housing. Although the *Washington Post* embraced his cause, Congress held back funds until passage of the National Housing Act of 1949. Even as money finally became available Ihlder reported that his agency was facing the problem of where to rehouse low-income occupants.[78]

In subsequent years Ihlder found himself constantly pressing redevelopment authorities for plans to rehouse those whose homes would be torn down for better housing. Even as he retired in 1952, he continued to describe himself as a beleaguered champion of those whom the private market was not serving adequately.[79] Before passage of the 1949 housing act, the NCHA had built a significant role for itself, but by then the emphasis on rebuilding Washington had shifted from attention to low-income needs to the broader concept of urban renewal. As the subsequent history of the redevelopment of the Southwest indicated, Ihlder's worst fears of the inadequacy of such an approach would be realized.

The people converging daily on the central business and government district of Washington are important. Not just as every individual in America is important, but more especially because the hope of the world rests in the hands of those administrators and their assistants through whom the goods of our factories and the products of our fields are flowing to rehabilitate a war-torn world. The energies of these men and women should be devoted to their important tasks, not to the enervating grind of fighting unnecessary traffic tangles.

> *Transportation Plans for Washington,* Report
> to the Board of Commissioners, December 20,
> 1946, J. E. Greiner Co., Deleuw, Cather & Co.

Washington is about to launch one of its greatest ventures in redevelopment since Major L'Enfant laid out the original plan for the city. The transformation of the Southwest . . . will not only wipe out a depressing slum area; it will also give the city a new and attractive downtown area and town center.

> *Washington Post,* editorial, April 7, 1956

As world war gave way to cold war, Washington and the nation entered a period of prosperity that loosened constraints on consumer spending and resulted in an outpouring of homebuying and homebuilding. Increases in federal employment—now widely praised as central to the cold war effort—made Washington one of the fastest growing metropolitan areas in the country. Yet as Washington residents joined the national suburban trend, government officials worried about the deterioration of inner-city areas, many of them close to concentrations of federal jobs. In the effort to revitalize the urban core, they seized on new tools for redevelopment and highway construction. While the impetus for such policy came from the federal government, which openly worried that urban slums could encourage communist subversion,[1] it received a warm welcome in the Washington press and from many builders and architects, and from some civic groups. Left out of the partnership, however, was the city's growing black population. Ultimately what was intended to serve locally as both a solution to federal needs and a national model for urban revitalization proved instead to be inflammatory, as racially charged social conflict rose to new levels, ultimately contributing to the tragic civil disturbances of 1968.

The suburban challenge to Washington's predominance in the metropolitan area was a common national phenomenon, but for a while it appeared that the city might utilize its hold on federal employment to escape the decline facing other older urban centers. With income rising at a rate higher than even New York or Los Angeles, Washington was widely compared to the booming cities of the South and West, sharing with its Sunbelt counterparts a powerful boost from the development of a national defense industry and an information-system economy.[2] The District of Columbia continued to attract new residents equal in number, if not in proportion, to the suburbs into the late 1940s. And while the 1950 census showed a drop in both the city's absolute and proportionate share of the metropolitan population, from 68.5 percent to 53 percent (table 3), most local commentators viewed suburbanization as a healthy development.

Stressing the perception that "Washington and its environs are now one integrated urban region," the *Star* argued that decentralization could proceed without harm to the city, to which a *Post* editorial added, "This is a big country, and there is good reason why its inhabitants should spread out and enjoy it, instead of cooping themselves within city walls."[3] The Washington Board of Trade gained assurance in the late 1940s from reports that 86 percent of metropolitan area retail sales took place in the District[4] and from the belief, as one of their members put it, that "positive and intelligent action taken now can go far to avoid the worst features of decentralization experienced by other cities."[5] A 1946 transportation report to the District government recognized "no marked trend for the decentralization of either federal or private employment," prompting the prediction that "Washington is destined to remain, for an indefinite period, a city of concentrated activity in the area of federal buildings and the adjacent business district."[6]

If anything, federal planners worried that too much government concentration would negatively affect the city by adding to congestion. Interest in decentralizing federal agencies, which first emerged in the 1930s, influenced the decision to construct the Pentagon in northern Virginia during the war.[7] Persistent problems of traffic congestion led a number of enthusiasts of planned decentralization to recommend the phased dispersion of federal facilities on a regional basis. In making this case, Frederick Gutheim wrote in 1942 that continued centralization of government was hurting efficiency, noting that "the departments in Washington are swollen beyond any practical necessity by the hordes of operating bureaus clustered around them."[8] Arthur Rabuck of the Public Buildings Commission extended the argument in a memo he submitted to the NCPPC in 1948, writing:

Table 3
Population: Washington Metropolitan Areas

	White	Black	City Total	% Metro	Suburbs	Total Metro
1940	474,326	187,266	663,091	68.5	304,894	967,985
1950	517,865	280,803	802,178	53.1	708,000	1,510,985
	+9.2	+41.8	+36.2		+132	+56
1960	345,263	411,737	763,956	36.9	1,304,554	2,068,510
	−33.3	+49.8	−4.7		+84.2	+36.9
1970	209,272	537,712	756,510	26.4	2,104,000	2,860,510
	−39.4	+30.6	−4.8		+61.3	+38.2

Even a little decentralization may save this community many millions of dollars by reducing the mileage of express highways that may be needed. Moreover, continuance of the policy of centralization will make a subway system necessary. . . . Decentralization of homes is a natural trend in all American metropolitan areas. You may rest assured that no one is going to reverse it. The wise thing for planners to do is to readjust their plans to bring them into harmony with what the people need and want.[9]

After the war, planned dispersion received support from promoters of civil defense, foremost among them Tracy Augur, already an advocate of decentralized city development and redevelopment through highway construction in his work as a consultant to the Cincinnati Master Plan of 1948.[10] In joining the National Security Resources Board after the war, he popularized the theory of tying defense to urban decentralization. "A metropolitan area that is well organized in terms of the amenities of modern urban living and the efficient conduct of modern business," he told participants at the National Planning Conference of 1948, "will also be an area of decreased vulnerability to atomic bombs, and to other weapons of mass destruction."[11]

Although U. S. Grant III argued that the advantages for defense from dispersion should be weighed against the costs of administrative losses as well as initial capital expenditures, his successor as acting director of the National Capital Park and Planning Commission embraced government decentralization, describing the underlying principles of physical planning as the same, "whether the purpose is planning for dispersal to dodge bombs or decentralizing to get elbow room parking areas."[12] To objections from Washington businessmen who feared the effects of decentralization, Federal Buildings Commissioner William E. Reynolds responded that planned dispersion would help the city by keeping development from moving even

Redevelopment and Dissent

further out. In a speech before the Washington Board of Trade, Reynolds stressed the need "to plan for a motor age" with the construction of six-lane depressed highways to insulated federally created subcommunities of six thousand people each. The NCPPC's 1950 comprehensive plan for the capital region attempted to institutionalize such thinking by arguing that "there should be a definite policy to locate as many as possible of the required new employment places away from the center, and actually remove most of the existing temporary workplaces," a policy that was underscored by news that as many as one thousand new federal employees were being added each day with the outbreak of the Korean War.[13] In November 1950, the General Services Administration announced an ambitious plan tied specifically to the threat of atomic attack to disperse government agencies at eight sites along a twenty-mile radius from the central city.[14]

In line with such thinking, a number of government agencies migrated from city to suburb. But more ambitious plans for dispersal of federal employment nationwide and to the farthest reaches of the suburbs, beyond the threat of atomic explosion, never materialized as the exigencies of central place reasserted themselves.[15] Although the District's share of federal employment in the metropolitan area fell from 75 percent in 1947 to 66.8 percent in 1967, the change was much more modest than the decline in its share of private jobs, from 71 percent to 51 percent between 1954 and 1967. When Congressman Henry Reuss of Wisconsin attempted in 1961 to revive interest in decentralizing government agencies around the country as a means of dampening the population explosion in the Washington area, he was greeted by opposition from planners and the press, who claimed that federal employment no longer played a central role in the area's growth.[16]

The federal presence thus remained an anchor of stability for the District, and yet the city changed dramatically in the 1950s and the early 1960s. In 1953 Washington joined the list of the nation's dozen largest cities—including Pittsburgh, San Francisco, Boston, and Los Angeles—which held less than 50 percent of their metropolitan populations.[17] The 1960 census marked the city's first absolute decline in population, and by 1970 the District's share of metropolitan population had fallen to little more than a quarter. In 1957 Washington became the first major city in the country with a majority black population. The city's once unexceptional demographic profile diverged sharply from that of its suburbs, not just in racial composition but also in terms of age, marital status, and income distribution. Retail sales in the city dropped both in absolute terms and in proportion to the sales in the suburbs.[18]

Such dramatic changes prompted serious concern. The response of Washington's civic leaders, however, was not to abandon expectations that Washington could be different from other deteriorating urban centers but rather to redefine the nature of the urban problem. As early as 1958 the planning commission leadership abandoned the decentralist approach of its 1950 comprehensive plan,[19] and in 1961 the commission altered much of the earlier approach in its highly influential *Policies Plan for the Year 2000*. Urging the introduction of a mass transit system, which had been rejected first in 1944 for fear that it would add to congestion downtown and then in 1950 as inappropriate for the widely dispersed capital region,[20] the commission advocated directing growth along six transportation corridors radiating out from the historic city. This the commission redefined as the Metro Center, in line with its cosmopolitan vision of the metropolitan area as one integrated region.[21] The *Star* was among the enthusiasts for "the new Washington," an area it described as transformed "from a well-ordered city of three-fourths of a million people into a dynamic heart of a still growing regional community of two million."[22] The key to that transformation, as the *Star* was not alone in identifying, was the influx of federal funds from new national programs, especially for urban redevelopment and transportation improvements.

Although coordination faltered between plans for redevelopment and new urban roads made possible under the Highway Act of 1944, key figures in national planning circles were determined to forge a coherent program for the revitalization of the District of Columbia. Chief among these was the St. Louis planner Harland Bartholomew, who was most anxious to use the location of new freeways both to direct patterns of metropolitan growth and to define further the boundaries of in-town neighborhoods. As the chief consultant to the NCPPC in the formulation of its 1950 comprehensive plan, as the commission's chair from 1954 to 1960, and as the main force behind the landmark Mass Transportation Survey of 1959, Bartholomew proved a central figure in policy formulation for Washington in the 1950s. In these efforts he gained an ally dedicated to directing highway policy toward urban revitalization, Public Works Agency director Philip Fleming.[23] Other planners inside and outside Washington reiterated the theme of utilizing the District's status as a company town for directed regional development. And while Washington suffered serious problems in realizing the goal, the vision of providing through the city a national model for urban revitalization remained remarkably consistent throughout the 1950s.

In shaping national policies for redevelopment, Washington assumed central importance. Although other states passed enabling legislation earlier, Washington provided the first test of congressional will on the procedures that ultimately became institutionalized under Title I of the National Housing Act of 1949. The Redevelopment Land Agency (RLA), established to assemble land parcels for resale to developers, fell under the control of its chair, department store owner Mark Lansburgh, who conceived the agency's role as attracting higher-income buyers back to the downtown area.[24] Although during the debate over national housing in 1949 the *Washington Post* had stressed the importance of placing poor residents in new housing and protecting them from displacement, by 1952 it had shifted its editorial

155

focus, as exemplified in a series of articles promoting redevelopment which were pointedly titled "Progress or Decay? Washington Must Choose." Asserting that "the central civic problem in Washington today—as in every other major American city—is the flight to the suburbs," reporter Chalmers Roberts reiterated the enthusiasm of local developers for slum clearance, an inner-loop highway to bring shoppers back downtown, and new parking facilities to accommodate their cars.[25] Noting a concern for St. Dominic's parish in the Southwest, the *Catholic Standard,* in an editorial entitled "Return to Beauty," urged the complete redevelopment of the area, claiming that

> The Southwest, thoughtfully redesigned for quiet, uncrowded convenient living in an atmosphere of dignity and beauty, would serve as a model for projects in other sections. It could mark the beginning of a decline in the headlong flight to the suburbs, thus reducing the threat to intown business, churches, and the District's Treasury. If the rebuilding were of a kind calculated to encourage the minimum of general obsolescence, a section would be provided wherein families would be encouraged to send down the roots from which spring stability, healthy tradition, civic pride and responsibility.[26]

With editorial backing from the *Post,* the RLA selected for its first project the dramatic rebuilding of a 550-acre site in the city's Southwest sector, rejecting as too timid an alternative plan prepared by Elbert Peets, which, like the Goodwillie plan before it, stressed rehabilitation of existing properties in the area and the retention of the area's existing residents and businesses.[27] Harland Bartholomew submitted a plan to the planning commission in 1952 which also stressed rehabilitation,[28] but the most influential plan proposed for the Southwest was one envisioning wholesale redevelopment submitted by architects Chloethiel Woodard Smith and Louis Justement, president of the Washington Building Congress. Reiterating the enthusiasm he had revealed in the 1930s for slum clearance, Justement urged planners in his 1946 book, *New Cities for Old,* not to be stifled by the "dead hand of the past." He urged the complete rebuilding of cities "as a frontier for constructive achievement" and a chance to "banish the ugliness which is almost as revolting as the squalor of our urban surroundings."[29]

When several Southwest businesses contested their displacement, a three-judge panel ruled against their suit, stating nonetheless that the sole reason for condemnation was the removal or prevention of slums. Other goals, such as modernization, the panel suggested, were inappropriate, noting that "the poor are entitled to own what they can afford. The slow, the old, the small in ambition, the devotee of the outmoded have no less right to property than have the young, the aggressive, and the modernistic or futuristic."[30] In considering the case on appeal, the Supreme Court went a good deal farther to embrace Justement's modern approach to redevelopment, both as comprehensive and as suited to serve aesthetic as well as social purposes. "It is within the power of the legislature," Justice William Douglas wrote for a unanimous Court, "to determine that the community should be beautiful as well as healthy, spacious as well as clean, well-balanced as well as carefully patrolled." The Court ruled specifically that property which "standing, by itself, is innocuous and unoffending" could nonetheless be condemned for redevelopment in order to prevent the extension of blighted areas into slums. "If those who govern the District of Columbia determine the nation's capital should be beautiful as well as sanitary, there is nothing in the Fifteenth Amendment that stands in the way."[31] A report prepared for the District commissioners by James Rouse and Nathaniel Keith, issued in 1955 under the pretentious title *No Slums in Ten Years*, cited the Supreme Court decision in justifying the complete rebuilding approach exemplified in the Southwest. In this effort the authors saw the potential of realizing an "integrated approach" to urban renewal through the creation of vital, self-sufficient neighborhoods bounded by major highways to direct traffic around the area, not through it.[32]

Planners thus arrived in the 1950s at a consensus, backed by business organizations and the press, that made the linchpin of a revitalized central area a circumferential highway around the downtown, which would both define the area and direct through traffic from the suburbs away from the most congested part of the city. Louis Justement presented such a vision in his 1946 book, describing both an inner circumferential highway for the collection of downtown shoppers at parking garages along the route and an outer circumferential highway to which new business and government might be directed in the effort to relieve congestion further and to achieve a measure of planned decentralization.[33] Justement's enthusiasm for circumferentials was shared by Harland Bartholomew, who claimed to have introduced the concept into the important report of the Interregional Highway Committee returned in January 1944, which so directly influenced the National Highway Act of 1946.[34] Bartholomew was responsible for introducing a series of three circumferential highways into the 1950 comprehensive plan: an inner loop circling the White House at a distance of half a mile; another located some three to six miles from downtown; and a third, entirely outside the District, six to ten miles from the city center. A 1950 report of the Washington Metropolitan Chapter of the American Institute of Architects, signed both by Justement and by Chloethiel Smith, strongly endorsed the ring road concept and urged amendment of redevelopment laws to allow the use of highways to create new land-use patterns for strategic location of business and government. The transportation subcommittee of the Committee of 100 also endorsed the concept of radial and ring roads in a 1952 report signed by Tracy Augur as chair. Although the report recognized that District residents might question the utility of such roads, it warned that "unless people from an ever-expanding trade territory outside the District are brought to its center expeditiously—and accommodated comfortably when they get there—the city's economic and cultural life will dry up and its residents will have little reason for remaining."[35]

Until passage of the National Highway Act of 1956 increased federal funding from 50 percent to 90 percent, Washington area planners felt stymied in the most ambitious of their plans. But with the prospects of massive funding for long-delayed projects, District highway officials, backed by allies in the Bureau of Public Roads, pressed their efforts to locate and construct the interstate routes that would link downtown Washington with its Maryland and Virginia suburbs. Instead of helping realize long-anticipated goals, however, the influx of funding served instead to shatter consensus.

While a wide range of redevelopment supporters accepted the use of the Southwest leg of the Inner Loop freeway to redefine that completely redeveloped neighborhood's boundaries, many found it difficult to justify a six-lane freeway through the affluent upper Northwest as a means of connecting Maryland's new Interstate 70S through Montgomery County to the Inner Loop. Although Bartholomew kept pressing for this Wisconsin Avenue corridor plan, the Committee of 100, under the influence of several young lawyers whose Cleveland Park community was threatened by the route, attacked the concept, arguing that the highway would more effectively contribute to urban revitalization by following a route through the dilapidated neighborhoods on the other side of Rock Creek Park.[36] Another alternate route, proposed along the Potomac River, drew opposition from Bartholomew, who felt that it did not conform to his notion that freeways should enhance existing population trends, and from the National Park Service, which threatened to block the project by refusing to turn over needed parkland, which it wanted protected. Other planned projects, including an interstate connector between the Inner Loop and the Wisconsin Avenue radial through Glover-Archibold Park and a new bridge at Three Sisters Island between Georgetown and Arlington, which would have necessitated a huge cloverleaf in parkland, drew further opposition from the National Park Service and from residents on both sides of the river.[37]

Granted ultimate authority to redirect redevelopment as part of the comprehensive plan by the District Redevelopment Act of 1945, the commission attempted to project a pattern of controlled decentralization through its 1950 comprehensive plan. But a lack of authority to plan for suburban areas and competition from other government agencies for control over such crucial ingredients of the plan as the location of new federal office facilities compromised the NCPPC's ability to realize its goals. Traditionally, local governments resented federal intrusion into area affairs and remained, for the most part, fiercely independent of each other into the 1950s. In 1952 the *Star*'s Crosby Noyes felt justified in extending the cold war analogy to the lack of area cooperation in a series entitled "Our Own Iron Curtain." Whether it was a problem of local services or civil defense, Noyes reported, area cooperation was sadly lacking.[38]

In the same year, however, Congress authorized a plan, promoted as early as 1944 by the Bureau of the Budget, to strengthen the planning commission. The National Capital Planning Act of 1952 reorganized the commission, providing direct federal funding and responsibility for reviewing all federal decisions as they affected development and redevelopment of the entire capital region. To signify a shift in emphasis, the act dropped the term *park* from the commission's title and replaced the director of the Forest Service as an ex-officio member with the director of the Bureau of Public Roads. In addition to the commission's responsibility for redevelopment, the act added a call for plans for regional thoroughfares, which would also fall under the commission's continuous review. The act established a second agency, the National Capital Regional Planning Council, as a means of institutionalizing regional planning efforts by the area's different jurisdictions, each of which was to be represented on the council. Staff was to be provided by the planning commission itself.[39]

Such efforts helped promote regional cooperation. In 1954 the Maryland and Virginia assemblies signed an agreement with the District to plan for coordinated transportation facilities. For three years in the late 1950s, Harland Bartholomew provided the major direction to a survey of regional transportation needs jointly directed by the NCPC and the National Capital Regional Planning Council. Their report, issued in 1959 as the Mass Transportation Survey, endorsed a scaled-back but still substantial network of new interstate highways totaling 329 miles and a 33-mile rail system to serve District commuters. A new joint congressional committee on metropolitan Washington problems scheduled hearings on the report, and its support for a "balanced" system of highways and rapid rail transit added federal weight to apparent regional consensus. In 1960 Congress issued a resolution of intent, agreeing for the first time to coordinate formally with local planning agencies federal decisions affecting physical changes in the metropolitan area.[40] Stating his intent to make Washington a national model for coordinated metropolitan development, President John Kennedy named a liaison with the Washington Metropolitan Regional Conference early in his term, following in 1962 with the appointment of the first White House special assistant for national capital affairs.[41] It seemed only appropriate, then, that the *Policies Plan for the Year 2000* would choose to highlight President Kennedy's description of the city and its suburbs as "interdependent parts of a single community, bound together by a web of transportation and other facilities and by common economic interests."[42]

By the early 1960s, then, conflicts related to efforts to revitalize the central city appeared to have been resolved, and the transition had been made to the bold redefinition of the city as the heart of a larger metropolitan region. Yet for all the allusions to newfound unity, fissures had deepened within the metropolitan framework. At the heart of those problems lay the central question of race.

Redevelopment and Dissent

★ ★ ★

Washington's rigid segregation came under increasing national pressure in the postwar years, as reports from the President's Commission on Civil Rights in 1947 and the National Committee on Segregation in the National Capital in 1948 sharply criticized District practices, which confined black residents to overcrowded quarters in the blighted central portion of the city through strict adherence to racially restrictive covenants. But just as Eleanor Roosevelt's effort to promote integration of Washington's public housing had prompted local opposition, these national reports drew local criticism. In response to the 1948 report, the executive board of the Federation of Citizens' Associations issued a stinging critique, rebuking social scientists who, it claimed, had virtually no knowledge of the city for attempting to legislate change. When a few realtors, influenced by the efforts of Catholic activists to promote desegregation, sold homes to blacks in white areas, the all-white citizens' associations retaliated by circulating newsletters urging residents not to sell to blacks and forming pools to buy back homes that had fallen into the wrong hands. A particularly vocal critic of all efforts to desegregate, Federation of Citizens' Associations president Clifford Newell, called Washington a "haven for Negroes" and blamed outside agitators with communist sympathies for trying to make blacks discontented.[43]

In May 1948, the Supreme Court ruled that restrictive covenants could not be enforced by law, and other racial barriers—in recreation and public accommodations—fell thereafter.[44] But as late as 1959, restrictive covenants were still in place in sections of predominantly white Washington west of Rock Creek Park,[45] and the 1948 ruling did not effect immediate changes in residential patterns, in large part because of difficulties blacks had in securing loans from Washington banks. More important in effecting neighborhood change in some areas was the 1954 Supreme Court decision overturning Washington's racially separate school system.[46] Other policies, however—national in scope, but with local applications—were as significant as desegregation in the city's changing demography, namely the twin policies of redevelopment and transportation improvements.

Even as the city's racial and demographic profile changed radically in the 1950s and 1960s, national supporters of redevelopment and their local adherents clung doggedly to the vision of a revived central city. The city's black population, on the other hand, consistently opposed those efforts. With clear evidence that public and private redevelopment contributed to displacement, blacks openly expressed fears that further incentives to private investors would make the situation even worse.[47] Having failed to curb the private orientation of the District Redevelopment Act of 1945, blacks tried but also failed to secure a nondiscrimination clause in the redevelopment procedures that made their way into the 1949 housing act.[48]

Although Congress gave in to local protests against redeveloping the predominantly black Marshall Heights area in the far southeast corner of the District, the decision appeared to have more to do with protecting the prerogatives of several committee chairs who were bypassed in an effort to get appropriations to the Redevelopment Land Agency to execute the Marshall Heights plan.[49] Even as the *Post* applauded the appointment of the first black to the board of the National Capital Housing Authority, architect Hilyard Robinson, the *Pittsburgh-Washington Courier* labeled the agency "the city's most unenlightened, stubborn bulwark of the traditional segregation policy" for continuing to maintain segregated housing even after restrictive covenants on private dwellings had been struck down.[50] Although the city adopted a strict nondiscrimination law for new housing in the Southwest, redevelopment proved to have a devastating impact on the black community.

At issue in the Southwest was whether the area would be upgraded, as originally intended, to improve housing opportunities for existing low- and moderate-income residents near potential places of work; or whether, as Mark Lansburgh had argued in the 1940s, redevelopment would be used to attract a higher-income-level resident who would contribute to the local economy as a consumer and taxpayer. Although there was indisputable evidence of decay in the area,[51] there were nonetheless many signs that the blighted Southwest had the potential for rehabilitation. Both a survey by the Homebuilders' Association of Metropolitan Washington, which described houses in the Southwest "as sound and in many cases as large as fashionable homes in Georgetown," and the 1950 census revealed large numbers of structurally sound homes in black as well as white portions of the area designated for redevelopment.[52] Even the RLA's survey of the area noted a high level of residential stability, considered unusual for a blighted area.[53]

Throughout the initial stages in planning, policymakers attempted to reconcile two competing goals: to upgrade the whole neighborhood while at the same time making it possible for lower-income blacks to find suitable alternative housing in the area. Speaking at a meeting of the Joint Committee on the National Capital in 1952, Philadelphia housing reformer Oscar Stonorov stressed the need, in making the first redevelopment project in Washington a model for the nation, to avoid forcing current residents out of their neighborhoods, a theme John Ihlder reiterated as he pointed out that 76 percent of the Southwest's affected residents were black.[54] Harland Bartholomew's 1952 proposal to the NCPC, intended to serve as a compromise between the Peets approach and that of Justement and Smith, also stressed efforts to retain the indigenous population, a point that RLA executive director John Searles made repeatedly in early meetings with neighborhood residents.[55] The *Star* immediately commended the Bartholomew proposal for supporting construction of new housing within the means of displaced families. Both the AIA and Chloethiel Smith and Louis Justement sharply criticized the Bartholomew plan, calling the retention of low-income

An overview of Southwest Washington before redevelopment. Copyright *Washington Post;* reprinted by permission of the D.C. Public Library.

housing in the area "a very questionable asset" and accusing the NCPC of a "tired, unimaginative and defeatist" approach to the redevelopment of Southwest Washington.[56] Once the federal Housing and Home Finance Agency rejected the rehabilitation approach as insufficient to qualify for national funding,[57] local officials finally swung behind the total rebuilding approach to slum clearance. Even Bartholomew stated publicly that "piecemeal redevelopment is of limited value. We must rebuild by neighborhoods, not by individual blocks."[58] In the process, low-rent housing fell by the wayside.

The contradictory goals stated by the RLA split the community. While the Washington Board of Trade, the Committee of 100, and the all-white Southwest Citizens' Association, citing a need for high- as well as moderate-income housing units, endorsed redevelopment plans, the all-black Southwest Civic Association decried the lack of plans for low-income housing and described redevelopment "as a shameful un-American displacement program."[59] Joseph Curtis, chairman of the Southwest Civic Association's redevelopment committee, charged that planners had failed to take into account requests of local residents for more public housing, moderate rents, and assurances that they would have priority in buying and renting new properties.[60]

Curtis's skepticism toward planners' intentions reflected sentiment in the black community that went back more than a decade. In 1949, the *Pittsburgh-Washington Courier* spelled out its criticism of whites who, it claimed, had "decided that the pauperized underdogs of color are too close to the nation's seat of government" and who wanted to entice migrants from the Maryland and Virginia suburbs through "attractive houses and lavish apartments close to government jobs." The paper continued: "The plea that 'thousands of Negroes will lose their life savings and become renters or objects of charity; hundreds of Negro business enterprises will be wiped out; hundreds of Negro churches will be destroyed and their membership scattered; Negro professional men will lose their clientele' is seen as a poor excuse for not making Washington the most beautiful city in the world."[61]

Such criticism had little effect, however. Even among the staunchest advocates of civil rights, the *Post* pressed for stepped-up redevelopment efforts in a series of articles and editorials, noting in 1957, "No doubt many residents of the area will be loath to lose their homes despite the prevailing slum conditions. They should realize, however, that the net effect of this great redevelopment effort will be to make Washington a much more pleasant place in which to live and work."[62] By 1959 the RLA made its goal with regard to the suburbs overt, stating of the Southwest in its annual report, "Here is an opportunity for persons to live who prefer the amenities of . . . a highly convenient and attractive location to a long commuter's journey to a larger suburban lot." Two years later it added a story about a government official whose workload was eased because he could get home for dinner and still return to the office to work late because it was nearby.[63] In 1961 the *Post* pressed for stepped-up redevelopment efforts in a sequel to its "Progress or Decay?" series, and a year later its architecture critic, Wolf Von Eckardt, who was otherwise critical of many redevelopment projects, affirmed his sympathy with the Southwest project, claiming that it was succeeding in combining "suburban wholesomeness with urban stimulation."[64] However true this may have been, it would not be so for blacks, who found themselves pushed out of their homes.

Ninety-nine percent of the buildings in the Southwest were torn down. Of the 5,900 new units constructed, only 310 could be classified as moderate-income. Except for the Kober-Sternberg apartment complex, appropriately named for the pioneers in limited-dividend housing, no homes existed in

The Redevelopment Land
Agency provides relocation assistance to Southwest residents,
mid-1950s. Courtesy District of
Columbia Department of Housing and Community Devel-
opment.

the new Southwest for low-income families. More than a third of the population displaced found alternative homes in public housing, much of it
just outside the redevelopment area. Another 2,000 families moved into
private rental units, and only 391 purchased private homes, all in other
parts of the city.[65]

As an aggressive backer of the redevelopment process, the *Washington
Post* wrote enthusiastically in 1955 that the city relocation program "has
already meant as much 'renewal' in the lives of many of the displaced families as the physical rebuilding itself will mean to their old neighborhood."[66]
A subsequent independent study of some five hundred people relocated,
entitled *Where Are They Now?* provided one measure of confirmation for
this rosy picture, reporting that the overwhelming majority of those inter-

viewed lived in better physical conditions: "If one measures the impact of relocation solely in terms of physical rehabilitation the urban renewal program is a huge success." Socially, however, those displaced expressed high levels of alienation and regret over the loss of their old neighborhood setting. Only 14 percent reported that they now felt safe out alone after dark, and an extraordinary 25 percent reported that in the five years since their relocation they had not made a single new friend in their new neighborhood. "New Southwest may yet develop into the 'Good City,' but its birth has been at a cost," the report concluded. "It has risen over the ashes of what was a community of well-established, though poor, inhabitants."[67] Meanwhile, the large number of displaced Southwest residents began to flood into other black areas, ultimately spilling over into predominantly white neighborhoods, such as Anacostia, just across the river from the Southwest.[68]

Much the same kind of social turmoil followed from the way in which highway plans threatened black neighborhoods. Stressing the interconnection between highways and redevelopment, the RLA's 1959 annual report praised construction of the Southwest Freeway, commenting, "Fortunately the essential segment of the inner loop could be placed and integrated with it rather than passing through the area as an unrelated and uncongenial element."[69] Had plans for the Inner Loop been completed, however, it would have required the demolition of sixty-five thousand building units, one-fourth of the city's total,[70] much of it in areas where blacks had finally managed to escape confinement to the central city. According to estimates by the Mass Transportation Survey, peak traffic on an auto-dominant system as originally envisioned would have required thirty-lane interchanges where some northern freeways intersected the eight-lane Inner Loop, as well as the creation of eighty-five thousand new parking spaces downtown, covering one hundred acres of land.[71] By 1965 the *Post*'s Wolf Von Eckardt could write that if the current highway program were fully instituted, it would give the Washington metropolitan area twice the freeway mileage per square mile as well as per inhabitant as Los Angeles.[72]

Formidable opposition, much of it from members of Congress whose own homes were threatened, managed to kill the proposed Wisconsin Avenue Interstate in affluent Northwest Washington, but black residents on the other side of Rock Creek Park were faced with two Interstate connector routes, the North Central and the East Leg of the Inner Loop, which according to the Mass Transportation Survey would have displaced thirty-three thousand residents. Faced with inadequate housing inside the District and virtually complete housing discrimination in the suburbs, blacks had no alternative but to protest.[73] Initially opposed by government officials and the press, including the *Post*, which pointed out in a 1957 editorial that redevelopment would be strapped for funds without assistance made possible under the 1956 highway act,[74] blacks ultimately found white allies

Redevelopment and Dissent

who had also come to question the primary emphasis on highways for regional transportation.

The battle between highway and rapid transit interests flared in 1961 when President Kennedy's choice to administer the new National Capital Transportation Agency (NCTA), Darwin Stolzenbach, publicly questioned how "balanced" the Mass Transportation Survey's recommendations were for $1.8 billion in new highways and only $525 million for a subway.[75] Stolzenbach's pro-transit sympathies and Kennedy's decision to review highway plans for the District goaded highway supporters into action. Expressing "shock and disappointment" at Kennedy's action through its trade journal, the National Highway User Conference warned its constituents that "the campaign to supplant freeways with subways in Washington is the opening gun to what could lead to a national movement to slow down or curtail the highway program."[76] As rumors circulated that Stolzenbach's report would recommend the elimination of several freeways and the Three Sisters Bridge, highway supporters received encouragement from New York's Robert Moses, who offered a scathing critique in a Washington speech of "sideline kibitzers and creatures who never build anything." And as if to confirm his continued faith in a redevelopment plan tied to highways, *Washington Post* publisher Philip Graham urged a Board of Trade audience to heed Moses and "ignore the babel of strident voices that counsel delay and negativism."[77]

The 1962 NCTA report to Congress did reflect Stolzenbach's bias by proposing to reduce the number of projected miles of new highways in the District to eighty-four and to increase the rail system to eighty-three miles. By retaining the North Central Freeway and the East Leg of the Inner Loop in the recommended plan, the Stolzenbach report left open the possibility for racial conflict, while at the same time providing an open challenge to highway builders and users' organizations. But as the debate grew more intense during the 1960s, it was the National Capital Planning Commission that found itself increasingly under pressure from highway proponents as its leadership passed from Bartholomew to Elizabeth Rowe, who questioned the tenets of housing and highway redevelopment as they had been presented in the 1950s.

In 1965 the commission included in its comprehensive plan the full range of highway projects advanced by District Engineer Commissioner Charles Duke. But following an independent report, requested by President Lyndon Johnson and issued by the Arthur D. Little Company in March 1966 describing the D.C. Highway Department's plans as unjustified, the commission voted 8-3 to eliminate from its proposed 1985 comprehensive plan the North Central and East Leg freeways, along with the Three Sisters Bridge.[78] Goaded into action once again, highway proponents countered with an extensive pro-highway report, drafted by Lloyd Rivard of the Automotive Safety Foundation and released through the pro-development Federal City Council. Their position received strong support from the *Star* and even from the *Post*, which welcomed the report's recognition of the displacement problem, which the paper was stressing had to be solved as the price of further highway development.[79]

In calling for a virtual freeze on new highway construction, the Little report stressed the need to minimize the potential ill effects of highways on the aesthetic and social character of the city. To the latter issue, Duke responded with a proposal, widely circulated but never implemented, to form a semipublic housing corporation with responsibility for building new low-income housing along highway rights-of-way for those displaced in the area.[80] On the issue of aesthetics, he worked out an agreement with National Park Service director George Hartzog, publicized in mid-May, to minimize the impact of freeways on parks by running selected portions underground.[81] With Hartzog as an ex-officio member of the NCPC thus ready to shift his vote, NCTA administrator Walter J. McCarter was brought into line by threats from Congressman William Natcher of Kentucky, chairman of the House District Appropriations Subcommittee, that funding for the subway would be withheld if the District highway program failed to go forward.[82]

The social and racial implications of such moves could not have been clearer. Even as *Star* editorials endorsed the Hartzog agreement and expressed sympathy with Congressman Natcher's frustration over delays in freeways, a column on an inside page headed "The Bitter Taste of Freeways" chronicled the angry reaction of the black Federation of Civic Associations. Among those blacks who took up the highway issue was Marion Barry, local coordinator of the Student Non-Violent Coordinating Committee, who said he was shocked that a "racist Congressman from Kentucky would try to blackmail the city in this way." When the District Commissioners failed to attend a 1966 highway hearing, Barry likened them to slave masters, charging that "the white and black slaves are going to revolt."[83] While a *Post* editorial described the pact as "a reasonable and enlightened program of new construction that will greatly strengthen the city's ties to the surrounding suburbs at a minimal cost in disruption," a *Post* column by Wolf Von Eckardt ran under the headline "Highway Agreement Ignores Social Impact: Enhances City's Beauty at Expense of Displaced Families."[84]

As chair of the NCPC, Elizabeth Rowe wanted to stand by the commission's earlier vote to delete the controversial transportation projects. But at the commission's September 15 meeting, by vote of all six ex-officio members over the opposition of the four appointed members, the commission restored the freeways and the Three Sisters Bridge to the 1985 comprehensive plan. The best Rowe could salvage from the meeting was a commitment from the full commission to hold hearings on the proposed transportation changes.[85] As if to affirm that Congress would have its way regardless of any opposition that surfaced, Congressman Natcher made good his threat on the eve of the hearings by denying the city funds for subways until

Highway protest outside the District Building, 1967. Copyright *Washington Post;* reprinted by permission of the D.C. Public Library.

1967

the highway proposals were fully secured. This in turn prompted militant responses from black organizations in particular, who denounced Natcher's move as racist and directly counter to democratic principles. Despite angry and sizable protests at the hearings, the commission again confirmed its support by a vote of six to four for the controversial plans.[86]

The battle did not stop there, however, as the Federation of Civic Associations joined forces with other District citizens' groups to file suit, claiming that the NCPC and the commissioners had acted illegally in authorizing the new freeways without sufficient public hearings. On February 9, 1968, the U.S. Court of Appeals sustained the objection and issued an injunction halting any further action whatsoever on the contested freeways. Acting in retaliation, Congress attempted to intervene again, as Congressman John

Kluczynski of Illinois introduced an amendment to the Federal Highway Act of 1968 compelling the District of Columbia to carry out the Highway Department's freeway plan.

In public hearings during the early days of April, one Washington organization after another bitterly protested the bill. Pointing to the provision that directed the secretary of transportation to proceed with the highways "notwithstanding any other provision of law, or any court decision or administration action," witnesses castigated the bill's supporters for encouraging cynicism about law. Asking why highway proponents failed to exercise the normal options of appealing the Court of Appeals ruling to the Supreme Court or proceeding with the requisite public hearings on the comprehensive plan, representatives of the Black United Front and various civic groups repeatedly charged the bill's supporters with sowing the seeds of racism and possible disorder.[87] In fact, even before the subcommittee could hear the last friendly witnesses for the bill, Martin Luther King Jr. lay dead, and the city of Washington was in flames. By the time peace had been restored, seventy-six hundred people had been arrested. More than twelve hundred buildings had burned, with property damage at $24.7 million, more than any riot except for those in Watts in 1965 and Detroit in 1967.[88]

Redevelopment and Dissent

Renewal, Reconstruction, and Retrenchment

Our Society will never be great until its cities are great and today, as we face the future, the frontier of imagination and innovation is inside these cities. . . . Washington as the nation's capital is a unique city with its Federal buildings and monuments, long avenues, beautiful vistas, and government activities. But this is almost a facade for another Washington. . . . All the problems of the urban condition are present. . . . One Washington cannot be separated from the other.

Annual Report of the Government of the District of Columbia, Fiscal Year 1965

During the mid-1960s national urban policy underwent a dramatic turning point, as under a proclaimed War on Poverty the federal government directed funds to neighborhood-based organizations with the intent of enabling local residents to improve their own lives. Spurred by the growing momentum of the civil rights movement, the nation promised a second era of reconstruction. As the leading example of a predominantly black city plagued by social problems while denied fundamental political rights, Washington offered a prime target both to test the ideas behind the Great Society and, as the 1965 District annual report suggested, to overcome the distance between the city of federal monuments and its residential areas. Like the nation's other major cities in the 1960s, however, Washington experienced the same cycle of rising expectations and disappointment. No experience better captured the hopes as well as the dashed expectations of the black community than that of urban renewal.

By the early 1960s, even as the Southwest program received accolades in the business community and the press, urban renewal was generating criticism. Bitterness about the program was becoming familiar to those in the black community who had protested the wholesale displacement and relocation that usually accompanied redevelopment, but the most prominent voices came at first from conservatives historically antagonistic to federal grants to urban areas. Ironically, such early criticism revolved around the effort of Washington's business community to secure authority to utilize the tools of redevelopment in the historic downtown area, between Fifteenth Street, N.W., and the Capitol.

Under the aegis of the Federal City Council, a new organization, Downtown Progress, formed in 1960. It secured voluntary contributions to plan for the redevelopment of the center city and sought congressional authority to use urban renewal powers downtown. The House of Representatives authorized the request, which had become largely standard in American cities, in 1962, and the Senate followed by accepting the provisions a year later.[1] House conservatives, however, led by John Dowdy of Texas and assisted by the chairman of the House District Committee, John McMillan of South Carolina, chose to use the request as an excuse to investigate the entire renewal process in the District. They added to the Senate version of the bill a number of amendments, considered crippling by the Federal City Council, including requirements for competitive bidding, that priority be given to displaced businessmen in urban renewal projects, that the District Commissioners make a specific determination that relocation housing would be available for displaced families within their income range, and placing a limit on the number of urban renewal projects that could be undertaken at any one time. Dowdy's subcommittee managed as well to gain acceptance for a redefinition of a blighted area that was so stringent that it made authorization of funds for the downtown unlikely.[2]

Calling development officials "heartless," Dowdy castigated them for allegedly "saying it is all right to uproot 5,000 families, bulldoze their homes and leave them with no place to go." Making the connection between urban renewal and "black removal" overt in an article in *Reader's Digest*, he nonetheless revealed the clear object of his attack, federal expenditures, which he claimed had skyrocketed and were associated with charges of graft, favoritism, waste, and arbitrary and illegal use of power.[3]

Significantly, defense of the downtown renewal bill came from liberals. Locally the Washington Planning and Housing Association, whose role had been critical in advancing public housing in Washington, decried the redefinition of blight and argued against competitive bidding.[4] Nationally, Robert Weaver, John Kennedy's controversial choice to head the Housing and Home Finance Agency in 1961, joined the argument. Having faced conservative opposition to his appointment for his known desire to mediate the ill effects of renewal on black communities, Weaver, himself a black, wrote Congressman McMillan to protest the new restrictions imposed on Washington and published an essay in the *Washington Post*, which was immediately reprinted and circulated by the Federal City Council. Identifying the enemies of renewal as "groups and spokesmen who were against it in the first place and who are even more vehement in their attacks now that it is well on its way to accomplishing its mission," Weaver cited the rebuilt Southwest, where he had taken an apartment on arriving in Washington, among other examples of success. While acknowledging that renewal had its disruptive effects on poor blacks, he argued that the program provided adequate assistance under requirement of law and, most important, opportunities to live in improved housing in desirable locations. Because it was "available without racial or religious bars," he stated, it had become "a potent force in breaking down the ghetto."[5]

The Senate finally managed to bypass Dowdy through an amendment to the national housing bill of 1965 by simply authorizing the Redevelopment Land Agency to conduct renewal programs on the same basis as similar agencies in other cities. To this the *Post* commented that Dowdy had never shown much sympathy for either the shift of the city's wealth and commerce toward the suburbs or the poor living in grossly overcrowded conditions because of the housing shortage.[6] In promoting renewal for downtown, however, neither the *Post* nor its liberal allies took up the arguments for greater protection for local residents. Renewal of the downtown was seen as yet another part of the effort to compete with the suburbs by making the area, like the Southwest, physically attractive as well as convenient. Such views revealed the depth of consensus among the business establishment, liberal politicians, and the press,who formed what John Mollenkopf has called the "progrowth coalition," which had such a great influence on urban Democratic politics in the post–New Deal era,[7] an ethos that stressed the cosmopolitan goals of generating more jobs and an expanded tax base over what was considered parochial resistance to redevelopment by individual residents and property owners.

When the District Health and Welfare Council offered a sharply contrasting point of view in November 1966, that one of the city's natural communities had been destroyed, James Banks, director of the city's antipoverty agency, the United Planning Organization, and former director of relocation in the Southwest, warned against being too nostalgic about the past. The *Star* called the report "pure bunk" and claimed that there was no room for debate about the old Southwest: "It was filled with disease, squalor, crime and hopelessness. In getting rid of it, the people who lived there, no less than the city as a whole, gained immeasurably."[8] But even as the approach to redevelopment in the Southwest maintained some support, the direction of renewal was shifting, as a result both of growing antagonism from the black community and of changing views within the renewal establishment itself.

The first area designated for renewal after the Southwest was a decaying portion of the eastern side of the city's Northwest sector, which had seen its largely immigrant population of the early twentieth century give way to a predominantly poor and black community after World War II. When uncertainty over the location of the North Leg of the proposed Inner Loop Expressway interfered with planning for the whole area, city officials designated a smaller ninety-acre area for renewal. Identified by planners as a possible site to relocate those being displaced from other parts of the city, initial plans for the area, while stressing the provision of low- and moderate-income housing, nonetheless called for demolition of up to 80 percent of the existing buildings in the area and the relocation of 80 percent of the resident population.

For two years planning for the area proceeded without much citizen opposition. But as they faced the twin problems of relocation and poor maintenance in homes taken over by the Redevelopment Land Agency and slated for demolition, residents in the area historically known as Swampoo-dle but designated as Northwest #1 turned out en masse at a 1965 meeting with redevelopment officials. Largely through the efforts of the Washington Urban League and with some assistance in Congress, especially from Representative William Widnall of New Jersey, residents managed to alter the direction of the plan. They secured commitments for greater reliance on conservation and rehabilitation, staged redevelopment so as to minimize the impact of displacement, priority for existing residents in new homes, and employment of those residents in construction work in the neighborhood.[9]

With the encouragement of the Urban League's Neighborhood Advisory Council, established in the area to monitor renewal, the Redevelopment Land Agency hired residents to serve as subprofessional aides to interpret relocation programs to residents and to communicate local complaints to the agency. Even as the *Star* was defending the top-down approach exemplified in the Southwest, the *Post*, under the title, "The New Renewal," praised the Northwest #1 project, stating, "The massive, scattered relocation campaigns of the past, which provided homes but destroyed communities will not be repeated. . . . The city's housing shortage is very much worse now than in the middle 1950s, when Southwest was cleared. The city now needs renewal carried out with specific concern for the residents, and a commitment to build for the same kinds of families that it evicts."[10] By 1966 the Redevelopment Land Agency, under the influence of the Great Society's emphasis on citizen participation, had made the Neighborhood Advisory Council its de facto vehicle for channeling such activity. Explaining the agency's policy in 1967, executive director Thomas Appleby stated, "In Southwest there was little planning with the people. . . . It is the policy of the RLA to carry out the Northwest #1 project with the full participation of the residents of the area. While this isn't the easiest way to operate, it will continue to be our policy."[11]

In nearby Shaw, an inner-city neighborhood just north of the old downtown, the Rev. Walter E. Fauntroy took the principle of citizen involvement to a new level. He did so in particular opposition to the Southwest experience. A native of Shaw, who on receiving his divinity degree from Yale University returned to the area to serve as minister to the New Bethel Baptist Church, Fauntroy was an early critic of redevelopment. At a 1960 rally of the National Association for the Advancement of Colored People he

Renewal, Reconstruction, and Retrenchment

described redevelopment as a "new reconstruction" in which "unscrupulous investment interests are planning to make untold billions of dollars through the shrewd manipulation of race prejudice." In a singular reinterpretation of block-busting tactics, Fauntroy used the example of the Southwest to demonstrate his belief that white businesses had used the powers of eminent domain to drive poor blacks from valuable in-town land into "politically ineffective Harlems" at the city's periphery. Calling in congressional testimony the following year for "full and effective" citizens' participation, "adequate and humane solutions" in relocation and rehousing families displaced by redevelopment, and more positive emphasis on neighborhood rehabilitation,[12] Fauntroy gained a chance to test his theories as he worked to locate an alternative site for his church. Discovering that prices had been pushed up artificially by absentee owners, he concluded that the only way local residents could benefit from redevelopment was to take control of the renewal process themselves.

As early as 1950, the National Capital Park and Planning Commission had recommended in a draft of its comprehensive plan the redevelopment of some parts of Shaw for moderate- and even high-income residents. That proposal drew the criticism of the National Capital Housing Authority's John Ihlder, who commented, "Theoretically that is good, provided that adequate and convenient locations are provided for the low income families. They are an integral and important part of the population and can't be disregarded. The great part should be rehoused in the areas where they are now living."[13]

More than a decade later, fired by the immediate experience in the Southwest, Fauntroy sought to give such concerns positive meaning within his own community through the creation of a coalition of 150 community organizations, churches, and a variety of civic groups, into the Model Inner City Community Development Organization (MICCO). In announcing the group's plans, he commented, "You will notice that I have very carefully avoided use of the term 'urban renewal' in referring to this project. This is not without good reason. This community's tragic experience with an urban renewal effort in Southwest which did not provide housing for the people displaced on the land renewed, and which did not provide adequate and humane relocation services, remains painfully etched in the memory of many residents of the area."[14] As Shaw's own planner, Reginald Griffith, put it in the MICCO newspaper, *Shaw Power*, "We have taken urban renewal, a tool often used to destroy black neighborhoods, and fashioned it into an instrument by which the people can preserve and upgrade their own community. We shall not be another Southwest."[15] The Shaw theme song made such pronouncements popular wisdom in the neighborhood by declaring, in part,

> Old Southwest, it lost its fight
> Old Southwest, did the thing wrong

Shaw will work as one big team
Tenants, unions, workers, all
We'll UNITE our Shaw to plan.[16]

The MICCO articles of incorporation filed in 1966 stressed the desire for residents to take charge of the physical as well as human renewal of the area:

This is our area. We not only live, work or serve in it, but we also pray and play within these boundaries. Often we have despaired and sometimes we die, too young and violently. . . . We are not wholly without assets. We have ourselves and high hopes. We have leadership, to give and to take. . . . This corporation is formed so that we can work effectively with our government in a partnership that will develop our area and our people into the kind of community and citizens that we and the City deserve. . . . All of the purposes and objectives of this corporation combine to enable it to assist the City and the nation in a bold frontal attack on our urban ghetto.[17]

No less a figure than Martin Luther King Jr., with whom Fauntroy had been closely allied through the Southern Christian Leadership Conference, helped launch the redevelopment effort by addressing a boisterous rally at Cardozo High School.[18]

Like the revised plan for Northwest #1, the Shaw project emphasized staged redevelopment through an emphasis on rehabilitation and a minimum of displacement. Acting with a black business organization, Uptown Progress, which also formed in reaction to the displacement generated in the Southwest,[19] MICCO gained the role not just as a vehicle for citizen participation but as the virtual agency for redevelopment. Having publicly assured residents that Shaw would not be another Southwest, the Redevelopment Land Agency granted $200,000 to the two organizations in February 1967 to prepare the application for redevelopment of the area for submission to the U.S. Department of Housing and Urban Development. A press release issued by the agency described the decision as providing for "establishing a method for the intimate involvement of neighborhood organizations, businesses and residents in the process of planning and for establishing new ways in which residents of the area who have never before participated in the making of decisions and the establishment of programs to become a part of that process [can do so]. . . . Further, a program of social and economic planning . . . is designed to parallel the physical development process and to provide for these needs."[20] In the following year, MICCO in particular assumed increasing control over the redevelopment process, as Fauntroy had originally hoped.

Shaw's leaders benefited from the growing notoriety that the Southwest approach to redevelopment was gaining, even beyond the black community. For example, the white Capitol Hill Citizens' Association proposed in 1966 that the RLA report to a watchdog committee of Congress every two

MICCO president Walter Fauntroy, speaking at Shaw Junior High School on May 8, 1969, unveils plans for the redevelopment of the surrounding neighborhood. Copyright *Washington Post;* reprinted by permission of the D.C. Public Library.

months on displacement in Shaw to "avoid the repetition of the Southwest catastrophe." Both the *Star* and the *Post,* in endorsing the Shaw approach, compared it favorably with Southwest, citing Fauntroy's comment before the National Capital Planning Commission, "People don't explode when they have legitimate reason to believe that help is coming."[21] In May the District Commissioners wrote the RLA that "based upon the prior experience in the Southwest area," the Shaw project "should provide maximum rehabilitation and minimum relocation of residents and businesses."[22]

The Shaw effort also benefited from the marked increase of liberalism which followed John Kennedy's assassination and Lyndon Johnson's succession to the presidency. Following Johnson's declaration of the War on Poverty, the creation of the Office of Economic Opportunity, and the Model

Cities programs, each with their requirements for citizen participation, the way opened for an organization like Fauntroy's to fill the role. When Phil A. Doyle served as executive director of the Redevelopment Land Agency, he disparaged citizen participation as late as April 1965, saying "you can't take a plebiscite about every official action or proposal." His successor, Thomas Appleby, who came from the highly regarded redevelopment program in New Haven, assumed a more open approach, assuring local residents that Show would not become another Southwest.[23]

To direct the Shaw effort from his agency, Appleby chose Frank Del Vecchio. A young Harvard-trained lawyer who worked with Boston Redevelopment Administrator Edward J. Logue, as director of the Charlestown, Massachusetts, urban renewal project, Del Vecchio had been identified with limited clearance and the right of residents to remain in their own neighborhoods.[24] To assist Del Vecchio, who was white, Appleby named two black ministers to the Shaw planning team, Arnor Davis, director of education at Fauntroy's New Bethel Baptist Church, and Douglas Moore, whose rise to head the militant Black United Front had been preceded by an active role in the Student Non-Violent Coordinating Committee. An outspoken critic of the planning process as it had unfolded earlier in Washington, Moore actively promoted the Shaw approach as an alternative means for blacks to seize control of their own destinies.[25]

Although the *Post* had described Fauntroy at the advent of the Shaw program as a "militant civil rights leader,"[26] he shared with increasing numbers of black leaders who chose to work within the establishment the problem of pressure from more militant constituents. John Duncan, for instance, the first black District Commissioner, appointed in 1963, was encouraged by the *Washington Afro-American* to take the position, only to come under increasing criticism from the paper, particularly from its outspoken columnist Chuck Stone. Criticizing "ceremonial colored leaders" who were incapable of energizing an entire community into a frontal assault on racial segregation, Stone singled out Duncan for not being aggressive enough. "Look around at our colored leadership in this community," Stone wrote. "Do they operate from a position of strength or do they pussyfoot from a posture of subservience?" "There isn't a colored person in this city who has not been aware of the explosive situation developing among the District's poor and deprived," he wrote early in 1967. "Welfare, crime, unemployment, housing, education, police brutality plague this community's colored citizenry, but where have our leaders been? Silent as the Nile River."[27]

Fauntroy faced similar pressures from several rival organizations formed soon after MICCO's inception, notably Community Rehabilitation Under Security and Trust (CRUST) and Shaw People's Urban Renewal Group (SPUR), both of which complained that the MICCO leadership, which included a number of directors who lived outside the Shaw area, was too middle class and out of touch with the community. As William Street, a recent architecture graduate of Howard University and director of one of MICCO's rivals put it, "MICCO can't speak for the people of Shaw when it works for the RLA. They can't get citizen participation by buying it."[28] Described by Reginald Griffith as organizations spawned by United Planning Organization neighborhood units "threatened if they couldn't control all the action in the area," CRUST and SPUR helped delay funding of MICCO until September 1967.[29] On another front John Immer, president of the whites-only Federation of Citizens' Associations, complained in the *Afro-American* about the 885 families expected to be displaced in Shaw. He charged that had the Board of Trade and not MICCO made the announcement it would have been picketed, but because blacks had assumed leadership, the negative consequences of the plan were accepted too easily.[30] Such criticism played on increased awareness of the housing crisis facing blacks and a growing skepticism that the white power structure would allow anything to be done about the problem, skepticism that was fueled by difficulties in attempting to designate excess federal land for public housing.

Housing advocates had two sites in mind, a 159-acre oasis in Northeast Washington, once the location of the National Training School for Boys but slated to be abandoned by the Justice Department, and the Bolling military airfield in the Anacostia section of Southeast Washington, which had been closed in 1962 because of conflicting air traffic at Washington National Airport. The Government Printing Office, seeking more space to lay out its vast plant, with the backing of the General Services Administration, claimed the Training School site for itself. When the National Capital Planning Commission voted to limit the printing office to 85 acres, it satisfied neither those who advocated using the entire site for the creation of a new town devoted to low- and moderate-income housing nor the Public Printer James L. Harrison, who rejected a request by the District Commissioners that he scale down the acreage he had requested.

When the planning commission voted to sustain its earlier decision, albeit by a split vote, pickets from both the Congress of Racial Equality and the newly formed Archbishop's Committee on Community Relations of the Catholic Archdiocese of Washington denounced the result.[31] The Ad Hoc Committee on the Housing Crisis, composed of twenty-seven community groups, demanded the entire site for housing, charging, "In a city devoid of vacant land necessary to satisfy the overwhelming need for inexpensive and decent housing, the National Capital Planning Commission cannot indulge the extravagant, expansionist whims of the public printer." Following stinging editorial criticism of the decision, the planning commission finally reversed its position in April 1966, but not without engendering a good deal of criticism and acrimony from social activists.[32]

At the Bolling airport site, congressional defiance of local wishes became even more extreme, when L. Mendell Rivers of South Carolina, chairman of the House Armed Services Committee, managed in 1966 to block plans to put eight thousand new housing units on the site by extending for five years exclusive military use of the land. Despite strong reactions against the decision, from the National Capital Planning Commission, the local press, and the city's Democratic party, which proclaimed that "the people of the District are fed up with being kicked around by unsympathetic and unfriendly Congressmen,"[33] Rivers refused to back down, forcing an unhappy Lyndon Johnson to sign the bill. While the president spoke vaguely about changing the situation in the next session of Congress, local activists, including Fauntroy, members of the NAACP, CORE, and SNCC, and white Episcopalian minister William Wendt, registered their anger by staging an overnight sit-in at the site.[34] The issue dragged on for several more years, as Rivers managed again to find other uses for the site, first for civilian aviation, then for a construction of a "little Pentagon," each time provoking the anger of Washington blacks and their white supporters.

Such points of contention appeared to be balanced somewhat in the year before the riots by a number of advances in black empowerment. In 1967, Lyndon Johnson, convinced that the city needed leadership closer to home, reorganized the District government, naming as mayor-commissioner the former head of the National Capital Housing Authority, Walter Washington, and creating an appointed city council to replace the District Commissioners.[35] Washington and a majority of the council members, which included Walter Fauntroy, were black. In addition, Johnson personally intervened in the controversy over the National Training School site to promote a new town to be known as Fort Lincoln, dedicated to housing up to fifteen thousand of the city's poor. Although the General Services Administration resisted giving up control over the land, Johnson insisted, establishing a cabinet-level task force at the same time to study the possibility of distributing federal sites in other cities. Locally, the project included from the start a strong commitment to racial and economic integration as well as community participation, goals that were boosted by the appointment of Boston's Edward Logue, considered a leader in the field in implementing citizen input to planning, as principal development consultant to the project.[36] A strong statement from RLA board chairman Neville Miller stressing the importance of citizen participation seemed to affirm that judgment. "It takes a lot longer to get urban renewal plans completed with citizens involved," Miller said, "because they have a hard time coming to a conclusion. But you have to do it that way now. Citizens demand it and if you don't let them participate, people will stretch out in front of bulldozers. Can you imagine that?"[37]

Nonetheless, testimony at congressional hearings in May 1968 on what had gone wrong in the city that resulted in the riots the previous month stressed over and over the sense that blacks still had not been sufficiently involved in the planning process. Among those promoting black militancy

Renewal, Reconstruction, and Retrenchment

was Marion Barry, then director of operations of Pride Incorporated, a self-help black enterprise organization formed in 1967. Anticipating the opening lines of the Kerner Commission report, written in the aftermath of the nationwide riots in 1968, he charged that the nation was divided into two cultures, one white, one black, and if the city was rebuilt the way it was for whites, it would be burned down again. Although more restrained, Howard University law professor Herbert Reid, later to become counsel to Barry as mayor, echoed the theme, testifying at congressional hearings:

> The recent disorders in Washington . . . have provided this community with an opportunity to rebuild and reconstruct our city in the political and social forms which are necessary for the creation of a decent and democratic society. In so doing we cannot simply recreate the same kind of city which was burned down and which by all projections will be burned again. We must provide new mechanisms and approaches to the reconstruction of this city, and in a pattern where it will furnish hope and aspirations for all of the people who live in it.

In summarizing hearings before the city council, its chairman, John Hechinger, who was white, noted that while black separatist voices were the most startling of those heard, "the ideas behind these firebrand attitudes are no different from the views of the vast majority of witnesses. In one way or another, what came through was the universal demand for the right of self-determination for the neighborhoods that need rebuilding." The council agreed, he reported, that "the black community of Washington should have a central and powerful role in the planning and implementation of policies for rebuilding and recovery. Policies must be realistic in recognizing the need for economic and political power in the Negro community, particularly in housing and business development."[38]

More comments ensued in a city quickly polarizing over what was to be done. A Shaw organization that was a rival of MICCO's appeared shortly after the riots and described the hearings as a sham, declaring, "The present political, economic, and physical violence against Black people is exceedingly more severe and greater in scope than the actions which the Black community must commit in order to survive and achieve self-determination."[39] A community meeting in Cardozo called right after the riots erupted when one member of the audience interrupted discussion of plans to replace liquor stores with apartment houses, shouting, "We'll plan this city with gasoline."[40] Circulars from the newly formed Build Black Incorporated calling for white merchants to turn over to blacks existing business sites for modest fees urged its potential audience to "Stop shufflin' and beggin' whitey. Build Black."[41] The *Star*, on the other hand, called black demands for neighborhood control "so fallacious in concept and so unworkable in practice that they should be repudiated by Mayor Washington and the City Council at the outset."[42] Northern Virginia congressman Joel

180

Broyhill was even blunter, telling an audience of police and firefighters that looters ought to be shot, saying, "We are going to restore law and order to this land . . . not by passing more civil rights bills . . . not by giving in to the demands of hoodlums with more spending programs . . . but by giving the American people what they are demanding . . . full protection under the law."[43]

In efforts to resolve the crisis brought on by the riots, Mayor Washington established a special advisory council on rebuilding the damaged areas, which was broadly representative both of citywide business groups and of disaffected neighborhoods. He also lobbied effectively for federal assistance and encouraged citizen participation at every level of the rebuilding process. The effort culminated August 28, the one hundredth day after the riots, with

Renewal, Reconstruction, and Retrenchment

the mayor's announcement that the Ford Foundation had provided a $600,000 grant to launch a Community Reconstruction and Development Corporation to "provide the initial thrust of our rebuilding efforts."[44]

Public effort was backed by an outpouring of sympathy and tangible involvement by private organizations, not the least of which were area religious institutions. Only days after the riots, the Catholic Archdiocese of Washington announced a halt to all new church and school construction in the area, with the savings redirected to deal with the chronic causes of poverty in the city. In addition, the church announced that it would engage black contractors and Build Black apprentices in acquiring and rehabilitating a number of low-rent houses in Northwest Washington.[45] Both St. Stephen and the Incarnation Episcopal Church at Sixteenth and Newton streets, N.W., under the leadership of its white pastor, William Wendt, and All Souls Unitarian Church, nearby at Sixteenth and Harvard streets, under the influence of its first black minister, David Eaton, responded to demands from the Black United Front to dedicate portions of its endowment to community needs. St. Stephen ultimately built seventy-two units of new moderate-income housing on its property for the benefit of the Cardozo neighborhood, while All Souls announced that it would invest $250,000— two-thirds of its endowment—to finance economic development projects on upper Fourteenth Street. The Jewish Community Council, speaking for many of the white businessmen whose buildings had been burned, while wary of black militants, accepted the principle of neighborhood participation in rebuilding the riot corridors.[46]

Even President Richard Nixon, who had conjured up the image of Washington as the "crime capital of the world" in his 1968 election campaign, felt the need to affirm some commitment to the spirit of the Great Society, when shortly after his inauguration he paid a surprise visit to city ceremonies marking the start of urban renewal in Shaw. Subsequently he reported that the Department of Housing and Urban Development had approved a $29.7 million urban planning grant for the area. In addition, HUD announced a $1 million interim grant to improve living conditions for residents in the riot corridors.[47] Taking advantage of the neighborhood planning provision of the National Housing Act of 1968, which removed cumbersome requirements that a full long-term plan be approved in advance of intermediate steps for renewal, neighborhood organizations in Washington helped generate one-year action plans to gain the federal funds needed to start the rebuilding process.

Events following the riots thus appeared to confirm the new direction set in the late 1960s for urban renewal through joint partnerships between planners and citizen organizations. A radio and television editorial aired in August 1968 praised the direction in which black power was heading in the city, stating:

Inside Washington's decaying vitals, where anger and frustration exploded in an ugly week last spring, there is stirring a new kind of energy—constructive, orderly, and potent. It is one manifestation of the "black power" about which we have heard a great deal; and in this case, at least, the ferment needs to be coaxed along. The enthusiasm surrounds efforts to change the course of urban renewal programs. . . . What's different and important about Shaw is that the people who live there—black people primarily—are being consulted and listened to on a scale never attempted or even considered before. . . . The black leadership is saying that bulldozers and bureaucrats must no longer treat people like so many faceless numbers in the big game of renewal. The remaking of Shaw will be a tremendously complex business, of course—one which cannot rely overly on amateurs for its execution. But ordinary citizens have some good notions on where and how they want to live; and to the extent that the health of the larger community is not compromised, these concepts can be incorporated into the charts and programs of the planners.[48]

At Fort Lincoln, negotiations to choose a developer continued, with active community input in the decision, even though the new Nixon administration reportedly had reservations about the new town concept. In January 1969 the National Capital Planning Commission approved the plan for Shaw developed within the neighborhood. It stressed staged redevelopment through rehabilitation, with the stated goal to "eliminate physical blight and deterioration . . . and by so doing, establish an environment in which, by maximum use of government programs, the socio-economic problems confronting the residents of the Project Area will be ameliorated and increased opportunities provided for employment and education, health and social services."[49] Projects in the Cardozo area and the Northwest #1 redevelopment area as well as Shaw received praise in the press. A year after he became the first black executive director of the Redevelopment Land Agency, Melvin Mister could proclaim that Washington's black population had come to see urban renewal differently: "People still say they don't want another Southwest. There's still some suspicion. But they're willing to look at it as a tool that can be used in different ways."[50]

★ ★ ★

There were already signs, however, that support for the keystone of the community-based approach to planning, citizen participation, was wearing thin, even among its strongest proponents. As early as September 1968, the *Washington Post*, referring to compromises in the planning commission's authority during the freeway controversy, warned against relinquishing too much authority to citizen organizations, charging that a city that had done its homework "would never find it necessary to turn over the basic function of planning to an outside body." Under the headline "Searing

Renewal, Reconstruction, and Retrenchment

Symbols of Inaction," the paper warned only months later against giving citizen groups a veto over reconstruction projects.[51]

Such reservations stemmed from increased jockeying among competing citizen organizations, spurred in part by promises of increased federal aid to the city. The problem emerged early in the Nixon administration when the president's staff, impressed with Fauntroy's leadership role in Shaw, encouraged him to draw up plans for reconstructing the riot corridors, not just in Shaw but also in the other two areas hardest hit, Fourteenth Street, N.W., and H Street, N.E. Fauntroy had made considerable progress in creating plans for the areas when opposition from other neighborhood organizations, and possibly from Walter Washington, blocked the signing of a contract giving Fauntroy's new planning organization, the Inner City Planning Association, authority to develop the initial plans.[52] Even more telling was the seemingly endless contest between two rival citizen organizations over which would serve as the primary agent for reviewing plans for the Fort Lincoln new town. Out of frustration stemming from trying to work with these groups, Mayor Washington finally created in 1970 an entirely new, citywide organization to serve as a forum for citizen input at Fort Lincoln, a move that evoked praise in the press but failed to resolve the problem.[53]

Not just citizen participation but the concept of pouring money into the inner city came under attack as well. In November 1970 *Post* architectural critic Wolf Von Eckardt suggested that the RLA, in attempting to redress the problems in the Southwest, had gone to yet another extreme in Shaw. Feeling "badly about *their* part in the so-called Southwest Negro removal," Von Eckardt wrote, HUD had overemphasized putting money into the ghetto, when a better solution lay in developing sites, like Fort Lincoln, on the city's perimeter.[54] When both the National Capital Planning Commission and outside consultants questioned favoring decentralized, neighborhood-based planning over the traditional method of centralized city control, Fauntroy responded angrily, "Any suggestions of return to the old style urban renewal with its massive displacement of the black and poor is totally unacceptable."[55]

In the following year, however, Fauntroy and his approach to redevelopment came under increasing pressure. Shortly after the RLA selected a consortium led by the Westinghouse Corporation as the sole developer for Fort Lincoln, the company announced a shift in its housing emphasis from lower- to higher-income occupancy, including in its target some white residents of Prince George's County with incomes in the $11,000 range. Citing the goal of providing 75 percent home ownership, the official plan for the area promised a fresh choice in a community that blended "the urbanity and diversity of city life with the suburban ideal of better living conditions and openness." Noting that while poor families would naturally be attracted to better living conditions at Fort Lincoln, the company prospectus claimed, "middle-income families have a wider choice of housing. Therefore, it is primarily to these people that our marketing effort must be directed if our objective of social and economic inclusiveness is to be met. These are the people who must be convinced that Fort Lincoln will be an exciting place to live."[56] Martha Derthick's 1972 book on new towns concluded that Fort Lincoln was too ambitious. Its supporters "sought innovation in every aspect of planning, design and development. In the end, this freight of social significance proved too much for Fort Lincoln to bear."[57] Planners also suggested encouraging higher land uses in both Shaw and Northwest #1 than had originally been anticipated. Indeed, it was in Shaw that citizen control over redevelopment came under the sharpest attack.

185

As the Shaw project area prepared to enter its third year under the neighborhood development program, representatives of both MICCO and the RLA became increasingly anxious to speed up housing starts. At a March 1971 board meeting of MICCO, Fauntroy coined a phrase that would be repeated throughout the year, that it was time to move beyond the planning state to "get the dirt flying." To advance that goal, Fauntroy authorized a staff reorganization, in anticipation of hiring a new executive director to assume daily direction of the organization following his election as the District's first nonvoting delegate to Congress in nearly a century.[58] Although remaining concerned about displacement, MICCO found itself pressing the RLA to hasten the relocation of a dozen or so families, whose continued presence on a potential site for new housing was holding up bidding.[59] For its part, the RLA tended to blame delays largely on the intricate process of citizen review. In addition, it expressed concern about MICCO's control over its own budgetary and administrative processes, a matter that James Woolfork, the RLA's Shaw project director, took up in July with William Stewart, MICCO's new executive director, who had joined the organization after directing the Model Cities program in Minneapolis.[60]

Such administrative concerns were not terribly unusual on the RLA's part. More significant was its decision in the summer of 1971 to shift its approach to development in Shaw from negotiated bidding, which community activists considered essential in the effort to recruit nonprofit housing sponsors from within the area, to competitive bidding, which the RLA hoped would accelerate construction by attracting more substantial national investors. To make such opportunities attractive, the RLA introduced in June the concept of packaged development, which involved combining several different lots in order to gain efficiencies of scale and thus reduce costs. The agency proposed offering "Package A," located above M Street between Fifth and Seventh streets, N.W., for competitive bids, putting in jeopardy MICCO's effort to recruit Boston's Development Corporation of America to develop the area as a joint venture with two local churches.

Citing DCA's commitment to make the remaining equities in the projects available to its nonprofit partners after twenty years, MICCO argued that such community control might be lost in competitive bidding.[61]

To make matters worse, MICCO, which since its inception had maintained a proprietary interest in having each project cleared in advance through its board, found itself overruled on a second site, on Seventh Street, where the RLA had accepted the offer made by a church group, which had been pending for some fourteen months, to build low-rise garden apartments. A late proposal from MICCO to develop the site for high-rise apartments gained support from the Model Cities Agency and a *Washington Star* columnist, who accepted MICCO's contention that a high-density project was more appropriate at a future subway stop.[62] The press paid more attention, however, to charges generated by MICCO's rival for the spot that Fauntroy's continued role as both president of MICCO and a member of Congress constituted a conflict of interest. Fauntroy denounced such charges, securing opinions from both the RLA and the Justice Department that no such conflict existed because he received no salary in his position as president of MICCO.[63] The issue continued to dog Fauntroy, however, after the *Post*'s Eugene Meyer reported in October that Fauntroy planned to resign as president of MICCO, a claim Fauntroy denounced in the strongest terms both publicly and in a circular to MICCO's board. Pointing to what he described as a conspiracy between a midlevel RLA staff member and the *Post*'s Meyer, Fauntroy charged, "Somebody has decided that the citizen participation process was not going to be around anymore and therefore he had to find reasons for these arguments."[64]

Despite such controversies, Fauntroy launched the new year on an upbeat note, pointing to the groundbreaking of several new housing projects as a sign that finally "the dirt is flying" and stating his intent not only to retain his role as MICCO's president but to "preserve citizen participation throughout the planning and building process in Shaw."[65] Yet in spite of having cleared Fauntroy on conflict-of-interest charges, the RLA contended that its continued assistance of MICCO hinged on Fauntroy's resignation. In a February 4 memorandum, RLA executive director Melvin Mister told Fauntroy, "It is not appropriate for an agency which is part of the executive branch of the government to negotiate a contract with an organization headed by a member of Congress. . . . The Agency will not approve a contract with MICCO until Reverend Fauntroy no longer holds an official position in the organization. This issue should not divert us from the important task of renewing Shaw."[66] On February 18 Fauntroy resigned, explaining to MICCO's board of directors, "If the creative process we have fashioned in Shaw is to be undermined and discarded, I cannot allow my presence on the Board to be used as the reason for not funding MICCO."[67]

The RLA extended MICCO's contract ten days later— noting, however, that the agency would exercise more control over administrative matters.[68] Given something of a reprieve, MICCO attempted to continue its role as the leading force in shaping the redevelopment of Shaw, but within the year the RLA finally terminated its contracts both with MICCO and Uptown Progress. Despite a number of protests, including a charge by MICCO's Noah Moore, who invoked the specter of the Southwest once again—that the decision was intended to remove MICCO as the best protection against the exploitation of Shaw by big-moneyed interests—the RLA stood its ground.[69] Having seen its effort to work within the establishment fall short, MICCO officials revived the kind of shrillness about the RLA that had characterized the period before MICCO's inception. Speaking as Fauntroy's successor as MICCO president, Charles Braxton told a District City Council hearing in February 1973:

> Notwithstanding the reasons furnished by the Agency for whatever plan it is following, the results are highly unsatisfactory to the residents. Whether or not the community is too impatient for the effecting of the grand design can be considered academic. These residents are confronted with an Agency that induced decline in the value as well as the environment of the area. These people are not particularly persuaded that the Agency has planned or planned well. If their reaction to plans and proposals are characterized as hostile, it is because of their frustration at the artful maneuvering they see under the guise of urban renewal.[70]

In effect, the rationale for RLA's decision had been laid even before Fauntroy was pressured to resign. Using an outside consulting agency, which he called on frequently to back his ideas, Melvin Mister released a report in September 1971 which criticized both citizen participation and the attendant practice of negotiated contracts. Pointing to Washington's lag behind other cities, notably Boston and Philadelphia, in developing extensive rehabilitation programs, the report favored use of limited dividend corporations, made attractive to parent corporations under the Tax Reform Act of 1969, for promising to "provide a more efficient production mechanism through provision of adequate working capital and infusion of professional developers' expertise." The report claimed that the Neighborhood Development Program, by making improvements in small increments, "makes it difficult to have the kind of impact on neighborhood character that will be necessary to make the area attractive again to middle- and upper-income residents during the early years of redevelopment." While the document reaffirmed the importance of minority participation, the Redevelopment Land Agency, it stressed, "has a responsibility to see that these provisions do not substantially impair the likelihood of successful projects within the resources available to the development teams."[71] The report bolstered Mister's desire not to accede to the plan favored by MICCO for high-rise apartments on Seventh Street and to award another contract to outside California investors over the bid of the locally based Neighborhood Development Corporation.[72]

Mister's conclusions received backing a year later from the report of a blue-ribbon citizen's commission advisory to the District City Council, which had been initiated by Sterling Tucker. Chaired by Washington Planning and Housing Association President Reuben Clark, a strong advocate of negotiated development contracts in the early 1960s, the report fully endorsed competitive bidding in Shaw as well as in other renewal areas. Blaming the lack of results in construction on conflicting authority, the panel urged a reconsideration of such systems of "checks and balances" as citizen organizations in light of the critical need to minimize delays and provide developers with a predictable schedule for development. Urging that development be returned to developers, the report, while favoring more technical assistance for neighborhood organizations, asserted strongly that they should not be given the authority for planning. It called the plan for Shaw totally inadequate, pointing out that only two hundred new housing units had been constructed and occupied in the area. While it reported another six hundred units under construction, it stressed that only fifty-five of four thousand planned rehabilitations had been completed. The report praised the RLA's effort to take back some authority from MICCO in the interest of reversing what it called a pattern of "purposelessness and drift."[73]

In a period that marked the unprecedented role of community direction of the redevelopment process, the report indicated a full swing back to vesting that authority in duly constituted officials, a theme that RLA board chairman John Gunther stressed in writing Fauntroy to explain why his agency, not MICCO, should have the final say in who should develop "Package A":

> We should not permit any private developer or would-be-developer to plan and pursue the development of parcels in a manner contrary to the decision of duly constituted public bodies made after extensive public hearings. No one developer has vested rights to exclusive or extensive land acquisition in any renewal area. To throw out the pending proposal, which is consistent with the use designation, at this late date in favor of a proposal contrary to the Plan and designated use would, in my view, indicate a disposition by the public agencies in this city to make public authority available to private parties.[74]

Although the citizens' committee report on urban renewal foreshadowed a new role for citizen participation constituted by the Home Rule Act of 1973 in the form of neighborhood advisory commissions, the era when neighborhood-based black organizations could direct and not just influence the reconstruction of their own communities had clearly passed.[75] As the locus of power shifted to large organizations and to elected city officials, the partnership between local and federal agencies dissolved, leaving as yet unmet the nation's best chance to use Congress's power of exclusive jurisdiction over the District to establish a model city for the rest of the country. Now it would be up to a new generation of local leadership to try to resolve the city's most persistent social problems.

Renewal, Reconstruction, and Retrenchment

The Limits of
Social Protest Politics

We want to free D.C. from our enemies, the people who make it impossible for us
to do anything about lousy schools, brutal cops, slumlords, welfare investigators
who go on midnight raids, employers who discriminate in hiring and a host of
other ills that run rampant through our city.

Marion Barry, speaking for the Free D.C.
Movement, 1966

The restoration of an elected city government in 1974 and the subsequent election of civil rights and home rule activist Marion Barry as mayor
brought promise that at last issues of social justice would gain the attention
they demanded in Washington. Barry established an ambitious social welfare program for the city and recruited talent from around the country to
put it in place. Continued federal meddling made Barry's task particularly
difficult, but such interference served at least to help maintain his political
support. By appealing both to local antagonism against the government
and to racial solidarity, he continued to dominate Washington politics,
even when he strayed far from his socially progressive agenda. Rather than
effecting social change or building local consensus, however, he left Washington even more bitterly divided by race and class than he found it.

Shortly after his election as nonvoting delegate to Congress, Walter
Fauntroy achieved one of his most important political victories. By directing funds and attention to an intense primary race in South Carolina in
1972, Fauntroy helped upset House District Committee chairman John L.
McMillan, thereby removing the single most entrenched opponent to home
rule for Washington. Even Republican president Richard Nixon endorsed
home rule for the city, and, with voter approval in 1973, Washington finally
gained back the right, denied since 1874, to elect its own local officials.
There were, however, several crippling limitations to local authority. Congress specifically prohibited one potentially important source of revenue to
the District, a commuter tax, while retaining control over the city's budget
and court system. Congress also retained the right to override District
legislation, and Washington remained without voting representation in

Congress. Home rule thus did not bring with it complete independence from federal oversight, but it gave local leadership its first opportunity in a century to take the initiative in setting its own policy agenda.

Although Fauntroy participated in shaping Washington's new era, the most important role fell to the executive officer of the new city government, the mayor. With the election of Walter Washington, the incumbent mayor-commissioner, to that position in 1974, the city entered a transitional period. As a career civil servant, who had served both on the National Capital Housing Authority and on the appointed city council when it was first named in 1967, Washington was well known to both federal and local organizations. His ability to navigate federal-city relations and his adeptness in dealing with the immediate crisis of the 1968 riots gained him considerable respect. Washington, however, found it difficult to turn the new city bureaucracy to long-term local needs. His appointments—many like him with federal credentials—were drawn largely from the city's comfortable black elite. Lacking the sense of urgency felt in the inner city, the Washington administration provoked criticism from neighborhood activists for failing to address a host of unmet social problems. In 1978 both city council chairman Sterling Tucker and at-large council member Marion Barry challenged Washington's reelection in the Democratic primary. In a particularly close race, Barry managed to win with just over a third of the vote. Endorsed by the *Washington Post*, Barry appeared to carry with him something of an establishment blessing. But his role as a civil rights activist, as a staunch home rule supporter, and as an advocate for reordering priorities to assist the inner-city poor promised a very different direction for the city.

The son of a Mississippi sharecropper, Barry was the first in his family to attend college, where he entered the civil rights movement through involvement in the campus chapter of the NAACP. "I took a chance on losing a scholarship or not receiving my master's degree," Barry said of his first sit-in at a segregated lunch counter while a graduate student in chemistry at Fisk University, in Nashville. "But to me, if I had received my scholarship and master's degree, and still was not a free man, I was not a man at all."[1] A founder of the Student Non-Violent Coordinating Committee and its first chairman, Barry moved to Washington to open a branch office in 1965 as part of SNCC's effort to extend its reach from the rural South to the nation's major cities.[2]

Barry's sharp mind and populist political style quickly established a visible place for him in Washington. In January 1966 he helped organize a highly successful one-day bus boycott involving 100,000 people in protesting a proposed five-cent fare hike, which he argued would burden the city's working poor. Attacking the primary issue facing the city, he challenged the Washington Board of Trade's opposition to home rule by organizing a "Free DC" movement, starting with a boycott of all businesses that refused

The Limits of Social Protest Politics

to display pro–home rule stickers. If Congress could not be forced to act on the city's behalf, Barry charged angrily, merchants could: "Southern white segregationists have gotten together with the moneylord merchants of this city to oppose our right to vote. . . . The merchants are in business because we support them with our money. If we withdraw our support, then they will no longer be around to oppose us."[3]

Barry's tactics sparked an angry response, as House District Committee chairman McMillan called hearings to examine whether the boycott had violated federal antiracketeering law by interfering with business through the threat of violence.[4] Although Barry backed off, he prompted black *Washington Post* columnist William Raspberry to describe him as "fast becoming the leading catalyst for change in Washington."[5] Indeed, criticism from the white establishment only further enhanced Barry's reputation in the black community, where his fight against highway programs threatening severe displacement kept him in the news.

In 1967 Barry left his SNCC position to deal with another pressing social issue by establishing Pride, Incorporated, a self-help organization designed to train and put to work unemployed black teenagers. When Congress finally authorized the city's first locally elected positions in the twentieth century, for school board, Barry built on an extended organizational network to win a seat as president in 1971. He subsequently gained election to an at-large seat on the first city council established under home rule.

Like Walter Fauntroy, who proved an early supporter, Barry reached beyond an earlier generation's emphasis on integration to embrace such community-based services as housing and land development. Openly impatient with traditional black leadership, with its emphasis on what political scientist James Q. Wilson has called the status ends associated with achieving integration in all phases of life, Barry stood apart from Washington and Tucker in the 1978 primary in his commitment to social welfare goals: tangible improvements in such areas as better schools, more low-income housing units, and an increase in black political power.[6] Barry carried his message to the poorest sections of the city. But in a race where his opponents had virtually locked up the support of the black middle class, Barry had to broaden his electoral base by appealing to white voters, a decision that proved crucial to his victory. While Barry carried only 27 percent of the black vote overall, as compared to 38 percent for Washington and 32.7 percent for Tucker, he outdistanced his rivals among whites with 53 percent of their support.[7]

Barry's victory thus sent a mixed message. Identified with the causes closest to the black power movement, he nonetheless had made himself acceptable to whites, a pattern he had already established while serving on the city council. When Mayor Washington proposed a business franchise tax in 1975 to help reduce the city's financial deficit, Barry responded to protests from his former antagonists at the Board of Trade by turning back

Marion Barry, the activist founder and director of Pride, Incorporated, with Mayor-Commissioner Walter Washington and Secretary of Labor Willard Wirtz in 1968, shortly after Wirtz engineered federal funding for Pride in an effort to blunt threats of civil disorder in the city. Copyright *Washington Post*; reprinted by permission of the D.C. Public Library.

the tax in favor of cuts in staff.[8] Such willingness to work with the establishment undoubtedly helped Barry secure the *Post*'s endorsement for mayor in 1978 and built his vote among white voters, but it also provoked criticism after his primary victory from those who feared Barry might compromise self-determination for the city's black majority. Lillian Wiggins put it most bluntly in a widely quoted article in the *Washington Afro-American*. Referring to Betty Ann Kane, a successful white candidate for an at-large seat on the city council, Wiggins warned against the implementation of a "master plan" intended by whites to "recapture the nation's capital." "Unless there are some changes in our voting patterns and egos," she warned, "four years from now we will be attending the inauguration of Washington's first white mayor." *Washington Post* columnist Milton Coleman reiterated the fear,

The Limits of Social Protest Politics

Walter Fauntroy endorses Marion Barry for election to the School Board, October 7, 1971. Copyright *Washington Post;* reprinted by permission of the D.C. Public Library.

noting that Barry's nomination in the Democratic primary "is seen as an ominous sign that black political power here, still in its infancy, is already on the wane."9

Such criticisms were not sufficient to dampen support for Barry's overwhelming election over his Republican opponent in November. Obviously sensitive to such charges, however, Barry made a point in his first term to reaffirm his ties to black Washington residents. Making the most of city patronage, Barry worked adroitly to transform the District from the sinecure it had once been for whites appointed by friends in Congress into an opportunity structure for local blacks. While aides subsequently regretted that he did not do more to prune the government of Walter Washington's appointments, he nonetheless moved to preempt both Washington and

Marion Barry and wife Effi greet well-wishers on January 2, 1979, on the way to Barry's first inauguration as mayor. In a fitting tribute to Barry's civil rights leadership, the oath of office was administered by Supreme Court Justice Thurgood Marshall, himself a leader of an earlier generation of rights activists. Copyright *Washington Post;* reprinted courtesy of the D.C. Public Library.

Tucker from challenging his authority by promoting some of their key allies to visible positions within the government. He set a goal to increase business with minority contractors from 10 to 35 percent and informed developers that they would have to include blacks in joint ventures if they wanted to build on city property.[10] To shore up his standing in the poorer neighborhoods, he worked with local clergy who had been cool to his election on such social concerns as housing and aid to the elderly. In a symbolic and highly publicized move, he shifted his residence from a racially mixed neighborhood on Capitol Hill to the politically strategic black middle-class Hillcrest section of Southeast Washington.[11]

At the same time, Barry addressed the issues that had dominated the concerns of whites during the 1978 election, promising an administration of

The Limits of Social Protest Politics

competence as well as compassion. Most immediately of concern were the city's bloated and largely unresponsive bureaucracy and a budget that had passed from the federal government to the city in 1974 with a substantial deficit. Required by the home rule charter to balance the budget and stunned by a federal cut in appropriations of $25 million four months into his administration, Barry immediately faced a fiscal crisis. To respond, he laid off more than four thousand of the city's sixty thousand employees, a cut of 6.5 percent, during the first two years of his term. To increase revenues, he pressed for greater efficiencies in tax collection, the introduction of tax-exempt bonds at an estimated savings of $211 million, and the attraction of new investment in the decaying sector of the old downtown east of Fifteenth Street.[12] Going beyond Walter Washington's ability to recruit local talent, Barry made a conscious effort to hire black managers from across the country whom he could showcase before the still-meddling Congress.

Despite achieving visible progress in the goal of making the city work more effectively, Barry remained vulnerable in the polls in the year before his reelection campaign. Cuts in the local workforce, while warmly embraced by the Washington Board of Trade, eroded his support among city employees, prompting him to pledge not to make any further cuts in a second term. Although he admitted that his style had changed as he was forced to work with the business and congressional establishments, he stressed his ongoing commitment to improving the economic well-being of the District's poorest residents. As he announced his candidacy in March 1982, he stressed his accomplishments in dealing with the social welfare concerns of crime, poor housing, and the creation of jobs.[13]

Barry's claims remained in dispute, and no less than three members of the city council announced their decisions to enter the Democratic primary for mayor, among them Betty Ann Kane, whose early interest in the race evoked more commentary that there was a plan among whites to reclaim political power in the District.[14] Kane's candidacy proved short-lived: failing to rise higher than third in the polls and to raise sufficient funds, she withdrew from the contest well before the primary. Race remained a factor in the campaign, however, even though all of Barry's remaining opponents were black. Finding himself trailing Patricia Roberts Harris, a former cabinet secretary of two departments under Jimmy Carter, Barry presented himself as the "blacker" of the two candidates. By attempting to taint Harris with her federal credentials and her association with Walter Washington's more affluent black supporters, Barry evoked protests from Harris's managers, who pointed to her working-class origins. Barry's strategy made sense, however, according to the *Washington Post*'s Juan Williams, who wrote, "In a town where a majority white Congress has dominated local black political life for decades, many blacks still blame Capitol Hill for the problems of the District government. Barry wants to attract all the racial sympathies that a black mayor can get to wipe away the memory of the problems that plagued his administration."[15]

In an effort to break Barry's hold on issues of social welfare, Harris released detailed position papers calling for improvements in programs related to housing, education, and crime. She could not, however, overcome Barry's superior organizational ability or his emotional appeal to the mass of Democratic voters. Barry trounced Harris in the primary, winning the majority of black votes in the middle- as well as lower-income areas. His appeal to white voters slipped badly, however, indicating his failure to hold them in his coalition.[16] His second term served to polarize the electorate even more sharply.

The extent of the challenge to his reelection prompted Barry to pursue a dual strategy in his second term. Looking to his solid base of support in lower-income wards, where appeals to race pride and symbolic gestures of striving for better social welfare had the greatest resonance, he continued to build grass-roots support, not the least among public housing tenants, who constituted some 10 percent of the city population. At the other end of the social spectrum he courted developers whose contributions were crucial to staving off yet another bruising primary. To the first set of constituents he promised more affordable housing by rehabilitating boarded-up public housing units. To the second he promised better management and greater opportunities for financial return by removing obstacles to investment.

Barry's most visible achievement came in promoting business in Washington. While in his first campaign for mayor he had supported the conversion of the Georgetown waterfront to a park, a strategy favored by preservationists, he subsequently encouraged the development of a large office and residential complex, Georgetown Harbour, on the site. He further challenged preservationists by strongly supporting a convention center downtown—feared as a threat to the existing Chinese-American community in the area—and development of a large office complex at the site of the city's oldest historic building, Rhodes Tavern.[17] He also promoted construction of the Techworld office building bridging Eighth Street, N.W., in the heart of the old downtown, over the opposition of preservationists who claimed the building would block a vista intended by the L'Enfant plan.[18] As a measure of Barry's success, the downtown underwent dramatic upgrading. By 1986 the city, which ranked sixteenth in the nation in population, ranked third in office space.[19]

Having drifted far from any concept of community control of valuable land, Barry justified his decisions to black constituents by arguing that development at least would create needed jobs. More central to his immediate needs, he managed to preempt possible primary opposition to his reelection by securing all the contributions he needed to stay in office. "Had an appointed mayor been as enamored with brick as the current

The Limits of Social Protest Politics

mayor," one critic charged, "Washington's activists would have yelled and screamed.... But because Barry is elected, and black, and comes from the civil rights movement, few seem to care that he is, at least when it come to development, indistinguishable from either the late Richard Daley of Chicago, or on an even grander scale, the late Nelson Rockefeller. He loves development."[20]

For his poorest constituents, however, Barry was less adept at delivering service. Despite the creation of forty thousand new jobs in the District between 1980 and 1986, one thousand fewer District residents were employed, as new positions routinely went to suburban commuters.[21] With employment opportunities restricted, those most in need continued to struggle to find decent housing at affordable prices. In March 1986 the U.S. Department of Housing and Urban Development, reacting to failures to correct problems identified in federal audits, designated an aide to oversee the District's public housing program. A city document issued several months later did the only thing a mayor could do in an election year—stress the historic legacy of inadequate housing in the city. But no historical account could hide the fact that the convergence of lost opportunities under Jimmy Carter and deep cuts under the Reagan administration, when combined with inefficient city management, were conspiring to put home ownership out of the reach of a majority of the city's black population. The lack of adequate private and subsidized housing heightened the need for public assistance. But delays in renovation left more than 2,000 public housing units out of a total of 11,400 unfit for habitation in 1986, while the waiting list for space was greater than the number of public units available.[22] Such substantive shortcomings were soon obscured, however, by allegations of Barry's misconduct.

★ ★ ★

During his first term, Barry's former wife, Mary Treadwell, was charged with stealing federal funds from Pride, Incorporated, and reports surfaced that the mayor might be accused as well. No public charges materialized, and although Treadwell was tried and sentenced, Barry did not suffer initially from the association.[23] During the second term, however, reports of personal as well as governmental impropriety began to accumulate. In 1983, shortly after he left his position as deputy mayor for operations, Ivanhoe Donaldson, Barry's closest political associate, was indicted for defrauding the government and obstructing justice. In December 1985 he pled guilty to illegally obtaining more than $190,000 in government funds, most of it from the Department of Employment Services. He subsequently received a seven-year prison term.[24]

While the mayor was quick to disassociate himself from Donaldson as he previously had done with Mary Treadwell, Barry too became the subject of a federal investigation, as he was called before a grand jury to answer questions about whether he bought cocaine from Karen Johnson, a woman with whom he admitted a personal, though nonintimate involvement. Johnson was sentenced and her jail term extended for contempt of court when she refused to answer questions before the grand jury. Reporters asked whether she was protecting Barry, but no charges were brought against the mayor, and he appeared vindicated.[25] In March 1986, however, Deputy Mayor for Finance Alphonse Hill resigned after acknowledging that he had received $3,000 in payments from a Chicago-based accounting firm that had been awarded a number of lucrative city auditing contracts. Like his former associate Ivanhoe Donaldson, he too went to jail.[26]

While the actual level of documented crimes in District government was low relative to other big cities such as New York, Barry's reputation had been tarnished. Although he cleared the Democratic primary in 1986 without trouble, the level of criticism of his administration continued to rise. In the months before the general election campaign another grand jury investigation opened, focusing again on Karen Johnson, particularly whether she received payment to withhold information on city officials. Again the investigation implicated the mayor through leaks to the press, prompting a sharp response from Barry that U.S. Attorney Joseph diGenova, a white Republican appointee, was engaged in a racist attack on his administration.[27] Barry's defense found some adherents in Washington, but criticism in the press extended nationally and even internationally, as the London *Economist*, for instance, pointed to poor schools and a failure to provide adequate housing as "in their own way as heinous as the official hands caught in, or hovering over, the till."[28]

When Ivanhoe Donaldson was prosecuted, *Washington Post* columnist Milton Coleman asked why there was not more criticism of the Barry administration. "Where is the outrage when black people use their positions of authority and trust to rip off the black community?" he quoted a local black activist. The answer, he suggested, was that blacks withheld their criticism so as not to give ammunition to white racists.[29] Many blacks in fact rallied to Barry's defense, but the most scathing criticism came from a young black reporter for the *Washington Post*, Juan Williams. Having gained considerable attention for his book, *Eyes on the Prize*, a study of the civil rights movement complementing the public television series of the same title, Williams accused Barry of forsaking the idealism of that struggle. Pointing to a disparity between programs benefiting a small number of black professionals and continued mismanagement in social welfare areas critical to the mass of the District's poor black voters, Williams charged:

> Barry did more for his people when he was working in the civil rights movement to gain power than he did after he had that power. The constant bouts with petty corruption have diverted attention from Barry's policy failures and from the larger agenda of reforms that black voters might demand of the

The Limits of Social Protest Politics

practically white development firms, real estate companies, banks and utilities. Consequently, the promise of black political power in Washington and the change it could bring for the city's black residents, particularly the poorest, has gone down the drain.[30]

The city's weak Republican party had not intended to field a candidate for mayor, but the only Republican member of the city council, Carol Schwartz, still in her first term, announced her candidacy and ran a spirited campaign. Undoubtedly aided by the charges of corruption in the Barry administration, she nonetheless focused on substantive welfare issues, working hard to build support outside her base in affluent and predominantly white Ward 3 on the west side of Rock Creek Park. Underfunded, outorganized, and lacking substantial credentials to run the city, Schwartz nonetheless attracted a respectable 33 percent of the vote, indicating that the contest was as much a referendum on Barry as it was a choice for mayor. Although the outcome of the election could scarcely have been in doubt, nearly half the city's eligible electorate voted, the highest turnout in a mayoralty race to date under home rule. Schwartz carried Ward 3 as expected, by an overwhelming 85 percent. She also edged Barry in racially mixed Ward 2 in the city's gentrifying in-town precincts, improving substantially on Patricia Harris's strong showing there four years earlier. Although she lost the other six wards in the city, she recorded as much as 14 to 16 percent in the city's two poorest wards, where there was virtually no Republican registration. While Barry triumphed with 61 percent of the vote, his mandate for a third term carried with it a clear warning of rising discontent.[31]

Once reelected, Barry attempted to strike a unifying theme by employing the widely accepted goal among Democrats of achieving full home rule under statehood. Attacking in his inaugural address what he called the last vestiges of colonial mentality in the city, he once again pledged a government of both efficiency and compassion.[32] Finally accepting advice he had received throughout his second term, he moved to establish a separate agency to deal with public housing, appointing a respected Cleveland administrator to tackle persistent problems of housing rehabilitation.[33] But even as he reactivated the progressive agenda of earlier years, his behavior became detached and, at times, bizarre.

During a snowstorm that virtually paralyzed the city in January 1987, while he was making an extended trip to the Super Bowl in California, Barry flippantly discounted the city's problems, suggesting in the process a lack of commitment to basic issues of governance.[34] Such conclusions were supported as the mayor failed to grapple with highly publicized problems with the city's ambulance and welfare services. Adding to policy difficulties were personal controversies, including reports of illegal back payments for a $4,500 fur coat for his wife. Barry claimed that an aide made a $1,500 payment out of city funds without his knowledge. The aide subsequently resigned his post and pled guilty to misuse of the funds, but questions of the mayor's personal finances persisted.[35]

During the summer of 1987 Joseph diGenova revived the grand jury investigation of Karen Johnson, implicating the mayor again as the investigation widened to cover possible corruption in the police department, the award of minority contracts, and the sale of municipal bonds. Again Barry attracted national attention, including a biting segment of the ABC television program *20/20* and a report from the *Los Angeles Times* that charged, "At a time when Congress is once again considering legislation to make most of the District of Columbia into New Columbia, the 51st state, the district's government is staggering under a barrage of scandals involving everything from fraud, bribery and extortion to cocaine use, philandering and faulty snow removal."[36]

With no indictment actually forthcoming against the mayor, Barry's defenders depicted the probes as racist, going so far as to bring Atlanta civil rights activist Hosea Williams to Washington to charge that the investigation was part of a nationwide effort by the Reagan administration to overthrow black elected officials. "There is unquestionably an effort to destroy and defame black leadership in this country," Williams told a Blacks in Government conference. "There was a failure by the white power structure to co-opt them. Blacks did not capitulate, and now there's an effort to destroy them."[37] Barry's legal counsel, Herbert O. Reid Sr., presented a similar defense to a meeting of the Congressional Black Caucus, pointing back to racist reactions during Reconstruction as a relevant lesson for the present.[38]

So prominent was attention to "the plan" to disfranchise blacks that a Washington television station presented a week-long series on perceptions of white efforts to curb black power. While various whites, including Betty Ann Kane, discounted the likelihood of conspiracy, several blacks interviewed claimed that white objections to the expansion of minority contracting, in particular, were attempts to discredit black politicians. Drawing from an updated study of harassment of black elected officials compiled by Iowa State University professor Mary Sawyer, they pointed especially to leaks from grand juries as a means of discrediting black politicians perceived by the white establishment as too powerful.[39] Barry's critics remained skeptical of conspiracy theories, and the *New York Times*, pointing to the eleven city officials who had been indicted and convicted, as well as almost a dozen additional officials who had quit or resigned under fire for misdoings, called Barry "one of the most controversial mayors in the United States, almost certainly the most controversial black mayor."[40] The greatest controversy in the Barry era, however, was yet to come.

The arrest of a close Barry associate, Charles Lewis, for drug use in the Virgin Islands and a subsequent raid on Lewis's hotel room in Washington

The Limits of Social Protest Politics

only moments after Barry had left the premises put the mayor in the storm of controversy once again. Barry relentlessly denied he used drugs, but he faced a wave of criticism. The new U.S. attorney, Jay Stephens, quickly summoned a grand jury to investigate Barry for possible drug use, and although Lewis refused to implicate Barry, the mayor's hold on office began to slip away. The press reported the unraveling of the coalition that had secured the allegiance both of the business community and of the city's poorest residents.[41] Although Barry announced his "irreversible" decision to run again, even his closest former associate, Ivanhoe Donaldson, urged him not to seek another term. By January 1990 Barry's vulnerability had attracted a slew of possible candidates to the Democratic primary, including Walter Fauntroy, who resigned the nonvoting delegate position in Congress he had held since 1971 to run for mayor, and Jesse Jackson, who moved his residence from Chicago to Washington to explore the race. Even Barry's police chief, Maurice Turner, resigned his position after clashing with the mayor and reregistered as a Republican to run for mayor.

Then, on January 18, FBI agents struck. Using an ex-girlfriend to lure the mayor to a hotel room where video cameras were concealed, agents caught the mayor inhaling crack cocaine. Police immediately arrested Barry. A grand jury subsequently indicted him on three felony counts for lying to a grand jury about cocaine involvement with Charles Lewis and five counts of cocaine possession. As he had done so often when under fire, Barry resorted to a racial defense, calling the federal case against him "a political lynching."[42]

Not all blacks endorsed such self-serving statements. Barry's most severe black critic, Juan Williams, responded to the crisis by writing:

> The city was racially divided before Marion Barry showed up. But what Barry has done is to really exacerbate those tensions—to the point where I think there is less communication, less of the kind of coalition-building so important to something like the quality of our public schools, the quality of our social welfare system, even the quality of our religious life. Things have become more and more split as black people have been put in the position of having to defend a man who in reality is indefensible.[43]

Many black activists, however, continued to defend Barry, charging again that he was the victim of a federal conspiracy to drive him from office, a charge sustained in part by reports that prosecutors would reduce charges against him if Barry would resign his position as mayor.[44] Barry's supporters carried that message to the Association of Black Mayors, an organization he had recently headed, at its April meeting. According to the Reverend George Stallings, a Catholic priest who had broken with the church to establish his own runaway sect, Barry's arrest represented a direct tie to the harassment of civil rights activists by J. Edgar Hoover's FBI during the 1960s. The retiring president of the organization, Atlantic City mayor James

Usry, charged that the Justice Department investigation of Barry was a "witch hunt" inspired by Barry's efforts to deliver city services to blacks, a theme reiterated several months later by NAACP executive director Benjamin Hooks.[45]

Barry's highly publicized trial continued to divide Washington. Responding to Barry's calculated effort to build his defense on a racial basis, a ready audience emerged among many blacks, though not whites. "This is our city," one participant told reporters at a pro-Barry rally shortly after his arrest. "It is a black city. And they want to take the mayor because the mayor has built it up."[46] "Many African Americans believe that a kind of cultural apartheid rules the nation," two *Washington Post* reporters said in July, "and their response is to assert their own identity."[47]

When the jury limited its conviction to just one count of drug possession, dismissing one other count and failing to reach a verdict on twelve other charges, Barry and his most loyal supporters claimed vindication, even though the court subsequently sentenced him to serve a six-month jail term. "The government has examined my conduct; now it must examine its conduct," Barry declared. His virtual exoneration represented a strike against the federal prosecutors and the federal judge who tried to bring Barry down, William Raspberry wrote. But divisions remained, even within the black community, he reported, separating those status-conscious blacks Barry had contested most of his career, "who place great weight on being well thought of by whites," from low-income residents who likely harbored "memories of their own unhappy encounters with authorities over whom they wield no influence" and saw Barry's deliverance as their own. Although he understood why Barry would evoke sympathy from blacks who felt besieged, Raspberry nonetheless urged Barry to "stop using poor residents of Washington the way a drug addict uses his family. . . . If he is serious about healing, let him gather up the mistrust, the shame and the racial and political division that have showered the city like feathers from a broken pillow and say: 'These are mine. I claim responsibility for them. Forgive me for making them yours.'"[48]

The initial result of the federal prosecution was to drive Barry out of the race for mayor. In his absence, Walter Fauntroy attempted to gain attention for the issues that had animated his tenure as director of MICCO, arguing against giving up land to developers, when it could serve instead as a source of empowerment and stability for indigenous black residents.[49] In doing so he attempted not just to revive the political themes of the mid-1960s but to expose the effects of Barry's effort to give special breaks to Jeffrey Cohen, his son's godfather, to develop a prime site in Shaw.[50] The issue could have revived the substantive debate over the direction of land use in the inner city. But as a measure of Fauntroy's own distance from the issues that had animated his earlier career and the way Barry's personal exercise of power had come to dominate local politics, Fauntroy's campaign never attracted

The Limits of Social Protest Politics

Marion Barry appearing at the pulpit of Union Temple Baptist Church in Anacostia shortly after his release from prison in April 1992. Wearing the African garb that became a trademark in this period of "redemption," Barry frequently returned to Union Temple, where he found comfort before the historical figures depicted on the church mural: the black Jesus surrounded by his twelve disciples, including those pictured here—Elijah Muhammad, Malcolm X, and Mary McLeod Bethune. Courtesy Darrow Montgomery.

significant attention. Instead media, especially the influential *Washington Post*, focused on outsider Sharon Pratt Dixon's promise to clean house by cutting the size of city government and eliminating cronyism.

Barry tried to maintain some power by running as an independent for an at-large seat on the city council. In this campaign he revived the social issues that had compelled his first elections. Describing himself to supporters as a "vote for the disenfranchised," he said in his announcement, "You've not heard anybody say, 'Look, something needs to be done to help people in public housing, to make sure the city government continues its commitment to the poor, the handicapped.'"[51] Although Barry's welfare-oriented message retained considerable force in the city's poorer neighborhoods, it lacked credibility elsewhere. His loss and Sharon Pratt Dixon's victory as mayor appeared to mark the end of the era of social welfare politics.

Dixon (who married and changed her name to Kelly in the first year of her administration), working with the new delegate to Congress, Eleanor Holmes Norton, quickly improved relations with the federal government. Together they attained a sizable federal supplement to the District budget to avert a fiscal crisis. The Democratic National Convention strongly endorsed statehood for the District in 1992. Bill Clinton's election as president and the defeat of Congress's effort to impose the death penalty on the District encouraged Mayor Kelly to proclaim that the day when the District would be politically free was at last clearly in sight. Together with Norton, she pressed hard for statehood in the early months of the new Clinton administration.

Barry's own election to city council in 1992 revealed, however, both the mayor's vulnerability and that of the city. While both the former mayor and his successor could unite behind a campaign for statehood, Barry's reemergence on the political scene served to highlight the unfinished social agenda before the District. Although Barry's comeback carried with it every measure of improbability, he managed to gain 70 percent of the vote against an incumbent council member in Ward 8, where he moved right after getting out of prison.[52] Wearing the African garb he had adopted since leaving the mayor's office in 1990, Barry succeeded in reviving the

socially progressive image of the activist days before his first election, when
he was so often seen in street demonstrations wearing a dashiki.[53] To un-
derscore his emphasis on neighborhood-based power, he told supporters
who crowded around him at his primary victory celebration at the symbolically appropriate Frederick Douglass Junior High School, "You have made
Ward 8 the most famous place in America. You have empowered yourselves. . . . You are a sleeping giant that has risen."[54]

As a member of the city council, Barry extended his agenda beyond
immediate problems in his ward to general issues of social concern, including guarantees of summer jobs for youth and defending subsidies for poor
tenants from Kelly's budget cuts. Such efforts rekindled some portions of
his old constituency, but it served as well to point up the city's problematic

The Limits of Social Protest Politics

relationship with Congress. Within only a month of his primary election in 1992, statehood supporters were forced to delay a vote on the issue until after the presidential election. When the issue finally came before the House of Representatives in November 1993, it failed by a wide margin, 277-153.[55]

Barry's comeback built upon a reversion to welfare-oriented politics. His support for statehood appeared to offer a means of securing welfare-related goals the federal government had failed to deliver, but it did nothing in itself to address the remaining structural problems facing the District. Race and class continued to divide the city in ways that made governing difficult. Although demonstrating the ability to bridge such differences at the outset of his administration, Barry reverted over time to utilizing a racially polarizing style as a means of shoring up his own personal and political standing. Such rhetoric helped to sustain his political career, but it stood in the way of advancing any long-term solutions to persistent social welfare problems.

In fact, the failures of the Barry years extended well beyond his personal problems, or even the obvious antagonism engendered between District government and the conservative Republican administrations of Ronald Reagan and George Bush. By the time power had finally begun to accrue to the District, its position in the region had clearly eroded. An overheated real estate market, which collapsed in the recession of the early 1990s, could mask but not hide the growing imbalance of city and suburb. Not only did the District population and share of area wealth continue to fall as it rose in the suburbs,[56] but Washington's shifting social composition heightened divisions inside the District. Failures to improve schools, provide affordable housing, or assure public safety encouraged the black middle class to follow the lead of whites a generation earlier to flee the city. By the end of Barry's third term as mayor, more than half the metropolitan black population lived in the suburbs, much of that just across the District line in Maryland's Prince George's County, where a process of resegregation began all over again.[57] Blacks remaining in the city tended to be among the region's poorest, bringing the District, as George and Eunice Grier reported, closer to a "two-class society" polarized between white and black, well-to-do and poor.[58]

During his last two terms as mayor, Barry campaigned to satisfy those residents in greatest need, but even as he did so he sacrificed social welfare to other priorities. Like white civic leaders a generation earlier, he sought, in promoting Techworld and other office development downtown, to build up investment in the District to maintain competitiveness with the suburbs. Rather than attempting to revive a neighborhood-based strategy like that pioneered by MICCO, he acceded in the concentration of capital downtown. In doing so, Barry helped further define what geographer Paul Knox describes as the contrasting landscapes of desire and despair, the result, he argues, of "a social geography that has become an exemplar of the congested,

fragmented and polarized urbanization of the postmodern metropolis."[59]
With increased tax revenues from such projects, Barry attempted to argue,
more could be done to solve persistent social problems. But while Barry
sustained such efforts sufficiently well to secure funding for his reelection,
he failed to effect social change. Drug-related violence was only the latest
and gravest of the problems that plagued the city's lower-income areas.
Inadequate housing and health care, teenage pregnancy, and welfare dependency were among the other problems that got worse, not better, during the
Barry years. As the *New York Times* reported in 1990, "there is little dispute that during Mr. Barry's tenure the city became a better place to work
and visit and, in many blue-collar and poor neighborhoods, a worse place
to live."[60]

When in trouble on social issues, both Barry and Kelly reverted to the
popular issue of statehood. That cause could always serve as a rallying cry
by satisfying emotional needs as well as promising long-denied fundamental political rights. Such support was understandable, given the long history
of federal meddling and interference in District affairs. The very success in
establishing a federal enclave that was physically set apart from the city to
serve as a specialized government and tourist center made it easier for local
residents to make their case for separation of city from capital. Prospects as
a city-state seemed preferable to any further insults like Senator Richard
Shelby's effort to impose the death penalty in 1992. It also promised some
measure of fiscal relief by lifting the prohibition on a commuter tax imposed by the Home Rule Act of 1973. But satisfying as statehood appeared
locally, it was a sure sign of the failure of urban policy. Neither efforts to
implement black power activism nor federal intervention had been able to
resolve the structural problems continuing to plague the city. Hope, not
reason, pointed to a better future for the District under statehood. Meanwhile, it was clear that any pretext the nation might have had to use Congress's power of exclusive jurisdiction over the District to establish a model
city for the rest of the country had failed.

Conclusion

The city, as one finds it in history, is the point of maximum concentration for the power and culture of a community. . . . here is where human experience is transformed into viable signs, symbols, patterns of conduct, systems of order. Here is where the issues of civilization are focused.

Lewis Mumford, *The Culture of Cities,* 1938

If any city in the United States has borne the burden of serving as a symbol of American aspirations and has simultaneously been the place, as Mumford says, where the issues of civilization have been focused, it has been the nation's capital. Given Congress's power of exclusive jurisdiction as well as the historical absence of powerful indigenous economic as well as cultural traditions, Washington invited efforts to mold it. Whether it was George Washington's determination to use Washington to bind the new republic together, Charles Sumner's effort to forge new opportunities regardless of race, or Marion Barry's determination to utilize black political power for social renewal, each generation embraced a "New Washington" where it could put to work its vision for urban development.

Within the framework of Washington's special relationship with the federal government, there have been creative periods, marked by activist, interventionist administrations inspired by the goal of addressing social needs. Reconstruction, Progressivism, the New Deal, and the Great Society all represented such eras. Each provided some hope for federal assistance in the resolution of persistent social problems. But more powerful and enduring among the forces determined to remake Washington were competing efforts to secure the city's beautification. Starting with L'Enfant and carrying through Alexander Shepherd's public works programs, the McMillan Commission, and the commission's successor agencies, Washington's measure of worthiness as the national capital came to be judged in terms of building a physically pleasing city. When Justice William Douglas's 1954 Supreme Court ruling cleared redevelopment of the Southwest by saying that legislatures had the power "to determine that the community should be beautiful as well as healthy," he merely amplified Daniel Burnham's claim fifty years earlier that "People bid their wise men . . . to remove and forever keep from view the ugly, the unsightly and even the commonplace."

Federal officials, in fact, achieved dramatic success in beautifying Washington, most particularly in carving out a distinctive federal enclave at the city's core. They did so, however, at the cost of adequately dealing with social issues identified with local needs. To the degree that the government addressed a compelling problem like inadequate housing, it did so on a primarily aesthetic basis by attempting to extend design controls from the capital enclave into residential quarters. Once granted the power to remove "slum dwellings," the government improved the city's appearance, but it failed to provide alternative housing at affordable prices to those it displaced. As redevelopment, with its aesthetic orientation and attempt to stem the flight of white taxpayers to the suburbs, succeeded public housing as the chief element of urban policy, the problem of displacement only worsened, and resentment mounted in the black community.

In 1967, asserting the importance of beautification in federally funded redevelopment programs, journalist Jeanne R. Lowe described Washington's Southwest renewal effort as one that "helped the city realize not only aesthetic and monetary values . . . but also spiritual or civic values."[1] The black power movement that crystallized in the aftermath of the riots of the following year shattered that concept of civic revitalization. Social justice succeeded social uplift as the rallying cry of those who had previously been excluded from shaping policies intended for their benefit.

The MICCO experience in Shaw paralleled the first era of reconstruction in Washington in that local groups worked with federal assistance to shape their own destinies. But it went further, because for a short time at least black leaders set the agenda, not white sponsors. While neighborhood leaders did not accomplish all they intended, they did demonstrate the capacity to provide better housing facilities at affordable costs without giving up control of the land to outsiders. In utilizing the tools of urban planning and development for their own purposes, activists demonstrated the capacity to affect the social as well as physical renewal of their neighborhood. Given the power as well as the money to develop programs central to their needs, Shaw residents did just that.

To its credit, the Clinton administration has learned the lesson of the past generation that programs designed for social improvement must engage the energies and secure the commitment of the intended beneficiaries. In stressing citizen empowerment within the Republican concept of enterprise zones, Clinton's urban advisers have sought to link the energies of local residents with the public and private resources brought to the redevelopment process. Given the fiscal constraints the national government continues to face, however, any such program runs the risk demonstrated so clearly in the Model Cities program of the 1960s, when available funds were spread too widely among competing constituencies. Moreover, the

Conclusion

political climate has changed, a fact underscored by the 1994 election returns.

Only two short years after Bill Clinton's and Marion Barry's election as president and city councilman respectively, Washington's future prospects took a dramatic turn. In what once would have appeared totally improbable after his drug conviction, Marion Barry was elected to a fourth term as mayor. Energizing his most fervent supporters with a powerful anti-establishment campaign, Barry trounced incumbent Sharon Pratt Kelly and City Councilman John Ray in the Democratic primary. He subsequently overcame widespread editorial criticism, especially in the *Washington Post,* and a spirited challenge from Republican former city councilwoman Carol Schwartz to win election with 56 percent of the vote.

Even as Barry claimed his own personal and political redemption, however, dramatic gains that put Republicans in control of both houses of Congress preempted any chance of a return to the hopeful period of Barry's first term as mayor. As if to symbolize the heightened division between city and capital so central to Washington's history, Senator Richard Shelby, who had tried in 1992 to impose capital punishment on the city, announced his switch of party allegiance to the Republican majority. In place of the creation of new jobs Barry had promised his strongest supporters, who were concentrated in the lower- and middle-income black neighborhoods, public commentary following the election focused on ways to cut back public spending in order to avert a fiscal crisis.[2]

Then, in a dramatic statement issued January 2, 1995, Barry himself virtually renounced the statehood cause by declaring that the city could no longer sustain the cost of functions normally absorbed by state government: courts, prisons, and Medicare. Less than two months later, Congress imposed a financial control board on the city that sharply curtailed the power of Washington's elected officials.[3]

In light of the shift to social as well as fiscal conservatism, Mumford's stirring picture of the importance of cities—and with it those attendant liberal federal initiatives directed at urban renewal—must be seen for what they are, artifacts of the past. Modern modes of communication and transportation have relentlessly undercut the forces that once made cities central to economic development. If cities have served historically as transforming agents of their cultures, there can be little doubt, as Robert Fishman writes, that the most powerful transformers today have migrated to the former suburbs: "Although American central cities are by no means bereft of skills or information, it is also clear that a whole world of advanced production and specialized consumption has grown up outside of them." Edge cities, as Joel Garreau calls them—those concentrations of commerce and residence more likely to be located near a suburban shopping center or a regional airport than a historic downtown—have become the new magnets of growth.[4] Overall, suburbs contain not only more residents but also more

Conclusion

jobs than cities. They hold the new balance of political power, and the great majority of those voters not only distrust welfare-oriented politics, they find themselves increasingly removed from the circumstances that produced such an ethos in the first place. The constituency for urban-oriented federal initiatives may still exist, but it is increasingly a minority position nationally.

For those Washington residents acutely aware of the ways in which past federal actions have exacerbated the city's social problems, the current constraints on government action in cities may not be regretted. Regarding the effort to combine city and capital as a failure, they call for a radical departure—statehood for the District of Columbia. Seen as an extension of the drive for home rule and an essential measure for assuring justice in light of federal policies perceived as inimical to the needs of the city's black population, the statehood cause has emerged nationally as well as locally as part of the current civil rights agenda. Certainly political independence is a necessary condition for any step Washington residents might themselves take to revitalize their civic life. Statehood offers an attractive solution to this political problem without, however, bringing with it attendant solutions to the city's social and fiscal problems. As appealing as such action has been to those fed up with government meddling in their lives, the timing is wrong.

Besides lacking any precedent in American history, the concept of a city-state flies in the face of every trend in the modern era. Those cities that have been successful in an era of diminished federal resources have survived by working effectively at the state and regional level. Central to their ability to deal with persistent social problems, former Albuquerque mayor David Rusk reports, has been their capacity to be elastic enough to extend their policy reach either through the annexation of adjacent territory or through the implementation of metropolitan compacts. Because the Constitution prohibits the expansion of its boundaries, Washington stands as literally the nation's most inelastic city and thus serves as the prime example of the problems Rusk identifies with cities in decline: a shrinking population and tax base, concentration of the poor, and polarization by race and class.[5] Statehood may bring with it, as its proponents argue, increased financial revenues through implementation of a commuter tax that the 1973 Home Rule Act specifically prohibited. But the tiny state of New Columbia—just 1/28th the size of Rhode Island—would still rely heavily on federal subsidy, even though it would no longer have the special relationship it has historically had with the national government. With such financial support uncertain, Washington would at the same time deprive itself of the diverse demographic and geographic resources typically offered by states.

Instead of trying to solve its problems through the politically attractive but economically suspect vehicle of statehood, Washington should take a

Conclusion

A flyer from the 1993 March on Washington showing that statehood for the District of Columbia has become identified as a national civil rights issue.

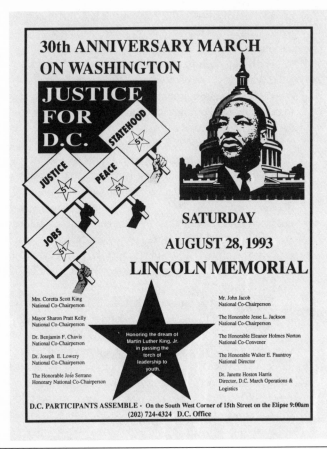

clue from the history of Alexandria County's retrocession to Virginia. Not only did Alexandria residents gain immediate political rights in 1846, but their economic aspirations also obtained a considerable boost. The retrocession of the remaining nonfederal enclave back to Maryland would provide Washington with similar opportunities. The designation in December 1992 of a single Washington-Baltimore demographic area points the way to a potentially powerful urban alliance. While the two cities have contrasting backgrounds, the one industrial and the other not, they have converged in recent years on many more fronts than just a common interest in the Orioles baseball team. Economic and residential development in Maryland's Montgomery and Prince George's counties is closely associated with patterns already established in Washington. Extending both those patterns

Conclusion

and that influence all the way to Baltimore would assure both political and economic powers largely denied Washington throughout most of its history.[6] At the very least, retrocession would provide a boost to greater regional cooperation, a factor that commentator Neil Peirce argues is essential to the solution of contemporary social problems.[7]

Although the idea of retrocession is not new, it has appeared most often in a partisan context not likely to advance a solution, from Republicans seeking to block the two new Democratic senators whom statehood would bring with it. It lacks a strong political constituency in Washington or in Maryland, which has historically been divided between the Baltimore area and its rural sector. The latter areas oppose expanding the urban influence in the state and undoubtedly remain suspicious of Washington's increasingly visible financial problems. Yet Washington's own Maryland suburbs gained sufficient influence, in alliance with Baltimore, to elect Parris Glendening, county executive of Prince George's County, governor of Maryland in 1994. As the balance of power in Maryland shifts to the Baltimore-Washington corridor, the prospects for retrocession improve. In the meantime, Washington remains a vital part of its own metropolitan region—which, it should be noted, contains the highest median income and the lowest poverty rate among the nation's leading urban centers.[8] If Maryland could be assured of the resolution of such federally induced problems as Washington's underfunded pension plan, it should be willing to see possible benefits from absorbing another city into its ranks. In the meantime, by becoming part of a state, Washington would at least enter an equal playing field with other cities, gaining access to all state and federal powers guaranteed by law. In such circumstances, the factors Rusk considers necessary for urban revitalization as well as improved prospects for social justice—coordinated regional economic development and uniform open housing and educational policies across jurisdictions—would be greatly facilitated. In fact, Rusk cites adjacent Montgomery County as a model for achieving ends that he considers virtually unattainable within the framework of city-suburb opposition.[9]

Caught between conflicting ideals of beauty and social justice, the District of Columbia stands as a powerful symbol of America's historical failure to develop adequate urban policies: housing programs with too little money to have sustained effect; tax policies that direct investment out of older, crowded areas into suburbs; redevelopment policies that compound divisions between rich and poor, black and white. We have built our physical cities effectively in what Jon Teaford calls an unheralded triumph.[10] But we have been less successful in dealing with persistent social problems, many of which have been and continue to be concentrated in our cities. If the future demands something other than simply encouraging cities to go back to federal sources for more money, the least the Congress can do is recognize its own failures in the one city under its direct control. It can do

Conclusion

more than just respond negatively by voting down statehood. It can set Washington free to enjoy, as part of the state of Maryland, the full range of political powers guaranteed other citizens under the Constitution. Given that opportunity, Washington will at least have a chance in the next century to show that the seemingly intractable problems that have beset it and other cities can be addressed better at the regional and state levels.

Conclusion

Note on Sources

Archival Sources, Documentary Collections, and Newspapers

Unlike most cities, Washington lacks a central historical archive, the product of its special relationship with the federal government. The District of Columbia Archives did not receive its first records until 1990. While it contains some potentially valuable record groups for tracing urban development, such as the Engineer Department files covering the years 1898 to 1950, and some government record groups covering portions of the work of the National Capital Housing Authority and the Redevelopment Land Agency, limited funding and staff have prevented the archives from becoming the central resource it was intended to be for the record of the city's modern history. More central to that and the city's early history is the National Archives, which, despite lacking specialized attention to Washington records, contains the most complete documentation of Washington's history. Particularly important are the record groups for the U.S. Senate and House of Representatives (46 and 233), the District of Columbia government (351), the National Capital Planning Commission (328), the National Capital Housing Authority (302), the Commission of Fine Arts (66), and the Office of Public Buildings and Grounds (42). Each of these record groups has a published finding aid, with the congressional records being treated most extensively in Robert W. Coren et al., *Guide to the Records of the United States Senate at the National Archives*, and Charles E. Schamel et al., *Guide to the Records of the United States House of Representatives at the National Archives*, both published by the National Archives and Records Administration, in 1989.

The Library of Congress holds the personal papers of several key figures in Washington history, most notably two contributors to the Senate Park Commission, Frederick Law Olmsted Jr. and Charles Moore. The library's holdings for Alexander Shepherd and Sayles Bowen are not nearly so complete, and I had to rely on other sources, most notably news accounts, to document their roles in shaping the city. Past historical work on Pierre L'Enfant has drawn on those of his papers in the library's collections that have survived. But they are notoriously incomplete, and it is widely believed that some of the most important documents recording his effort to design the District of Columbia are in private hands.

George Washington University's Gelman Library Office of Special Collections contains a few especially valuable manuscript collections for modern Washington. In addition to the Walter Fauntroy Collection, which is not yet open for public use, it holds an invaluable group of transportation-related documents compiled by Peter Craig. Darwin Stolzenbach's initial collection of documents recording the origins of the Metro subway system is also valuable. The Greater Washington Board of Trade Collection consists mostly of public reports, but the library lacks a run of the *Washington Board of Trade News*, a useful record of board policy, which can be found at the Historical Society of Washington and the D.C. Public Library. Jessica I. Elfenbein, *Civics, Commerce, and Community: The History of the Greater Board of Trade, 1889–1989* (Dubuque, Iowa: Kendall/Hunt Publishing Co., 1989) builds on those records. The Catholic University Archives holds some of the records of the Associated Charities.

The Historical Society of Washington collections are stronger for maps and photographs than manuscripts. The society holds, nonetheless, some papers pertinent to Washington's urban development, notably those of U. S. Grant III and John Nolen, planning directors for the National Capital Park and Planning Commission; Harry Wender, Southwest civic activist; and Charles Glover, parks enthusiast and banker. The D.C. Public Library is known especially for its extensive local history subject files as well as its photographic and print files from the *Washington Star*. More recently the library has sought out manuscript collections; among the promising records for future research are those of Julius Hobson Sr., social activist and civil rights leader whose leadership role in Washington corresponded with Marion Barry's early years in the city. Each of the major Washington collections is described in some detail in Perry G. Fisher and Linda J. Lear, *A Selected Bibliography for Washington Studies and Descriptions of Major Local Collections* (Washington, D.C.: GW Washington Studies no. 8, 1981). Also helpful as a guide is Kathleen Collins, *Washingtoniana Photographs: Collections in the Prints and Photographs Division of the Library of Congress* (Washington, D.C.: Library of Congress, 1989).

A particularly valuable source for the history of urban renewal in Washington has been the collection of the Department of Housing and Community Development, which contained extensive clipping files as well as many project reports relating to redevelopment. That collection has since been dispersed, with much of it sent to the District of Columbia Archives.

Because of Washington's national role, many personal records of those who have helped shape the city and its social relations are located in other parts of the country. Among the most important of these are the papers of Senator James McMillan at the Detroit Public Library; Daniel Burnham at the Art Institute of Chicago; John Ihlder and Frederic Delano at the Franklin D. Roosevelt Library in Hyde Park; and Arthur Capper at the Kansas State Historical Society. Additional material related to Ihlder can be found in the Delaware Housing Association Papers in the Urban Archives at Temple University.

The papers of early national leaders who did so much to shape the District of Columbia, notably George Washington and Thomas Jefferson, are readily available in print and in microfilm. I have relied especially on John C. Fitzpatrick, ed., *The Writings of George Washington,* 39 vols. (Washington, D.C.: Government Printing Office, 1939; reprint, Westport, Conn.: Greenwood Press, 1970), and Julian P. Boyd, ed., *The Papers of Thomas Jefferson* (Princeton: Princeton University Press, 1950–), especially volume 20, with its excellent essay on Jefferson's role in Washington. I have also drawn extensively on Saul K. Padover, ed., *Thomas Jefferson and the National Capital* (Washington, D.C.: Government Printing Office, 1946). Other valuable documentary collections are Elizabeth Kite, *L'Enfant and Washington* (Baltimore: Lord Baltimore Press, 1929), Donald B. Cole and John J. McDonough, eds., *Witness to the Young Republic: A Yankee's Journal, 1828–1870* (Hanover, N.H.: University Press of New England, 1989), and the series running under the general editorship of Ira Berlin, *Freedom: A Documentary History of Emancipation, 1861–1867.* The University of Maryland's Freedmen and Southern History Project, as sponsor of this effort, holds copies of many documents that have not been included in the published volumes.

Newspapers provide an invaluable source of information on Washington. For the earliest years, the *National Intelligencer* was most important. The *Alexandria Gazette* provided extensive coverage of its locale during the period in which it remained in the District of Columbia, and for a bit less than a decade, starting in 1835, the *Georgetown Metropolitan* provided a strong voice for that city's commercial aspirations. The *Washington Star,* known from 1941 to 1973 as the *Evening Star,* emerged in 1852 as a strong booster for private development and remained so until its demise in 1981. A number of specialized papers appeared during the Civil War and Reconstruction, the most important of which were the *Chronicle,* edited by Radical Republican John Forney, and the *National Republican.* The *New National Era,* edited by black abolitionists Sella Martin and Frederick Douglass, appeared for a short time after the war. The successor paper for the black community was the *Washington Bee,* edited by Calvin Chase with a caustic view of the slide in rights for blacks. The *Washington Afro-American* and the Washington edition of the *Pittsburgh Courier* have provided coverage of black life and issues of social concern in the twentieth century. The *Capital Spotlight* has also served the black community in modern times. Although today the *Washington Post* is dominant newspaper in the metropolitan area, it struggled to establish its importance until the mid–twentieth century, when a series of consolidations and aggressive marketing and editorial efforts made the *Post* one of the most important newspapers in the country. The *Washington Times* has never filled the role it has aspired to, to be a viable competitor for the *Post* in the aftermath of the *Star*'s demise. The

City Paper, though not carrying news reports as such, has provided lively and usually critical commentaries on city affairs in recent years.

Although Washington lacks a single coordinated locale for the collection of its history, thus making the retention and preservation of historical records more haphazard than it should be, historians can be thankful for the many government reports that have been published on Washington. In line with Congress's oversight of virtually every aspect of city life, these cover a wide range of subjects relating to social relations as well as physical development. These municipal reports, legislative reports and investigations, and records of petitions and other memorials have been published as part of the Congressional Serial Sets and are readily available in microfilm.

I have paid considerable debt in the Notes to graduate research done over the past forty years. Some of the more important work has appeared only in articles, and the dissertations from which this work appeared are worth consulting. See especially William Robert Barnes, "The Origins of Urban Renewal: The Public Housing Controversy and the Emergence of a Redevelopment Program in the District of Columbia," Syracuse University, 1977; Dennis E. Gale, "Restoration in Georgetown, Washington, D.C., 1915–65," George Washington University, 1982; Barbara Gale Fant, "Slum Reclamation and Housing Reform in the Nation's Capital, 1890–1940," George Washington University, 1982; William Brian Bushong, "Glenn Brown, the American Institute of Architects, and the Development of the Civic Core of Washington, D.C.," George Washington University, 1988; Joanna Schneider Zangrando, "Monumental Bridge Design in Washington, D.C., as a Reflection of American Culture," George Washington University, 1974; and William Anthony Tobin, "In the Shadow of the Capitol: The Transformation of Washington, D.C., and the Elaboration of the Modern U.S. Nation-State," Stanford University, 1994.

Books and Articles

Washington has been the object of a number of biographical treatments, the most comprehensive of the modern efforts being the two-volume history by Constance McLaughlin Green published in 1962 and 1963 and reissued as a single volume by Princeton University Press in 1976 under the title *Washington: A History of the Capital, 1800–1950.* A broad review of Washington which indiscriminately mixes federal and local history, Green's study came too early to be touched by modern approaches to African American history. As a result, these volumes, along with her subsequent book *The Secret City: A History of Race Relations in the Nation's Capital,* also published by Princeton, in 1967, tend to see race issues largely through the perspective provided by white observers. A notable example lies in the way she uncritically recounts the observations of social reformers on black residential patterns in the city's back alleys. James Borchert challenged this perspective frontally in his innovative study, *Alley Life in Washington: Fam-*

ily, Community, Religion, and Folklife in the City, 1850–1970 (Urbana: University of Illinois Press, 1980), thus paving the way for modern treatments of the subject. This approach is employed in the textbook prepared for use in Washington high schools, *City of Magnificent Intentions* (Washington, D.C.: Intac, 1983), compiled and edited by Keith Melder. Very sophisticated for its intended high school readers, the book nonetheless lacks the integrative narrative treatment or footnotes that could make it of use as a classroom text for advanced students.

Although it is much broader than its title suggests, Frederick Gutheim's *Worthy of the Nation: The History of City Planning for the National Capital* (Washington, D.C.: Smithsonian Institution Press, 1977) slights the social side of Washington history, not the least race. Rather, he builds on a worthy tradition of interpreting Washington as a largely monumental federal city, a process given its most important statements by John Reps, particularly in his *Monumental Washington: The Planning and Development of the Capital Center* (Princeton: Princeton University Press, 1967) and in the richly illustrated and documented volume prepared to coincide with the bicentennial anniversary of the L'Enfant plan for the city, *Washington on View: The Nation's Capital since 1790* (Chapel Hill: University of North Carolina Press, 1991). Also relating to this aspect of Washington's design are the essays compiled from a 1987 conference and edited by Richard Longstreth, *The Mall in Washington, 1791–1991* (Washington, D.C.: National Gallery of Art, 1991). Of special importance are the essays by Pamela Scott on Pierre L'Enfant, Therese O'Malley on the midcentury Andrew Jackson Downing plan, and Jon A. Peterson on the Senate Park Commission. Peterson's earlier essay on that subject, prepared as part of a larger treatment of the history of comprehensive planning, remains the most incisive comment on the subject: "The Nation's First Comprehensive City Plan: A Political Analysis of the McMillan Plan for Washington, D.C., 1900–1902," *American Planning Association Journal* 51 (Spring 1985): 134–50. Although Mel Scott's landmark history, *American City Planning since 1890* (Berkeley: University of California Press, 1971), gave ample attention to Washington's role in the evolution of urban and regional planning, two more recent studies published by the Johns Hopkins University Press virtually ignore the city, despite the its obvious relationship to their subjects: William H. Wilson, *The City Beautiful Movement* (1989) and Jon C. Teaford, *The Rough Road to Renaissance: Urban Revitalization in America, 1940–1985* (1990).

Despite the lack of complete records, Pierre L'Enfant's role in planning the city continues to attract attention. Of particular note is the special bicentennial issue of *Washington History* 3 (Spring/Summer 1991), especially articles by Pamela Scott and Don Hawkins. The latest addition to the literature has been prepared by Richard Stephens, whose years of work in the Geography and Map Division of the Library of Congress drew him to L'Enfant's plan: *"A Plan Whol[l]y New": Pierre Charles L'Enfant's Plan of the*

Note on Sources

City of Washington (Washington, D.C.: Library of Congress, 1993). That L'Enfant's intent continues to be richly debated is illustrated in J. L. Sibley Jennings, "Artistry as Design: L'Enfant's Extraordinary City," *Quarterly Journal of the Library of Congress* 6 (Summer 1979): 225–78. For a thorough examination of the context out of which the new federal district emerged, see Kenneth R. Bowling, *The Creation of Washington, D.C.: The Idea and Location of the American Capital* (Fairfax, Va.: George Mason University Press, 1991).

Lacking the industrial setting where class issues have most often been manifest, Washington has not produced much of the kind of social history that has proved so prominent in the historical profession over the past quarter century. That has recently changed with publications built on dissertation research: Elizabeth Clark-Lewis, *Living In, Living Out: African American Domestics in Washington, D.C., 1900–1940* (Washington, D.C.: Smithsonian Institution Press, 1994), and Kathryn Allamong Jacob, *Capital Elites: High Society in Washington, D.C. after the Civil War* (Washington, D.C.: Smithsonian Institution Press, 1994). Also pertinent to social history are two neighborhood studies, both sponsored by George Washington University's Center for Washington Area Studies: Suzanne Berry Sherwood, *Foggy Bottom, 1800–1975* (Washington, D.C.: GW Washington Studies no. 7, 1975) and Kathryn Schneider Smith, *Port Town to Urban Neighborhood: The Georgetown Waterfront of Washington, D.C., 1880–1920* (Dubuque, Iowa: Kendall/Hunt Publishing Co., 1989). The volume edited by Smith for the Historical Society of Washington, *Washington at Home: An Illustrated History of Neighborhoods in the Nation's Capital* (Northridge, Calif.: Winsor Publications, 1988), offers considerable information on urban development. Brett Williams's ethnography, *Upscaling Downtown*, although not intended to treat the city's Mount Pleasant neighborhood in specific terms, provides an important record of this socially diverse community at a time of difficult transition. Another source, though not a traditional one, is Edward P. Jones's book of short stories, *Lost in the City*, originally published by William Morrow in 1992.

Over time the Columbia Historical Society, now known as the Historical Society of Washington, has provided an essential chronicle of the city's history. *The Records of the Historical Society of Washington*, published in fifty-one volumes, contain a number of original documents as well as a wide range of interpretive essays. The society's successor journal, *Washington History*, although more scholarly in some respects, combines a commitment to advanced research with the goal of reaching a general audience. Some of the essays that have appeared in the first six volumes represent the best research currently being conducted on the city.

The city-federal relationship has been surprisingly neglected over time, the few exceptions being James Sterling Young's *The Washington Community, 1800–1828* (New York: Columbia University Press, 1966) and Nelson

Polsby's "The Washington Community, 1960–1980," in Thomas E. Mann and Norman J. Ornstein, eds., *The New Congress* (Washington, D.C.: American Enterprise Institute, 1981), pp. 7–31. This subject took a major step forward with Alan Lessoff's thoroughly documented examination of the critical transition the city made to modern status as it was placed under the commission form of government, *The Nation and Its City: Politics, "Corruption," and Progress in Washington, D.C., 1861–1902* (Baltimore: Johns Hopkins University Press, 1994). Carl Abbott has been investigating a more broadly based view of the city's modern development, stressing cultural and regional as well as political themes. His essays "Perspectives on Urban Economic Planning: The Case of Washington, D.C. since 1880," *Public Historian* 11 (Spring 1989): 5–21 and "Dimensions of Regional Change in Washington, D.C.," *American Historical Review* 95 (December 1990): 1367–93 provide a foundation for a forthcoming study of the city as an international center. By way of indicating just how hard it has been to place Washington culturally, Abbott identifies Washington as part of the Sunbelt in his book *The New Urban America: Growth and Politics in Sunbelt Cities*, rev. ed. (Chapel Hill: University of North Carolina Press, 1987), while Steven Diner provides a chapter on Washington for the volume *Snowbelt Cities*, edited by Richard M. Bernard for Indiana University Press in 1990.

In the way of more specialized studies, James D. Dilts has added a useful account of the B&O Railroad, *The Great Road: The Building of the B&O, The Nation's First Railroad* (Stanford: Stanford University Press, 1993) to complement the old standard on its rival C&O Canal, Walter S. Sanderlin's *The Great National Project* (Baltimore: Johns Hopkins Press, 1946). There is solid work on the Reconstruction era, notably by James H. Whyte, *The Uncivil War: Washington during the Reconstruction, 1865–1878* (New York: Twayne Publishers, 1958), and William M. Murray, *Alexander "Boss" Shepherd and the Board of Public Works* (Washington, D.C.: GW Washington Studies no. 3, 1975). Also useful is Robert Harrison's essay, "The Ideal of a 'Model City': Federal Society Policy for the District of Columbia, 1905–1909," *Journal of Urban History* 15 (August 1989): 435–63. Dennis Gale's *Washington, D.C.: Inner-City Revitalization and Minority Suburbanization* (Philadelphia: Temple University Press, 1987) examines some key social trends of the modern period.

Two journalistic accounts of Marion Barry's rise and fall have recently appeared: Jonathan I. Z. Agronsky, *Marion Barry: The Politics of Race* (Latham, N.Y.: British American Publishing, 1991), and Harry S. Jaffe and Tom Sherwood, *Dream City: Race, Power, and the Decline of Washington, D.C.* (New York: Simon and Schuster, 1994). While the latter volume provides some new information on Barry, it does not place him as much as it might in the context of the city he has dominated for so long. See also David Remnick, "The Situationist," *New Yorker*, September 5, 1994, 87–101. For a scholarly assessment of the intersection of race and District politics, see

Note on Sources

Jeffrey R. Henig, "Race and Voting: Continuity and Change in the District of Columbia," *Urban Affairs Quarterly* 28 (Spring 1993): 544–70. Pamela Scott and Antoinette J. Lee's *Buildings of the District of Columbia* (New York: Oxford University Press, 1993), though concerned primarily with individual buildings concentrated near the federal core, provides a good deal of information about physical development generally, including the emergence of Rock Creek Park.

222

Note on Sources

Notes

CHAPTER 1. City of Failed Intentions

1. L'Enfant cited in Kenneth R. Bowling, *Creating the Federal City, 1774–1800: Potomac Fever* (Washington, D.C.: American Institute of Architects Press, 1988), p. 12.

2. L'Enfant to Jefferson, April 4, 1791, in Saul K. Padover, ed., *Thomas Jefferson and the National Capital* (Washington, D.C.: Government Printing Office, 1946), p. 57.

3. L'Enfant cited in John W. Reps, *Monumental Washington: The Planning and Development of the Capital Center* (Princeton: Princeton University Press, 1967), p. 14. Reps draws on the note attributed to L'Enfant by Elizabeth Kite, *L'Enfant and Washington* (Baltimore: Lord Baltimore Press, 1929), pp. 43–48, believing it was written on L'Enfant's arrival in Georgetown on March 29, 1791.

4. The commissioners announced their intent to name the city Washington and the entire federal area the District of Columbia on September 9, 1791. Padover, *Jefferson and the National Capital*, p. 74.

5. The extent of the federal city was revealed in an article of July 5, 1791, published in Brown's *Federal Gazette*. A subsequent commentary in Bache's *General Advertiser* for July 12, 1791, noting that something had been given rival groups of property owners competing for advantage in Georgetown and Carrollsburg "to quiet them, without sufficient regard to the general good or to public opinion," complained of the inconvenience of placing Congress a mile and a half from the president's house and other government buildings. Julian P. Boyd, ed., *The Papers of Thomas Jefferson* (Princeton: Princeton University Press, 1990), 20: 29–30.

6. Cited in Reps, *Monumental Washington*, p. 16. See also Boyd, *Papers of Thomas Jefferson*, 20: 29.

7. L'Enfant to Jefferson, April 4, 1791, in Padover, *Jefferson and the National Capital*, p. 57.

8. Lewis Mumford, *The City in History: Its Origins, Its Transformations, and Its Prospects* (New York: Harcourt Brace and World, 1961), pp. 403–4; J. P. Dougherty, "Baroque and Picturesque Motifs in L'Enfant's Design for the Federal Capital," *American Quarterly* 26 (March 1974): 24, 26.

9. Pamela Scott, "'This Vast Empire': The Iconography of the Mall, 1791–1848," in Richard Longstreth, ed., *The Mall in Washington, 1791–1991* (Washington, D.C.: National Gallery of Art, 1991), pp. 39–40.

10. "Essay on the City of Washington," *Gazette of the United States*, reprinted in the *Washington Gazette*, September 23, 26, November 19, December 7, 1796,

cited by Pamela Scott, "L'Enfant's Washington Described: The City in the Public Press, 1791–1795," *Washington History* 3 (Spring/Summer 1991): 110.

11. John Lauritz Larson, "'Bind the Republic Together': The National Union and the Struggle for a System of Internal Improvements," *Journal of American History* 74 (September 1987): 366. By 1794 Washington's property included an estimated twenty thousand acres on or accessible to the Potomac River. Donald Sweig, "A Public Broadside and Private Intrigue: How Alexandria Became Part of the National Capital," *Virginia Magazine of History and Biography* 87 (January 1979): 76. Washington's commitment to the Potomac Company went well beyond his role in its establishment, as he continued to publicize its potential impact on trade as the company's president through 1789. Kenneth R. Bowling, *The Creation of Washington, D.C.: The Idea and Location of the American Capital* (Fairfax, Va.: George Mason University Press, 1991), pp. 119, 125.

12. Joseph H. Harrison Jr., "*Sic Et Non*: Thomas Jefferson and Internal Improvement," *Journal of the Early Republic* 7 (Winter 1987): 337; Bowling, *Creation of Washington, D.C.*, p. 115.

13. John C. Fitzpatrick, ed., *The Writings of George Washington* (Washington, D.C.: Government Printing Office, 1939), 31: 271.

14. "Jefferson Note," November 29, 1790; "Jefferson Opinion relative to locating the Ten Mile Square for the Federal Government, and building the Federal City," March 11, 1791, in Padover, *Jefferson and the National Capital*, pp. 31, 48. Despite his reputation as an agrarian, as early as 1776 Jefferson had pressed the Virginia House of Delegates to move the state capital to Richmond from Williamsburg because, he argued, Williamsburg could never be a great town that would attract "manufacturers, trade and husbandry." Peter Nicolaisen, "Thomas Jefferson's Concept of the National Capital," in Lothar Hönnighausen and Andreas Falke, eds., *Washington, D.C.: Interdisciplinary Approaches* (Tübingen: Francke Verlag, 1993), p. 106.

15. Jefferson to L'Enfant, April 10, 1791; Jefferson to Washington, April 10, 1791, in Padover, *Jefferson and the National Capital*, pp. 59, 60.

16. Boyd, *Papers of Thomas Jefferson*, 20: 18.

17. Ibid., p. 26; Reps, *Monumental Washington*, p. 14.

18. Boyd, *Papers of Thomas Jefferson*, 20: 19. On p. 16 Boyd describes Jefferson's sketch as emphasizing "public parks, gardens and walks facing the river and providing long vistas downstream. . . . Jefferson's concept of extensive public parks and gardens along the waterfront, its possibilities thus enhanced by transference intact to a more appropriate terrain, may rightly be regarded as the origin of what would eventually become one of the chief glories of the national capital."

19. Boyd argues that the removal of the fifteen state squares was necessary to avoid what would have been "a virtual guarantee that continuing and divisive debate would take place in every part of the nation." *Papers of Thomas Jefferson*, 20: 67. In fact, retention of the state squares would have been fully in line with L'Enfant's symbolic representation of the nation within the plan, a suggestion of implied inclusiveness rather than the kind of division Boyd suggests. For the most complete examination of the changes Jefferson authorized in L'Enfant's plan, see Richard W. Stephenson, *"A Plan Whol[l]y New": Pierre Charles L'Enfant's Plan of the City of Washington* (Washington, D.C.: Library of Congress, 1993), pp. 38–47.

20. The extent of the changes in L'Enfant's plan is the subject of considerable

controversy, as illustrated most extensively in J. L. Sibley Jennings, "Artistry as Design: L'Enfant's Extraordinary City," *Quarterly Journal of the Library of Congress* 6 (Summer 1979): 225–78. Pamela Scott, "L'Enfant's Washington Described," 106, concludes convincingly, however, that changes suggested by George Washington and Thomas Jefferson and executed by Andrew Ellicott did not materially alter L'Enfant's intent.

21. Reps, *Monumental Washington*, p. 18; Boyd, *Papers of Thomas Jefferson*, 20: 26.

22. See Bowling, *Creation of Washington, D.C.*, especially chaps. 5–7.

23. In a set of notes drawn up November 29, 1790, regarding the implementation of the Residence Act, Jefferson recorded discussions with the commissioners, that owing to the controversy over the location of the new capital "it would be dangerous to rely on any aids from Congress, or the assemblies of Virginia or Maryland." Padover, *Jefferson and the National Capital*, p. 34.

24. Boyd, *Papers of Thomas Jefferson*, 20: 33–37, 44–49.

25. Washington to L'Enfant, December 2, 1791, cited in Stephenson, "*A Plan Whol[l]y New*," p. 34.

26. Boyd, *Papers of Thomas Jefferson*, 20: 47. Boyd alludes to Washington's communication with Daniel Carroll of Duddington but does not cite Washington's message delivered December 2, 1791: "What has been done cannot be undone, and it would be unfortunate in my opinion, if disputes amongst the friends to the federal City should Arm the enemies of it with weapons to wound it." Fitzpatrick, *Writings of George Washington*, 31: 433.

27. Jefferson to L'Enfant, February 22, 1792; L'Enfant to Jefferson, February 26, 1792; Jefferson to L'Enfant, February 27, 1792, in Padover, *Jefferson and the National Capital*, pp. 93–94, 98–99, 100.

28. Declaration of President Washington, March 6, 1792. Jefferson defended the loan in a letter to commissioner Thomas Johnson, March 8, 1792. Padover, *Jefferson and the National Capital*, pp. 107, 111.

29. Cited in Constance McLaughlin Green, *Washington: Village and Capital, 1800–1878* (Princeton: Princeton University Press, 1962), p. 23.

30. Cited by Gibbs Myers, "The Founding of Modern Washington" (Ph.D. diss., Yale University, 1943), p. 32.

31. Allen C. Clark, "The Mayoralty of Robert Brent," *Records of the Columbia Historical Society* 33–34 (Washington, D.C.: Columbia Historical Society, 1932), p. 272; Edward Carter II, John C. Van Horne, and Lee W. Fromwalt, eds., *The Journals of Benjamin Henry Latrobe, 1799–1820* (New Haven: Yale University Press, 1980), 3: 217.

32. Myers, "Founding of Modern Washington," p. 114.

33. Green, *Village and Capital*, pp. 61–68.

34. Myers, "Founding of Modern Washington," p. 119; John W. Reps, *Washington on View: The Nation's Capital since 1790* (Chapel Hill: University of North Carolina Press, 1991), p. 56. According to an 1830 description of Washington, "These daily inconveniences were amazing to the members of Congress, and they were in ill-humor when any call for money was made for the city; and it was evident that the dislike to Washington, as a permanent seat of government, was fast advancing to a determination to remove it. The goodly streets and comfortable rooms in the dwelling houses of Philadelphia were remembered, and nothing but reverence for

the name of Washington kept those feelings from breaking out into acts of legislation." Ignatius Loyola Robertson [Ignatius Lorenzo Knapp], *Sketches of Public Characters* (New York: E. Bliss, 1830), p. 87.

35. Green, *Village and Capital*, pp. 172–73.

36. Alexander White to Jefferson, June 10, 1802; Jefferson to Daniel Carrol, Daniel Brent, and Charles Minifie, May 28, 1803, in Padover, *Jefferson and the National Capital*, pp. 274, 301–2.

37. Jefferson to Robert Brent, March 10, 1807, responding to Brent's letter to Jefferson, March 9, 1807, seeking authority to improve Delaware and Maryland avenues from the Capitol to the Potomac River, in ibid., pp. 384–85.

38. In a letter to Jefferson dated September 25, 1803, City Surveyor Nicholas King complained that the completion of more than 130 building additions without authority of the plan had sharply compromised the beauty and health of the city. Jefferson responded by making an extensive review of his powers in notes dated October 12, 1803. As late as 1806, however, he accepted the difficulty, noted by King in 1803, in overturning private decisions. More central to his concern was the discovery in 1808 that Benjamin Latrobe, acting as surveyor of public buildings, had exceeded his appropriation. In ibid., pp. 313, 322–34, 365, 415.

39. *National Intelligencer,* December 29, 31, 1800, cited in Green, *Village and Capital*, p. 25.

40. Ordinance, February 24, 1804, *Acts of the Corporation of the City of Washington, D.C.* (microfilm, D.C. Public Library).

41. Ordinances, October 6, 1806, October 28, 1806, October 7, 1809, July 26, 1815; Linda M. Arnold, "Congressional Government of the District of Columbia, 1800–1846" (Ph.D. diss., Georgetown University, 1974), p. 123.

42. William Bogart Bryan, *A History of the National Capital* (New York: Macmillan Co., 1916), 2: 19.

43. Ordinance, July 24, 1804.

44. Bryan, *History of the National Capital*, pp. 605–6.

45. Green, *Village and Capital*, p. 95. Even as late as 1993 Congress continued to assert its prerogative over the presumably local function of fire stations by insisting that Fire Station no. 3, located near congressional offices on New Jersey Avenue, stay open despite objections from the District government since 1987 that it was outmoded and unnecessary to public safety. Kent Jenkins Jr., "The Long Road to New Columbia," *Washington Post Magazine*, July 4, 1993, p. 19.

46. Ordinance, August 28, 1828.

47. Ordinance, May 30, 1844.

48. Sarah Pressey Noreen, *Public Street Illumination in Washington, D.C.* (Washington, D.C.: GW Washington Studies no. 2, 1975), pp. 5–6; Bryan, *History of the National Capital*, 2: 14.

49. *Gales & Seaton's Register of Debates in Congress,* December 31, 1827, p. 862.

50. Ibid., June 6, 1834, p. 4394.

51. *National Intelligencer,* July 24, 1835.

52. While New York City asserted the right to regulate animals in the streets as early as 1818, in what was a clear sign of the city's substituting modern legal forms for common custom, typically cities allowed such practices to continue well into the century. Hendrik Hartog, *Public Property and Private Power: The*

Corporation of the City of New York in American Law, 1730–1870 (Chapel Hill: University of North Carolina Press, 1983), pp. 140–42.

53. Stanley K. Schultz, *Constructing Urban Culture: American Cities and City Planning, 1800–1920* (Philadelphia: Temple University Press, 1988), pp. 115–16; Iver Bernstein, *The New York City Draft Riots: Their Significance for American Society and Politics in the Age of the Civil War* (New York: Oxford University Press, 1990), p. 200. Baltimore took its first steps to liberalize municipal funding for street improvements in 1834, finally assuming full responsibility for cleaning the streets in 1845. Gary Lawson Browne, *Baltimore in the Nation, 1789–1861* (Chapel Hill: University of North Carolina Press, 1980), pp. 155, 200. Eric H. Monkkonen, *America Becomes Urban: The Development of U.S. Cities and Towns, 1780–1980* (Berkeley: University of California Press, 1988), p. 94, reports that it was not until the last decade of the nineteenth century that extensive government investment in hard surfaced roads became common.

54. Nelson M. Blake, *Water for Cities: A History of the Urban Water Supply in the United States* (Syracuse: Syracuse University Press, 1956); Joel A. Tarr and Josef W. Konvitz, "Patterns in the Development of the Urban Infrastructure," in Howard Gillette Jr. and Zane L. Miller, eds., *American Urbanism: A Historiographical Review* (Westport, Conn.: Greenwood Press, 1987), p. 199.

55. Hartog, *Public Property and Private Power,* pp. 97–99, 127–29, reports a growing but easy reliance of New York City public works projects on state approval in the period before the Civil War. Although the 1868 ruling by Iowa Supreme Court Justice John F. Dillon that "municipal corporations owe their origin to, and derive their powers and rights wholly from the legislature" confirmed the power of states over cities, Stanley Schultz reports that the courts subsequently encouraged cities to regulate uses of urban land to benefit public health, safety, and civil order. Schultz, *Constructing Urban Culture,* pp. 66–78. "State legislative interference is one of the chief bogeys in American urban history," Jon C. Teaford reports. "For though state legislatures were potentially masters of the city, throughout much of the United States they were actually compliant servants of urban spokesmen." *The Unheralded Triumph: City Government in America, 1870–1900* (Baltimore: Johns Hopkins University Press, 1984), pp. 83–84.

56. *Hartford Courant,* April 11, 1791, cited in Boyd, *Papers of Thomas Jefferson,* 20: 21–22.

57. "Observations on the Intended Canal in Washington City" [1804], reprinted in *Records of the Columbia Historical Society* 8 (Washington, D.C.: Columbia Historical Society, 1905), pp. 161–62. The pamphlet anticipates Jacob M. Price's argument for the relative success of Baltimore as against tobacco trading towns, in "Economic Function and the Growth of American Port Towns in the Eighteenth Century," *Perspectives in American History* 8 (1974): 164–74.

58. *National Intelligencer,* March 25, 1801. Barlow subsequently returned to Washington, where he became a major promoter of nationally funded internal improvements. Jefferson read Barlow's poem *The Vision of Columbus,* which declared, "Canals, long-winding, ope a watery flight / And distant streams and seas and lakes unite," while "New paths, unfolding, lead their watery pride / and towns and empires rise along their side." Ronald E. Shaw, *Canals for a Nation: The Canal Era in the United States, 1790–1860* (Lexington: University Press of Kentucky, 1990), p. 22.

59. Jefferson cited in Harrison, *"Sic Et Non,"* p. 341.

60. Larson, "Bind the Republic Together," pp. 372–73; James D. Dilts, *The Great Road: The Building of the B&O, The Nation's First Railroad* (Stanford: Stanford University Press, 1993), p. 18.

61. Shaw, *Canals for a Nation,* p. 229.

62. Larson, "Bind the Republic Together," pp. 372–86; Shaw, *Canals for a Nation,* p. 200.

63. *Gales & Seaton's Register,* House of Representatives, May 13, 1828, p. 2670.

64. Green, *Village and Capital,* p. 127; Carter Goodrich, *Government Promotion of American Canals and Railroads, 1800–1890* (New York: Columbia University Press, 1960), p. 77. In addition, Goodrich reports, individuals subscribed just over $600,000.

65. 20 Cong., 1 sess., H. Rept. 112, January 30, 1828.

66. Mayor Joseph Gales, message to councils, June 8, 1829, Washingtoniana Division Archives, D.C. Public Library.

67. *Alexandria Gazette,* quoted in the *National Intelligencer,* April 12, 1831.

68. *Alexandria Gazette,* June 26, 1830, cited in Thomas F. Duffy, "The Decline of the Port of Alexandria, Virginia, 1800–1861" (master's thesis, Georgetown University, 1965), p. 85.

69. *National Intelligencer,* May 14, 1831; see also editorial for May 10, 1831. A subsequent note in the *Intelligencer* for December 1, 1834, reported that one canal boat could haul what it would take fifty-six horses to move by land, exclaiming, "Is there any rail-road exploit to equal this?" Such claims, though proved empty by historical perspective, were widespread at the time, not just in America but abroad. As Cecil O. Smith Jr. reports in "The Longest Run: Public Engineers and Planning in France," *American Historical Review* 95 (June 1990): 665, the Erie's success was "the magnificent exception proving the geographic rule that inland barge canals were not the wave of the future. Nowhere else on earth was there the possibility of digging a long canal with a Great Lakes at one end and a slow, deep naturally navigable Hudson River on the other and, at the end of the route, the port of New York and the Atlantic Ocean—with no mountain divide to cross, few locks per mile, and, above all, plenty of water along the way."

70. Walter S. Sanderlin, *The Great National Project* (Baltimore: Johns Hopkins Press, 1946), pp. 83–88.

71. 22 Cong., 2 sess., H. Doc. 117, February 22, 1833. The canal had its own powerful influence in Congress, not the least from its first president, Charles Fenton Mercer, an aggressive advocate of internal improvements and after 1817 an influential member of the House of Representatives. While president of the C&O Canal he also served as a member or chairman of the House Committee on Roads and Canals. It was Mercer who both engineered Congress's initial $1 million subscription in canal stock and blocked a similar request from the B&O. Dilts, *The Great Road,* pp. 29–30, 106.

72. *Gales & Seaton's Register,* February 4, 1835, pp. 1167, 1176.

73. A petition submitted to Congress on February 22, 1828, complained that "the plan of this City, in its spacious public squares, avenues and streets, was adopted by the public functionaries, almost solely in reference to national objects, whilst the convenience and interests of its future population could scarcely have entered into the contemplation of its founders." 20 Cong., 1 sess., S. Doc. 119.

74. 23 Cong., 2 sess., S. Rept. 97, February 2, 1835; Green, *Village and Capital*, pp. 130–31.

75. Arnold, "Congressional Government of the District of Columbia," p. 123.

76. 20 Cong., 2 sess., S. Doc. 119, February 22, 1828.

77. *National Intelligencer*, July 30, 1835.

78. 24 Cong., 1 sess., S. Doc. 11, February 2, 1836.

79. Green, *Village and Capital*, p. 129.

80. 26 Cong., 2 sess., S. Doc. 30, December 28, 1840.

81. Goodrich, *Government Promotion of American Canals*, p. 81.

82. See the glowing report of the railroad's arrival in the *National Intelligencer*, August 27, 1835; Edward Hungerford, *The Story of the B&O Railroad, 1827–1927* (New York: G. P. Putnam's Sons, 1928), chap. 10; and Bryan, *History of the National Capital*, 2: 117, who reports that the railroad shortened the trip to Baltimore to two hours, ten minutes, half the time it took by stage.

83. 25 Cong., 2 sess., S. Rept. 366, April 10, 1838.

84. *Congressional Globe*, app., 29 Cong., 1 sess., May 8, 1846, p. 896. For analysis of the debate that pitted Alexandria and Georgetown against each other over whether the Potomac would be spanned by a bridge or blocked by a dam, see John Lauritz Larson, "A Bridge, A Dam, a River: Liberty and Innovation in the Early Republic," *Journal of the Early Republic* 7 (Winter 1987): 353–75.

85. *Alexandria Gazette*, September 3, August 19, 1846.

86. Sanderlin, *Great National Project*, p. 182.

87. *Alexandria Gazette*, September 7, 1846.

88. Ibid., May 30, 1846.

89. *National Intelligencer*, June 1, 1849.

90. Ordinance, May 20, 1848; Betty L. Plummer, "A History of Public Health in Washington, D.C., 1800–1890" (Ph.D. diss., University of Maryland, 1984), pp. 63–64, 68, 70.

91. Ordinances, April 26, 1850, June 5, 1852, May 27, 1858.

92. Noreen, *Public Street Illumination*, pp. 8–9, reports that Washington businessmen attempted, without success, to organize a gas light company as early as 1816. Baltimore, however, became the first city, in 1816, to introduce such a measure, with Boston (1822), New York (1823), and Philadelphia (1836) following shortly behind. Bryan, *History of the National Capital*, 2: 16, 295–300.

93. Green, *Village and Capital*, p. 209.

94. Ibid., p. 210.

95. David Schuyler, "The Washington Park and Downing's Legacy to Public Landscape Design," in George B. Tatum and Elisabeth Blair MacDougall, eds., *Prophet with Honor: The Career of Andrew Jackson Downing, 1815–1852* (Washington, D.C.: Dumbarton Oaks Research Library and Collection, 1989), p. 293; "Report of the Secretary of War Relating to the Mall," 34 Cong., 1 sess., S. Exec. Doc. 88, July 3, 1856.

96. Therese O'Malley, "'A Public Museum of Trees': Mid-Nineteenth Century Plans for the Mall," in Longstreth, *The Mall in Washington*, pp. 64, 71; David Schuyler, *The New Urban Landscape: Redefinition of City Form in Nineteenth-Century America* (Baltimore: Johns Hopkins University Press, 1986), pp. 67–74.

97. Schuyler, "Washington Park," pp. 294–95.

98. Reps, *Washington on View*, pp. 114, 128.

99. William Tindall, *Standard History of the City of Washington* (Knoxville, Tenn.: H. W. Crew and Co., 1914), p. 237.

100. 21 Cong., 1 sess., H. Rept. 344, April 5, 1830. Mills arrived in Washington in 1830, where he secured commissions to design several federal customhouses in New England, a bridge over the Potomac River, and subsequently a new Treasury building and a patent office. Reps, *Washington on View*, pp. 85–87.

101. Mills had reported that Washington had previously relied for water on what he optimistically called the "rich gifts of nature of underground springs, which rise up whenever a well is dug," springs, however, which were undoubtedly not so pure. Russell F. Weigley, *Quartermaster General of the Union Army: A Biography of M. C. Meigs* (New York: Columbia University Press, 1959), pp. 59–60.

102. *National Intelligencer*, August 10, 19, 1849. In the first of a series of historical sketches for the *Intelligencer* dated August 29, 1849, covering the provision of water from ancient Rome to the present, Mills noted that Boston, Baltimore, Philadelphia, and New York had far outdistanced Washington in securing an adequate supply. In making his case for a new aqueduct system, he cited, above all, the government's duty to protect valuable national records from possible fire.

103. Frederick Gutheim, *Worthy of the Nation: The History of Planning for the National Capital* (Washington, D.C.: Smithsonian Institution Press, 1977), p. 56; Weigley, *Quartermaster General*, p. 59; Harold K. Skramstad, "The Engineer as Architect in Washington: The Contribution of Montgomery Meigs," *Records of the Columbia Historical Society* 47 (Washington, D.C.: Columbia Historical Society, 1971), p. 268.

104. Green, *Village and Capital*, p. 210.

105. Ordinances of June 21, 1859, April 11, 1864.

106. Comparing Washington to Baltimore is particularly instructive. Both sought the advantage of harbors situated on rivers some days' sail inland from the open sea. Both faced the obstacle of traversing mountain ranges in seeking improved transportation routes westward, Baltimore facing a 2,700-foot ascent over the Alleghenies. Each city, however, could claim advantage over cities to the north by virtue of their greater proximity to the trans-Allegheny West, Baltimore lying 150 miles closer than Philadelphia and 200 miles closer than New York. Each city suffered divided political loyalties, as the Maryland legislature split its allegiance between the canal and the railroad, while members of Congress maintained their prime interest in local constituencies. The ultimate triumph of railroad interests in Maryland provided the essential ingredient to boost Baltimore's dominance. See Browne, *Baltimore in the Nation*, especially chaps. 4 and 8.

CHAPTER 2. The Specter of Race

1. Wilhelmus Bogart Bryan, *A History of the National Capital* (New York: Macmillan Co., 1914), 1: 548; Letitia Woods Brown, *Free Negroes in the District of Columbia, 1790–1846* (New York: Oxford University Press, 1972), pp. 43, 63. For a summary of laws in Virginia and Maryland, see Jane Freundel Levey, "Segregation in Education: A Basis for Jim Crow in Washington, D.C., 1804–1880" (master's thesis, George Washington University, 1991), pp. 25–27. Leonard P. Curry, *The Free Black in Urban America, 1800–1850: The Shadow of the Dream* (Chicago: University of Chicago Press, 1981), p. 5, reports that as of 1850, 60 percent of Washington's free black population had been born in Maryland and Virginia and

that as much as 80–90 percent "may have been drawn from a contiguous area no larger than the state in which every one of the other [major border] cities was located."

2. Act of December 16, 1812; Act of April 14, 1821; Linda M. Arnold, "Congressional Government of the District of Columbia, 1800–1846" (Ph.D. diss., Georgetown University, 1974), pp. 76, 78; Curry, *The Free Black in Urban America*, p. 86.

3. Letitia W. Brown, "Residence Patterns of Negroes in the District of Columbia, 1800–1860," *Records of the Columbia Historical Society* 47 (Washington, D.C.: Columbia Historical Society, 1971), p. 74.

4. Constance McLaughlin Green, *Washington: Village and Capital, 1800–1878* (Princeton: Princeton University Press, 1962), p. 99; Richard Sylvester, *District of Columbia Police* (Washington, D.C.: Gibson Bros., 1894), p. 24.

5. Bryan, *History of the National Capital*, 1: 141–42. Lundy spent only a few years based in Washington, much of that time on the road. Levey, "Segregation in Education," p. 65.

6. Neil S. Kramer, "The Trial of Reuben Crandall," *Records of the Columbia Historical Society* 50 (Charlottesville: University Press of Virginia, 1980), pp. 123–39.

7. *National Intelligencer*, August 27, 28, 1835; Green, *Village and Capital*, pp. 141–42; Stephanie Cole, "Changes for Mrs. Thornton's Arthur: Patterns of Domestic Service in Washington, D.C., 1800–1835," *Social Science History* 15 (Fall 1991): 374–75.

8. *Georgetown Metro*, November 18, 1835. Georgetown further restricted free blacks by an ordinance of August 22, 1845, requiring each to carry a certificate of freedom at all times, secured "with two freehold securities in the penalty of five hundred dollars, conditioned for him or her 'and every member of his or her existing family's' good and orderly conduct." Curry, *The Free Black in Urban America*, p. 17, notes that while other such laws had been suggested but not implemented in Baltimore and Charleston and introduced in Louisville in 1839, Washington's code was the most extreme effort to place restrictions on free black employment. For restrictions placed on free blacks in nearby Baltimore, where after 1831 out-of-state freedmen were prohibited from taking up residence and where blacks were generally excluded from a host of licensed jobs, see Joseph Garonzik, "Urbanization and the Black Population of Baltimore, 1850–1870" (Ph.D. diss., State University of New York at Stony Brook, 1974).

9. Dorothy Provine, "The Economic Position of the Free Blacks in the District of Columbia, 1800–1860," *Journal of Negro History* 58 (January 1973): 66–67, 71; Curry, *The Free Black in Urban America*, p. 31. More than 72 percent of a sample taken from the 1860 census by Melvin Williams fell in the categories of laborers, laundresses, servants, and domestics. While blacks constituted 16 percent of the population of Washington that year, they held only 1.85 percent of the wealth. Melvin R. Williams, "A Statistical Study of Blacks in Washington, D.C. in 1860," *Records of the Columbia Historical Society* 50 (Charlottesville: University Press of Virginia, 1980), pp. 173–74. Allan John Johnston presents somewhat different but complementary figures, noting that in 1860 more than half of all black property owners in Washington owned less than $500 and 89 percent of the entire black population owned none at all. In all, although the assessment of free black property holdings amounted to close to $759,000, that amount represented less than 1.5 percent of the city's total property value. "Surviving Freedom: The Black

Community of Washington, D.C., 1860–1880" (Ph.D. diss., Duke University, 1980), pp. 120, 130.

10. Gary B. Nash, *Forging Freedom: The Formation of Philadelphia's Black Community, 1720–1840* (Cambridge, Mass.: Harvard University Press, 1988), p. 253; Bruce Laurie, *Working People of Philadelphia, 1800–1850* (Philadelphia: Temple University Press, 1980), p. 65; David A. Gerber, *Black Ohio and the Color Line, 1860–1915* (Urbana: University of Illinois Press, 1976), p. 7; Leon F. Litwack, *North of Slavery: The Negro in the Free States, 1790–1860* (Chicago: University of Chicago Press, 1961), pp. 158–60. Lacking the magnet of industrialization, Washington failed to attract the number of immigrants that fueled Northern industrial cities. Not only did that relieve the city of some of the antagonism that flared over white exclusion of blacks from trade associations, it reduced the number of immigrant wives who might otherwise have served as servants and maids.

11. Green, *Village and Capital*, pp. 182, 184; Litwack, *North of Slavery*, p. 156.

12. Brown, "Residence Patterns of Negroes," p. 70; Samuel Krislov, *The Negro in Federal Employment: The Quest for Equal Opportunity* (Minneapolis: University of Minnesota Press, 1967), pp. 9–10.

13. Kramer, "Trial of Reuben Crandall," p. 125; Leonard L. Richards, *Gentlemen of Property and Standing: Anti-Abolitionist Mobs in Jacksonian America* (New York: Oxford University Press, 1970), p. 52.

14. *National Intelligencer*, August 7, 15, 1835.

15. Ibid., September 15, 1835.

16. Ibid., September 3, October 1, 1835.

17. Ibid., August 25, September 3, 1835.

18. 24 Cong., 1 sess., February 8, 1836, app., *Gales & Seaton's Register of Debates in Congress*, pp. 104–14. Arnold, "Congressional Government of the District of Columbia," p. 176, reports that the first motion to allow for gradual abolition in the District, introduced in 1808, was tabled without debate and that the focus of abolitionist effort on Washington gathered intensity after submission of a scathing attack on the institution by Jessey Torrey in 1817. See also David L. Lewis, *District of Columbia: A Bicentennial History* (New York: W. W. Norton and Co., 1976), p. 44. Since Pinckney was a strong defender of Missouri's right to bar, in its new constitution, free blacks and mulattoes from entering the state, his strong position could hardly have been surprising. More important to Washington history is that local residents did not challenge the report. On Pinckney's role in the Missouri Compromise, see Litwack, *North of Slavery*, pp. 35–37.

19. 20 Cong., 1 sess., S. Doc. 215, March 24, 1828.

20. Levey, "Segregation in Washington," p. 62.

21. 25 Cong., 3 sess., S. Doc. 191, February 7, 1839.

22. Although a congressional committee appeared ready to recommend repeal of a Maryland law requiring freedmen to carry papers certifying their status at all times, a minority report warned that the action would "have the effect of overrunning the District with hordes of free negroes and runaways. Already the free negroes of the District have arrived to the enormous number of 8361; and to repeal the laws, as proposed, could not fail to add to the number." 29 Cong., 1 sess., H. Rept. 29, January 13, 1844; Resolution of Councils, February 21, 1844.

23. Levey, "Segregation in Washington," p. 122.

24. The *National Intelligencer* for May 4, 1831, reported a meeting of blacks

opposing colonization, about which an editorial defended the American Colonization Society and its efforts as "a scheme devised by purest philanthropy, for the improvement of their condition whether here or in Africa." See also Brown, *Free Negroes*, p. 141, for local opposition; see Curry, *The Free Black in America*, pp. 232–37, and Nash, *Forging Freedom*, p. 238, for black opposition in other areas.

25. Stanley C. Harrold Jr., "The Pearl Affair: The Washington Riot of 1848," *Records of the Columbia Historical Society* 50 (Charlottesville: University Press of Virginia, 1980), p. 154.

26. *Congressional Globe*, 30 Cong., 2 sess., December 18, 1848, p. 55.

27. 31 Cong., 1 sess., July 8, 1850, app. to *Congressional Globe*, p. 1633. Linda M. Arnold reports that debate over the slave trade in Washington extended as far back as 1820 in the debate relating to the admission of Missouri to the union as a slave state. "Congressional Government of the District of Columbia," p. 176.

28. *Washington Star*, May 28, 31, 1854. For reports of clashes over the Fugitive Slave Act, see the *National Intelligencer*, August 10, 13, 1854.

29. Curry, *The Free Black in America*, pp. 159–60.

30. Josephine F. Pacheco, "Myrtilla Miner," in Philip S. Foner and Josephine F. Pacheco, *Three Who Dared: Prudence Crandall, Margaret Douglass, Myrtilla Miner—Champions of Antebellum Black Education* (Westport, Conn.: Greenwood Press, 1984), p. 116. Cook headed Washington's largest school in 1835, when the riots forced him to flee the city. He later returned to Washington to regain a leading role in educating blacks. Green, *Village and Capital*, p. 145.

31. Druscilla Null, "Myrtilla Miner's 'School for Colored Girls': A Mirror on Antebellum Washington," *Records of the Columbia Historical Society* 52 (Charlottesville: University Press of Virginia, 1989), pp. 116, 123.

32. *National Intelligencer*, May 6, 1857, in Levey, "Segregation in Education," p. 132; Pacheco, "Myrtilla Miner," pp. 160–61.

33. Pacheco, "Myrtilla Miner," p. 141.

34. Ibid., p. 196. Another founder of Washington's Republican party, Benjamin Brown French, politely received Minor and a friend in his capacity as president of the Board of Aldermen. "They are engaged in a good cause, and I say God speed them," he wrote in his diary for January 8, 1852. He could not help adding, however, that although they appeared to be sensible and ladylike girls, "I must say I do not admire their taste in the selection of an occupation!" Donald B. Cole and John J. McDonough, eds., *Witness to the Young Republic: A Yankee's Journal, 1828–1870* (Hanover, N.H.: University Press of New England, 1989), p. 226.

35. Litwack, *North of Slavery*, pp. 114–15; Gerber, *Black Ohio and the Color Line*, p. 4.

36. Litwack, *North of Slavery*, pp. 129–31; Philip S. Foner, "Prudence Crandall," in Foner and Pacheco, *Three Who Dared*, p. 44.

37. Litwack, *North of Slavery*, pp. 143–51.

38. Gerber, *Black Ohio and the Color Line*, p. 5.

39. Litwack, *North of Slavery*, p. 279.

40. Pacheco, "Myrtilla Miner," pp. 196–97.

41. Melvin R. Williams, "A Blueprint for Change: The Black Community in Washington, D.C., 1860–1870," *Records of the Columbia Historical Society* 48 (Charlottesville: University Press of Virginia, 1973), pp. 375–76.

42. James H. Whyte, *The Uncivil War: Washington during the Reconstruction, 1865–1878* (New York: Twayne Publishers, 1958), p. 20; *Washington Star*, May 28, 1860.

43. *Washington Chronicle*, November 24, 1863. The paper carried many reports on schools founded by missionary organizations for blacks, summarizing their efforts in a long report on September 19, 1864.

44. *Washington Star*, December 11, 1861.

45. Levey, "Segregation in Education," p. 79.

46. *Washington Star*, March 29, 1862; *National Intelligencer*, March 27, 1862. An editorial in the *Intelligencer* for April 5, in pointing to efforts in the North to bar free blacks from entering their states, urged that emancipation be coupled with colonization.

47. *Washington Chronicle*, April 6, 20, 1862; Green, *Village and Capital*, p. 275. "While stressing this incompatibility of free and slave labor," Litwack reports, "most Republicans also denied any intention to extend political rights to free Negroes and expressed revulsion at the idea of social intercourse with them. Full legal protection should be accorded both races, but according to Republican logic, it did not necessarily follow that Negroes should be granted the right to vote, sit on juries, or testify in cases involving whites." *North of Slavery*, p. 270. See also Richards, *Gentlemen of Property and Standing*, p. 143.

48. *Washington Star*, March 4, 1862. Supporters of the bill, confirming the general consensus in the city, avowed that they too opposed granting freedmen the franchise.

49. *National Republican*, May 16, 22, 1862. This paper was founded by Lewis Clephane in 1860 as a successor to Gamaliel Bailey's *National Era*, where Clephane had been employed as manager. Levey, "Segregation in Education," p. 71.

50. *Washington Star*, June 6, 1862.

51. *Washington Chronicle*, June 12, 1863.

52. Ira Berlin, Barbara J. Fields, Thavolia Glymph, Joseph P. Reidy, and Leslie S. Rowland, eds., *The Destruction of Slavery*, ser. 1, vol. 1 of *Freedom: A Documentary History of Emancipation, 1861–1867* (Cambridge: Cambridge University Press, 1985), p. 164.

53. Ibid., p. 166. A District court upheld this right in 1863 against defense efforts to dismiss evidence from a black on the grounds of the "irreliability of negro testimony in all its bearings." *Washington Chronicle*, April 10, 1863.

54. Margaret Leech, *Reveille in Washington, 1860–1865* (New York: Harper and Brothers, 1941), p. 252.

55. *Congressional Globe*, 37 Cong., 1 sess., February 24, 1862, p. 918; 37 Cong., 2 sess., May 8, 1862, p. 2020. *Washington Star*, December 5, 1861.

56. David Donald, *Charles Sumner and the Rights of Man* (New York: Alfred A. Knopf, 1970), pp. 158–60; James M. McPherson, *The Struggle for Equality: Abolitionists and the Negro in the Civil War and Reconstruction* (Princeton: Princeton University Press, 1964), pp. 230–36.

57. Williams, "Blueprint for Change," p. 375. Curry, *The Free Black in America*, p. 90, reports that while blacks were admitted to horsecars in Brooklyn, they were excluded in New Orleans and relegated to places on the outside platform in New York City until the mid-1850s.

58. The origin of the term *contraband* followed from a decision by General Benjamin Butler to give refuge to blacks after his capture of Fortress Monroe in

the Tidewater section of Southeastern Virginia in May 1861. Moved by practical rather than moral necessity, Butler's policy to treat fugitives as property gained grudging acceptance by federal authorities. The immediate result at Fortress Monroe was a rapid influx of refugees. Finding Northern states unreceptive to appeals to place the newcomers on farms in their region, Butler's successor gained approval to send a number of able-bodied blacks, along with their families, to serve under General George B. McClellan in Washington to assist in the capital's defense. In July General Joseph K. F. Mansfield, commander of the Department of Washington, applied the term to slaves who had escaped to Washington from Virginia. Louis S. Gertein, *From Contraband to Freedman: Federal Policy toward Southern Blacks, 1861–1865* (Westport, Conn.: Greenwood Press, 1973), pp. 11–19; Ira Berlin, Steven F. Miller, Joseph P. Reidy, and Leslie S. Roland, eds., *The Wartime Genesis of Free Labor: The Upper South*, ser. 1, vol. 2 of *Freedom: A Documentary History of Emancipation, 1861–1867* (Cambridge: Cambridge University Press, 1993), pp. 127, 245.

59. Berlin et al., *Wartime Genesis*, p. 245.

60. *Washington Star*, April 6, 1862.

61. Robert J. Brugger, *Maryland: A Middle Temperament, 1634–1980* (Baltimore: Johns Hopkins University Press, 1988), p. 299.

62. Berlin et al., *Wartime Genesis*, pp. 248, 78–79; Joseph P. Reidy, "'Coming from the Shadow of the Past': The Transition from Slavery to Freedom at Freedmen's Village, 1863–1900," *Virginia Magazine of History and Biography* 95 (October 1987): 405–6.

63. Whyte, *The Uncivil War*, p. 31; Richard Wallach to William E. Foster, Provost Marshal, October 29, 1862. Mayor's Correspondence Record Group 351.2, National Archives; Page Milburn, "The Emancipation of the Slaves in the District of Columbia," *Records of the Columbia Historical Society* 16 (Washington, D.C.: Columbia Historical Society, 1913), p. 115.

64. Berlin et al., *Wartime Genesis*, pp. 249–50.

65. Ibid., pp. 252–53.

66. Chief Quartermaster of the Department of Washington Elias M. Greene to Acting Quartermaster General Col. Charles Thomas, December 17, 1863, "Contraband Fund," Consolidated Correspondence File, ser. 225, Central Records, RG 92 (Quartermaster General), National Archives, copy Freedmen and Southern History Project, University of Maryland.

67. Greene to Commander of Department Major General S. P. Heintzelman, May 5, 1863, in ibid., copy Freedmen and Southern History Project.

68. Donald, *Charles Sumner*, p. 192.

69. *Washington Chronicle*, December 8, 1865.

CHAPTER 3. Reconstruction: Social and Physical

1. James H. Whyte, *The Uncivil War: Washington during the Reconstruction, 1865–1878* (New York: Twayne Publishers, 1958), p. 45, notes that only six states in the North and West granted black suffrage, and New York restricted it to those who owned at least $250 in property.

2. David Donald, *Charles Sumner and the Rights of Man* (New York: Alfred A. Knopf, 1970), p. 181; Constance Green, *Washington: Village and Capital, 1800–1878* (Princeton: Princeton University Press, 1962), p. 284; *Washington Star*, December 12, 1865.

3. Donald, *Charles Sumner*, pp. 281–82. Sumner's bill stating conditions for the return of Southern states to the Union included the "suppression of all oligarchical pretensions" and the complete enfranchisement of all citizens regardless of color or race. *Washington Chronicle*, December 5, 1865.

4. *Washington Chronicle*, December 19, 1865. For the text of the resolution, see William Tindall, "A Sketch of Mayor Sayles J. Bowen," *Records of the Columbia Historical Society* 18 (Washington, D.C.: Columbia Historical Society, 1915), pp. 33–35. Such racially tainted remarks were common in the immediate postwar period, especially among Southern whites, but also in the North. William Gillette, *Retreat from Reconstruction, 1869–1879* (Baton Rouge: Louisiana State University Press, 1979), pp. 238–39.

5. *Washington Star*, December 20, 1865. In charging that Congress intended to "thoroughly Africanize the District," it claimed that the city was burdened with thousands of contraband, who, it charged, "were ignorant and incapable of the duties of citizenship." Ibid., December 5, 8, 1865. The *Chronicle* was founded in 1861 at the request of President Lincoln to counter Radical influence within the Republican party, but by 1863 the paper had embraced Radical doctrine. James LeRoy Oxford, "John W. Forney, The *Washington Chronicle*, and the Civil War Era" (Ph.D. diss., University of New Mexico, 1952), pp. 62, 147.

6. *Washington Chronicle*, December 16, 19, 1865. A petition dated January 17, 1865, from established black leaders John Cook and Lewis Douglass, among others, while urging enfranchisement without regard to color, nonetheless was willing to accept an educational qualification. See ibid., December 12, 1865. Green, *Village and Capital*, p. 288, describes *Chronicle* editor John Forney's hard-line editorial policy, portraying Washington as "a city virtually captured from her rebel inhabitants and thus properly subject to all the punitive measures the Union army employed in the South."

7. *Washington Chronicle*, December 22, 1865.

8. Green, *Village and Capital*, p. 305. As chairman of the House Committee on Public Lands, Julian was a strong proponent of land reform, arguing that Southern society had to be remade according to the principles of "radical democracy." See Eric Foner, *Reconstruction: America's Unfinished Revolution* (New York: Harper and Row, 1988), p. 68.

9. Tindall, "Sketch of Mayor Sayles J. Bowen," pp. 33–35; Green, *Village and Capital*, p. 298; Whyte, *Uncivil War*, p. 49. The *Washington Chronicle* for December 18, 1865, urged that no one favoring universal freedom participate and thus give the color of legality to what it called a mock election.

10. *Washington Star*, December 22, 1865. The *Star* for January 19, 1866, reiterated the theme, arguing that if Congress chose to "make the national capital a negro Utopia," blacks would swarm to the area, making Congress "suffer fully their share of any inconveniences from such surroundings."

11. Ibid., February 7, 1866. According to his most recent biographer, Douglass went into the meeting already disgusted with Johnson's Reconstruction politics and did everything he could to put down the president, invoking the grandeur of his predecessor in office and claiming that Lincoln had called blacks to enlist in the Union cause so they might ultimately be given the vote "with which to save ourselves." William S. McFeely, *Frederick Douglass* (New York: W. W. Norton and Co., 1991), pp. 246–47. See also James M. McPherson, *The Struggle for Equality:*

Abolitionists and the Negro in the Civil War and Reconstruction (Princeton: Princeton University Press, 1964), pp. 343–46.

12. Morton Keller, *Affairs of State: Public Life in Late Nineteenth Century America* (Cambridge, Mass.: Harvard University Press, Belknap Press, 1977), pp. 63–64; *Washington Star,* February 7, 1866.

13. *Washington Chronicle,* February 20, 1866. Foner, *Reconstruction,* pp. 247–48, reports the national argument contained in the *Chronicle,* that with this veto Johnson appeared ready to turn back every measure of congressional reconstruction. Although the *Star* worried that Johnson's permissive policy of encouraging the restoration of the Southern states would result in turning power back to the white oligarchy, which had brought on the war, it supported the veto, charging that to secure self-sufficiency for the freedmen, it was necessary to let the laws of supply and demand "which govern labor and regulate wages elsewhere do for the emancipated slaves what legislative actions could never do." *Washington Star,* February 20, 1866. See also Keller, *Affairs of State,* p. 71.

14. *Washington Star,* December 10, 1866, quoting Senator Waitman Willey of West Virginia. Granting grudgingly that Congress as the sole judge in the matter was intent on adopting manhood suffrage, the *Star* recommended restrictions to make the act more palatable, in addition to requiring voters to be able to read and to pay a school tax four months in advance of the election.

15. Ibid., January 7, 1867.

16. Ibid., January 7, 8, 22, 1867.

17. Ibid., February 27, 1867.

18. *Washington Chronicle,* May 27, 1867.

19. *Washington Star,* May 30, 31, 1867. The *National Intelligencer* for May 25, 1867, reported a Democratic meeting that claimed the country would be watching to see whether whites would submit to the indignity Congress had imposed on them. A May 29 editorial in the same paper urged voters to "forever settle the question whether the citizens of Washington stand under their own government or leave their destinies in the hands of the motley crowd of mendicants who have been attracted hither by the largesse of the Freedmen's Bureau."

20. *Washington Star,* May 31, June 4, 1867.

21. Tindall, "Sayles Bowen," pp. 26–28; *Washington Chronicle,* December 18, 1865.

22. *Washington Chronicle,* May 9, 1868.

23. *National Intelligencer,* May 28, 1868.

24. *Washington Star,* June 1, 1868, *Washington Chronicle,* April 29, 30, 1868. A petition complaining about Republican efforts to keep soldiers off the rolls contained a number of Irish names, presumably Democrats. June 28, 1868, Senate Papers 40A-H51.1 DC, National Archives.

25. Whyte, *Uncivil War,* p. 67; Thomas R. Johnson, "Reconstruction Politics in Washington: 'An Experimental Garden for Radical Plants,'" *Records of the Columbia Historical Society* 50 (Charlottesville: University Press of Virginia, 1980), p. 183; *Washington Chronicle,* April 26, 29, 30, 1868.

26. *Washington Star,* June 3, 1868.

27. Ibid., May 22, 1868.

28. Green, *Village and Capital,* pp. 321–22. In line with its conservative social orientation, the *Star* editorialized on June 7, 1869, against the public accommoda-

237

tions bills, which it argued would prove offensive to visitors to the city. The complaint of the colored people, the paper claimed, was not that they were barred from mixing with whites but that they wanted more support for their own social and fraternal organizations: "The colored people are acquiring a good deal of self-respect, and are not disposed to thrust themselves, socially, where they are not wanted. What they would probably ask is that they may be admitted to equally eligible seats with the whites, but probably they would prefer to have their own quarter in each part of the house." Only three Northern states—Massachusetts, New York, and Kansas—passed anti-discrimination provisions similar to those adopted in Washington. Half the Southern states and virtually all border states, as well as Pennsylvania, Ohio, and Indiana, enacted laws enforcing racial segregation in public schools. Gillette, *Retreat from Reconstruction,* p. 194.

29. *Washington Star,* July 28, 1869.

30. For an interpretation of the importance of party patronage in the period, see Richard L. McCormick, "The Party Period and Public Policy: An Exploratory Hypothesis," *Journal of American History* 66 (September 1979): 279–98.

31. Among the petitions submitted to Congress by blacks seeking work, one dated January 15, 1868, painted a particularly stark picture of employment, charging that "the white laborers of this city refuse to work upon jobs with the colored man, unless he is employed as a mere helper or hod-carrier, and by thus combining against us they deprive us of nearly all profitable and permanent employment, and secure to themselves a monopoly of nearly all the skilled and remunerative labor of this District." Senate Papers 40A-H5.1 DC, National Archives. Republican leaders responded through participation in philanthropic as well as political organizations, as revealed in a petition sent from the Provident Aid Society to members of the Senate District Committee on January 28, 1868. Noting that the committee had raised $5,000 already, it sought further assistance, pointing to the fact that those most in need had migrated to Washington recently from other parts of the country. Sharing the fear that too much charity might attract "hundreds and thousands" of other needy to the city, the petition stressed putting the money into public improvements, "thus affording to the able bodied poor an opportunity by their labor of obtaining sustenance." Senate Papers 40A-E.3 DC, National Archives. See also *Washington Chronicle,* May 16, 1868.

32. *Washington Chronicle,* June 30, 1868.

33. Both Bowen and his wife were active in voluntary associations to assist the needy freedmen who had poured into the District. See, for instance, the petition of the National Freedmen's Relief Association, January 9, 1868. Senate Papers 40A–H5.1 DC, National Archives.

34. See resolutions for removal of the capital from Washington, by the Kansas legislature, which called for a site at Fort Leavenworth, and by Iowa, which requested "some point in the great valley of the Mississippi." 41 Cong., 2 sess., S. Misc. Doc. 28, January 26, 1869; 41 Cong., 2 sess., S. Misc. Doc. 73, March 17, 1870.

35. *Washington Star,* editorials, June 5, 1868, January 5, 1869.

36. *Washington Chronicle,* May 16, 1868.

37. Ibid., May 29, 1868.

38. *Washington Star,* October 1, 1869, May 17, 1870.

39. Ibid., May 11, 1870; report of the clerk of the House Committee for the District of Columbia, July 12, 1870, Senate Papers 41A-E5 24 DC, National Archives.

40. *Washington Chronicle,* May 6, 1870.

41. *Washington Star,* May 7, 14, 1870.

42. Ibid., November 12, 1869.

43. *Washington Chronicle,* April 27, 1870.

44. *Washington Star,* May 2, 1868.

45. Tindall, "Sayles Bowen," p. 28.

46. A. Sergent to Senator Charles Sumner, July 13, 1867, Senate Papers 40A-E4 DC, National Archives; Tindall, "Sayles Bowen," pp. 27–28. Washington's first Board of Trade made improved transportation facilities the heart of its agenda but floundered within a few years over disagreements about the means to achieve those ends. See Elizabeth J. Miller, "Dreams of Being the Capital of Commerce: The National Fair of 1879," *Records of the Columbia Historical Society* 51 (Charlottesville: University Press of Virginia, 1984), pp. 71–72. Washington County encompassed the relatively undeveloped area of the District of Columbia, excluding the cities of Washington and Georgetown.

47. *Washington Star,* May 25, 1870.

48. *New National Era,* June 16, 1870.

49. *Washington Chronicle,* December 25, 1865; *Washington Star,* January 25, May 22, 1866.

50. *Washington Star,* February 26, March 15, 1867.

51. 41 Cong., 1 sess., S. Misc. Doc. 24, April 7, 1869.

52. *Washington Chronicle,* January 19, 27, 1870.

53. *Washington Star,* February 2, 1870.

54. *New National Era,* January 27, 1870; see also *Chronicle* editorial, February 23, 1870.

55. *Washington Chronicle,* January 18, 24, 1870.

56. Ibid., January 21, 1871.

57. Ibid., March 4, 1870. A *Washington Star* editorial dated May 30, 1868, declared on the eve of local elections, "The city must make up its mind to have to shoulder mainly the work of municipal improvement. Congress may make appropriations in driblets, but nothing sufficient to carry out our improvements on any systematic comprehensive scale." An editorial dated January 1, 1871, pressing for a new government, stressed the importance of a board of public works "charged with the duty of establishing comprehensive and systematic plans for all general improvements."

58. William M. Maury, *Alexander "Boss" Shepherd and the Board of Public Works* (Washington, D.C.: GW Washington Studies no. 3, 1975), p. 4; Green, *Village and Capital,* pp. 335–36.

59. *Congressional Globe,* 41 Cong., 3 sess., January 21, 1871, p. 642. Senator George Edmunds of Vermont made a similar point a few days later in aruging that Congress had a responsibility to assert its power when local authorities were lax enough to allow animals to continue to run free on the streets. Ibid., January 24, 1871, p. 687. The *Star* for January 25, 1871, denied allegations that the new government had anything to do with compromising the rights of freedmen to vote, since "by the bill the colored men have precisely the same rights of suffrage as white men."

60. *Washington Chronicle,* March 3, 1871; *Washington Star,* March 8, 1871; Whyte, *Uncivil War,* pp. 22–23.

61. *Washington Chronicle,* March 30, 1871. For a profile of Chipman, see C. R. Gibbs's essay in the *Washington Post,* March 2, 1989.

62. *Washington Chronicle,* January 6, 1872, March 13, 1872; Laws of the Legislative Assembly, June 26, 1871; Green, *Village and Capital,* p. 372. Thomas Johnson reports as well that under the territorial government, about one-third of city employees, working as lamplighters, street sweepers, garbage collectors, and the like were black. Johnson, "Reconstruction Politics in Washington," pp. 188–89.

63. July 20, 1871, Joint Committees relating to the District of Columbia, 40–45 Congress, box 1, RG 128, National Archives.

64. Maury, *Shepherd,* pp. 9–10.

65. *Washington Star,* November 23, 1871; *Washington Chronicle,* July 8, 1871. Among other positive endorsements for the new government was that of the *New York Times* for December 12, 1871, which praised District residents "instead of sitting supinely still as heretofore" for deciding "to go ahead and help themselves."

66. *Washington Patriot,* March 22, 1871, July 3, 1872, referring to the Franco-Prussian War.

67. Chauncey Hickox, "The New Washington," *Lippincott's* 11 (March 1873): 306. The *Philadelphia Press* compared Shepherd to Haussmann in an article published September 20, 1872. The essay was probably written by Emily Briggs, who wrote Shepherd on April 29, 1873, of her determination to describe Shepherd's role in converting "a mere winter resort into [one] of the most substantial places in the Union." "I believe in you Mr Shepherd," she closed, "and if I don't make others see as I do it will be because I don't know how to use the pen." Alexander Shepherd Papers, box 4, Library of Congress. Haussmann's success in bypassing a French commission set up to supervise public works so that he could report directly to Napoleon III and his manipulation of loans to carry out the work of rebuilding the heart of Paris set a strong precedent for Shepherd. David H. Pinkney, *Napoleon III and the Rebuilding of Paris* (Princeton: Princeton University Press, 1958), pp. 26, 174–209.

68. *Washington Star,* February 5, 1872.

69. *Washington Chronicle,* January 23, 1872; *Washington Patriot,* January 25, 1872.

70. 42 Cong., 2 sess., H. Rept. 72, May 13, 1872; Maury, *Shepherd,* pp. 39–40.

71. Maury, *Shepherd,* p. 42.

72. *Washington Star,* September 13, 1873.

73. Ibid., October 15, 1873.

74. *Annual Report of the Board of Public Works,* November 1, 1872.

75. Green, *Village and Capital,* p. 359; *Annual Report of the Board of Public Works,* November 1, 1873; 43 Cong., 1 sess., S. Rept. 647, June 16, 1874.

76. *Washington Star,* May 20, 29, 1874. Merrick was an active Democratic partisan at the height of Radical strength, as he took the lead in 1867 in challenging Republican registry lists for the first election under the expanded franchise. *National Intelligencer,* June 15, 1867.

77. *Washington Star,* June 19, 1873.

78. Maury, *Shepherd,* p. 48.

79. *Washington Chronicle,* June 6, 1874.

80. The report, submitted by Senator Lot Morrill, described the committee's hopes for the capital as establishing "that common ground where the fervor of patriotism will rise above the zeal of partisanship, and the laws, appropriations,

and appointments to office will be made in relation to its real wants, and cease to be shaped by partisan aspirations or local interests." 43 Cong., 2 sess., S. Rept. 479, December 15, 1874, p. 3. While the investigative report issued on June 16 did not specifically endorse a federal payment to the District, it nonetheless pointed to such a practice in stating, "The committee here also recommends that the joint select committee to provide a form of government should settle and determine the proportion of expenses which should be borne by the District and the United States respectively." 43 Cong., 1 sess., S. Rept. 647, p. 29.

81. A minority report signed by George E. Spencer of Alabama from the Joint Select Committee to Form a Government for the District of Columbia charged that the elimination of the elective franchise in Washington represented "the entering wedge to the overthrow of representative government throughout the United States," recommending instead adoption of "a simple municipal government in the form common to American communities." 44 Cong., 2 sess., S. Rept. 572, January 11, 1877.

82. *Washington Patriot*, September 26, November 21, 1872.

83. *Washington Chronicle*, February 9, 1872; Jane Freundel Levey, "Segregation in Education: A Basis for Jim Crow in Washington, D.C., 1804–1880" (master's thesis, George Washington University, 1991), pp. 237–42.

84. Gillette, *Retreat from Reconstruction*, pp. 238–39.

85. See petition from the National Executive Committee of Colored People, signed by Lewis Douglass, Sella Martin, and John Cook, among others, seeking public instruction in Washington without regard to color. 41 Cong., 2 sess., S. Misc. Doc. 130, April 29, 1870; Levey, "Segregation in Education," pp. 243–44; Whyte, *Uncivil War*, pp. 164–65.

86. The *Chronicle* shifted its hard-line radical position after John Forney left as editor in January 1871, defending the concept of the territorial government and—finally—its termination, along with the franchise for Washington voters. Gillette, *Retreat from Construction*, p. 196, cites an editorial of August 25, 1873, from the *National Republican*, founded as an abolitionist voice by Lewis Clephane, warning against any further efforts "to make of Washington a sort of Hayti where black men shall rule." Clephane may have foreshadowed the shift in Republican ideology.

87. Joseph West Moore, *Picturesque Washington* (Providence, R.I.: J. A. and R. A. Reid, 1884), p. 52. For a further account of the improvements, which listed virtually the same features, although in more flowery language, see Mary Clemmer Ames, *Ten Years in Washington* (Cincinnati: Queen City Publishing, 1874), p. 73. Shepherd's achievement in constructing 120 miles of sewer lines, 150 miles of improved roads, 30 miles of water mains, and 39 miles of gas lines, as well as filling in the notorious Washington Canal, compared favorably with the other major city undergoing a reconstruction at the same time, Chicago, which had 140 miles of sewer lines in 1871. Maury, *Shepherd*, p. 51; Jon C. Teaford, *The Unheralded Triumph: City Government in America, 1870–1900* (Baltimore: Johns Hopkins University Press, 1984), p. 225.

88. The most thorough assessment of the corruption in the Shepherd regime is provided by Alan Lessoff, who shows that while no member of the territorial government was ever indicted for any action related to the comprehensive plan, as much as 20 percent of spending from the plan went to friends and business

associates of members of the Board of Public Works. Lessoff, *The Nation and Its City: Politics, "Corruption," and Progress in Washington, D.C., 1861–1902* (Baltimore: Johns Hopkins University Press, 1994), pp. 79, 95.

89. *Washington Patriot,* September 26, November 21, 1872.

90. *Washington Star,* April 25, 1896.

CHAPTER 4. Making a Greater Washington

1. *Washington Star,* December 12, 1900.

2. Quoted in Alan Lessoff, "The Federal Government and the National Capital: Washington, 1861–1902" (Ph.D. diss., Johns Hopkins University, 1990), p. 218.

3. Alan Lessoff, *The Nation and Its City: Politics, "Corruption," and Progress in Washington, D.C., 1861–1902* (Baltimore: Johns Hopkins University Press, 1994), p. 123.

4. *Washington Star,* December 23, 1879, January 13, 1880. The *Star* revealed its continuing conservatism on race in opposing all forms of integration in an editorial appearing on September 30, 1890. The patronizing attitude toward blacks in official Washington is further illustrated in a local guidebook, which, while noting that Washington had more "well-to-do colored people than any other American city," charged, "it must be admitted that many are improvident, unreliable, careless of the future, and are quite content if they have a ragged coat to wear, a crust to eat, and plenty of leisure to enjoy the sunshine." Joseph West Moore, *Picturesque Washington* (Providence, R.I.: J. A. and R. A. Reid, 1884), p. 248.

5. According to a *Star* editorial for November 29, 1889, "The time and labor and money which others spend on their political machines, we save for other purposes." See also *Star* editorials, January 8, November 18, December 21, 1891. An editorial for June 28, 1901, on Philadelphia's upcoming election, for instance, attacked big-city machines, charging, "The whole body of the nation is threatened with blood pouring from these local sores." A *Star* editorial for November 18, 1901, "The Best Governed City," identified Washington's nonpartisan government as the key to its success, while a subsequent editorial for December 21, 1901, claimed that federal surveillance over the city raised "local administration to the same high plane as that occupied by the federal government." Constance Green, *Washington: Capital City, 1879–1950* (Princeton: Princeton University Press, 1963), p. 60, cites an article from a 1900 issue of *Atlantic Monthly* as an example of the national respect given Washington's form of government. See also Lessoff, *Nation and Its City,* pp. 203–4.

6. "The New Washington," *Harper's* 50 (February 1875): 314.

7. *Congressional Record,* 43 Cong., 2 sess., February 12, 1875, p. 1207, cited in Lessoff, "Federal Government and National Capital," p. 178.

8. John Addison Porter, *The City of Washington: Its Origin and Administration* (Baltimore: Johns Hopkins Press, 1885), pp. 43–44, quoted in Lessoff, *Nation and Its City,* p. 99.

9. *Washington Star,* May 29, November 2, 1893, November 8, 1890, May 4, 1903. In a special supplement marking the paper's fiftieth anniversary in 1902, G. A. Lyon wrote under the title "The *Star*'s Part in the National Development of Washington," "What L'Enfant planned and government approved Shepherd tried to the limit of local means to develop and perfect."

10. Lessoff, "Federal Government and National Capital," pp. 170–72.

11. Stetson Hutchins and Joseph West Moore, *The National Capital: Past and Present* (Washington, D.C.: Washington Post Publishing Co., 1885), p. 303. In *Democracy: An American Novel*, published in 1880, Adams tells the story of Mrs. Lightfoot Lee, who having tired of society in New York, looks for amusement in the more provincial but enticing city of Washington.

12. Moore, *Picturesque Washington*, pp. 240–41. The continuity with the Shepherd era is well demonstrated in comparing Moore's description with an editorial in the *Washington Star*, "Washington as a Central Winter Residence," January 6, 1872. The attractions of art galleries, libraries, and the new Smithsonian Institution, the *Star* said, must "be greatly increased as the city is adorned, improved, and made equal in comfort and elegance to its natural advantages of position and climate. For the first time in the history of Washington the city has streets sufficiently well paved to allow of pleasure-driving every day through the winter, and the brilliant spectacle on Pennsylvania Avenue of an afternoon is a foretaste of what the future will show when the wealth of the country shall congregate here, as it is beginning to do, for its winter Newport or Saratoga."

13. Lessoff, *Nation and Its City*, pp. 86–87; *Annual Report of the Engineer Commissioner*, November 30, 1875, pp. 54, 46.

14. Stanley K. Schultz, *Constructing Urban Culture: American Cities and City Planning, 1800–1920* (Philadelphia: Temple University Press, 1989), pp. 184–85, points out that St. Louis had to reconstruct its water supply system and Cincinnati its sewer system within ten years of completion as well; the *Annual Report of the Commissioners of the District of Columbia* for 1875, p. 50, while not so incisive in its criticism, complained that aside from the principal mains, Shepherd appeared not to have followed plans for sewers laid out for him by the engineer assigned to the Board of Public Works. See also Stanley K. Schultz and Clay McShane, "To Engineer the Metropolis: Sewers, Sanitation, and City Planning in Late-19th Century America," *Journal of American History* 65 (September 1978): 397; Lessoff, *Nation and Its City*, p. 91.

15. Aneli Moucka Levy, "Washington, D.C. and the Growth of Its Early Suburbs: 1860–1920" (master's thesis, University of Maryland, 1980), p. 68; Patrick Haynes Newell, ed., *Planning and Building the City of Washington* (Washington, D.C.: Ransdell, 1932), pp. 142–43. Jon A. Peterson, "The Impact of Sanitary Reform upon American Urban Planning, 1840–1890," *Journal of Social History* 13 (Fall 1979): 83–103, identifies the challenge of building sewers as a necessary first step in the creation of a comprehensive urban planning process.

16. *Annual Report of the Engineer Commissioner*, November 30, 1875; *Annual Report of the Commissioners of the District of Columbia*, 1878, p. 92.

17. *Washington Star*, January 29, 1879.

18. Frederick Gutheim, *Worthy of the Nation: The History of Planning for the National Capital* (Washington, D.C.: Smithsonian Institution Press, 1977), pp. 92–94.

19. Howard Gillette Jr., "Old Anacostia," in Kathryn Schneider Smith, ed., *Washington at Home: An Illustrated History of Neighborhoods in the Nation's Capital* (Northridge, Calif.: Winsor Publications, 1988), pp. 97–105.

20. *Washington Star*, January 10, 1863.

21. Ronald M. Johnson, "LeDroit Park," in Smith, *Washington at Home*, pp. 139–41.

22. *Washington Chronicle*, May 29, 1870; Howard Gillette Jr., "The Emergence

of the Modern Metropolis: Philadelphia in the Age of Its Consolidation," in William W. Cutler III and Howard Gillette Jr., eds., *The Divided Metropolis: Social and Spatial Dimensions of Philadelphia, 1800–1975* (Westport, Conn.: Greenwood Press, 1980), pp. 3–25.

23. Melissa McLoud, "Craftsmen and Entrepreneurs: Builders in Late-Nineteenth Century Washington, D.C." (Ph.D. diss., George Washington University, 1988), p. 70; Levy, "Washington and Its Early Suburbs," p. 42; [John P. Coffin], *Washington: Historical Sketches of the Capital City of Our Country* (Washington, D.C.: John P. Coffin, 1887), p. 318.

24. Carl Abbott, "Perspectives on Urban Economic Planning: The Case of Washington, D.C., since 1880," *Public Historian* 11 (Spring 1989): 10.

25. *Washington Star,* December 14, 1867; Cindy Sondik Aron, *Ladies and Gentlemen of the Civil Service: Middle-Class Workers in Victorian America* (New York: Oxford University Press, 1987), pp. 20, 22. The *Star* for March 12, 1887, estimated that a government salary of $1,200 was sufficient to buy a house valued at $2,500, somewhat below the price asked in new developments like LeDroit Park, where costs fell between $3,500 and $7,000, but adequate to allow purchases in most other residential areas. See Barbara Hightower, "LeDroit Park: The Making of a Suburb, 1872–1888" (master's thesis, George Washington University, 1982), pp. 86–87.

26. *Washington Star,* June 10, 1882.

27. Moore, *Picturesque Washington,* p. 247. "Ten years ago," a writer claimed in a 1901 issue of the *Architectural Record,* "the majority of government officials lived in hotels. Many still do, but the social demands are fast becoming so various and elaborate that those who would be counted as factors in the society of the capital find it desirable to command the facilities for entertaining that a house alone affords." "Recent Domestic Architecture in Washington, D.C.," *Architectural Record* 10 (April 1901): 425.

28. Table 2 adapted from Lessoff, "Federal Government and Capital." Aron, *Ladies and Gentlemen,* p. 5, presents similar figures from different but comparable years. For a contemporary review of the growing opportunities for government clerks, see the *Washington Star* for March 31, 1894.

29. Writing in 1889, the noted statistician Carol D. Wright stated that the job stability offered by the act made civil servants feel safe in purchasing rather than renting their homes. Susan H. Meyers, "Capitol Hill, 1870–1900: The People and Their Homes," *Records of the Columbia Historical Society* 49 (Charlottesville: University Press of Virginia, 1976), p. 289; Levy, "Washington and Its Early Suburbs," p. 96.

30. Thomas Eugene Prince, "Washington, D.C.'s Streetcar Suburbs: A Comparative Analysis of Brookland and Brightwood, 1870–1900" (master's thesis, University of Maryland, 1979), pp. 39, 44; *Washington Star,* August 30, 1894. See also John N. Pearce, "Brookland: Something in the Air," in Smith, *Washington at Home,* pp. 171–79, and George W. McDaniel and John N. Pearce, *Images of Brookland: The History and Architecture of a Washington Suburb* (Washington, D.C.: GW Washington Studies no. 10, 1988), p. 17.

31. *Washington Star,* May 18, 1889.

32. Katherine Grandine, "Brightwood," in Smith, *Washington at Home,* pp. 93–94.

33. Judith Helm Robinson, "Chevy Chase," Emily Hotaling Eig, "Kalorama,"

and Kathleen Sinclair Wood, "Cleveland Park," in Smith, *Washington at Home*, pp. 181–213.

34. *Washington Star*, March 26, 1887, quoted in McLoud, "Craftsmen and Entrepreneurs," p. 117.

35. *Baltimore Sun*, October 19, 1886.

36. *Washington Star*, March 1, April 29, 1890.

37. S. L. Phillips, president, Metropolitan Railroad Co., to Senate District Committee, March 31, 1896; Victor Kauffman to Senate District Committee, December 24, 1896, Senate Papers 54A-F8 28 DC, National Archives.

38. W. F. Mattingly, Minutes of the District Commissioners, May 16, 1899, RG 351, Records of the Government of the District of Columbia, National Archives.

39. *Annual Report of the Commissioners of the District of Columbia*, 1879, p. 7.

40. *Washington Star*, May 17, 1898.

41. Ibid., December 20, 1893.

42. Lessoff, *Nation and Its City*, p. 242.

43. *Washington Star*, March 23, 1887.

44. *Annual Report of the Commissioners of the District of Columbia*, 1888–89, pp. 30, 255.

45. *Washington Star*, January 1, 1890; Grandine, "Brightwood," p. 94.

46. *Annual Report of the Engineer Commissioner*, 1888–89, p. 266.

47. Johnson, "LeDroit Park," p. 141. The *Washington Star* for September 14, 1888, put the racial implications of the fence in stark terms, noting, "Through the giant cracks in the fence one can see Howardtown, and Howardtown sometimes thrusts a shining head through the cracks." LeDroit's racial composition changed dramatically, from white to black, after the fence came down. By 1930, according to one account, only one white family remained in the area. Charles A. Hamilton, "Washington's First Residential Suburb," *Nation's Capital Magazine* 1 (December 1930): 29.

48. See the report of a special committee of the Board of Trade on highway extensions in the *Washington Star*, February 20, 1896. It describes the legislation of 1888 and 1893 as necessary because Washington was "in danger of being surrounded by straggling villages with a labyrinth of streets, narrower in general than those in the city, in many instances not being extensions of the city streets, and even not conforming to each other."

49. District of Columbia Commissioners to J. W. Babcock, chairman of the Committee on the District of Columbia, House of Representatives, January 12, 1898. Senate Papers 55A–F6–F7 50 DC, National Archives. In fact, Alan Lessoff points out, of the other large cities in the eastern United States, only Philadelphia had clear legal authority to compel subdividers to adhere to preconceived patterns of development. *Nation and Its City*, p. 243.

50. *Washington Star*, January 19, 1901. Noyes pointed to a clause in the most recent highway act in which Congress had attempted to deny its responsibility for improvements in Washington County. While the offensive measure was removed in 1900, it was being discussed again in 1901.

51. Lessoff, *Nation and Its City*, p. 245.

52. *Washington Star*, October 19, 1904. The *Star* for January 7, 1906, notes that before the act, ninety-three different subdivisions could name their own streets, with the result that the same street could change names several times within the

space of a few blocks. See also Alexander B. Hagner, "Street Nomenclature of Washington City," *Records of the Columbia Historical Society* 7 (Washington, D.C.: Columbia Historical Society, 1904), pp. 237–61.

53. *Washington Star*, November 15, 1890.

54. Ibid., April 30, 1887.

55. Ibid., April 6, 1887.

56. Washington Board of Trade, *Sixth Annual Report*, 1896, p. 17.

57. *Washington Star*, December 7, 1901, April 4, 1903. In 1897 the *Star* announced that it would deliver papers to Georgetown and Tenleytown, several miles farther out into Washington County, at the same price as in the city, commenting that both communities had become virtually part of the city.

58. D. W. Flagler to Senate District Committee, December 21, 1896, Senate Papers 54A-F8 26 DC, National Archives.

59. Senate Papers 56A-F7 47 DC, National Archives.

60. *Washington Star*, June 1, 1889.

61. The *Washington Star* for May 18, 1889, identifies Truesdell as "the father" of Washington Heights and an active promoter of the new road that would connect that area with the city by filling in the ravine that separated the area from Kalorama.

62. Irwin B. Linton, president, North Capitol and Eckington Citizens Association, to Senator James McMillan, April 26, 1900, Senate Papers 56A-F7 47 DC, National Archives; Memorial of North Capitol and Eckington Citizens Association, 54 Cong., 2 sess., S. Doc. 53, January 11, 1897.

63. Information on Eckington taken chiefly from an unpublished paper in the author's possession by Helen P. Ross, "The Capital's First Electric Streetcar Suburb: Eckington and Its Development, 1888–1908," December 10, 1986. For information on other citizens' association contests as reported here, see Grandine, "Brightwood," p. 94; *Suburban Citizen*, April 1, 1893; *Washington Star*, March 20, 26, 28, 1896.

64. *Washington Star*, May 23, 1894.

65. Ibid., May 16, 1896, April 21, 1904; Lessoff, *Nation and Its City*, p. 206.

66. *Washington Star*, June 9, 1888, May 18, 1889. A local guidebook described Parker as taking up various government positions in Washington after moving to the city upon his discharge from the army in 1865, during which time, the guide noted, "he was constantly handling real estate. He sold all of Columbia Heights and University Park, and during October of this year will plan Petworth, a suburban addition, in the market." Coffin, *Historical Sketches*, p. 276; Lessoff, "Federal Government and National Capital," p. 376; Green, *Capital City*, pp. 29, 31–32; Jessica I. Elfenbein, *Civics, Commerce, and Community: The History of the Greater Washington Board of Trade, 1889–1989* (Dubuque, Iowa: Kendall/Hunt, 1989), pp. 2–3. Lessoff, *Nation and Its City*, pp. 243–44, describes the Board of Trade support, led by Truesdell and Parker, favoring a comprehensive approach to platting the whole county as soon as possible.

67. Lessoff, *Nation and Its City*, p. 209.

68. Washington Board of Trade, *Sixth Annual Report*, 1896, p. 34, cited in Lessoff, *Nation and its City*, p. 223.

69. Washington Board of Trade, *Sixth Annual Report*, 1896, pp. 4, 9. The board indicated its desire to exercise control over development at an 1894 meeting

at which officers complained of suburban development, which constituted a "stranglehold with a belt of subdivisions of land laid out between 1866 and 1888 which have choked the city growth and retarded the march of improvements."

70. Elfenbein, *Civics, Commerce, and Community,* pp. 13–14.

71. *Annual Report of the Commissioners of the District of Columbia,* 1885, p. 122; *Washington Star,* November 11, 1889; William Bushong and Piera M. Weiss, "Rock Creek Park: Emerald of the Capital City," *Washington History* 2 (Fall/Winter 1990– 91): 20–22; *Washington Star,* November 11, 1889, September 27, 1890.

72. Lessoff, *Nation and Its City,* p. 234; *Washington Star,* September 27, 1890.

73. *Washington Chronicle,* January 21, 1871; *Washington Patriot,* March 29, April 1, June 21, 1871.

74. 57 Cong., 1 sess., S. Rept. 982, April 3, 1902.

75. Statements from Southwest Citizens and Fred D. McKenney, November 14, 1900, Minutes of the District Commissioners, vol. 17, RG 351, National Archives.

76. *Washington Star,* May 3, 1890. See also January 28, 1893; Dian Olson Belanger, "The Railroad in the Park: Washington's Baltimore & Potomac Station, 1872–1907," *Washington History* 2 (Spring 1990): 21–24.

77. *Annual Report of the Commissioners of the District of Columbia,* 1878, p. 17.

78. Belanger, "Railroad in the Park," p. 22. She reports that President James Garfield made the first call for a union station. See also *Washington Star,* August 9, 1890.

79. *Washington Star,* May 21, 1890.

80. Washington Board of Trade, *Fourth Annual Report,* 1894, p. 39. Although Washington's railroad problem was particularly visible and protracted, the city was not alone in suffering such indignity. A *New York Times* editorial for December 23, 1900, complained that the slow rate at which the grade issue was being addressed in New York meant that with only $100,000 allocated by the legislature in 1899, it would take four hundred years to solve the problem. Massachusetts, in contrast, had allocated $5 million to be spent at $500,000 a year to deal with the issue.

81. *Washington Star,* January 13, November 4, 1893, February 7, 1894, November 1, 1898.

CHAPTER 5. The New Washington: City Beautiful

1. Jon A. Peterson, "The Nation's First Comprehensive Plan: A Political Analysis of the McMillan Plan for Washington, D.C., 1900–1902," *Journal of the American Planning Association* 51 (Spring 1985): 134–50.

2. Charles Moore, ed., *The Improvement of the Park System of the District of Columbia,* 57 Cong., 1 sess., S. Rept. 166 (Washington, D.C.: Government Printing Office, 1902), p. 16.

3. Charles Moore, intro., dated April 24, 1901, to Glenn Brown, comp., *Papers Relating to the Improvement of the City of Washington,* 56 Cong., 2 sess., S. Doc. 94, pp. 7–9. See also Moore's reference to what he called "necessary measures of civil housekeeping," when he states, "The city that L'Enfant planned has outgrown its boundaries, and now the task is to extend to the entire District of Columbia as comprehensive and as well-considered treatment as he gave to the forests and plains with which he was called to deal." "The Making of a Plan for the City of Washington," paper read before the Columbia Historical Society, January 6, 1902, printed in *Records of the Columbia Historical Society* 6 (Washington, D.C.: Columbia Historical Society, 1903), p. 14.

4. Informal hearing before the subcommittee of the Senate Committee of the District of Columbia; Park Improvement Paper no. 5, in Charles Moore, comp., *Park Improvement Papers: A Series of Seventeen Papers Relating to the Improvement of the District of Columbia* (Washington, D.C.: Government Printing Office, 1902).

5. Jessica I. Elfenbein, *Civics, Commerce, and Community: The History of the Greater Washington Board of Trade, 1889–1989* (Dubuque, Iowa: Kendall/Hunt Publishing Co., 1989), p. 14; *Washington Star*, February 29, 1896.

6. *Washington Star*, August 19, 1893.

7. J. F. Harder, "The City's Plan," *Municipal Affairs* 2 (March 1898): 25–45. See also *Washington Star*, editorial, "The Lessons of Municipal Art," April 14, 1898.

8. *Washington Star*, May 26, 1898, February 26, 1900; Washington Board of Trade, *Eighth Annual Report*, 1898, pp. 27–28. For an evaluation of the connection between the Spanish-American War and Progressivism, see Howard Gillette Jr., "The Military Occupation of Cuba, 1899–1902: Workshop for American Progressivism," *American Quarterly* 25 (October 1973): 410–25.

9. Peterson, "First Comprehensive Plan," p. 135.

10. Ibid.; John W. Reps, *Washington on View: The Nation's Capital since 1790* (Chapel Hill: University of North Carolina Press, 1991), p. 237; F. W. Fitzpatrick, "Beautifying the Nation's Capital," *Inland Architect* 35 (March 1900): 10–14. In a subsequent article Fitzpatrick claimed that the Centennial Avenue, once lined with government buildings, would undoubtedly become "one of the grandest vistas and the most imposing streets one could find in the world." "Centennial of the Nation's Capital," *Cosmopolitan* 30 (December 1900): 112.

11. *Washington Star*, February 22, March 5, 19, 1900.

12. When the amendment was introduced in the Senate, McMillan explained that it had been unanimously recommended by the Bicentennial Committee. He used the occasion as well to reiterate his idea "to open up the Mall by means of a handsome avenue to connect the White House grounds with the Capital grounds." *Congressional Record*, 56 Cong., 1 sess., May 29, 1900, p. 6222.

13. *Washington Star*, May 25, 1900. In this the *Star* echoed Fitzpatrick's call for "a grand avenue, one side park, shade and rest; upon the other nothing but great Government buildings; not a hodge-podge of shanties, flashy stone fronts, galvanized iron facades, interspersed with massive granite federal buildings, attempting to look dignified but failing on account of the company they are in; but solely and exclusively a Government avenue." Fitzpatrick, "Beautifying the Nation's Capital," p. 14.

14. Washington Board of Trade, *Ninth Annual Report*, 1899, p. 26.

15. *Washington Star*, February 23, 1900.

16. Smith's detailed plan for Washington was printed by Congress at the request of Senator George Frisbie Hoar, 56 Cong., 1 sess., S. Doc. 209, February 12, 1900. Frederick Gutheim, *Worthy of the Nation: The History of City Planning for the National Capital* (Washington, D.C.: Smithsonian Institution Press, 1977), p. 114, and Reps, *Washington on View*, pp. 209, 237, 239, accord Smith only relatively brief treatment, given the extent and the ultimate relevance of the plan to those actually adopted in Washington over the next quarter century.

17. *Washington Star*, December 1, 1900; Gutheim, *Worthy of the Nation*, p. 115; 56 Cong., 2 sess., H. Doc. 135, December 6, 1900, p. 8.

18. Peterson, "First Comprehensive Plan," 137–38. In a telegram to General William Sewell dated February 28, 1900,, Cassatt complained that the plan for the new Centennial Avenue "cuts our station lot in two and practically destroys the station as it will be impossible for us to get a station of sufficient length between the New Avenue and Virginia Avenue." Senate Papers 56A-F7 46 DC, National Archives.

19. *Washington Star*, November 17, 1899. The *Star* for November 7, 1897, had noted that while Cassatt was new to the railroad, he "understands the value of the Washington terminal and the prospect that its importance will greatly increase as the capital becomes a distributing center for this country."

20. Ibid., January 29, 1900.

21. Report of the Commissioners of the District of Columbia on S. 2329, Senate Papers 56A-F7 47 DC; 56 Cong., 1 sess., S. Rept. 928, April 10, 1900.

22. *Congressional Record*, 56 Cong., 2 sess., May 26, 1900, p. 6091.

23. Ibid., p. 6092.

24. Ibid., December 18, 1900, p. 404.

25. As something of a corrective to the long-held belief that the interest in developing a park system came from national rather than local interest, the December 3, 1900, petition to Senator McMillan from owners of property adjoining Garfield Park claims that "it is the sentiment of the best people of our section and of our city that the park system of Washington should be extended rather than curtailed," arguing in addition that Garfield Park should be a connecting link between the Mall and the park to be improved with the reclamation of the Anacostia Flats. Senate Papers 56A-57 46 DC, National Archives; *Congressional Record*, 56 Cong., 2 sess., December 18, 1900, p. 397. The decision to go through Garfield Park was initially the result of a compromise intended to settle the controversy over whether to approach the rail station on the Mall above or below grade. *Washington Star*, April 10, 1900.

26. Gutheim, *Worthy of the Nation*, p. 115. Brown, who described Bingham's effort to enlarge the White House as "monstrous," had personal as well as professional reasons to mount a campaign against Bingham, whom he described as having pirated plans that Brown had prepared for providing the White House with new plumbing. Glenn Brown, *Memories, 1860–1930: A Winning Crusade to Revive George Washington's Vision of a Capital City* (Washington, D.C.: W. F. Roberts Co., 1931), pp. 106–7; Glenn Brown, "A Suggestion for Grouping Government Buildings: Landscape, Monuments, and Statuary," *Architectural Record* 7 (August 1900): 89–94. For Brown's role in marshaling the energies of the AIA in support of making Washington a City Beautiful, see William Brian Bushong, "Glenn Brown, the American Institute of Architects, and the Development of the Civic Core of Washington, D.C." (Ph.D. diss., George Washington University, 1988), especially chapters 3–4. While the controversy garnered national attention, it by no means favored the architects' position. A *New York Times* editorial for December 16, 1900, for instance, defended the Bingham plan, contending that the AIA position stemmed more from trade unionism than from aesthetic principles.

27. *Washington Star*, December 12, 1900. Had the good work of the founding fathers been carried on continuously, the paper claimed, "Washington would long ago have met the ideal of the nation as a city worthy of emulation by all the world." The *Washington Post* for the same date struck a similar theme, stating, "As

Washington has grown from a wretched, straggling, dirty village—a sandstorm in dry weather and a quagmire in wet—as Washington has thus developed into at least the promise of a splendid and majestic Capital—so has the whole civilized world moved onward toward a goal of material perfection."

28. Brown, *Papers Relating to the Improvement of the City of Washington,* pp. 36, 59, 67, 85–86, 30, 34. Neither McKim nor Burnham, who would join Olmsted on the Senate Park Commission, attended the conference, although Brown did his best to coax Burnham into it. Bushong, "Glenn Brown," p. 118; Reps, *Washington on View,* p. 239. Brown offered his own alternative to Centennial Avenue, which he argued would destroy the beauty of the park. Howard Walker was listed, along with Daniel Burnham, as a regular contributor to *Inland Architect,* which in its issue for April 1900 called on Congress to adopt "the plan we and many of the leading dailies of the country have adopted in regard to the group of buildings in Washington." For background on *Inland Architect,* which was published from 1883 to 1908, and Burnham's association with it, see Ross Miller, *American Apocalypse: The Great Fire and the Myth of Chicago* (Chicago: University of Chicago Press, 1990), p. 223.

29. Cass Gilbert, in Brown, *Papers Relating to the Improvement of the City of Washington,* p. 81; *American Architect* 71 (January 19, 1901): 19–20.

30. *Congressional Record,* 56 Cong., 1 sess., May 29, 1900, p. 6222.

31. *Inland Architect* 71 (February 2, 1901): 46; Bushong, "Glenn Brown," pp. 122–23.

32. *Washington Star,* December 17, 18, 1900.

33. One former Shepherd associate, Hallet Kilbourn, took the architects to task for completely ignoring Shepherd at their December meeting. Hardly a disinterested observer, having been Shepherd's partner in a number of building enterprises, Kilbourn used the occasion to note that had he the authority he would have placed a statue of Shepherd atop the Washington Monument. *Washington Post,* December 14, 1900.

34. District Commissioners Report on Senate Resolution 139 and Senate Bill 5195, January 15, 1901, Senate Papers 56A-57 46 DC, National Archives.

35. 56 Cong., 2 sess., S. Rept. 1919, January 18, 1901. Franklin Smith, although also commending the "splendid architectural success of the World's Fair, at Chicago," argued that a small commission offered the prospect of encouraging self-promotion. In words some might have seen in retrospect as applying to Daniel Burnham, he charged, "An ambitious member of the architectural profession, with a landscape map in his pocket, may, with some knowledge of wire-pulling and a strong array of political backing, bag the plum which this bill so temptingly displays, and lay the foundations of a possible greater and more golden career—at the nation's expense." 56 Cong., 1 sess., S. Doc. 209, February 12, 1900, Add. 11.

36. Peterson, "First Comprehensive Plan," p. 143; Gutheim, *Worthy of the Nation,* p. 118; Bushong, "Glenn Brown," p. 122.

37. Gutheim, *Worthy of the Nation,* p. 108.

38. Burnham to Lyman Gage, April 10, 1901, Burnham Papers, Art Institute of Chicago.

39. Charles Moore, *Daniel Burnham: Architect Planner of Cities* (Boston: Houghton Mifflin, 1921), 1: 149, 154–55; Thomas S. Hines, *Burnham of Chicago: Architect and Planner* (New York: Oxford University Press, 1974), p. 148; Reps, *Washington on View,* p. 241; Moore, *Improvement of the Park System,* p. 15.

250

40. *Washington Star,* December 20, 1900. The *Washington Post,* in commending passage of grade legislation on December 20, 1900, chose to consider the additional expenditure involved positively, writing, "The passage of these bills not only means the abolition of the grade crossings, so essential to the development of the city, but it means also the expenditure of $1,000,000 in improvements in Washington—an outlay that will assuredly augment the present prosperity of the city."

41. Cynthia R. Field, "The McMillan Commission's Trip to Europe," in Antoinette J. Lee, ed., *Historical Perspectives on Urban Design: Washington, D.C., 1890–1910,* Occasional Paper no. 1 (Washington, D.C.: Center for Washington Area Studies, George Washington University, 1984), pp. 19–24; Susan L. Klaus, "'Intelligent and Comprehensive Planning of a Commonsense Kind': Frederick Law Olmsted, Junior, and the Emergence of Comprehensive Planning in America, 1900–1920" (master's thesis, George Washington University, 1988), pp. 105–7; Moore, *Improvement of the Park System,* pp. 82, 85, 104, 109.

42. Richard Guy Wilson, "The Great Civilization," in Brooklyn Museum, *The American Renaissance, 1876–1917* (New York: Pantheon Books, 1979), p. 31.

43. In a letter to Moore dated January 30, 1902, Olmsted sought to minimize the number of illustrations, citing for contrast Franklin Smith's elaborate presentation to Congress. A handwritten postscript complained that the use of full plate illustrations rather than small inserts in the text increased "the embarrassment of overillustration." Moore Papers, box 2, Library of Congress.

44. For information about costs, see Peterson, "First Comprehensive Plan," pp. 144–45. Senator McMillan reminded Moore in a letter dated September 12, 1901, that he had strenuously objected to the high costs associated with the models, noting that "although Mr. Burnham seems to have gotten the impression that I assented to it provided the depot was taken from the Mall; anything I did say was rather in the nature of a remark than an agreement. Possibly I did say that if he could get the Mall cleared we would could do most anything." Moore Papers, box 1.

45. McKim, reporting to Burnham on August 28, 1901, about an early meeting with Root, praised his interest in the plan, adding that Root felt that government purchase of land along the south side of Pennsylvania Avenue, though "not essential to the report," should be inserted into the commission report to help overcome opposition from "certain quarters," undoubtedly referring to the Board of Trade and the *Star.* Root wrote McMillan on April 11, 1902, "Of course you understand correctly that I want to see every peg possible driven in to fasten the future development of the city down to the line of the commission's plans." Moore Papers, box 1.

46. Moore, *Improvement of the Park System,* p. 17; Gutheim, *Worthy of the Nation,* p. 125.

47. Burnham to Senator William B. Stewart, July 20, 1903, Olmsted Papers, job 2823, Library of Congress.

48. Frederick Law Olmsted, "Beautifying a City," *Independent* 54 (August 1902): 1870. "There is probably a more widespread interest at present in the municipal development of the city of Washington than in that of any other place in the country," he claimed. "This is mainly because the country at large has something of the pride of possession in it that it cannot have with regard to a great commercial metropolis with commanding local interests of its own."

49. Charles Moore, "The Improvement of Washington," *Century* 63 (Febru-

251

ary/March 1902): 621–28, 747–57. Glenn Brown, "Twentieth Century Washington," *House and Garden* 11 (February 1902): 39–56. Daniel Burnham, Park Improvement Paper no. 10, "Extract from a Paper on the Commercial Value of Beauty," in Moore, *Park Improvement Papers.* Burnham first made his presentation in Chicago, as reported by the *Chicago Tribune,* February 11, 1897, under the headline, "For a Paris by the Lake." Citing a $60 million annual profit from tourism in Paris, Burnham argued for lakefront improvements along the lines of the 1893 fair, saying, "The city could be made to excel Paris in its attractiveness and at even less cost. Such work would arouse civic pride, would make us glory in our city, would keep us and our money at home, and draw others here from all over the world to leave their money with us. We can quickly and cheaply make this city fastidiously clean and exquisitely beautiful if we will." Such a theme caught on in other cities, as when San Francisco mayor James Phelan declared, "If cities are made attractive, they will draw homeseekers and visitors, which make prosperity. . . . Municipal art is not a dream of the dilettante, but should be the concern of the practical men of every community." Judd Kahn, *Imperial San Francisco: Politics and Planning in an American City, 1897–1906* (Lincoln: University of Nebraska Press, 1979), p. 70.

50. Daniel Burnham, "White City, Capital City," *Century* 63 (February 1902): 62.

51. Montgomery Schuyler, "The Nation's New Capital," *New York Times Magazine* suppl., January 19, 1902. The leading architectural critic of his era, Schuyler served on the editorial staff of the *Times* from 1883 until his retirement from active journalism in 1907. William H. Jordy and Ralph Coe, eds., *American Architecture and Other Writings by Montgomery Schuyler,* abridged ed. (New York: Atheneum Publishers, 1964), p. 9. The *Washington Star* for February 27, 1894, reported Schuyler's interest in seeing the architectural ideals of the Chicago fair applied to Washington.

52. *Washington Star,* March 11, 1902. In a letter to President Theodore Roosevelt dated February 10, 1904, Charles McKim claimed that Cannon had no objection to individual members of the commission, but that "his real opposition arose from the Senate's independent action in going ahead without the concurrence of the House." Moore Papers, box 7.

53. *Washington Star,* April 1, 1902. The *Star* subsequently made the argument circulating increasingly in City Beautiful circles that expenditures on physical improvements had been proven a good investment in the Paris of Napoleon III. Some say it would be a great expense, the paper argued, "but it will not cost a tithe of what Paris spent to beautify that city under Louis Napoleon, and there is not a Frenchman anywhere who is not proud of that act. . . . The French tore down old buildings of hundreds of years standing and put up buildings of fine character, and made great, wide streets where there had been narrow ones." March 30, 1904.

54. Moore, *Improvement of the Park System,* p. 16; Theodore Starett, "The Washington Terminal," *Architectural Record* 18 (December 1905): 435.

55. Olmsted to Moore, August 28, 1902, Moore Papers, box 7.

56. Ibid., October 6, 1903.

57. McKim to Olmsted, February 11, 1903; Olmsted to McKim, February 12, 1903, Moore Papers, box 7.

58. Burnham to Secretary of the Treasury Leslie B. Shaw, July 24, 1903, Olmsted Papers, job 2828. Burnham's strong emphasis on George Washington's role in

providing the design for the Mall was reinforced by his discovery, communicated to Olmsted on November 27, 1903, that Washington had laid out a small town near Connellsville, Pennsylvania, in "the same system of radiating streets as the City of Washington. This, if true, will prove that the plan of the Capital of the country is Washington's own and not Major L'Enfant's." Olmsted Papers, job 2823. Olmsted provided a similar rationale in notes provided for Congressman Samuel J. Powers on November 28, 1904, writing that "unless Congress puts a positive limit to the encroachment of such buildings on the Mall, not only is the original plan of a grand vista leading to the Capitol likely to be blocked for all time . . . but . . . the actual size of the area devoted to park purposes is likely to be seriously curtailed." Moore Papers, box 17.

59. James Wilson to Representative Sereno E. Payne of New York, February 16, 1904, Olmsted Papers, job 2828.

60. Hearings on regulating buildings on the Mall, March 12, 1904.

61. Moore to Olmsted, Olmsted Papers, job 2823.

62. Charles Eliot to Representative Joseph Cannon, February 15, 1904; Nicholas Murray Butler to Senator Francis Newlands, March 14, 1904. In response to Robinson's stated concern about the Department of Agriculture controversy in letters dated February 25 and March 9, 1904, Olmsted wrote Robinson on March 15, 1904, "I hope you will put everyone to work whom you can get hold of to bring pressure to bear upon members of the House." Olmsted Papers, job 2828. Charles Mulford Robinson, "New Dreams for Cities," *Architectural Record* 17 (May 1905): 411. For information on Robinson, the American Park and Outdoor Association, and the association's merger into a newly named American Civic Association, see Mel Scott, *American City Planning since 1890* (Berkeley: University of California Press, 1971), pp. 65–67; William H. Wilson, *The City Beautiful Movement* (Baltimore: Johns Hopkins University Press, 1989), pp. 36–50.

63. Olmsted Papers, job 2828. Burnham wrote Olmsted on April 28, 1904, urging a public relations campaign to reach several hundred daily newspapers on behalf of the Park Commission's vision. "You cannot expect to avoid unjust criticism when you touch public life," he wrote. "This is the reason I have shrunk from public work. However, we are in this thing and must do our duty." Olmsted Papers, job 2823.

64. Roosevelt cited in Sally Kress Tompkins, *A Quest for Grandeur: Charles Moore and the Federal Triangle* (Washington, D.C.: Smithsonian Institution Press, 1993), p. 7.

65. Bushong, "Glenn Brown," pp. 148–51.

66. Moore to Olmsted, April 21, 1904, Olmsted Papers, job 2828.

67. *Washington Star*, October 10, 17, 1907, January 14, 1908. Bushong argues that this attack on the commission was probably encouraged by Cannon. "Glenn Brown," pp. 163–64.

68. Reps, *Monumental Washington*, p. 144; Gutheim, *Worthy of the Nation*, p. 131.

69. Burnham to Olmsted, June 10, 1908, Burnham Papers.

70. Sitting as chairman of the Fine Arts Commission at its seventh meeting, Burnham reported that he had asked a member of his firm to prepare sketches for a Lincoln Memorial site between the Capitol and Union Station at the request of members of Congress. Minutes of the Fine Arts Commission, March 17, 1911.

71. Burnham to Elliott Woods, January 22, 1909, Office of the Architect of the Capitol.

72. Burnham to Moore, February 16, 1907, quoted in Moore, *Burnham*, 2: 21.

73. Charles Moore draft MS, "Makers of Washington," chap. 21, "Presidents Roosevelt and Taft Induce Congress to Create a Commission of Fine Arts," Moore Papers, box 22. Only parts of this story appear in Moore's published account, *Burnham*, 2: 118–20.

74. Sue A. Kohler, *The Commission of Fine Arts: A Brief History, 1910–1984* (Washington, D.C.: Commission of Fine Arts, n.d.), p. 5; Tompkins, *Quest for Grandeur,* p. 8. For Glenn Brown's role in establishing the commission, see Bushong, "Glenn Brown," pp. 181–93. Other members of the commission with connections to the fair were Daniel Chester French, sculptor; architect Cass Gilbert, who had served on the jury of fine arts for the fair; and Thomas Hastings, of the firm of Carrere and Hastings, also a contributor to the fair.

75. Isaac F. Marcosson, "The New Washington," *Munsey's* 46 (December 1911): 321, 328.

76. William H. Wilson, "J. Horace McFarland and the City Beautiful Movement," *Journal of Urban History* 7 (May 1981): 323.

77. Gutheim, *Worthy of the Nation,* p. 135.

CHAPTER 6. Reform: Social and Aesthetic

1. Although the Park Commission responded to Weller's comments on the improvement of the Anacostia Flats, it ignored his plea either to deal with the city's alley dwellings or to fill the James Creek Canal, which he described as "an open sewer, so dangerous, unwholesome, and hideous that this community has no right to inflict it upon the southwest portion of the city which it now pollutes." Statement of the Associated Charities and Citizens' Relief Association, August 19, 1901, in Charles Moore, comp., *Park Improvement Papers: A Series of Seventeen Papers Relating to the Improvement of the District of Columbia* (Washington, D.C.: Government Printing Office, 1902). Charles McKim responded in a letter to Weller dated August 26, 1901, "Your letter will be brought before the Commission at an early meeting, and it is unnecessary to assure you, will receive the consideration it deserves." Moore Papers, box 2, Library of Congress; Charles Moore, ed., *The Improvement of the Park System of the District of Columbia,* 57 Cong., 1 sess., S. Rept. 166 (Washington, D.C.: Government Printing Office, 1902), pp. 80, 125–26.

2. Moore, *Improvement of the Park System,* pp. 37, 7.

3. The Cleveland plan called for the elimination of older housing to make way for a centrally located civic center complex, while the Chicago plan mentioned housing only by urging that space be set aside for future residences. Peter Marcuse, "Housing Policy and City Planning: The Puzzling Split in the United States, 1893–1931," in Gordon E. Cherry, ed., *Shaping an Urban World* (New York: St. Martin's Press, 1980), p. 28.

4. Charles Mulford Robinson, *Modern Civic Art, or the City Made Beautiful,* 2d ed. (New York: G. P. Putnam's Sons, 1904), pp. 257–58.

5. Betty L. Plummer, "A History of Public Health in Washington, D.C., 1800–1890" (Ph.D. diss., University of Maryland, 1984), p. 161, reports that the Board of Health declared 1,665 dwellings unfit and condemned another 141 between 1873

and 1877. The *Washington Chronicle* for January 20, 1872, in commending the Board of Health for undertaking sanitation work and condemning unfit buildings, urged more attention to the city's back alleys, asking rhetorically, "Have the majority been wedded so long to filthy alleys, poisonous back yards, unwholesome allies for the poor, and the lawless straggling of pigs and cows on the public thoroughfares, that they actually regret to be deprived of them?"

6. In 1905 George M. Kober called for a restoration of the board's power of condemnation, quoting a powerful statement from the board's 1877 report: "Our experience in dealing with filth . . . and disease among these people during the past four years, has taught us that the great public economy, viz., the preservation of public health, is defeated by allowing these filthy, worthless, dependent class of humanity to congregate in the alleys and byways out of sight, and therefore out of mind, until a direful epidemic, incubated and nourished among them, spreads its wings over the homes of the whole city." As Weller was to do later, he emphasized the need to contain the possible spread of disease, citing as well the threat of the James Creek Canal specifically and alley housing more generally. "The Health of the City of Washington," *Charities and the Commons* 14 (March 3, 1906): 8.

7. See, for instance, Francis E. Leupp, "Washington as a City of Pictures," *Scribner's* 31 (February 1902): 144, which describes in picturesque terms a row of shanties occupied by blacks, with "Uncle and Auntie, all rags and tatters, smoking their pipes demurely beside a little bonfire" while "a dozen solemn-faced pickaninnies" dance around them. "It is a bit of the South of forty years ago thrown out on the picket line of to-day."

8. *Becoming the Capital City: DeLancy Gill's Washington* (Washington, D.C.: Exhibit Guide of the Historical Society of Washington, 1992).

9. *Washington Star*, January 23, 1890.

10. Constance McLaughlin Green, *Washington: Capital City, 1879–1950* (Princeton: Princeton University Press, 1963), p. 45; James Borchert, *Alley Life in Washington; Family, Community, Religion, and Folklife in the City, 1850–1970* (Urbana: University of Illinois Press, 1980), p. 13. Borchert's revisionist account is intended to penetrate the reformers' accounts in order to identify the forms of social organization that escaped their attention. He manages to suggest a different level of experience than those recorded in the press and public reports. In tracing evolving efforts to intervene in the situation, however, my focus is as much on the rhetoric and the perceptions of reformers as on the conditions they deplored.

11. *Washington Star*, April 4, 1896.

12. Roy Lubove, *The Progressives and the Slums: Tenement House Reform in New York City, 1890–1917* (Pittsburgh: Pittsburgh University Press, 1962), pp. 87–88.

13. *Washington Star*, March 15, May 27, 1893. Efforts to establish public baths were part of the larger movement of sanitary reforms seeking to improve social behavior through environmental intervention. According to Marilyn Thornton Williams, "Although sanitary reformers did not abandon the effort to achieve a cleaner slum environment through effective garbage collection, streetcleaning, sewer systems, and other means, they stressed the role played by the infected individual as a bearer of disease." *Washing "The Great Unwashed": Public Baths in Urban America, 1840–1920* (Columbus: Ohio State University Press, 1991), p. 23.

14. 56 Cong., 1 sess., H. Rept. 324, February 13, 1892.

15. *Washington Star*, May 26, 1894.

16. Ibid., January 12, 1897; Katherine Hosmer, "What Women Have Done in Washington's City Affairs," *Municipal Affairs* 2 (September 1898): 514–22; George M. Kober, "Report on the Housing of the Laboring Class in the City of Washington," app. E, *Annual Report of the Commissioners of the District of Columbia, 1898–99*, pp. 111–12; Laurie May, "The Woman's Anthropological Society, 1885–1899: Earnest in the Search for Truth" (master's thesis, George Washington University, 1988), p. 82; Elizabeth Hannold, "'Comfort and Respectability': Washington's Philanthropic Housing Movement," *Washington History* 4 (Fall / Winter 1992): 26.

17. *Washington Star,* January 13, 1897.

18. Elizabeth Anne Hannold, "'Philanthropy That Pays': Washington, D.C.'s Limited-Dividend Housing Companies, 1897–1954" (master's thesis, George Washington University, 1988), p. 36.

19. *Annual Report of the Commissioners of the District of Columbia, 1901–2*, p. 15; *Washington Star,* April 3, 5, 1897.

20. Hearings before a subcommittee of the Senate Committee on the District of Columbia, April 14, 1904.

21. Gould's role as author of *The Housing of Working People*, a study of social conditions in the United States and Europe published by the Department of Labor in 1895, undoubtedly brought him to the attention of Washington housing activists. Convinced that urban government in America was too corrupt to solve the problem, Gould favored laws setting minimum standards for dwellings supplemented by limited-dividend companies. To put his beliefs to work, he helped found in 1896 the City and Suburban Homes Company in New York City. He served as president of the company until his death in 1915. Anthony Jackson, *A Place Called Home: A History of Low-Cost Housing in Manhattan* (Cambridge, Mass.: MIT Press, 1976), p. 109; Lubove, *Progressives and the Slums*, pp. 101–4.

22. Hannold, "Philanthropy That Pays," pp. 36–38, 47, 49, 51.

23. Hannold, "Comfort and Respectability," p. 32. The Washington approach was fully consistent with an emerging philosophy in the field of philanthropic housing described as the "filtration" process, in which each class would move up the housing scale as new housing became available. Eugenie Ladner Birch and Deborah S. Gardner, "The Seven-Percent Solution: A Review of Philanthropic Housing, 1870–1910," *Journal of Urban History* 7 (August 1981): 405. The attitude toward helping only the worthy poor led in Washington as well as in other cities to efforts to rationalize charitable work by consolidating different organizations and pooling their information. See Roberta Baxter Holt, "The Associated Charities of Washington, D.C.: A History of Activity and Decrees of the Board of Managers" (D.S.W., Catholic University, 1986), pp. 40–42.

24. Hannold, "Philanthropy That Pays," pp. 52–54. In addition to Sternberg, Kober, and Weller, signers of the petition seeking congressional authority to incorporate the new company included a full roster of Washington's leading businessmen and officers of the Board of Trade: S. W. Woodward, Crosby Noyes, Brainard Warner, Charles Glover, John Joy Edson, Simon Wolf, H. A. and C. H. Willard, E. Francis Riggs, and Alexander Graham Bell. 56 Cong., 2 sess., H. Rept. 2478, April 14, 1904.

25. *Washington Star,* December 8, 1906. See also George Sternberg, "Housing Conditions in the National Capital," *Charities* 12 (July 23, 1904): 762–64.

26. Theodore Roosevelt, message to Congress, December 3, 1901, *Presidential Addresses and State Papers of Theodore Roosevelt* (New York: P. F. Collier and Son, 1902), 2: 547; *Annual Report of the Commissioners of the District of Columbia*, 1901–2, p. 15. See also *Washington Star*, editorial, December 3, 1901. Roosevelt reiterated his concern in his next address to Congress, delivered on February 2, 1902, stating, "The evils of slum dwellings, whether in the shape of crowded and congested tenement-house districts or the back alley type, should never be permitted to grow up in Washington. The city should be a model in every respect for all cities of the country." *Addresses and Presidential Messages of Theodore Roosevelt, 1902–1904* (New York: G. P. Putnam's Sons, 1904), p. 374.

27. Charles Weller, serving as secretary for the committee, announced that Wood would actually meet with the committee when he was in Washington in May 1902. *Washington Star*, April 14, 1902. For the importance of Wood's sanitary reforms in Cuba, see A. Hunter Dupree, *Science in the Federal Government* (Cambridge, Mass.: Harvard University Press, 1957), p. 266. Committee member George Sternberg may well have been interested in what happened in Cuba because of his own investigation of sanitary conditions in Cuba in 1879, a pioneering study of its kind. See Jon A. Peterson, "The Impact of Sanitary Reform upon American Urban Planning, 1840–1890," in Donald A. Krueckeberg, ed., *Introduction to Planning History in the United States* (New Brunswick, N.J.: Center for Urban Policy Research, Rutgers University, 1983), p. 37.

28. Proceedings of the Civic Center, 1907, vertical files, Washingtoniana Division, D.C. Public Library.

29. A member of the first board of directors of the Washington Sanitary Improvement Company, Woodward made a similar comment shortly after the McMillan report was issued, saying, "The movement would also take part in the beautification of the capital city." *Washington Star*, March 21, 1902. Woodward's efforts were reported in *Charities* 10 (June 13, 1903): 585, under the title "A Capital City of Broad Streets but Evil Alleys."

30. Hannold, "Philanthropy That Pays," p. 38; *Washington Star*, January 1, 1902.

31. *Washington Star*, December 2, 1902. Weller's continuity with the first efforts to eliminate alley dwellings can be seen in his reiteration of the idea suggested by Clare de Graffenried in 1896 that alleys on small blocks be converted into small parks, playgrounds, and open spaces. The Washington Civic Center submitted a similar plea to the Park Commission on March 23, 1901, calling for additional parks and playgrounds and public toilet facilities. The statement was signed by George Kober as chairman. Moore, *Park Improvement Papers*.

32. Minutes of the Committee on the Improvement of Housing Conditions of the Associated Charities, December 4, 1902, Papers of the Associated Charities of Washington, Catholic University of America (CUA).

33. *Washington Star*, December 15, 1903. See also excerpts from Riis's address to the Associated Charities, "The Housing Problem Facing Congress," *Charities and the Commons* 12 (February 6, 1904): 163.

34. *Washington Star*, December 15, 16, 1903.

35. William Loeb Jr. to Charles Weller, January 12, 1905, Papers of the Associated Charities.

36. John E. Hayford, assistant secretary, Committee on Housing Conditions of the Associated Charities, to Senator William M. Stewart, February 7, 1905. Papers of the Associated Charities.

37. *Washington Star*, December 27, 1906.

38. Lawrence Veiller to S. W. Woodward, April 10, 1902. See also letters from Veiller's close associates in housing reform circles, Robert W. DeForest, president of the Charity Organization Society of New York City, April 7, 1902, and Robert Hunter, University Settlement Society of New York, April 10, 1902, Papers of the Associated Charities. For a profile of Veiller, see Lubove, *Progressives and the Slums*, pp. 127–32.

39. *Washington Star*, March 31, 1902. Weller's comments were very close to those communicated by Veiller in his April 10, 1902, letter to Woodward: "No one who has worked for any time among the poor can help being impressed with the fact that little can be accomplished for their permanent betterment unless the homes of the poor are such as to foster and develop a strong and healthy domestic atmosphere. This is almost axiomatic. As long as you have bad housing conditions in any city you are bound to have an unnecessary amount of poverty, disease, crime, immorality and sickness."

40. In a landmark article entitled, "The City Beautiful," George Kriehn writes, "Why should not the American people be taught patriotism, to a far greater extent than at present? . . . nothing would be a more effective agent in making good citizens of our foreign population than such monuments. Many of them cannot read English books, but they can read monuments which appeal to the eyes." *Municipal Affairs* 3 (December 1899): 600. Burnham made virtually the same point in the 1909 plan for Chicago, writing, "Chicago, in common with other great cities, realizes that the time has come to bring order out of chaos incident to rapid growth, and especially to the influx of many nationalities without common traditions or habits of life. Among the various instrumentalities designed to accomplish this result, a plan for a well-ordered and convenient city is seen to be indispensable." Cited in Ross Miller, *American Apocalypse: The Great Fire and the Myth of Chicago* (Chicago: University of Chicago Press, 1990), p. 208.

41. Charles Frederick Weller, *Neglected Neighbors: Stories of Life in the Alleys, Tenements, and Shanties of the National Capital* (Philadelphia: John C. Winston Co., 1909), p. 257.

42. *Hearings before the Subcommittee of the Committee on the District of Columbia*, House of Representatives, 68 Cong., 1 sess. (Washington: Government Printing Office, 1924), pp. 11–12.

43. For information on Reynolds and his ties to New York housing reformers, see Lubove, *Progressives and the Slums*, pp. 81–82, 126. Minutes, Committee on Housing of the Associated Charities, January 6, 1908, CUA.

44. *Washington Star*, December 27, 1908. See also editorials of May 6, 20, 30, 1907.

45. Ibid., March 17, 1908. Modeled after a Boston organization of the same name founded in 1888, the Monday Evening Club had as its central goal the social uplift of the deserving poor. Ibid., April 24, 1910; Dorothy A. Mohler, "The Monday Evening Club of Washington, D.C.: A Pioneer Social Organization," *Records of the Columbia Historical Society* 50 (Charlottesville: University Press of Virginia, 1980), pp. 367–82.

46. *Washington Star*, May 6, 1907; Preliminary Report of the President's Homes Commission, 60 Cong., 2 sess., S. Doc. 599, December 17, 1908, p. 17.

47. President's Homes Commission Report, 60 Cong., 2 sess., S. Doc. 644, January 8, 1909, pp. 16, 110–11.

48. *Washington Star,* May 22, 1909. The *Star* captured the dual intent of the planning meeting under the headline, "More Parks and No Slums."

49. Olmsted to Moore, May 26, 1909, Moore Papers, box 7, reporting Harvard President Charles Eliot's reaction to Addams. In addition to Eliot, Olmsted, and Addams, the call to the first national meeting on city planning was signed by social activists Robert DeForest and Mary Simkhovitch; District Commissioner Henry B. F. McFarland; AIA president Cass Gilbert; and William Gude, president of the national Chamber of Commerce. Olmsted attached copies of the conference resolution on Washington as well as Coolidge's memo, also dated May 26, 1909. In a letter to Burnham dated July 26, 1909, Charles Moore indicated that Olmsted as well as Coolidge was responsible for the Washington resolution, adding that he had been asked to write the memorial to Congress on behalf of the 1909 planning convention. Burnham Papers, Art Institute of Chicago.

50. Hearing before the Committee on the District of Columbia, June 1, 1909, 61 Cong., 2 sess., S. Doc. 422. Kober was even more specific in his 1906 article, "The Health of the City of Washington," when he wrote that the first goal for the national capital should be the protection of the health of its people: "Its beautifying is essential, but of secondary importance."

51. Washington Board of Trade, *Nineteenth Annual Report,* 1909, p. 125. In this, the Board of Trade was merely extending a point made in the District Commissioners' annual report for 1907, which, even as it praised continuing efforts to beautify Washington, stated that local authorities would fail their duty "if they were content with the mere physical improvement of the capital" (p. 6). While the board in 1913 commended the creation of Potomac Park "out of unsightly and unhealthful flats," it still urged that the highest priority be given "to those working to transform the hideous disease-ridden alleys of the city into open spaces or into buildings suitable for the abode of human beings." Washington Board of Trade, *Twenty-third Annual Report,* 1913, p. 63.

52. Borchert, *Alley Life,* p. 47; *Washington Star,* July 30, 1911, July 7, 1913, November 15, 1914. Jacob Riis had instituted just such an approach in the notorious Mulberry Bend section of New York City in the late 1890s. Paul Boyer, *Urban Masses and Moral Order in America, 1820–1920* (Cambridge, Mass.: Harvard University Press, 1978), p. 233.

53. *Washington Star,* July 14, 1910, July 11, 1911.

54. Grace Vawter Bicknell, *The Inhabited Alleys of Washington, D.C.* (Washington, D.C.: Committee on Housing, Women's Welfare Department, National Civic Federation, 1912), p. 16.

55. Barbara Gale Howick Fant, "Slum Reclamation and Housing Reform in the Nation's Capital, 1890–1940" (Ph.D. diss., George Washington University, 1981), pp. 62–71.

56. *Washington Star,* May 27, 1913.

57. *Congressional Record,* 61 Cong., 1 sess., May 27, 1913, pp. 1786–93. Edith Elmer Wood, who would come to play a prominent national role in housing reform, after testifying on the issue before Congress, wrote glowingly on the Washington effort: "Never before have the women of the capital risen in a body, encouraged by the presence and example of the mistress of the White House, to demand the eradica-

259

tion of the alley evil. . . . Congress is at last thoroughly aroused and will, it is believed, treat the matter as a national, not merely a local issue. For it seems obvious that Washington should be a model for the nation—not a warning." "Four Washington Alleys," *Survey* 31 (December 6, 1913): 46. On Wood's background and her congressional testimony, see Fant, "Housing and Slum Reclamation," pp. 44–48.

58. *Washington Star,* December 13, 1913. The Board of Trade annual report for 1913 urged the highest priority be given "to those working to transform the hideous disease-breeding alleys of the city into open spaces or into buildings suitable for the abode of human beings" (p. 63).

59. *Outlook* 108 (September 30, 1914): 240–41.

60. *Washington Star,* January 3, March 29, 1918. A letter sent to newspapers on June 9, 1919, and included with a statement given to Congress by Washington's Emergency Housing Association argued that once the first half of its work of eliminating slums by abolishing inhabited alleys was done, the rest should be completed by providing model housing. Hearings on the discontinuance of alley dwellings in the District of Columbia, Senate Committee on the District of Columbia, February 21, 24, 1922.

61. Hannold, "Philanthropy That Pays," p. 69.

62. John Ihlder [report on housing conditions], suppl., *National Capital Park and Planning Commission Annual Report,* 1930; *Washington Daily News,* editorial, "Alleys in the Back Yard of the City Beautiful," May 27, 1927.

63. In undated notes prepared for the initial meeting of the Senate Park Commission, Burnham urged a comprehensive survey of existing buildings in the city with the intent of designating those structures that in whole or in part should be demolished with the intent of creating a harmonious appearance for the whole city. Burnham Papers, Art Institute of Chicago. Urging establishment of a national bureau of fine arts with powers to supervise private as well as public building, Schuyler claimed that "the full realization of this iridescent dream of the 'most beautiful capital city in the world' cannot be had so long as the right of a man to do what he likes with his own is held to include the right to vulgarize or vandalize his city." "The Nation's New Capital," *New York Times Magazine,* suppl., January 19, 1902. Schuyler reiterated his belief in a subsequent article, writing, "Uniformity and conformity are sufficiently provided for in public buildings by the proposal of the Commission that such buildings shall have a common material, a common cornice line, and a common classicism of style. But there is no use doing these things by halves. The individual owner must be prevented, in the general interest, from using his own taste so as to injure another, when the injury pertains to the appearance of the city." "The Art of City-Making," *Architectural Record* 12 (May 1902): 22. Charles Robinson added his own endorsement of the concept, arguing that a uniform architectural style was necessary to restrain eccentricity in building. *Modern Civic Art,* p. 283.

64. Henry B. F. MacFarland, "The Rebuilding of the National Capital," *American City* 1 (September 1909): 3–13.

65. *Washington Star,* January 21, 1910.

66. Schuyler reported that the city's Engineer Commissioner wanted to designate certain area streets for special aesthetic restrictions to assure the city's "beautiful and harmonious appearance." "The New Washington," *Scribner's* 51 (February 1912): 145–46.

67. Commission of Fine Arts, *Annual Report,* 1916, p. 31.

68. Commission of Fine Arts, *Annual Report,* 1919; Frederick Gutheim, *Worthy of the Nation: The History of Planning for the National Capital* (Washington, D.C.: Smithsonian Institution Press, 1977), pp. 160–61, 164. For more background on the implementation of zoning in Washington, see 66 Cong., 1 sess., H. Rept. 108, July 11, 1919.

69. *Washington Star,* March 19, 1919; Gutheim, *Worthy of the Nation,* p. 161. Brown's establishment of the first Committee of 100 followed a speech he gave on the Lincoln Memorial to the District of Columbia Chamber of Commerce, December 13, 1910. William Brian Bushong, "Glenn Brown, the American Institute of Architects, and the Development of the Civic Core of Washington, D.C." (Ph.D. diss., George Washington University, 1988), p. 194. Among the members of the original Committee of 100 who joined the new organization were Frederic Delano, former AIA president Gilbert Cass, former Board of Trade president Cuno Rudolph, and social activist Archibold Hopkins. In an address before the Chicago Planning Association on November 2, 1923, Delano indicated that the American Civic Association had asked him to "reform" the earlier Committee of 100. "Regional Planning Next!" *National Municipal Review* 13 (March 1924): 147.

70. *Preliminary Report of the Committee of 100 on the Federal City to the American Civic Association,* January 3, 1924, pp. 12, 26–27.

71. *Washington Star,* January 4, 1924. See also ibid., editorials for March 22, October 8, 1924.

72. *Hearings before the Subcommittee of the Committee on the District of Columbia,* House of Representatives, 68 Cong., 1 sess., on H.R. 8055 (Washington, D.C.: Government Printing Office, 1924), pp. 2–10. Coldren and Delano in this respect extended the concern of the Park Commission, especially of Olmsted. See his letter to E. D. Shaw, March 16, 1906, Olmsted Papers, job 2823, Library of Congress.

73. 68 Cong., 1 sess., S. Rept. 245, March 12, 1924.

74. *Congressional Record,* 68 Cong., 1 sess., May 26, 1924, pp. 9561–62, 9564, 9567.

75. *Washington Star,* May 28, June 9, 1924.

76. Ibid., July 12, 1925.

77. 68 Cong., 1 sess., S. Rept. 1050, February 3, 1925; 68 Cong., 2 sess., H. Rept. 149, February 16, 1925.

78. Olmsted to Frederic Delano, telegram, November 28, 1925, Olmsted Papers, job 2844.

79. Harlean James, executive secretary, American Civic Association, to Olmsted, February 18, 1925, Olmsted Papers, job 2844; 69 Cong., 1 sess., H. Rept. 204, February 5, 1926.

80. Rep. Charles Lee Underhill of Massachusetts, *Congressional Record,* February 8, 1926, p. 3575.

81. *Washington Star,* March 20, 30, 1904. In the latter article, the paper revived the model of Haussmann's Paris, saying, "There is not a Frenchman anywhere" who was not proud of the way Louis Napoleon directed that old buildings give way to grand new structures and boulevards.

82. Washington Board of Trade, *Eighteenth Annual Report,* 1908, pp. 169–70. The *Annual Report of the Public Buildings Commission* for 1926 reports that the Triangle plan had been called for as early as 1899 by Col. Theodore Bingham. In fact, the *Star* had been pressing for just such changes for most of a decade. See editorial for April 15, 1890.

83. For further details on the foundation of the Public Buildings Commission, see Sally Kress Tompkins, *A Quest for Grandeur: Charles Moore and the Federal Triangle* (Washington, D.C.: Smithsonian Institution Press, 1993), pp. 26–27.

84. *Annual Report of the Public Buildings Commission,* 65 Cong., 2 sess., S. Doc. 155, December 18, 1917, p. 59.

85. Grant cited in Tompkins, *Quest for Grandeur,* p. 38.

86. Gutheim, *Worthy of the Nation,* pp. 172–74.

87. *Washington Star,* December 31, 1926; *Annual Report of the Public Buildings Commission,* 1927, p. 8.

88. U. S. Grant III address, October 18, 1928, Peter S. Craig Collection, Special Collections, Gelman Library, George Washington University. Representative Arthur Capper quoted President Hoover as saying, "Washington is not only the Nation's Capital; it is the symbol of America. By its dignity and architectural inspiration we stimulate pride in our country . . . the complete Capital of the Nation can not be alone a man-made city of buildings and boulevards and marble memorials. It must combine in perfection the man-made wonders with the natural charms which come from the creator." Speech attached to flyer issued by the American Civic Association, February 1930, "A Danger to Be Averted—An Opportunity to Be Grasped," Committee of 100 Papers, Gelman Library.

89. Gutheim, *Worthy of the Nation,* pp. 198, 200.

90. *National Capital Park and Planning Commission Annual Report,* 1930, p. 7.

91. Harlean James, "Architectural Control Now a First in Washington," *American City* 43 (July 1930): 148, cited in Tompkins, *Quest for Grandeur,* p. 61.

92. Cited in the *Washington Star,* January 9, 1930.

93. Charles W. Eliot II, "A Great and Effective City," *American Magazine of Art* 31 (August 1931): 131, 136. The nephew of the leading figure in developing the 1890 metropolitan park plan for Boston, Eliot made clear his debt to the 1893 fair and the Park Commission, writing in the same article, "The term 'city beautiful' was the inspiring motto of those who went forth to war against disordered cities after the World's Fair of 1893 and was the battle-cry in 1901 when the McMillan Plan for Washington was prepared. In many quarters, however, that phrase became associated with namby-pamby aesthetes, impractical idealists, and dreamers, so that it came into fairly general disrepute. But the principles motivating those who sought to get the ideals of the city beautiful established in the American consciousness still prevail."

CHAPTER 7. A New Deal for Washington

1. Mark I. Gelfand argues that while the New Deal "rescued local government from financial ruin and revolutionized federal-municipal relations," it "never came to grips with the city as an economic and social entity. . . . The Roosevelt Presidency, if not intentionally then at least by necessity, transformed the urban political universe, but American ideology and federal bureaucratic structure lagged far behind." *A Nation of Cities: The Federal Government and Urban America, 1933–1965* (New York: Oxford University Press, 1975), pp. 69–70. Frederick Gutheim charges, "Despite concern with unemployment and recovery, and a liberal orientation to social problems, the New Deal in Washington, as in many metropolitan areas, was not innovative. Fundamental urban problems were largely ignored; unable to function in the vacuum, city planning became almost totally

262

ineffective." *Worthy of the Nation: The History of Planning for the National Capital* (Washington, D.C.: Smithsonian Institution Press, 1977), p. 213.

2. Grant to Olmsted, October 11, 1939, Olmsted Papers, job 2844, Library of Congress.

3. According to an account by Barbara Fant, Mrs. Hopkins confronted Grant one day when, as director of Public Buildings and Grounds, he called at her home to remove to Rock Creek Park a copper beech tree that had grown too large for her yard. Hopkins used the occasion to thrust a handful of pamphlets on alley conditions at him. Subsequently, in 1926, she brought him to a meeting at her home of a group that had worked with Ellen Wilson on alley clearance. They urged Grant to get the National Capital Park and Planning Commission to sponsor alley clearance. "Slum Reclamation and Housing Reform in the Nation's Capital, 1890–1940" (Ph.D. diss., George Washington University, 1982), p. 72.

4. William Henry Jones, *The Housing of Negroes in Washington, D.C.: A Study in Human Ecology* (Washington, D.C.: Howard University Press, 1929), p. 40. In addition to Mrs. Hopkins, the sponsoring committee included white civic leader Anson Phelps Stokes, Episcopal bishop of Washington, and black civic leaders Nannie Helen Burroughs and Mary Church Terrell.

5. *Washington Star,* February 1, 1925.

6. Fant, "Slum Reclamation and Housing Reform," pp. 147–50; Olmsted to President Calvin Coolidge, April 13, 1926, Olmsted Papers, job 2844; John F. Bauman, *Public Housing, Race, and Renewal: Urban Planning in Philadelphia, 1920–1974* (Philadelphia: Temple University Press, 1987), pp. 10–11; Roy Lubove, *Twentieth Century Pittsburgh* (New York: John Wiley and Sons, 1969), pp. 65–68.

7. John Ihlder, "A Housing Program for the District of Columbia," Report to the National Capital Park and Planning Commission, September 21, 1929, John Nolen Jr. Papers, RG 302, box 41, National Archives. John Nolen was named city planner for the District on October 6, 1931, and served in that capacity for many years.

8. John Ihlder, "Progress Report on Housing," November 19, 1932, app., NCPPC Minutes. Ihlder to Grant, March 15, 1932, Papers of the NCPPC, RG 302, box 204, National Archives, cited by Fant, "Slum Reclamation and Housing Reform," p. 168.

9. John Ihlder, "Housing and Assessed Values," app. F, NCPPC Minutes, December 16, 1932, Papers of the NCPPC. A *Washington Star* editorial for January 17, 1929, in commenting on William Jones's report on black housing, had made the same point by urging that the poor be removed from alley dwellings as long as it was done gradually and with fair notice.

10. John Ihlder, "Housing and Slum Clearance: Opportunities in Washington under the Public Works Administration," NCPPC Minutes, App. H, July 1933, Papers of the NCPPC. Ihlder made a similar point in meeting with the Community Affairs Committee of the Washington Board of Trade, by saying that while the city had a legal obligation to clear alleys, it also had a moral obligation to provide new dwellings for those forced out of their homes. *Washington Star,* January 16, 1935.

11. *Washington Star,* editorial, "Clean the Capital," April 20, 1930.

12. Ibid., November 7, 1930.

13. Louis Justement, "Housing in the District of Columbia," report to the

American Institute of Architects, n.d., Nolen Papers. For coverage of the report, see the *Washington Star,* November 20, 1931.

14. *Washington Post,* October 28, 1933.

15. See Howard Gillette Jr., "The Evolution of Neighborhood Planning from the Progressive Era to the 1949 Housing Act," *Journal of Urban History* 9 (August 1983): 421–44.

16. Lawrence Veiller to Donald H. Sawyer, temporary administrator of Public Works, memorandum, July 3, 1933, Nolen Papers.

17. *Washington Star,* April 24, 1932.

18. Eleanor Roosevelt to Charlotte Hopkins, March 21, 1933, box 41, Nolen Papers.

19. Ihlder to Arno B. Carmerer, NCPPC, January 2, 1934, Nolen Papers.

20. *Washington Star,* September 22, 1932.

21. Ibid., April 2, 1933.

22. *Washington Herald,* November 6, 1933.

23. 72 Cong., 2 sess., S. Rept. 1361, Alley Dwelling Act, March 3, 1933.

24. *Washington Star,* June 12, 1934.

25. *American City* 47 (December 1934): 67. See also article by Ihlder and ADA attorney Maurice V. Brooks, "Use of the Power of Eminent Domain in Slum Reclamation," *Journal of Land and Public Utility Economics* 12 (November 1936): 355–60, which describes the inadequacies of police power alone to clear slums.

26. *Washington Star,* May 30, 1934.

27. *Washington Post,* October 11, 1934.

28. Delano to Ihlder, June 2, 1933, Ihlder Papers, Roosevelt Library, Hyde Park, cited by Fant, "Slum Reclamation and Housing Reform," p. 118.

29. Report of the Conference on Better Housing among Negroes, April 18, 1936, in the *Housing Newsletter,* October 1, 1936, Nolen Papers. The attitude that an improved physical environment could uplift individuals and groups is well illustrated in two excellent case studies of housing reform in the period: Bauman, *Public Housing, Race, and Renewal,* and Robert B. Fairbanks, *Making Better Citizens: Housing Reform and the Community Development Strategy in Cincinnati, 1890–1960* (Urbana: University of Illinois Press, 1988).

30. Jerome Page and Margaret Reuss, "Safe, Decent, and Affordable: Citizen Struggles to Improve Housing in the District of Columbia, 1890–1982," in Steven J. Diner, ed., *Housing Washington's People: Public Policy in Retrospect* (Washington, D.C.: University of the District of Columbia, 1983), p. 78.

31. *Washington Star,* May 2, 1925. In reporting the effect of lifted rent controls, a *Washington Post* editorial for February 1, 1934, cited a report of the city's Public Utilities Commission that while the supply of better-class homes had grown to exceed demand since World War I, "the supply of houses for the lower-paid workers has been negligible."

32. See Thomas S. Settle, memorandum on proposed amendments to the Alley Dwelling Act, December 27, 1935, Nolen Papers.

33. *Washington Star,* November 20, 1931.

34. Ibid., May 31, 1934.

35. Dennis E. Gale, "Restoration in Georgetown, Washington, D.C., 1915–65" (Ph.D. diss., George Washington University, 1982).

36. Minutes, Alley Dwelling Authority, March 29, 1937. For details on the

St. Mary's complex as constructed, see Suzanne Berry Sherwood, *Foggy Bottom, 1800–1975* (Washington, D.C.: GW Washington Studies no. 7, 1974), p. 21.

37. *Washington Tribune,* July 24, 1937.

38. Minutes, Alley Dwelling Authority Meeting, October 7, 1937, Nolen Papers. See file marked E. F. Harris, Papers of the National Capital Housing Authority, Speeches and Addresses of John Ihlder, RG 302, ser. 1, especially the copy of the letter from Harris to President Roosevelt, January 29, 1938. Harris to Senator Arthur Capper, May 30, 1940; Capper draft response to Harris, 1940, Arthur Capper Papers, Kansas State Historical Society.

39. Under the headline, "ADA Charged with Colonizing?" the *Washington Tribune* for September 23, 1939, repeated Harris's criticism of plans for one site where fifty-six homes were to be removed to make way for parking facilities for automobiles.

40. Ibid., December 28, 1940.

41. Resolution adopted by the Lincoln Civic Association on March 4, 1942, vertical subject files, Washingtoniana Division, D.C. Public Library.

42. John Ihlder diary, vol. 18, January 14, 1940, p. 4, cited in Fant, "Slum Reclamation and Housing Reform," p. 287.

43. *Washington Star,* March 5, 1942.

44. Ibid., May 16, November 18, 1942.

45. Ibid., December 5, 1941.

46. Ibid., December 13, 1941.

47. Ibid., December 9, 1941, January 19, 1942.

48. Ibid., January 13, 1942; Gutheim, *Worthy of the Nation,* pp. 232–33. In a letter to NCPPC chairman Frederic Delano, dated January 20, 1942, Goodwillie described his plan as a means of producing "a large pool of low cost housing, in which low income workers can be domiciled after the war, at rent levels that will reflect little or no subsidy, thus increasing the number of families which are self-sustaining." RG 328, Records of the National Capital Planning Commission, box 4, National Archives.

49. *Washington Star,* March 5, 1942.

50. See reports of the *Washington Daily News,* February 15, 1944, *Washington Star,* August 13, 1944.

51. *Washington Star,* March 26, 1943.

52. Ibid., May 23, 1943.

53. Ihlder to members of the Senate Committee on the District of Columbia, May 6, 1943; memorandum on alleys, July 4, 1943, Capper Papers. For complete itineraries and commentary on a number of tours conducted by the NCHA, see NCHA Records, RG 302, box 32. These tours continued into the fall, indicated by a memorandum dated October 14, 1943, addressed by Ihlder to key members of Congress and reported in the *Star* on October 17, 1943, Capper Papers.

54. *Washington Star,* January 21, 1944.

55. Ibid., January 25, 29, February 9, 1944.

56. "Report of the Housing and Rent Control Committee of the Federation of Citizens' Associations of the District of Columbia on Slum Reclamation and Low Cost Housing," December 4, 1943, Capper Papers; *Washington Star,* December 8, 1943.

57. The result of eliminating the National Capital Housing Authority, the *Post*

claimed editorially on December 8, 1942, would be that "the inhabitants would be put out in the street with nowhere to go."

58. *Washington Star,* February 4, 1944.

59. Statement of Joseph H. Deckman, chairman, District of Columbia Federation of Citizens' Associations, Committee on Housing and Rent Control, hearings on the elimination of alley dwellings, May 23, 1944.

60. John Ihlder citing the December 17, 1943 issue of the Homebuilders Association of Metropolitan Washington newsletter, NCHA Records, RG 302, box 43.

61. *Washington Star,* February 1, 1944.

62. Nelson to Ihlder, May 24, 1935; Confidential Weekly Letter, NAREB, October 31, 1938; Nelson to Ihlder, November 26, 1938, NCHA Records, RG 302, ser. 1.

63. Nelson to Ihlder, March 21, 1940, NCHA Records, RG 302, ser. 1.

64. Ibid., December 23, 1940. Nelson carried his campaign against public housing to Congress in the 1940s, charging that it destroyed the American way of life and even linking Republican Senator Robert Taft to Communism for his support of the program. Gelfand, *Nation of Cities,* p. 113.

65. *Washington Star,* February 8, 1944.

66. Ibid., March 10, 1944.

67. *Washington Post,* January 29, 1944, cited in William Robert Barnes, "Origins of Urban Renewal: The Public Housing Controversy and the Emergence of a Redevelopment Program in the District of Columbia" (Ph.D. diss., Syracuse University, 1977), p. 118.

68. *Washington Post,* May 17, 1944.

69. See Joseph D. Cannon, acting regional director, CIO, Kentucky, letter dated June 7, 1944, to members of the Senate District Committee, declaring that realtors "are interested in neither improvement nor adequate housing. Their purposes are rents and higher rents and increasing real estate prices." See also Harry Bate, chairman, Housing Council of the American Federation of Labor, and Lee F. Johnson, executive vice-president, National Housing Council, telegrams dated September 24, 1945, to Senator Arthur Capper; Sydney Maslen, director, National Council of Housing Associations, to Capper October 11, 1945, charging that if public housing were weakened in the District of Columbia, it would provide an unfortunate national precedent. Capper Papers.

70. Wender testimony cited by Barnes, "Origins of Urban Renewal," p. 114. As president of the Southwest Citizens' Association in the 1930s, Wender had welcomed public housing as a means of offering both blacks and whites affordable accommodations. *Washington Herald,* June 28, 1935. By the 1940s, however, as Barnes points out, whites increasingly viewed public housing as housing for poor blacks, and thus their opposition to such programs heightened.

71. Geneva Valentine testimony, June 10, 1944, cited in Barnes, "Origins of Urban Renewal," p. 124. Traditionally, in Washington, black neighborhood organizations were identified as civic associations, while similar white organizations carried the name citizens' associations.

72. NCHA Records, RG 302, box 43.

73. U. S. Grant III to Arthur Capper, April 7, 1945, Capper Papers.

74. A pioneer city planner, Bettman had come to believe by World War II that privately funded redevelopment downtown was a necessary counterweight to suburban development. He is credited with influencing his fellow Cincinnatian

Senator Robert Taft to embrace federal intervention in housing policy. Laurence C. Gerkins, "Bettman of Cincinnati," in Donald A. Krueckeberg, *The American Planner: Biographies and Recollections* (New York: Methuen, 1983), pp. 141–43.

75. Ihlder Diary, July 28, 1946, cited in William R. Barnes, "A National Controversy in Miniature: The DC Struggle over Public Housing and Redevelopment, 1943–46," *Prologue*, 9 (Summer 1977): 102.

76. Arnold R. Hirsch, *Making the Second Ghetto: Race and Housing in Chicago, 1940–1960* (Cambridge: Cambridge University Press, 1983), pp. 112, 136.

77. W. E. Washington, "Urban Redevelopment in the District," *Washington Tribune*, September 21, 1946. See also a report dated August 10, 1949, for the NCPPC detailing the role that government building played in contributing to the shortage of low-cost housing. "It must be emphasized that the only remedy for this situation is the construction of more low-rent housing. It would not be a remedy to continue the occupancy of existing unfit dwellings—that was permissible only in time of war. It, therefore, should also be emphasized that those who displace or cause the displacement of low-income families and persons have a responsibility for aiding in properly rehousing them. This means that, to the extent displaced families cannot be provided for in acceptable private housing, the agencies responsible for displacement should effectively and courageously aid the National Capital Housing Authority in providing additional dwellings." Nolen Papers, box 34.

78. *Washington Post*, March 15, 1948; *National Capital Housing Authority Annual Report*, 1949.

79. In announcing his resignation on July 11, 1952, Ihlder claimed that "there never has been a time when the Authority, and I as its executive, have not been under attack by one or more special interest group." While he would like to continue as a participant "in the present conflict," he said, he feared he might lose his zest, even without knowing it. *National Capital Housing Authority Annual Report*, 1952.

CHAPTER 8. Redevelopment and Dissent

1. In commenting on Washington's redevelopment, *Newsweek* for March 29, 1954, claimed, "A favorite communist propaganda picture shows some dirty Negro kids playing in a yard of garbage against a backdrop of the sharply focused Capitol dome."

2. John Blum notes that wartime family income, which was rising nationally, was highest in Washington at $5,316, compared to $4,044 in New York City and $3,716 in Los Angeles. *V Was for Victory: Politics and American Culture during World War II* (New York: Harcourt Brace Jovanovich, 1976), p. 92. The *Washington Post* noted on September 13, 1940, that Washington was the third fastest growing city in the country, after Miami and San Diego. Carl Abbott associated Washington with Sunbelt cities in *The New Urban America: Growth and Politics in Sunbelt Cities* (Chapel Hill: University of North Carolina Press, 1981), pp. 26, 43.

3. *Washington Post*, January 28, August 23 1949; *Washington Star*, November 23, 1949, July 8, 1950.

4. *Washington Board of Trade News*, suppl., May 1947.

5. Max Wehrly of the Urban Land Institute summarizing a meeting of the Washington Board of Trade on the subject of decentralization, reported in the *Washington Board of Trade News*, February 1948.

6. *Transportation Plans for Washington: Report to the Board of Commissioners*

(Washington, D.C.: J. E. Greiner Co. and DeLeuw, Cather and Co., December 1946), p. 4.

7. A congressional resolution presented August 3, 1937, called for a halt to government building in the District and its dispersion to the states. 75 Cong., 1 sess., H.R. 475, John Nolen Jr. Papers, National Capital Park and Planning Commission, RG 302, box 29, National Archives. On wartime interest in decentralization of government facilities, see the *New York Times,* November 16, 1941.

8. Frederick Gutheim, "Washington Needs Decentralization," *New Republic* 106 (June 15, 1942): 827.

9. Arthur Rabuck to William E. Reynolds, NCPPC, memorandum, July 2, 1948, "Decentralization vs. Centralization of Government Employment in the Washington Metropolitan Area." Nolen Papers, box 31.

10. Mark H. Rose, *Interstate: Express Highway Politics, 1941–1956* (Lawrence: Regents Press of Kansas, 1979), p. 21; Laurence C. Gerckens, "Bettman of Cincinnati," in Donald A. Krueckeberg, ed., *The American Planner: Biographies and Recollections* (New York: Methuen, 1983), p. 142.

11. Tracy Augur, "Decentralization—Blessing or Tragedy?" in *Planning 1948: Proceedings of the Annual National Planning Conference* (Chicago: American Society of Planning Officials, 1948), p. 32. See also Augur, "Role of the General Services Administration in the Dispersal of Government Offices at Washington," *American Planning and Civic Annual* (Washington, D.C.: American Planning and Civic Association, 1952), pp. 21–28, and Augur, "The Organized Dispersal of the Urban Population," *American Planning and Civic Annual* (Washington, D.C.: American Planning and Civic Association, 1955), pp. 114–22.

12. U. S. Grant III to John Nolen, director, National Capital Park and Planning Commission, September 1, 1948, Nolen Papers, box 31. A. E. Demarey, quoted in the *Washington Star,* November 20, 1950.

13. National Capital Park and Planning Commission, *Washington: Past and Future, A General Survey of the Comprehensive Plan for the National Capital and Its Environs* (Washington, D.C., Government Printing Office, April 1950), 1: 10. *Washington Star,* February 17, 18, 1947. The idea for satellite federal facilities originated in a study done by two of Reynolds's employees at the Public Buildings Commission, Spencer E. Sanders and A. J. Rabuck, which appeared as *New City Patterns* (New York: Reinhold Publishing Co., 1946).

14. *Washington Star,* November 26, 1950. The dispersion policy stood in marked contrast to previous government policy. When departments were asked at the end of World War I whether they would consider leaving the District to ease the demand for space, not a single agency favored an alternative location. 62 Cong., 2 sess., S. Doc. 297, October 28, 1918.

15. Among those agencies to migrate were the Atomic Energy Commission to Germantown, Maryland; the Central Intelligence Agency to Langley, Virginia; the National Bureau of Standards to Gaithersburg, Maryland; and the National Security Agency to Ft. Meade, Maryland. These followed precedents for suburban siting initiated during World War II, starting with the Pentagon and including the Naval Medical Center and the Naval Ordnance Laboratory at White Oak, Maryland. Frederick Gutheim, *Worthy of the Nation: The History of Planning for the National Capital* (Washington, D.C.: Smithsonian Institution Press, 1977), pp. 335–37.

16. See *Washington Post*, editorials, July 23, December 4, 1961.

17. Ibid., July 30, 1950.

18. Homer Hoyt Associates, *Economic Survey of Montgomery and Prince George's County, Maryland* (Washington, D.C.: Homer Hoyt Associates, 1955), pp. 42, 65; Eunice S. Grier, *People and Government: Changing Needs in the District of Columbia, 1950–70* (Washington, D.C.: Washington Center for Metropolitan Studies, 1973). The *Washington Post* reported on January 27, 1961, that between 1948 and 1960, District retail sales dropped from 80 percent of sales in the metropolitan region ($137 million) to 46 percent ($126 million).

19. See the report of planning commission director William E. Finley's speech before the Washington Building Congress in Gutheim, *Worthy of the Nation*, p. 287.

20. For a report of the 1944 transportation plan, see the *Washington Post*, October 24, 1944. For one of the many objections to the subway's potential to add to congestion, see "Report to the Washington, D.C. Chapter of the American Institute of Architects of the Committee on Transportation," April 12, 1945, Peter S. Craig Collection, Special Collections, Gelman Library, George Washington University. Volume 5 of the 1950 Comprehensive Plan, *Moving People and Goods*, concluded that "neither the existing nor the probable future population pattern contains sufficiently high population densities over a large enough area to warrant the extremely high cost involved in the development of a rapid transit system." (Washington, D.C.: National Capital Park and Planning Commission, 1950), p. 25.

21. *A Policies Plan for the Year 2000* (Washington, D.C.: National Capital Planning Commission and National Capital Regional Planning Council, 1961). Noting that the Washington plan inspired Year 2000 plans in other cities, William Whyte suggested that the report assumed that planning could do too much. *The Last Landscape* (Garden City, N.Y.: Doubleday and Co., 1968), p. 149.

22. *Washington Star*, September 17, 1961. The 1961 annual report for the National Capital Housing Authority picked up the same theme. The concept of metropolitan Washington, it should be noted, was central to Harland Bartholomew's recommendations for planners. In 1949, for instance, in a speech to the American Society of Civil Engineers, he called the Washington metropolitan area the "New National Capital," the components of which "must find ways and means for adequate unified policy and control of government." *Washington Star*, November 4, 1949.

23. Rose, *Interstate*, p. 57, cites Bartholomew's 1949 address, "The Location of Interstate Highways in Cities," in *American Planning and Civic Annual* (Washington, D.C.: American Planning and Civic Association, 1949), pp. 73–78. Fleming spoke at the same conference, and his speech, "Federal Works and Community Planning," can be found in the same volume. See Rose, *Interstate*, pp. 61–62.

24. *Board of Trade News*, February 1948, quotes Lansburgh as saying that "to maintain purchasing power in the central business district it is necessary to develop housing near the area for the higher income groups." In this position Lansburgh shared a philosophy reported by Dero A. Saunders in "Race for the Suburbs," *Fortune* 44 (December 1951): 170, that downtown stores could continue to prosper by "giving rigorous encouragement to slum clearance, superhighways, better parking and similar efforts to rehabilitate downtown."

25. For the *Post*'s early position on relocation, see editorials for January 10

and June 22, 1949. For Roberts's quote, see ibid., January 27, 1952. The title for the series may have been borrowed from a similar series in St. Louis that ran in March 1950.

26. *Catholic Standard*, May 30, 1952.

27. Gutheim, *Worthy of the Nation*, pp. 232–33, 314–15.

28. *Washington Star*, May 30, 1952.

29. Louis Justement, *New Cities for Old* (New York: McGraw-Hill, 1946), pp. 3, 8. See also the report of Justement's testimony at a hearing before the District Commissioners, *Washington Times-Herald*, November 13, 1953. Justement's desire to eradicate blight, not just improve existing conditions, was a particularly powerful but not unique expression of an emerging viewpoint. A widely circulated 1943 article for the *Architectural Forum*, for instance, in asking how to fix decay, answered, "The way a dentist does—by clearing out the infected area and guarding it against further trouble." Cited by Norman M. Klein, "The Sunshine Strategy: Buying and Selling the Fantasy of Los Angeles," in Norman M. Klein and Martin J. Schiesl, eds., *Twentieth Century Los Angeles: Power, Promotion, and Social Conflict* (Claremont, Calif.: Regina Books, 1990), p. 14.

30. *Washington Star*, November 15, 1953.

31. *Berman v. Parker*, reported in ibid., November 22, 1954; Roger A. Cunningham, "Supreme Court Decision on Constitutionality of Redevelopment Interpreted," *Journal of Housing* 12 (December 1955): 445–47. The case has since become identified as a landmark in preservation law. See comments in Jacob H. Morrison, *Historic Preservation Law* (Washington, D.C.: National Trust for Historic Preservation, 1965), pp. 27, 45.

32. James W. Rouse and Nathaniel Keith, *No Slums in Ten Years* (Washington, D.C., 1955), p. 3. The report was required as a "workable" plan under provisions of the 1954 Housing Act, which stressed the need to include rehabilitation as well as clearance and required better assistance for the relocation of displaced persons. Having supported Dwight Eisenhower's election in 1952, Rouse was appointed to Eisenhower's Advisory Committee on Government and Housing Policies and Programs, which recommended modifications contained in the 1954 Housing Act. Keith had served as director of slum clearance and redevelopment in the Housing and Home Finance Agency from passage of the 1949 Housing Act until 1953, when he left to enter private consulting in Washington. Mel Scott, *American City Planning since 1890* (Berkeley: University of California Press, 1969), pp. 465, 498–501; *Washington Star*, September 17, 1949, September 12, 1953.

33. Justement, *New Cities for Old*, pp. 128–36.

34. For a description of the Interregional Highway Committee's report, see Rose, *Interstate*, pp. 19–21. Bartholomew claimed to have convinced the committee to accept the concept of in-town ring roads in an interview with Darwin Stolzenbach, director of the Metro History Project, March 27, 1979. Bartholomew described his own theory of how to use highways to promote recentralization in an assessment of his work in St. Louis, "The Location of Interstate Highways in Cities," *American Planning and Civic Annual* (Washington, D.C.: American Planning and Civic Association, 1949). See also the editorial and text of a speech given in Washington reported in the *Washington Star*, November 3, 4, 1949; Norman J. Johnson, "Harland Bartholomew: Precedent for the Profession," in Krueckeberg, *The American Planner*, pp. 279–300; and John F. Bauman, "Expressways, Public

Housing, and Renewal: A Blueprint for Postwar Philadelphia, 1945–1960," *Pennsylvania History* 57 (January 1990): 48–49.

35. Washington Metropolitan Chapter, American Institute of Architects, "Of Plans and People: Planning the City of Washington for Its People as a Worthy Symbol of a Great Nation," May 1950, and "Report of the Subcommittee on Transportation of the Committee of 100," December 18, 1952. Both documents are part of a compilation of transportation reports in the Craig Collection.

36. *Washington Post*, February 10, 1950; *Washington Star*, May 11, 1959.

37. *Washington Post*, December 31, 1957.

38. *Washington Star*, March 30–April 6, 1952.

39. "The National Capital Park and Planning Commission: A Study of the Organization for Planning the National Capital," prepared by the Bureau of the Budget, May 1944. Project files, Metro History Project, Gelman Library, George Washington University; Gutheim, *Worthy of the Nation*, pp. 256, 338.

40. *Washington Star*, July 7, 1960.

41. *Washington Post*, August 17, 1961; *Washington Star*, August 19, 1961, July 20, 1962.

42. *A Policies Plan for the Year 2000*, p. 26.

43. *D.C. Citizen*, July 1947; *Washington Star*, October 15, December 9, 1947. "Segregation in Washington," report of the Executive Board of the Federation of Citizens' Associations, 1948.

44. *Washington Star*, May 4, 30, 1948; Marvin Caplan, "Eat Anywhere!" *Washington History* 1 (Spring 1989): 25–39.

45. *Washington Post*, February 6, 1959.

46. See Martha Swaim, "Desegregation in the District of Columbia Public Schools" (master's thesis, Howard University, 1971), and Part 1, "Washington: Showcase of Integration," in Raymond Wolters, *The Burden of Brown: Thirty Years of School Desegregation* (Nashville: University of Tennessee Press, 1984), pp. 9–63.

47. In addition to testimony reported by William Barnes in the 1945 hearings cited in Chapter 7, see the charge by Joseph Lohman, secretary of the National Committee on Discrimination, who wrote with Edwin R. Embree in 1947 that planned capital improvement "with its irresponsible disregard for displaced Negroes, has fostered a corresponding growth in restrictive covenants." "The Nation's Capital," *Survey Graphic* 36 (January 1947): 33.

48. Mark Gelfand, *A Nation of Cities: The Federal Government and Urban America* (New York: Oxford University Press, 1975), pp. 212–13, citing George B. Nesbit, "Relocating Negroes from Urban Slum Sites," *Journal of Land Economics* 25 (August 1949): 275–88, and Charles Abrams, "Human Rights in Slum Clearance," *Survey* 86 (January 1950): 28. A draft memo in the files of the National Capital Park and Planning Commission in the National Archives from John Ihlder dated June 24, 1949, suggested that the antidiscrimination clause was actually encouraged by opponents of the bill who hoped the provision would help defeat it.

49. On June 30, 1949, the *Washington Times-Herald* reported that the House Appropriations Subcommittee had knocked out the $2 million requested by President Truman for use by the Redevelopment Land Agency, citing the high incidence of home ownership in the area and noting in light of the shortage of homes for black occupancy in the city, "many of these unfortunate people would be dispossessed without any prospect of securing a home." The committee's action, however, appeared to have come in reaction to efforts to bypass the committee by

tacking funds for the RLA onto another bill. In retaliation, House District Committee chairman John L. McMillan of South Carolina, who proved to be the staunchest congressional opponent of home rule, secured a provision prohibiting any federal housing funds for the District which had not been approved by the Appropriations Committee. *Washington Post*, June 24, 30, 1949.

50. *Washington Post*, July 2, 1949; *Pittsburgh-Washington Courier*, October 29, November 5, 1949.

51. William S. Harps Jr., one of the city's few black appraisers, surveyed 113 city blocks of the Southwest following his appointment in 1952. He described the conditions in the area as miserable in a December 11, 1983, interview.

52. *Washington Star*, June 19, 1949. An undated tract-by-tract analysis of the 1950 census held in the Washingtoniana Division of the D.C. Public Library shows wide discrepancies among contiguous tracts in Southwest Washington.

53. *Washington Star*, November 29, 1953.

54. Meeting of the Joint Committee on the National Capital, October 10, 1952, transportation reports, 1952, Craig Collection. See also Ihlder's response to Chalmers Roberts's "Progress or Decay" series on January 27, 1952, and the exchange of letters between Frederick Gutheim and Ihlder in the *Washington Post*, December 2, 10, 1950.

55. The Redevelopment Land Agency originally accepted the more modest goal of improving the area for its existing residents and remained confident that those displaced could be relocated. See report of the community meeting on Southwest in the *Washington Star*, November 21, 1952. Between 1951 and 1954, however, the agency's first executive director, John Searles, under the influence of the Federal City Council and *Washington Post* publisher Philip Graham, became convinced that the NCPC did not realize the full potential of the area and was "selling it short." He thus encouraged planners to shift to "the maximum-optimum" development proposal offered by New York real estate developer William Zeckendorf. John Searles to James Goode, July 15, 1983, copy in author's possession. Searles made the same point in an interview included in the film *Southwest Remembered*, released by Lamont Productions in 1991. Searles also mentioned the influence of Justement and Frederick Gutheim, whose treatment of the Southwest redevelopment in *Worthy of the Nation* is understandably positive. In addition to the *Post*, other papers recognized and supported the more dramatic wholesale approach. The *Star* for May 11, 1952, for instance, described the Justement and Smith plan under the front-page headline, "Costlier Housing in SW Is Aim of Bold New Slum Plan." Unlike earlier slum plans, it reported, "it proposes to make the Southwest one of the city's top-flight middle and upper-income residential sections." Similarly, a *Washington Daily News* editorial on May 23, 1952, in citing the architects' report stated, "Redevelopment can be used to arrest and reverse the tendency to municipal bankruptcy. There are many areas located so strategically with respect to the central city that they can be made most attractive for high-income as well as low-income families."

56. *Washington Star*, May 30, July 19, October 15, November 21, 1952. Smith and Justement's approach found favor nationally, in a report appearing in *Architectural Forum*. Although providing a statement from John Ihlder questioning the propriety of offering "a luxury type of dwelling for a high-income group," the

article praised the proposal for offering "a section capable of reversing the flow of high-income population out west beyond the city boundaries, bringing back the tax income to the city by which alone the city's contribution to redevelopment could be both diminished and recouped, and the rebuilding of lower-income areas . . . without disastrous public cost." Mary Mix Foley, "What Is Urban Redevelopment?" *Architectural Forum* 97 (August 1952): 131, 126.

57. *Washington Daily News*, September 18, 1952.

58. *Washington Post*, September 26, 1955.

59. Statement by Horace W. Peaslee, Committee of 100 on the Federal City, December 12, 1956, Committee of 100 Papers, Gelman Library, George Washington University; *Washington Star*, December 18, 1952; *Washington Daily News*, May 15, 1956.

60. *Washington Times-Herald*, December 18, 1952.

61. *Pittsburgh-Washington Courier*, June 4, 1949. See also July 21, 1951, for testimony of longtime black residents against their displacement.

62. *Washington Post*, January 5, 1957.

63. Redevelopment Land Agency, Annual Report, 1959, p. 15; Annual Report, 1961, p. 25. The 1963 Annual Report, p. 9, in noting that the area's black population now constituted only 10 percent, chose to stress Southwest's cosmopolitan residents: diplomats, government workers, and, as early proponents of wholesale redevelopment had hoped, "some who have moved to the Southwest from the nearby suburbs."

64. *Washington Post*, August 20–26, 1961; Von Eckardt quote from a paper by Keith Melder, "In the Capitol's Shadow: Two Neighborhoods," August 1978. A *Time* magazine report entitled "The Capital: Washington Reborn" was similarly uncritical. Citing Pierre L'Enfant's early expectations for the city, it concluded, "It has taken an awfully long time, but at last L'Enfant's dream seems about to come true." *Time* 78 (November 17, 1961): 22. See also comments by Chloethiel Smith defending the lack of low-cost housing being provided in the Southwest. *Washington Post*, November 25, 1965.

65. *Washington Star*, September 23, 1962, *Washington Post*, June 2, 1969.

66. *Washington Post*, November 30, 1955.

67. Daniel Thursz, *Where Are They Now?* (Washington, D.C.: Health and Welfare Council of the National Capital Area, 1966), pp. 28, 54, 57, 93.

68. Anacostia's white population fell dramatically, from 82.4 percent to 14 percent between 1950 and 1970. Thomas J. Cantwell, "Anacostia: Strength in Adversity," *Records of the Columbia Historical Society* 49 (Charlottesville: University Press of Virginia, 1976), p. 348. In a first-person account of changes in the working-class neighborhood Congress Place, S.E., in the *Washington Post*, May 25, 1986, Teresa Rogers blamed the deterioration of the neighborhood on crowding that followed when displacees from Southwest, many of them on welfare, moved into the area.

69. Redevelopment Land Agency, *Annual Report*, 1959, p. 10.

70. Suzanne Sherwood, *Foggy Bottom, 1800–1975* (Washington, D.C.: GW Washington Studies no. 7, 1978), p. 46. Among the most affected neighborhoods, Brookland faced the loss of seventy homes along Tenth Street, N.E. *Washington Post*, August 1, 1991.

71. Stolzenbach, "The History of the Mass Transportation Survey"; Carl Feiss and Boyd T. Barnard, *Reconnaissance Study of the Downtown Business Area, Washington, D.C.* (Washington, D.C.: Urban Land Institute, 1958), p. 42.

72. *Washington Post,* July 11, 1965.

73. See report of the Federation of Civic Associations meeting which urged the defeat of the proposed Inner Loop on the grounds that it would cause displacement, which would "convert the District into an automobile jungle." *Washington Star,* April 28, 1962.

74. *Washington Post,* editorial, "Homes vs. Freeway," September 18, 1957.

75. *Washington Star,* March 5, 1961; Stolzenbach, "The History of the Mass Transportation Survey."

76. *Highway User,* June–July 1962, cited in an unsigned article by Andrew Hamilton in *Congressional Quarterly,* October 10, 1963, 1733.

77. Moses's speech to the Regional Transportation Advisory Board was reported in the *Washington Star,* along with a favorable editorial in the same edition, September 20, 1962. For Graham's remarks, see the *Washington Post,* November 11, 1962.

78. *Washington Post,* March 24, 1966.

79. Ibid., April 24, 1966; *Washington Star,* May 2, 1966. Judith Hennessee, "A Layman's Who's Who on the Freeway Donnybrook," *Washingtonian Magazine* (May 1968): 47.

80. *Washington Post,* April 29, 1966; *Washington Star,* October 15, 1967.

81. *Washington Star,* May 27, 1966.

82. Interview with Darwin Stolzenbach, January 16, 1984.

83. A *Washington Star* editorial for May 27, 1966, described the pact as "a package which no one but an unalterable opponent of highways, in any form, could reasonably oppose." The *Post* editorial was also dated May 27, 1966, while articles critical of the agreement appeared in the *Star* on May 28 and in the *Post* on May 29. Barry's comments were reported in the *Post,* September 15, 1966, and in the *Star,* November 17, 1966.

84. *Washington Post,* May 27, 29, 1966.

85. Ibid., September 16, 1966. Rowe became aware of the problems with redevelopment and highways through her work with Child Services in Southwest, where she perceived the problems of relocation directly. Interview, June 21, 1985.

86. *Washington Star,* February 9, 1968.

87. "The Interstate System in the District of Columbia." Hearings before the Subcommittee on Roads of the Committee on Public Works, House of Representatives, 90 Cong., 2 sess. Testimony of Charles Cassel, Black United Front, p. 55; of Reginald Booker, Chairman, Emergency Committee on the Transportation Crisis, p. 14.

88. *Washington Post Magazine,* April 3, 1988, 23.

CHAPTER 9. Renewal, Construction, and Retrenchment
1. "Status Report on Downtown Urban Renewal Legislation for the District of Columbia," presented to the Federal City Council, March 27, 1964. RG1, Records of the Federal City Council, box 7, District of Columbia Archives (DCA).

2. See copy of letter from Rep. John McMillan to fellow members of Congress, June 16, 1964, Records of the Federal City Council.

3. *Washington Post,* January 31, 1964, report of a Dowdy speech delivered in

Dayton; John Dowdy, "The Mounting Scandal of Urban Renewal," *Reader's Digest* (March 1964): 51–53, copy in the Records of the Federal City Council.

4. Reuben Clark, president, Washington Planning and Housing Association, to John McMillan, chairman, Committee on the District of Columbia, House of Representatives, May 5, 1964. An attached statement from the Washington Planning and Housing Association argued against competitive bidding because, while it brought in more cash immediately, it had the effect in raising the value of land to push up rents, a problem identified with the redevelopment of the Southwest. Records of the Federal City Council, box 19. The association had argued as far back as 1950 for more reliance on rehabilitation as a means of keeping rents in redeveloped areas down and for the establishment of a relocation center to assist those forced to move as a result of redevelopment. *Washington Post*, October 12, 1950.

5. *Washington Post*, April 5, 1965, as reprinted by and preserved in the Records of the Federal City Council, box 19. For the controversy surrounding Weaver's appointment, see Mark Gelfand, *A Nation of Cities* (New York: Oxford University Press, 1975), pp. 309–15.

6. *Washington Post*, July 15, 30, 1965.

7. John H. Mollenkopf, *The Contested City* (Princeton: Princeton University Press, 1983), p. 43, argues that programs such as urban renewal were central to Democratic politics: "By making economically vital physical changes possible, federal urban development programs could create local coalitions of producer interests. The disparate urban constituencies of the national Democratic Party— machines as well as reform groups, big business as well as labor, blue collar ethnics as well as minorities—could each find reasons to be united behind a program of growth and development."

8. Daniel Thursz, *Where Are They Now?* (Washington, D.C.: Health and Welfare Council of the National Capital Area, 1966); *Washington Post*, November 29, 1966, *Washington Star*, December 5, 7, 1966.

9. "Preliminary Draft Urban Renewal Plan Northwest #1 Urban Renewal Area," November 1957. Frederick Routh, "Northwest #1: An Interim Report," October 1972, credits the Urban League's effect on redevelopment policy in the area, beginning September 1965. As early as 1958, District Commissioner Robert McLaughlin wrote Harland Bartholomew, chairman of the National Capital Planning Commission, urging a shift from the Southwest approach to one of "maximum conservation and rehabilitation." Noting that as many as half of the area residents might not be able to afford privately rehabilitated housing, he complained that "even in low-cost land areas, the few new dwelling units which have been constructed recently to sell or rent cheaply are of such standards as to create more problems than are solved." Peter S. Craig Collection, Special Collections, Gelman Library, George Washington University. Members of the board of the National Capital Housing Authority also discussed such an approach. Minutes, National Capital Housing Authority, May 25, 1960, DCA.

10. *Washington Post*, December 2, 1966. Unlike the *Star*, the *Post*, on May 2, 1967, accepted the implications of the *Where Are They Now?* relocation report, as well as in its summary of the redevelopment process, published June 2, 1969.

11. Thomas Appleby, statement before the Potomac Chapter of the National Association of Housing and Real Estate Officials, June 8, 1967. Library Collection of the Department of Housing and Community Development (DHCD) of the

District of Columbia, DCA. See also Appleby profile, *Washington Star*, November 27, 1967.

12. Walter E. Fauntroy, "The New Reconstruction," speech before the NAACP, August 10, 1960; Fauntroy before Subcommittee 1, on H.R. 6712, amendment to the District Redevelopment Act of 1945, July 27, 1961, collected as a notebook of materials sent to Jeffrey Cohen, August 17, 1989, Walter E. Fauntroy Papers, box 163, Gelman Library, George Washington University.

13. *Washington Post*, January 9, 1950.

14. Ibid., April 8, 1966.

15. *Shaw Power*, October 1969, Shaw vertical file, Washingtoniana Division, D.C. Public Library. Griffith was still working on a planning degree at MIT when he joined MICCO. In the thesis he completed somewhat later, Griffith reiterated the antagonism among Washington blacks to the Southwest experience with redevelopment, writing, "Washington, D.C.'s black communities look upon the Southwest Urban Renewal Project as a glaring and dismal failure. They see the results of the Project as typical of urban renewal's injustice to poor people in general and black people in particular. . . . These people who were 'outside' the influential decision-making camp . . . people without power or even the ability to comprehend urban renewal forces, were scattered to the winds. The new residents of the new Southwest were mostly white and affluent. The black community cries, 'No more Southwests.'" Reginald Wilbert Griffith, "The Influence of Meaningful Citizen Participation on the 'Urban Renewal' Process and the Renewal of the Inner-City's Black Community: Case Study—Washington, D.C.'s 'Shaw School Urban Renewal Area': MICCO A Unique Experiment" (master's thesis, MIT, 1969), p. 14.

16. Fauntroy Papers, box 409.

17. Articles of incorporation, MICCO, April 15, 1966, Shaw vertical file, D.C. Public Library.

18. A *Washington Post* editorial, "MICCO on the March," for March 21, 1967, praised the Shaw parade marking the event as "a symbol of a far wider alliance for neighborhood rehabilitation than has ever been attempted before in Washington. The character and scale of renewal in this city, for many years into the future, depends upon the success of this experiment."

19. In announcing formation of the Uptown Progress organization, R. N. Norton, a mortician, as chair said that it had been formed to "prevent what happened in Southwest from being repeated." The feeling is widespread, he charged, "that present long-range planning imposes deliberate disadvantages upon Negroes." *Washington Star*, December 5, 1965.

20. *Washington Post*, June 15, 1966, *Washington Star*, February 20, 1967. Press release, February 15, 1967, Shaw file, DHCD Library Collection, DCA.

21. *Washington Star*, June 4, October 29, 1966, *Washington Post*, editorial, April 29, 1966.

22. F. E. Ropshaw, secretary to the Board of Commissioners, memorandum to Thomas Appleby, executive director, Redevelopment Land Agency, May 6, 1966, reporting the decision of the April 21 board meeting. DHCD Library Collection. According to a report in the *Star* for April 21, Commissioner John Duncan said, in urging approval of the $2.8 million application for federal funds for Shaw, "We cannot make the same mistake we made in the Southwest. The Southwest was not just slum clearance. It cleared out people as well."

23. *Washington Post* headline, June 15, 1966, "Shaw Civic Group Told Its Area 'No Southwest'"; *Washington Star*, November 28, 1967.

24. The *Washington Post* for September 21, 1966, quoted Del Vecchio as saying, "Low-income families should have the opportunity to live close to town in pleasant surroundings rather than ten miles out where the market often forces them to live." Alan R. Talbot, *The Mayor's Game: Richard Lee of New Haven and the Politics of Change* (New York: Harper and Row, 1967), p. 136, described Logue's work in New Haven as neighborhood renewal "with a scalpel, not a bulldozer."

25. *Washington Afro-American*, November 26, 1966. According to a profile in the *Afro-American* on April 15, 1969, Moore had already organized sit-ins in his native North Carolina before coming to Washington to study theology at Howard University.

26. *Washington Post*, April 8, 1966.

27. *Washington Afro-American*, January 15, 19, 1963. The criticism of Duncan served as a measure of change among black activists. In 1949 Duncan took a leading role in questioning the redevelopment of Marshall Heights without an overall redevelopment plan for the city. *Washington Star*, February 25, 1949. Such criticism from Stone would never have emerged that early, and even early in 1963 one could consider him outside the mainstream. By 1967, however, even James Banks, as much an establishment figure as existed among blacks in the social policy arena, speaking as director of the United Planning Organization, accused middle-class blacks of being almost as heedless of the plight of the poor as middle-class whites. *Washington Post*, December 16, 1967. In a March 3, 1992, interview with me, Fauntroy said his trial by fire in the civil rights struggles in Selma and Birmingham, Alabama, should have commended him to militants, but he was still accused of being a dupe for whites who planned to take over valuable land in Shaw.

28. Quoted in Ellen Perry Berkeley, "People: The New Voice in Renewal," *Architectural Forum* 127 (November 1967): 75.

29. Griffith, "Meaningful Citizen Participation," pp. 61–62.

30. *Washington Post*, May 14, 1966; *Washington Afro-American*, May 28, 1966.

31. *Washington Star*, August 3, 5, 1965; *Washington Post*, August 7, 11, September 7, 10, 1965. The Catholic organization was the product of white activist priest Geno Baroni, who served on the original board of directors of MICCO. When the Government Printing Office later threatened to move its plant to the suburbs, Baroni described the move as "madness," pointing out that the plant provided vital economic opportunities in the heart of a Model Cities area. William Raspberry column, *Washington Post*, January 29, 1968. See also Lawrence M. O'Rourke, *Geno: The Life and Mission of Geno Baroni* (New York: Paulist Press, 1991), pp. 54–55.

32. *Washington Post*, November 26, 1965. A March 6, 1966, *Post* editorial attacked the initial planning decision for its inability to "reconcile the public interest with the narrow ambitions of the Federal agencies." The *Washington Afro-American* for March 12, citing poor living in buildings "fit only for cattle," argued that the decision provided a case for home rule.

33. *Washington Post*, July 27, 1966. See also the *Star* editorials for July 28, August 7, 18, and the *Post* for August 14, 1966.

34. *Washington Post*, August 3, 1966, August 6, 1969.

35. According to the account of Special Assistant Joseph Califano, Johnson

was moved by the Watts riots in 1965 to believe that some form of home rule was essential in heading off social disturbances in Washington. He wanted more power for the District government but was unable to secure sufficient backing from Congress to provide an elected city council. Joseph A. Califano, *The Triumph and Tragedy of Lyndon Johnson: The White House Years* (New York: Simon and Schuster, 1991), pp. 228–29; Charles A. Horsky, comments, 20th annual D.C. Historical Studies Conference, *Washington Post*, March 4, 1993.

36. Among those pressing most strongly for integration was Attorney General Ramsey Clark. Martha Derthick, *New Towns In-Town* (Washington, D.C.: Urban Institute, 1972), pp. 4–6, 29. *Washington Post* architectural critic Wolf Von Eckardt, who had written an open letter to Johnson on February 7, 1965, urging just such a plan, claimed in a column for September 3, 1967, that with bold planning, this project could become as influential as Weissendhof Village, near Stuttgart, Germany, had been fifty years earlier, when Walter Gropius, Miles van der Rohe, and Le Corbusier, among others, were given the chance to realize their most advanced ideas. *Washington Post*, January 3, 1968.

37. *Washington Post*, profile of Miller, former mayor of Louisville, March 21, 1968.

38. *Washington Afro-American*, April 16, 1968; Hearings before the Senate Subcommittee on Business and Commerce of the District of Columbia, 90 Cong., 2d sess., pt. 2, app.: Report of City Council Public Hearings on the Rebuilding and Recovery of Washington, D.C. from the Civil Disturbances of April 1968, May 10, 1968, DHCD Library Collection, DCA. While siding with greater citizen participation, the council set itself apart from black separatists, such as R. H. Booker, who spoke as chairman of the Emergency Committee on the Transportation Crisis, defending the looting by asking rhetorically how it was possible to steal something from a thief.

39. *Shaw's Last Stand*, May 1968, Shaw file, DHCD Library Collection, DCA.

40. *Washington Star*, April 13, 1968.

41. Ben W. Gilbert, *Ten Blocks from the White House: Anatomy of the Washington Riots of 1968* (New York: Praeger Publishers, 1968), p. 216.

42. *Washington Star*, April 21, 1968; see also the *Star* editorial for April 15, 1968, criticizing those at a CHANGE meeting who blamed whites for the riots, saying that with such an attitude, there would be no money for rebuilding.

43. Ibid., May 20, 1968.

44. Veteran *Post* reporter Jack Eisen called Washington's approach a clean break with the centralized and basically authoritarian planning tradition that dated from the days of Pierre L'Enfant. *Washington Post*, August 29, 1968. A *Star* editorial for September 2, 1968, called the approach a "people's plan."

45. *Washington Post*, April 15, 17, 1968. Although O'Rourke does not report this event, which Geno Baroni clearly helped orchestrate, he does trace Baroni's close ties to Protestant activists Wendt and Fauntroy, as well as to All Souls' James Reeb. *Geno*, pp. 35–38.

46. Kim Klein, "100th Anniversary for St. Stephen and the Incarnation Episcopal Church," *Washington History* 5 (Spring/Summer 1993): 85; *Washington Informer*, October 16, 1969; *Washington Star*, January 11, July 12, 20, 1970; *Washington Post*, June 9, 1970; Gilbert, *Ten Blocks from the White House*, p. 215.

47. According to a report in the *Washington Post* for February 1, 1969, President Nixon commented, "This is our capital city; we want to make it a beautiful

city in every way," to which Mayor Washington replied, "With the kind of help you are visibly demonstrating today, I think we can make this a model city." See also the *Washington Afro-American*, February 4, 1969, *Washington Star*, February 1, 1969, *Washington Post*, March 19, 1969.

48. WTOP editorial, August 22, 23, 1969, Fauntroy Papers, box 310.

49. Urban Renewal Plan for Shaw School Urban Renewal Area, 1969, 3–2.

50. *Washington Post*, September 13, 1969, January 12, 1970; Mister quoted in *Washington Star*, February 1, 1970.

51. *Washington Post*, September 2, 1968, April 14, 1969.

52. *Washington Star*, March 3, 21, April 6, 1969. A June 24, 1970, article by the *Post*'s Wolf Von Eckardt gave credit to Daniel Patrick Moynihan, then special adviser on urban affairs, for the suggestion that Fauntroy be put in charge of rebuilding the H Street, N.E., and Fourteenth Street, N.W., riot corridors.

53. In announcing the initial HUD planning and survey grant of $887,000 for Fort Lincoln, Washington had promised "maximum citizen participation in all phases of development." See Derthick, *New Towns In-Town*, pp. 27–28. A *Washington Star* editorial for June 13, 1970, commended the mayor's decision to bypass the competing local organizations, stating that "the stakes are too high to allow this valuable project to be further jeopardized by adhering to a course of action that has proved clearly to be unworkable," to which the *Post* for June 15 added, "Fort Lincoln's neighborhoods have a legitimate and proper interest in aspects of the planning that may affect their well-being, but they are not entitled to a veto." In response to reports that the Nixon administration was backing away from supporting Fort Lincoln, the *Post* added that "by securing acceptance of this citywide approach, Mayor Washington should be able to counter those in the national administration who would scrap the controversy-ridden, but nevertheless promising project." See *Post* reports on June 5, 8, 1970. See also *Post*, June 2, 1969, "Troubles Beset Model Cities."

54. *Washington Post*, November 25, 1970.

55. *Washington Afro-American*, November 21, 1970. In supporting Fauntroy, the paper praised the kind of advocacy planning practiced in Shaw, reiterating the belief that "such renewal efforts as that in Southwest Washington worked largely to the disadvantage of the people who were already there, but not because the planners didn't know what the people wanted. The planners simply didn't care what the people wanted." In a letter printed in the January 1971 issue of *Shaw Power*, NCPC acting director G. Franklin Edwards denied any effort to revive the "old urban renewal tactic of large scale planning of entire neighborhoods by planners from outside the area."

56. The *Washington Post* for September 17, 1970, reported that the Redevelopment Land Agency had decided to place development of Fort Lincoln in the hands of a single private developer, following the model of Columbia, Maryland, discarding the public corporation that Logue had recommended. This decision provoked sharp criticism from liberal gadfly Sam Smith in an article entitled, "The Fall of Fort Lincoln," *D.C. Gazette*, April 14, 1971. The *Post* reported a shift to a middle-class constituency on June 25 and December 30, 1971. Derthick, *New Towns In-Town*, p. 30, reports that Logue, because he was committed to building an integrated community, was uneasy with the emphasis on public and assisted housing, as were residents of the predominantly middle-class black neighbor-

hoods in the immediate vicinity. *Fort Lincoln New Town, Washington, D.C.: Report of the BSI/Westinghouse Joint Venture* (January 1972), pp. 11, 17, 45, 63. Wolf Von Eckardt, an ardent supporter of the Fort Lincoln concept, concluded sadly about the plan's unfulfilled promise, "There was, and is, no one with power in this city who really believes, as President Johnson did, that Washington deserves 'the best in community planning.'" *Washington Post,* January 26, 1980.

57. Derthick, *New Towns In-Town,* p. 92.

58. Minutes, MICCO Board of Directors meeting, March 31, 1971, Fauntroy Papers, box 310.

59. Statement of Stan Barry, director of community participation, MICCO, before Housing and Urban Development Committee, District City Council, August 9, 1971, Fauntroy Papers, box 310.

60. James Woolfork to MICCO Board of Directors, May 17, 1971, Fauntroy Papers, box 310. RLA's Melvin Mister wrote Fauntroy on August 27, 1971, "I think the general matter of budgeting, budget control, and budget support for proposals, is one which needs considerable attention by MICCO and RLA. Although much good work has been done recently by Bill Stewart and Jim Woolfork, there is still much to be done." Fauntroy Papers, box 310.

61. Fauntroy to Mister, August 31, 1971, Reading File, Melvin Mister, RG 14, box 10, DCA. Statement of Charles S. Holloway, executive director, Uptown Progress, before Housing and Urban Development Committee, District Council, August 9, 1971, Fauntroy Papers, box 310. In an analysis dated November 15 of the RLA meeting of November 10, 1971, at which MICCO representatives voiced their opposition to RLA's plan to encourage competitive bidding, Edwin Haynes, MICCO counsel, wrote to executive director William Stewart, "The MICCO process is more than just building housing. It is a process of land reform. The contribution of absentee land owners to deprived communities is well known. One of the important goals of the MICCO process is to have land ownership returned to the Shaw community. Competitive bidding would make the profit motive the dominant force and prime consideration among the bidders. The community's priority on land ownership would have very little value to the construction corporation which gets the job and the community would be powerless to promote its interests. Negotiative bidding allows the community to do the negotiating and gives the community power to promote its priority of community ownership and other priorities, e.g., contractual and employment practices." Fauntroy Papers, box 409.

62. Stephen Green, *Washington Star,* October 9, 1971.

63. James van R. Springer to Marjorie Lawson, August 13, 1971; Mike Levey to Ralph Werner, General Counsel, RLA, memorandum, September 9, 1971; Leon Ulman, Deputy Assistant Attorney General, to Walter Fauntroy, December 30, 1971, Fauntroy Papers, box 409.

64. *Washington Post,* October 3, 1971. In a memo to MICCO board members, October 4, 1971, Fauntroy charged, "It is obvious that people like Eugene Meyer do not want to see us own the land or learn to use the system instead of being used by it." Fauntroy Papers, box 310.

65. Fauntroy speech at annual MICCO meeting, January 29, 1972, Fauntroy Papers, box 409.

66. Melvin A. Mister to Walter E. Fauntroy, February 4, 1972, and attach-

ment, "RLA Board Policy on MICCO Contract," RG14, DCA; copy also in Fauntroy Papers, box 409.

67. Walter Fauntroy to MICCO board members, February 18, 1972, Fauntroy
Papers, box 409.

68. RLA review of MICCO contract, February 4, 1972, Fauntroy Papers, box 409.

69. *Washington Post,* January 11, 17, May 20, 1973.

70. Statement of Charles R. Braxton before the Housing and Urban Renewal
Committee, District City Council, February 22, 1973. See also letter from Nor-
man Wood Jr., president of MICCO, to Senator Birch Bayh, November 29, 1973,
Fauntroy Papers, box 409.

71. "Opportunities and Constraints Related to Housing Production in NDP
Areas: Renewal Action to Increases in Housing Production in NDP Areas," Linton, Mields and Coston, May 1971, DHCD Library Collection; *Washington Star,*
September 22, 1971. See also paper dated November 10, 1971, "Marketing and Development of Shaw Sites," RLA files-Shaw, DHCD Library Collection, DCA.

72. The award went to a group of black architects based in San Francisco over
the bid of the Washington-based Housing Development Corporation headed by
Channing Phillips, who charged that RLA's desire was an effort to "keep the big
guys bidding." *Washington Star,* October 7, 1971; *Washington Post,* October 7, 1971.

73. Report of Special Citizens Advisory Committee on Urban Renewal to the
D.C. City Council, September 25, 1972, pp. 6, 13, 32. These figures conformed
closely to RLA's own figures released January 6, 1972, with announcement of the
groundbreaking for New Bethel Church's Foster House, a 73-unit building at
Rhode Island Avenue, between Eighth and Ninth streets. Only Lincoln-Westmore-
land on Seventh Street, between R and S, with 108 units had been completed at
that time. Gibson Plaza on Seventh between N and O, with 217 additional units,
was still under construction. RLA files, RG 14, DCA.

74. John Gunther to Fauntroy, September 3, 1971, Fauntroy Papers, box 409.

75. The Special Report of September 29, 1972, in calling for home rule and
structured reorganization of city government, argued that "ultimately, home rule
should recognize those civic concerns and those public decisions that are largely
neighborhood-centered in character. It should delegate authority to deal with
such concerns to submunicipal units of government, elected by and responsible
to the people of the neighborhoods themselves" (p. 82). At its height, the Shaw
planning process embodied a broadly shared goal among urban blacks to achieve
authoritative political power and not mere influence, in line with the comment
that "in black power advocates, maximum feasible participation came to mean
capture of institutional self-development rather than the mere fact of formal
representation." J. David Greenstone and Paul E. Peterson, *Race and Authority in
Urban Politics: Community Participation and the War on Poverty* (New York:
Russell Sage Foundation, 1973), p. 94. The Shaw approach may be placed in the
tradition of redistribution, as opposed to development or allocation dominated
either by elites or by bargaining between generally equal forces. See comments of
Clarence E. Stone and Haywood T. Sanders on Peterson's book *City Limits,* "Reex-
aming a Classic Case of Development Politics: New Haven, Connecticut," in
Stone and Sanders, eds., *The Politics of Urban Development* (Lawrence: University
Press of Kansas, 1987), p. 160.

CHAPTER 10. The Limits of Social Protest Politics

1. Quoted in Jonathan I. Z. Agronsky, *Marion Barry: The Politics of Race* (Latham, N.Y.: British American Publishing, 1991), p. 97.

2. Clayborne Carson, *In Struggle: SNCC and the Black Awakening of the 1960s* (Cambridge, Mass.: Harvard University Press, 1981), pp. 24, 168.

3. Quoted in Steven J. Diner, *Democracy, Federalism, and the Governance of the Nation's Capital, 1790–1974* (Washington, D.C.: Studies in D.C. History and Public Policy no. 9, University of the District of Columbia, 1987), p. 52. Barry was among those SNCC leaders who urged the Democratic and Republican national conventions in 1960 to grant self-government to the District. Carson, *In Struggle,* p. 26; Agronsky, *Marion Barry,* p. 103.

4. Agronsky, *Marion Barry,* p. 125.

5. Ibid., p. 126.

6. James Q. Wilson, *Negro Politics: The Search for Leadership* (Glencoe, Ill.: Free Press, 1960), p. 185. Barry's style initially fit the pattern described nationally by James Jennings, "The Politics of Black Empowerment in Urban America," in Joseph M. Kling and Prudence S. Posner, eds., *Dilemmas of Activism: Class, Community, and the Politics of Local Mobilization* (Philadelphia: Temple University Press, 1992), pp. 114–15. See also an early interview Barry gave as a student activist, reprinted in the *Washington Post,* December 10, 1978.

7. Jeffrey R. Henig, "Race and Voting: Continuity and Change in the District of Columbia," *Urban Affairs Quarterly* 28 (Spring 1993): 554.

8. *Washington Post,* March 10, May 13, 1975; John R. Tydings, executive vice-president, Greater Washington Board of Trade, interview by author, May 11, 1987.

9. *Washington Afro-American,* September 30, 1978; *Washington Post,* October 19, 1978.

10. Harry S. Jaffe and Tom Sherwood, *Dream City: Race, Power, and the Decline of Washington, D.C.* (New York: Simon and Schuster, 1994), p. 130.

11. *Washington Post,* August 2, 1982, December 20, 1979.

12. The fiscal problems inherited from the federal government are dealt with in a report prepared for the 1986 Barry campaign by the Mayor's Office of Policy and Program Evaluation, "A Summary of the Programs, Progress, and Plans of the Barry Administration," October 1986, pp. 16–17. See also the commentary by Gladys Mack, assistant city administrator for budget and resource development, in the *Washington Post,* November 7, 1981.

13. *Washington Post,* January 14, 1981, March 28, 1982.

14. A reporter writing for the *Washington Post,* August 3, 1982, commented, "Any Kane mayoral race would automatically conjure up images—already prevalent in some sections of the black community—of a white-backed 'master plan' to regain political control of the nation's capital. With many blacks already fearful of whites moving into formerly black neighborhoods like Capitol Hill and Shaw, and with those new 'urban pioneers' becoming increasingly active in local politics, subscribers to the conspiracy theory may see a Kane candidacy as fulfilling a prophecy of Barry as the last black mayor."

15. Ibid., July 1, August 30, June 22, 1982.

16. Ibid., November 7, 1982. Barry carried only 34.3 percent of the white vote, compared to the 52 percent he carried in 1978. Henig, "Race and Voting," 554.

17. *Washington Post,* June 13, June 27, 1987; Dawn Monica Eichenlaub, "Rhodes

Tavern and Square 224, 1978–83: A Case Study of Preservation Practice in Washington, D.C." (master's thesis, George Washington University, 1983).

18. *Washington Post*, November 27, December 1, 1984, June 14, 1986, September 2, 1989. The *Post* architectural critic Benjamin Forgey wrote no less than three critical columns on the project, June 2, 1984, March 1, 1985, and November 17, 1990.

19. Mayor Marion Barry, interview, *Regardie's*, June 1986, suppl., p. 10. Barry's former special assistant, Mary Lamson, stressed Barry's concern about the threat of suburban competition as a motivating factor in giving developers breaks. Interview by author, June 1, 1987.

20. Richard Cohen, "Home Rule: The First Decade," *Washington Post Magazine*, December 30, 1984. In Chicago, another black mayor, Harold Washington, also stressed job creation as a criterion for supporting new development, but unlike Barry he made a point of balancing neighborhood with downtown interests. Jennings, "Politics of Black Empowerment," p. 125; Jaffe and Sherwood, *Dream City*, pp. 155–60.

21. Sam Smith, "Post-Reconstruction Blues: Reflections on Marion Barry and the Struggles of Black Power," *Progressive Review* (March 1989). Smith met Barry in the 1966 boycott and worked on his campaigns for school board, city council, and, in 1978, for mayor. He dated his break with the mayor to the first term when, he argued, "black power cut a deal with white power. The middle class and poor of either race weren't part of the deal although they were mightily affected by it."

22. *The Barry Administration Reports to the Public on Public Housing* (June 1986). See editorials on housing in the *Washington Post* for February 23, 1985, February 20, 1986, and the articles "Neglect Scars D.C. Public Housing," March 2, 1986, and "D.C. Public Housing Vacancy among the Highest," April 27, 1986.

23. *Washington Post*, February 5, 1981.

24. See ibid., December 12, 1985, January 12, 1986. Like Barry, Donaldson had been an activist in the Student Non-Violent Coordinating Committee, joining sit-ins in Mississippi while a student at Michigan State University. He got his start in politics working for Julian Bond's election to Congress in Atlanta before organizing for SNCC in Columbus, Ohio, and Washington. Carson, *In Struggle*, pp. 80, 166–68, 305. After directing Barry's 1978 upset in the Democratic primary, Donaldson joined the first Barry administration as a special assistant, first gaining a good reputation as an administrator by revamping a disorganized summer jobs program and then by straightening out the troubled D.C. Department of Employment Services.

25. *Washington Post*, July 24, August 11, 1984, April 4, 1985. On Barry's apparent vindication, see the *Post* editorial, "The End of Mr. Barry's Ordeal," April 5, 1985.

26. Ibid., January 16, 1987.

27. Ibid., May 29, June 7, 1987.

28. *Economist*, March 2, 1986.

29. *Washington Post*, December 18, 1985.

30. Juan Williams, "A Dream Deferred: A Black Mayor Betrays the Faith," *Washington Monthly* (July–August 1986): 39. Barry administration officials attempted to dismiss the article by charging that Williams's private school training and what they considered his covert support of Patricia Harris while he covered

the mayoralty campaign in 1982 disqualified him as an unbiased observer. Mary Lamson, interview by author, June 1, 1987, Dwight Cropp, interview by author, July 20, 1987. Williams told me in a telephone conversation in December 1987 that Barry's staff had urged him to cease his criticism in light of the fact that he was too young to have experienced the struggles of the civil rights era and thus could not understand what the Barry administration was up against.

31. *Washington Post,* November 6, 1986. In an interview just before the election with *Post* editorial staff member Robert Asher, Barry attributed his lack of support in predominantly white Ward 3 to a limited view of government. In poorer wards, he said, government played a much more extensive role in residents' lives through public health and housing facilities, summer jobs, and public schooling. Receiving such an array of services, "they see the improvements, they see the benefits." Any failure of integrity in his administration, he said, were "matters of the heart, not of the head." October 26, 1986.

32. Ibid., January 3, 1987.

33. Ibid., September 17, November 3, 1987. The new housing director, Alphonso Jackson, although he held the position eighteen months, was the fifth permanent director of housing along with four acting directors in the first ten years of Barry rule. Although city officials managed to get the vacancy rate in public units below 16 percent from a high of 17.6 percent in April 1986, by 1989 it had risen to 19 percent, third in the nation and outranked only by Newark and Cleveland. A series of critical articles in the *Post* in March 1989 reported that the Department of Housing and Urban Development considered the District housing authority to be one of the worst-managed in the country. If the District's own subsidy did not exceed that of every other major city in the country, it quoted a HUD official, "they would be bankrupt." *Washington Post,* April 10, 1987, March 26–27, 1989.

34. Barry's reported reaction to the snow was that he would be taking more time off in the future, to which the *Post* replied in a stinging editorial, "Yes, it was extraordinarily wicked weather—but mayors elsewhere have lost office for less. The public anger will not be soothed by any more false balm. This was a disaster. It still is." Ibid., January 23, 28, 1987.

35. For a summary of the other policy controversies that plagued the outset of Barry's new term, see Juan Williams, "The Imperial Mayor," *New Republic,* October 26, 1987, pp. 21–23, *Washington Post,* January 12, 1988.

36. *Los Angeles Times,* July 6, 1987. See also the report in the *New York Times,* "Washington Mayor Defiant as Attacks and Rumors Grow," September 3, 1987.

37. *Washington Post,* August 9, 1987.

38. Williams, "The Imperial Mayor."

39. WRC-TV Channel 4, week of November 6, 1987; Mary R. Sawyer, "Harassment of Black Elected Officials: Ten Years Later," published by Voter Education and Registration Action, Inc., Washington, D.C., September 1987. One of the most prominent affirmations of the belief that such efforts to discredit black officials have continued from the 1960s to the present is offered by Colgate University's Manning Marable, *Black American Politics: From the Washington Marches to Jesse Jackson* (London: Verso, 1985), pp. 139, 185–86. See also the article by Eric Pianin and Courtland Milloy in the Outlook section of the *Post* for October 6, 1985, "Does the White Return to D.C. Mean 'The Plan' Is Coming True?"

40. *New York Times,* January 24, 1988, September 3, 1987.

41. Ibid., March 6, 1989; *Washington Post,* March 13, August 31, 1989.

42. *Washington Post,* February 16, 1990.

43. "D.C's Day of Shame: Facing Up to the Jape," Outlook section, ibid., July 1, 1990. Civil rights activist and George Mason University professor Roger Wilkins made a similar statement in a column in the *Post* on July 15, 1990, saying, "As a former Justice Department official, I have been disgusted by their heavy-breathing and leaking prosecutorial style. But simply to scream 'racism!' 50 times a day does not lift Marion Barry out of the cesspool he created for himself. Nor does it make his defenders saviors of the race. We must have standards in the black community."

44. Among the most visible evidence of Barry's support was a rally of some two thousand people. Among the speakers was Abdul Alim Muhammed, a top official in the Nation of Islam and a candidate for Congress in Maryland, who reiterated Barry's characterization of the federal prosecution as a lynching. *Washington Post,* July 3, 1990. Of particular concern to some of Barry's supporters was that if he resigned, one of the announced candidates for mayor, City Council chairman Dave Clarke, would become acting mayor. Their opposition to Clarke reportedly stressed the unacceptability of handing him such an advantage because he was white, sentiment that was revealed when a predominantly black audience booed Clarke upon his introduction at a rally for South African leader Nelson Mandela. Ibid., July 15, 1990. For a review of the reaction to Barry's arrest in the Washington area black press, see Paul Ruffin, "The Black Press Dilemma," in the Outlook section of the *Post,* July 8, 1990. When he finally decided not to run for reelection, Barry made a point of conveying the news exclusively through the black media. Ibid., June 15, 1990.

45. Ibid., April 8, July 10, 1990. A survey of 800 voters reported in the *Post* on March 15, 1990, revealed that while 87 percent of white voters thought Barry should resign, only 41 percent of blacks surveyed agreed. While 97 percent of the whites said they would not vote for Barry, only 51 percent of blacks took the same position.

46. Jaffe and Sherwood, *Dream City,* pp. 275–76, 281, *Washington Post,* February 18, 1990.

47. *Washington Post,* July 22, 1990.

48. Ibid., August 12, 13, 1990.

49. Walter E. Fauntroy, interview by author, March 3, 1992. Fauntroy's platform, released in July 1990, addressed the major social issues of the time, including efforts to provide safe and affordable housing, dealing with drugs and violence, improving health care, and expanding economic opportunity in the inner city.

50. For a glowing report of Cohen's plans to channel some of the profits from his office/retail project back into the Shaw project, see Jonathan Walters, "Big Inner-City Plan," *Historic Preservation* (September/October 1987): 74–76. After receiving more than $12 million in advances from the District government, Cohen's financial problems finally overwhelmed the project, forcing him to declare bankruptcy. *Washington Post,* November 26, 1986, April 17, 1988, March 28, 1991.

51. *Washington Post,* September 18, 1990.

52. The *Washington Post,* among other media, was absolute in its opposition to Barry's election, charging in a September 12, 1992, editorial, "whatever difficulties the city in general and Ward 8 in particular are now encountering, putting Marion

Barry back in city hall would be a sorry response—a setback for the ward and the rest of the city." For profiles of Ward 8, see ibid., August 18, 1988, August 27, 1992.

53. When pressed whether such dress wasn't just political posturing, he retorted, "It's not just fashion, it's ideology." Ibid., May 10, 1993.

54. Ibid., September 16, 1992.

55. Ibid., November 22, 1993.

56. According to a report in the *Post* for December 30, 1992, Washington's population had fallen to 589,000, the lowest total since the Depression, while suburban Virginia and Maryland marked substantial gains in the early 1990s, continuing the trend that began in the 1980s. A further report, published in the *Post* on October 7, 1994, revealed that as middle-income residents left the city, the proportion of those living in poverty rose from 20.3 percent to 26.4 percent in the single year of 1993.

57. During the 1970s, Washington led the nation in the rate of black suburbanization, as the percentage of Washington area blacks located in the suburbs rose from 30 percent to more than 50 percent. Ibid., June 21, 1989. In response to the outmigration of blacks from the District into Prince George's County, 30 percent of the white population, 130,000 people, left the county in the same period, leaving the area immediately adjacent to Washington mostly black. The area of Hillcrest Heights, for example, listed only 27 blacks among 13,885 residents in 1960. In 1970 the town was 14 percent black. By 1980 it was 67 percent black. As one of the first towns to attract the black middle class, Glenarden is now 95 percent black, many of its residents employed at supervisory levels in the federal government. Ibid., October 4, 1981, October 23, 1982, December 1, 1987.

58. Eunice S. Grier and George Grier, "Changing Faces of Washington," ibid., June 17, 1980. A planning report for the Marshall Heights area in the eastern portion of the District, prepared in 1981, showed that this black area lost thirteen thousand people or 18 percent during the 1970s, leaving the remaining population of the area skewed between older and younger residents. Sam Smith, "Divided We Stand," *City Paper*, September 23, 1988, reported a loss of 8 percent of the city's middle-class taxpayers since 1975, with increases of 5 percent among the poor and 7 percent among the wealthiest city residents. An assessment of the 1990 census in the *Post*, April 23, 1992, while noting a drop in the number of poor households counted, nonetheless pointed to increased disparities between rich and poor in Washington and the metropolitan area.

59. Paul L. Knox, "The Restless Urban Landscape: Economic and Sociocultural Change and the Transformation of Metropolitan Washington, DC." *Annals of the Association of American Geographers* 81 (June 1991): 188.

60. *New York Times*, July 12, 1990. As a further sign of the national attention given Washington, see also Marianne Szegedy-Maszak, "D.C.: The Other Washington: One City with Two Cultures and Many Tensions," *New York Times Magazine*, November 20, 1988. For local data, see the 1988 report of the Greater Washington Research Center, "Opportunity Ladders: Can Area Employment Possibilities Improve the Prospects for Washingtonians in Long-term Poverty?" Summary Report, pp. 1–3. A report in the *Washington Post* for August 1, 1990, indicated that the waiting list for rent subsidies and public housing had risen to fifty thousand people. Another report in the *Post* for September 25, 1990, revealed that an estimated seventy-six thousand people in Washington, 13 percent of the total population, had a drug

problem. For a thorough review of the problems of teenage pregnancy in Washington, see the series by Leon Dash in ibid., January 26–31, 1986.

CONCLUSION

1. Jeanne R. Lowe, *Cities in a Race with Time: Progress and Poverty in America's Renewing Cities* (New York: Random House, 1967), p. 200.

2. Not only Republicans called for fiscal constraints. The same day that Senator Shelby switched to the Republican majority, Washington Democratic delegate to Congress Eleanor Holmes Norton announced an emergency plan covering $300 million in budget cuts intended to close the city's deficit and thereby secure congressional confidence in Washington's local leadership. *Washington Post*, November 10, 1994.

3. Ibid., February 3, April 18, 1995.

4. Robert Fishman, "Urbanity and Suburbanity: Rethinking the 'Burbs,'" *American Quarterly* 46 (March 1994): 37; Joel Garreau, *Edge City: Life on the New Frontier* (New York: Doubleday and Co., 1991).

5. Rusk's description of the tendency of inelastic cities to rely on federal subsidies rather than to share the financial burden with their suburbs is especially true of Washington. By contrast, Rusk writes, "Often city governments of elastic cities are better financed than are outlying jurisdictions. Poor minorities are not heavily concentrated within the central city. . . . Under such conditions mayors usually choose to handle local problems with local revenues rather than seek federal urban aid." David Rusk, *Cities without Suburbs* (Washington, D.C.: Woodrow Wilson Center Press, 1993), pp. 32–33.

6. On the merging financial interests of the two cities, see the commentaries by *Washington Post* business analyst Rudolph Pyatt, April 6, 1987, and September 25, 1989, and by Joel Garreau, October 10, 1992.

7. Neal R. Peirce, "No City Is an Island," Outlook section, *Washington Post*, March 27, 1994.

8. Analysis of the 1990 census reported by the *New York Times*, August 1, 1992, compared favorably the Washington metropolitan area median income of $46,884 and poverty rate of 6.4 percent with Los Angeles at $36,711 and 13.1 percent; Chicago at $35,918 and 11.3 percent; New York at $38,445 and 11.7 percent; San Francisco at $41,459 and 8.6 percent; and Boston at $40,666 and 8.1 percent.

9. Rusk, *Cities without Suburbs*, pp. 64–65.

10. Jon C. Teaford, *The Unheralded Triumph: City Government in America, 1870–1900* (Baltimore: Johns Hopkins University Press, 1984).

Index

290

Index

Index

297

Index